Four Leagues of Pecos

Four Leagues of Pecos

A Legal History
of the Pecos Grant, 1800 - 1933

G. Emlen Hall

New Mexico Land Grant Series

John R. Van Ness, Series Editor
University of New Mexico Press
Albuquerque

Library of Congress Cataloging in Publication Data

Hall, G. Emlen, 1942–
  Four leagues of Pecos.

  (New Mexico land grant series)
  Includes bibliographical references and index.
    1. Pueblo Indians—Claims—History.   2. Pueblo Indians
—Land tenure—History.   3. Indians of North America—
New Mexico—Claims—History.   4. Indians of North
America—New Mexico—Land tenure—History.   5. Land
grants—New Mexico—History.   I. Title.   II. Series.
KFN4105.5.P9H34   1984   346.73'08997   83-23505
ISBN 0-8263-0710-8   347.3068997

A portion of Chapter 1 appears in an expanded version as "Mexican
Liberals and the Pueblo Indians, 1821–1829," by G. Emlen Hall and
David J. Weber, *New Mexico Historical Review,* V. 4 No. 1 (January
1984): 5–32.

Contents

Illustrations

Maps

MAP 1. The Pecos Pueblo Grant and Its Environs

Except for the relatively small, 573 acre Alejandro Valle Grant, the Pecos Pueblo Grant lay closer to the headwaters of the Pecos River than any other grant originating under Spain or Mexico. Formal settlement of the area east of the Rio Grande Basin did not begin until 1794 with the making of the huge 350,000 acre San Miguel del Bado Grant. By 1803 the Hispanic towns of San Miguel del Bado and San Jose del Bado had taken root. By 1815 government officials had completed the legal creation of the 9,647 acre Los Trigos Grant, immediately south of the Pecos Pueblo Grant.

Foreword

Four Leagues of Pecos is a historical study of the legal relationships between man and land in Pecos, New Mexico. Control of land and water was the foundation of the economic and social order in New Mexico, and consequently uncertain land tenure caused enormous confusion, social conflict, and, at times, violent upheaval. This study of land tenure—the laws and customs governing landholding and use as well as the application of the principles—enables us to understand the human need to occupy land and exploit the earth's resources to secure a livelihood.

Land tenure has long been a crucial issue in New Mexico. From an ecological perspective, this may be attributed to the meager resources of its semiarid land, particularly the limited amount of irrigable land for farming found in the narrow river valleys. During periods of rapid population growth, these scarce natural resources engendered intense, and frequently, bitter competition among New Mexico's residents. It is this struggle for land that every student seeking to understand the region must come to appreciate.

New Mexico's multiethnic heritage under three sovereigns—the colonial Spanish Empire, the Mexican Republic, and the United States—defies full understanding until the evolution of land tenure is comprehended. An adequate synthesis of this vital dimension of New Mexican history can only be written after a number of detailed local studies, which reveal the range of geographic, ecologic, and social variations in land tenure, have been made. To date, the only such studies we have are those devoted to a single region, the territory encompassed by the Maxwell land grant. This second volume in the New Mexico Land Grant Series is the only study ever to trace an active land grant problem through three sovereigns. The sources are drawn mainly from primary and untapped documents held in a variety of locales in this country that have materials from Spain, Mexico, and the United States. These sources are richly supplemented by Pecos oral history.

Four Leagues of Pecos is local history at its finest. It is the product of the author's decade-long residence in Pecos, coupled with considerable practical experience with New Mexico's land and water law as an attorney in the State Engineer's Office in New Mexico. G. Emlen Hall, the author, conveys a vivid sense of the land—the special place that is Pecos—as well as the many subtle nuances of the Spanish, Mexican, and United States's governmental and legal regimes which have, in sequence, attempted to sanction and regulate man's presence on the Pecos Pueblo grant lands.

Only Hall could have written this book. Continuing a remarkable New Mexican tradition, Hall is an Eastern-trained lawyer whose fascination with the events and people in the state's past inspired him to take up the historian's pen. I will venture to predict, and I believe the reader will agree, that Em Hall is destined to achieve a place among the distinguished group of lawyer-historians that includes William A. Keleher, L. Bradford Prince, and Ralph E. Twitchell.

Hall is obviously at home with the massive body of administrative and legal records pertaining to Pecos. Thus, he is able to guide the reader skillfully through the labyrinth that is the grant's legal history. In the end, perhaps the greatest achievement of this minutely detailed, exhaustive examination of the interminable struggle for the Pecos grant lands is that Hall conveys more completely and profoundly than ever before the tremendous social, political, and economic costs incurred by New Mexico as a consequence of uncertain or clouded land titles.

This study is, however, much more than local history, and it will be of interest to scholars and other readers from several broad perspectives. For students of Latin American land and society, the volume provides a much needed study of regional land tenure on the far northern frontier of New Spain and, after 1821, the Mexican Republic. As a proper study should, it sets the local land history in the wider context of New World Hispanic land tenure laws and practices and, in particular, the consequences of the land reforms instituted by the Spanish Cortes of 1810–13. The volume will complement the considerable literature on the *latifundio* or the large agrarian estate in Latin America, represented by the *hacienda* on the northern frontier of New Spain. This book bears comparison with William Taylor's history of land and society in colonial Oaxaca. Along with Taylor's work and other regional land tenure studies yet to come, the *Four Leagues of Pecos* will help to broaden our understanding of an enduring theme in Latin American history: the centuries-long contest between Indian and Hispano, *pueblo* (land-holding community) and *hacienda*, and the *minifundio* and the *latifundio* for control over scarce land resources.

In a regional frame of reference, this study is an important new work on Hispanic land grants. It treats the careers of the principal land speculators who began to have an impact on New Mexico land grants during the Mexican Period. In doing so, it also outlines the little understood role of the Mexican *diputación* in land administration.

Of equal significance is the treatment of the colossal confusion in land administration that reigned throughout the United States territorial period and the untangling of financial deals by a group of early New Mexico figures who were able to profit personally from this disgraceful state of affairs. Operating during the 1850s and 1860s, this group might be called the "early Santa Fe land grant ring," for it preceded Thomas B. Catron and his cronies who became famous only during the latter decades of the nineteenth century.

Finally, the book merits special attention as a study of Hispanic and, later, Anglo encroachment on Pueblo grant lands. Myra Ellen Jenkins has been the leading historian in this field, and Hall has been able to build successfully on the fine foundations she and others have laid. The closely intertwined question of the Pueblos' legal status under American rule—were they to be considered full citizens or wards of the government—is also extensively treated. While ever mindful of his principal subject, Pecos, the author skillfully weaves together the wider legal and political forces at play, highlighted by a detailed review of the famous *Joseph* decision in 1877 and culminating with an analysis of the Pueblo Lands Board, which carried out its work in the 1920s. Students of Pueblo Indian history will be grateful for this incisive analysis of a vast and difficult subject.

A few words of caution to the reader who is not well acquainted with New Mexico's Hispanic land grant history are in order. As is to be expected, this history relies mainly on the study of the formal administrative and legal records of the Pecos Pueblo grant lands. However, during the nineteenth century the vast majority of those who claimed and settled on the grant were illiterate, so customary, informal land tenure practices prevailed over codified law. Also a large number of land transactions most likely took place without the creation of a formal written record. Under Spanish law, in fact, land transfers could be executed verbally. These customary practices endured long after the end of the Spanish colonial and Mexican administrations. Thus, the *whole* history of Pecos land tenure can never be retrieved.

Although the Pecos story holds much in common with the history of the other Pueblo land grants as well as the non-Indian grants, it was also quite unique in many respects. It always presented special problems to those who attempted to claim it as well as to the many government officials, judges, and others responsible for regulating land and settling land disputes in New Mexico. By no means have all Hispanic land grants entailed conflict with Pueblo land claims. Further, varying and, in some instances, entirely different social, economic, and political forces were present in other land grant histories. Thus, the reader must be careful not to over generalize. (For a comprehensive overview of the Hispanic land grants of the Upper Rio Grande region, the first volume in this series, *Mercedes Reales* by Victor Westphall, is highly recommended.)

With these words of caution well taken, I commend this remarkable study to the reader. He will find in the pages that follow a most engrossing story presented skillfully and elegantly. Em Hall brings clarity to an incredibly complex legal history and, through his penetrating analysis of Pecos, provides many new insights into the nature of the relationships between man, land, and society in New Mexico.

John R. Van Ness
Series Editor

December 15, 1983
Ardmore, Pennsylvania

Preface

I wrote *Four Leagues of Pecos* between 1972 and 1982. But in one day, Thanksgiving 1980, I shot Pecos Pueblo's league.

Nobody had hunted the league for more than a hundred years. But in its time, the league dominated Pecos. American Pecos, by way of nineteenth-century Mexico and eighteenth-century Spain, traces its lineage directly to Pueblo Indian Pecos, acknowledged by all three sovereigns. Pecos Pueblo had existed long before the whirlwind succession of foreign governments that began with Spain, in 1540. In hunting Pecos Pueblo's league, I stalked the elusive dividing line between Pecos Pueblo Indian and non-Indian worlds. At one time, the league was used to delineate an eighteen-thousand-acre square, land that Pecos Pueblo supposedly owned. If you knew the league's location, you knew what land belonged to the Indians and what land did not. In Pecos today, there are no formal worlds like that to divide. But I shot Pecos Pueblo's league anyway, to make some sense of a project I had struggled with since 1972.

I did it with a 277 foot rope and in the company of the 10 year-old Pecoseño Kenge Ruiz and the 187 year-old San Miguel del Vado *alcalde* don Vicente Villanueva. Villanueva had shot the Pecos Pueblo league in 1818. Someone probably had killed him for his efforts. In 1980 I followed in his footsteps. But that gets me ahead of my story. Besides, the complex tale that follows will explain my rope, its length, Pecos Pueblo's league, and my hero, Vicente Villanueva. It will tell you about the Pecos Pueblo ruins, now a national monument, sitting at the very northern edge of a pear-shaped, rocky ridge that commands a view of the upper Pecos Valley around it. You will then know exactly what Kenge Ruiz and I had in mind on Thanksgiving Day 1980. For the moment, take my word for it: We had come to this precarious point at the northern edge of Pecos Pueblo National Monument to shoot Pecos Pueblo's league.

From that point, Pecos Valley spreads out around you. The red sandstone face of Rowe Mesa rises precipitously to the west. Pecos Baldy and Santa Fe Baldy peer down from the north. To the east the terrain rises into jagged hills and then more rugged mountains. You cannot see the Hispanic village of Pecos or the river from here. But to the east, plumes of smoke from wood stoves mark the location of other people, different settlements.

From our vantage point, the only nearby building you can see is behind you, to the south. The roofless top of the old Pecos church still looms over the pueblo ruins where Kenge and I stand, ready with our rope. If you look carefully to the east and south, you may spot the chimneys of the Fogelsons' mansion, near the Pecos River. But if you miss the chimneys or do not know exactly where to look, the hills and mesa below you seem to run together eventually. Just at that point you can make out the small, narrow opening that funnels the Pecos world out onto the eastern plains that roll on, like the ocean, to Kansas.

But Kenge and I go north to hunt the Pecos Pueblo league with our rope, in the footsteps of don Vicente Villanueva. Our texts told us we would have the league if we took fifty lengths of our rope. When Villanueva did it in 1818, he had set out from this same spot with Pecos Pueblo leaders and Spanish settlers calling the length count as they went along. I take a bead on Pecos Baldy, due north of the pueblo ruins, and send Kenge running out with the first of fifty 277 foot lengths.

He disappears over the side of an enormous boulder, reappears at the bottom of a barren red ravine, and starts up the ravine's other side. The rope goes taut against the pueblo wall, but twists and bends on its way to Kenge. Three more 277 foot shots cover the same barren, broken terrain. Then, on the fourth 100 vara length, Kenge struggles up a dirt wash and emerges onto a flat plain, covered with sparse New Mexico grass.

Uprooted piñon trees, tossed carelessly aside by some beastly machine, dot the barren terrain. Occasional *No Trespassing* signs identify the owner as the Dallas millionaire E. E. Fogelson and his wife, the actress Greer Garson. For the next fifteen rope lengths we move across the plain with no houses in sight. Then Kenge and I hit an old, seemingly endless east-west cedar-post-and-wire fence. Thirty-one 100 vara lengths remain to the northern shot of Pecos Pueblo's league. But we have already hit one dividing line between worlds.

In the 1860s Pecos Pueblo Indian survivors, by then living with their kinsmen at Jemez Pueblo, sold the eighteen-thousand-acre grant for the second time, to a Las Vegas, New Mexico, merchant, for five thousand dollars. Shortly thereafter the merchant died. The probate of his estate in New Mexico began a series of Pecos Pueblo grant transfers that sent the title to New York for almost twenty years.

Before dying, the Las Vegas merchant had posted large, red linen signs on the old fence where Kenge and I now stood. The signs warned Hispanic settlers, who had been creeping onto Pecos Pueblo land from the canyon to the north for more than fifty years, to come no farther. They had not.

But while title to the whole grant, north and south of this fence, made its way around the markets of Manhattan, north of the fence Hispanic Pecos continued to grow. The Pecos Pueblo survivors then at Jemez respected this Spanish presence. They had sold the entire eighteen thousand acres once to Mexicans and a second time to New Yorkers. Now, in the 1870s and 1880s, they returned occasionally to sell small tracts in the northern portion of the grant for a third time, to Hispanic trespassers identified by the Pecos survivors as "nuestros hermanos."

By the time the federal government got around to straightening out the mess, in the 1930s, Tex Austin, the famous western singer, owned the two-thirds of the Indian grant that lay south of the fence and had a legal claim to the heavily populated northern one-third as well. Neither the Hispanics nor Austin wanted to fight that battle. Instead, they split the Indian land at this fence and cut the Pueblos out of the deal altogether.

The Fogelsons' estate now lies south of that ancient fence. Modern Spanish Pecos lies north of it. Neat dirt roads and clear, modern fences mark sharply divided one-acre tracts, dotted with trailers, mobile homes, and flat-roofed houses, all signs of twentieth-century Pecos. Old, historic Pecos, with its pitched-roofed, adobe houses huddled around the irrigation ditches that circumscribe the rich farmland at the heart of town, lies a mile to the east.

Ten more rope lengths through modern Pecos and Kenge hits the one paved road that runs east to the old village and west to the four-lane highway to Santa Fe. We cross the road. By my count we have come thirty lengths of 100 varas each. Pecos Pueblo's league required twenty more.

For the next ten of those, Kenge and I pass through land more twisted and contorted than any we have seen since leaving the pueblo ruins. Deep gullies, running from east to west, cut savagely through a pine barren. Twice Kenge, rope in hand, disappears into the bottom of quasi-lunar craters, dry, barren, the pale green color of spent copper.

Here, thirty years ago, the American Metals Company built tailings ponds to catch waste water and acid from the mills. The mine ran profitably through the Depression and into the 1940s. Then a bitter, violent strike ensued, pitting Hispano miners against Anglo owners. By the time the battle ended, American Metals had left town. Today only these dry tailings ponds remain.

Kenge scrambles off the far side of the last one, anxious to escape the foul odor the ponds still give off, and disappears into another pine barren. In the middle of the forty-third rope shot, he screams. I tie my end down and run to join him at the other, worried that he has hurt himself.

Instead, I find him at the edge of an almost vertical east-west cliff. A hundred feet below us the Pecos River cascades in its parallel course, hugging the canyon's rocky southern wall. From the top of that cliff, Kenge and I look straight up the main, north-south stretch of Pecos Canyon, into the snowcovered face of Pecos Baldy again. Below us the canyon abruptly turns east-west, along with the river.

The Hispanos have always called this oldest, hidden part of Pecos *El Rincón,* both the "nook, or inside corner" and the "lurking place." To the north of the rincón sits the Benedictine monastery. To the south, the much more open, obviously Pueblo Indian *Ciénaga de Pecos.* On this secret, off-set appendage to the Pecos Pueblo grant, Hispanic encroachments had first taken hold, around 1824.

We scramble down the steep cliff in front of us, dodging boulders as we go. At the bottom we jump from rock to rock, across the thirty-foot wide Pecos River and run into the middle of the green fields beyond, dragging our rope behind us. The forty-seventh of fifty lengths finds us in the middle of a world we have not seen before on this hunting trip.

In front of us, the late autumn grass still stands knee-deep and thick. Small furrows running perpendicular to the river mark the irrigation ditches. On the high side of the fields, an irrigation ditch still runs with water. Just above the ditch, small, neat adobe homes sit in a ragged line. The Zamora, Ortiz, Varela, and Roybal families now live here.

A large man approaches from behind one of the houses. I recognize him as Steve Roybal, a direct descendant of Jose Polonio Roybal, the first recorded non-Indian from Pecos to be baptised in the pueblo church. Steve Roybal now earns his living caretaking a large, New York–owned summer ranch up the Pecos River, where Frank Lloyd Wright had built one of his first homes.

"What are you doing?" Roybal asks suspiciously, in Spanish. "Agrimensando," I carelessly reply, picking a word for "surveying" that carries much too technical and legal an implication for my antiquated shot of the Pecos league. I explain in more detail, to a man whose father, grandfather, and great-grandfather have had to deal with various official attempts by Spain, Mexico, and the United States to pin down Pecos Pueblo's league. But when I have finished on this afternoon, Steve Roybal laughs and says, "You mean you came with that rope from way over there?" pointing in the direction of the pueblo ruins.

We turn around. The vertical cliff Kenge and I have just descended now rises sharply above us in the afternoon sun. From the fields below, the cliff obliterates the world to the south. We can just see the sharp, horizontal line of Rowe Mesa from here. We can see nothing of the pueblo land beneath it.

But here we are, in the heart of Hispanic Pecos and still well within Indian land. The three remaining 100 vara measurements carry us anticlimactically to a huge boulder and a gnarled piñon tree. We have shot the Pecos Pueblo league.

The following day I took my rope out at home and checked it against a standard rule. Battered, torn, and abraded, my 277 foot rope now measured 296 feet long. One of my companions, don Vicente Villanueva, had made the same shot in 1818. Four years later Spanish settlers found him dead, killed, they swore, by raiding Apaches from the east. Shooting the Pecos Pueblo league had proved dangerous for him. It was inaccurate for me. But, after all, nineteenth-century Mexican surveyors had never called their determinations of Pueblo boundaries surveys. Instead, they called them *vistas de ojos,* a way of getting a rough estimate of the terrain to be covered.

Four Leagues of Pecos surveys that same Pecos Pueblo terrain from

1803 to 1936, in greater detail and, I hope, with more accuracy. The unlikely hero of this book is an eighteen-thousand-acre tract of high Sonoran desert land in San Miguel County, New Mexico. The drama centers on the Spanish, Mexican, and United States versions of legal title to the tract. Between sovereigns, the vision of that title changed. Within the hegemony of each sovereign, the vision often wavered. Through all the permutations, the land remained in some sense Indian country, until the end of this tale. The dual Indian and sovereign focuses, the first constant, the second protean, have bent, refracted, altered, and confused the image of the Pecos Pueblo grant. No clear portrait emerges.

No consistent human occupation clarifies the picture of this tract of land. John Kessell's magnificent *Kiva, Cross, and Crown* tells the history of the living Pecos Pueblo. *Four Leagues of Pecos* picks up the story of the dying Pecos Pueblo, and follows it through the legal legacy left by a departed people. Between 1803 and 1936, the period with which this book is specifically concerned, other peoples occupied the Pecos Pueblo grant. But their hold on it was always tenuous and their imprint was obscured by the lingering image of Pecos as Indian country.

As a result, this book deals with the legal history of a particular tract of land owned by a departed people and occupied by a succession of interlopers. This is legal history with a vengeance: more often than not, the Pecos Pueblo debate centers on jurisdiction, always a boon to lawyers and a bane to everyone else. This is local history with a vengeance: *Four Leagues of Pecos* is primarily concerned with the history of an obscure New Mexico town now known, if at all, because it happens to sit at the entrance to the much more famous Pecos Wilderness. And this story deals not with all New Mexicans, but with Pecos Hispanics and Pecos Pueblos and the few others who showed an interest in the Pecos Pueblo grant over the years. In other words, this book does not even pretend to encompass the magnificent sweep of southwestern history from 1800 to 1936.

And yet, I am convinced that the Pecos Pueblo grant provides a key to New Mexico history precisely because the grant was so vulnerable during this period. The decline and final disappearance of Pecos Pueblo and the growth and final establishment of Hispanic and Anglo Pecos followed along with the changes from Spanish to Mexican to United States sovereignty in New Mexico. The grant, with its incredibly rich water resources, was always a tantalizing prize during the period. Like a lightning rod, the Pecos Pueblo grant drew to itself those interests in New Mexico land which drove the history of the period forward. To understand Pecos is to understand New Mexico during these chaotic but critical years.

I have tried to breathe life into this fascinating and obscure tale by concentrating on the life and times of particular principals in the ongoing battle over ownership of Pecos Pueblo's deserted land. Pedro Bautista Pino, Domingo Fernández, Juan Estevan Pino, Preston Beck, Jr., Donaciano Vigil, Manuel Varela, John Ward, James Seymour, D. C. Collier, Francis C. Wilson, and John Collier all strut and march across this Pecos Pueblo stage, playing their various parts in the drama of identity and ownership of the Pecos Pueblo grant. This book belongs to them, with all the claims they made, the battles they fought, the lawsuits they filed, the laws they passed, the victories they won, the losses they suffered, the friends and enemies they made.

And the papers they left behind. Pedro Bautista Pino published a book about New Mexico, in 1812. John Collier published one about New Mexico Indians, in 1963. All the intervening actors also left written evidence of their roles. Those papers litter archival collections from New Haven to Palo Alto, from Denver to Mexico City. Most of the documents are untranslated, unindexed, and virtually untouched. In recent years, William Taylor, of the University of Virginia, has reexamined documents in the Spanish Archives of New Mexico dealing with Pueblo Indian land and water. David Weber, of Southern Methodist University, and Daniel Tyler, of the University of Colorado at Ft. Collins, have made significant inroads into the Mexican Archives of New Mexico. Lawrence Kelly, of North Texas State University at Denton, has done invaluable work on Pueblo Indian materials in the National Archives. These pioneering scholars have barely begun to explore existing documents. None has focused on the Pecos Pueblo grant.

And new sources keep appearing. For years, members of Francis C. Wilson's family steadfastly maintained that their father had left no papers documenting his intricate political and legal life, part of which deeply involved the Pecos Pueblo grant, between 1911 and 1924. The Sena Plaza, in Santa Fe, a stately building where Wilson maintained his office, changed owners in 1981. In cleaning up, movers discovered in the basement several cubic feet of Wilson's papers, unknown even to his family. The New Mexico State Records Center wisely accessioned them. Archivists are now organizing them. I have checked the Wilson papers for this book, as I have checked most other sources of which I am aware; I think the book mines primary sources not heretofore explored in New Mexico history. But I am also aware that this book has not exploited everything that may be available. Regard *Four Leagues of Pecos* as a preliminary shaft into an incredibly rich lode whose exact contents and dimensions no one yet knows.

I should say a few words about the terms I use for the peoples who are really the main characters of this book. In the documents, *Pueblo* and *pueblo* are used interchangeably to mean a Pueblo Indian, the culture as a whole, and some particular Pueblo Indian village. To distinguish between the two basic meanings, I have used *Pueblo* for the culture and its members and *pueblo* for a corporate group of Pueblo Indians and their village. Thus "the pueblos" refers to what might otherwise be called the tribes of Pueblo Indians and their associated villages, while "the Pueblos" refers to the Pueblo Indians, as opposed to Navajo or Apache Indians, for example.

The terms used for the people who settled in the Pecos Pueblo grant and whose descendants still live there can be equally confusing. In order to emphasize the continuity of their culture, I refer to them as *Hispanos,* with the adjective *Hispanic,* regardless of what nation happens to have sovereignty over them. When I use *Spanish* or *Mexican,* I am referring to specifically political or legal conditions, not to the people.

As I have said, I have worked on this book for the past decade. In the process I have accumulated many debts, partially the result of a richly chaotic life, partially the result of having lived and worked in Pecos from October 1970 to June 1981. As a student of American civilization, I have come to believe that this country's best histories have been forged in personal experience, not, initially at least, in the nation's archives. Pecos forged this book and, hopefully, tempered its steel. Pecos haunts me; I am haunted by Pecos. I dedicate *Four Leagues of Pecos* to Pecos, to its bars and battles, its dogs and trout, its people and its language.

I owe the beginnings of this book to others: to Tom Giles, retired superintendent of the Pecos National Monument, and Marion Werner, of Washington, D.C., both of whom helped launch this sometimes woebegone project, years ago; to the Pecoseños Pete Vigil, George Adelo, Sr., and Verna Hutchinson, who all encouraged me to follow the history of their town and told me what they knew; to the Pecoseño

Adelaido Quintana, who encouraged me to follow the history of his town and constantly reminded me of what I did not know; to Anselmo Tijerina, of Tierra Amarilla, who showed me what New Mexico history was; and to John Kessell, of Albuquerque, who showed me how to write it.

I owe the stuff of this book to others: to State Engineer Steve Reynolds, who sent me on other business to the National Archives and the Sterling Library and allowed me to pick Pecos material while working for him there; to the lawyer Peter White, the historian Larry Kelly, and the archivists Richard Salazar and Myra Ellen Jenkins, for their help; to Melody Webb and the National Park Service for patience and financial support; to Chama Ruiz for her sharp tongue and quick pen; to Malcolm Ebright and Jim Bensfield for their editorial and artistic support over the long haul; and, above all, to my father, I. Davis Hall. He traipsed around northern New Jersey for gravestones and through the labyrinths of New York City for death certificates, all in an effort to pin down the New York financiers who hawked the Pecos Pueblo grant in the 1870s, 1880s, and 1890s.

But I owe my greatest debt to Jude Pardee. I owe to myself and her the completion of this book and a large part of my life. I learned from her the hard rules of pronoun case and the harder rules of mortality. Like Raymond Chandler, I now live for syntax. The grammar of *Four Leagues of Pecos* belongs to me. Its existence belongs to both of us. I am indebted to her and to our daughter, Delaney, for this book.

So much for the vista de ojos. Now, on with the agrimensura.

G. E. H.

Four Leagues of Pecos

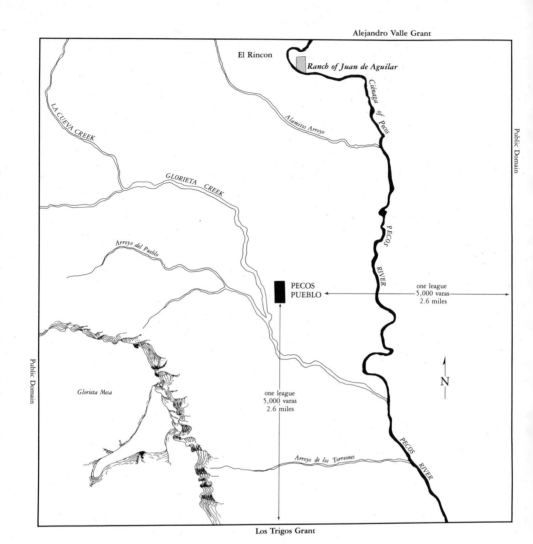

MAP 2. Pecos Pueblo Meets Its Neighbors, 1815–1818

By 1815 Spanish officials in Santa Fe had established non-Indian land grants on both the northern and southern borders of the Pecos Pueblo's acknowledged "league." In order to establish the northern boundary of the Los Trigos Grant and the southern boundary of the Alejandro Valle Grant, Santa Fe *alcalde* Matias Ortiz claimed to have measured the given Pecos Pueblo league of 5,000 Castilian *varas,* or 2.6 miles, both to the north and to the south. In response to Pecos Pueblo complaints in 1818, San Miguel del Bado *alcalde* Vincente Villanueva came to Pecos Pueblo and re-measured the Pueblo's northern league. Villanueva determined that non-Indian Juan de Aguilar had in fact established a ranch within the Pecos Pueblo league. Indicated on Map 2 is the location of Aguilar's claim and designates its non-Indian nature by shading.

ONE

Pecos Pueblo Falters
under Waivering Spanish Rule

Ya suben los dos compadres
hasta las altas barandas
dejando un rastro de sangre
dejando un rastro de lágrimas

—Federico García Lorca

In mid-March 1803, the *alcalde* ("magistrate") Pedro Bautista Pino left
his home base in Santa Fe and began an eastward journey to two Pecos
river communities thirty-five miles away, San Miguel del Vado and San
José del Vado. Spanish settlers in the upper Pecos Valley would complain later about the area's unforgiving climate—eight months of winter
("ocho meses de invierno") and four months of intolerable summer heat
("cuatro meses de infierno"). Local wags would dub March, the month
of Pino's journey, *"marzo loco"* for its often intemperate, always fickle
ways. But in early 1803, Spanish settlement had just taken hold in
the upper Pecos Valley. The month marked the time to prepare for the
first plantings: to make and clean the irrigation ditches, to break the
long dormant soil, to move into new homes. Alcalde Pino came under
orders from the governor of New Mexico, Fernando Chacón, for the
first time to confirm individual Spanish settlers in their ownership of
irrigated lands within the Pecos River's first community land grant.[1]

Nine years before, in 1794, Chacón had approved the San Miguel
del Vado land grant. The vast, ill-defined tract brought the initial non-
Indian colonists to the Pecos Valley. They settled at the town of San
Miguel del Vado where, as the name implies, a ford across the river
recommended the site. The settlement sat somewhere near the center
of the new grant. Where its outer boundaries lay, nobody knew for
sure. To the east, west, and south, obscure natural monuments marked
the end of the grant and the beginning of what remained public domain.

To the north, upriver, a place called *El Gusano* represented San Miguel del Vado's boundary. Just to the north of that lay Pecos Pueblo and its lands. Spanish officials had conferred with Pecos officials in 1794 and had secured the pueblo's approval of the El Gusano boundary. Wherever it lay, the Spanish grant's northern boundary should bring no trouble from the pueblo to the fifty-two original applicants.[2]

But the original 1794 grant had specifically kept the large grant open for more settlers and other communities within its outer boundaries. Between its establishment and Pedro Bautista Pino's arrival, in 1803, a second small town had sprung up in the grant. This town, San José del Vado, sat in a bend of the Pecos River, about three miles above San Miguel, in between the original settlement and Pecos Pueblo, to the north. Clearly expansion meant movement upstream, to the north, toward the lands of Pecos Pueblo. Pedro Bautista Pino came to confirm the existence of both non-Indian towns and incidentally to bless the movement toward Pecos land and resources that their presence portended.

Once outside Santa Fe, Pino's journey took him east, into the Galisteo drainage. Sixteen miles from the city, he reached Apache Canyon, a natural cut in the massive barrier that divides the Galisteo and Pecos drainages. Pino rode out of the canyon, up over Glorieta Pass, and then dropped into the upper Pecos Valley from the northwest.

From this vantage point, Pino would have been able to see the entire bowl of the valley. Snow-covered mountain peaks, the Santa Fe and Pecos baldies, loom over the valley's northern edge and form the bowl's rim on that side. Cradled between the two peaks, the Pecos River starts its descent to the relatively open valley below. A less precipitous range, east of the south-flowing river, forms the bowl's eastern edge and gives it definition, as the stunted mountains sweep down from north to south and then around, toward enclosure, from east to west. A steep, flat-topped mesa, jutting abruptly off the bowl's western floor, marks its western rim in a strong, horizontal line. As that line continues from west to east, it meets the mountain line that sweeps from east to west, neatly sealing the upper Pecos Valley. In the far distance, Bernal Peak emerges from the Sonoran desert floor and blesses the intersection. The upper Pecos Valley closes naturally on itself.

In 1803 Pedro Bautista Pino would have known that Pecos Pueblo stood on a rocky knoll near the center of that spaciously enclosed world. Northeast of the pueblo site, between its massive buildings and the narrow canyon that confines and nurtures the Pecos River, there lay, Pino also knew, the first open expanse of easily irrigable land on the river. The five hundred acres of river bottom land located there were so rich in precious water that the tract had long since come to be known as the *Ciénaga* ("swamp") de Pecos. Pino was aware that Pecos Pueblo had hardly used the ciénaga for twenty-five or more years. But he also realized that the ciénaga, or at least the largest part of it, lay well within Pecos Pueblo's league, that troublesome areal measurement of land supposedly owned by each New Mexico pueblo.[3]

That March Pedro Bautista Pino's route to San Miguel and San José took him just past what everyone had once recognized as New Mexico's greatest, most powerful, and most feared Indian pueblo. As late as 1826, Pecos Pueblo officials still boasted that "since the [Spanish] conquest, we have acquired more merits than all the Pueblos of this province and with more distinction." But by the time of Pino's visit many guessed and some hoped that the divided and dwindling pueblo of Pecos was losing its battle for survival. In 1706 estimates had placed the Pecos population at "about a thousand Christian Indians, children and adults." By 1803 only 125 Pueblos still lived at Pecos. The decline surely indicated a weakening of the pueblo's hold on its land.[4]

Pedro Bautista Pino helped speed that decline and further weaken that hold when he arrived at the town of San Miguel del Vado on 12 March 1803 and apportioned irrigated lots there to the heads of fifty-eight resident families. For the first time, non-Indian colonizers, sanctioned and confirmed by the Spanish government, had settled on the Pecos River, connected to the Pecos Pueblo upstream by sixteen miles of high Sonoran desert and the thin but infinitely more important thread of the river. The town itself lay outside the expansively enclosed Pecos Pueblo world, lying hidden, as it were, just behind the mesa that formed that Indian universe's western edge.

Two days later, on 14 March 1803, Pino moved three miles upstream to perform the same ritual confirmation at San José del Vado. There he distributed irrigated tracts to forty-eight additional non-Indian resident heads of families.

As at San Miguel del Vado, Pino and his assistant, José Miguel Tafoya, first measured the entire length of the area irrigated with Pecos River water. Pino classified that land as "tierra de pan yebar [*sic*]" ("wheat land"), a term for irrigated land common enough in central Mexico but not much used on the northern frontier. Next, again as at

San Miguel del Vado, Pino divided the total irrigated land by the number of family heads. These subdivided tracts he called *suertes* ("chances"), to emphasize the random nature of their distribution. The act of distribution Pino named a *reparto,* or *repartimiento* ("sharing"), to indicate the communal beginnings of the now privatized and individualized ownership. Finally, also as at San Miguel del Vado, Pedro Bautista Pino concluded the San José ceremony by admonishing the new property owners to mark their boundaries in stone ("mojoneras de piedra"). He reminded them that while they now owned their land, under Spanish law they could neither sell nor mortgage it for ten years.[5]

The Spanish had come to the upper Pecos River to stay. The difference between the towns of San Miguel del Vado and San José del Vado did not lie in any arcane distinction in the ritual incantations Pedro Bautista Pino used to bless them. Nor did the difference lie in the short three miles along the Pecos River that separated the two new towns. But the town of San Miguel del Vado lay just outside Pecos Pueblo's circumscribed universe and San José del Vado, not hidden by the massive mesa on its west, lay within it. San José del Vado broke the pueblo's natural circle.

Over the next 150 years, that non-Indian entrance would bring enormous changes to the upper Pecos Valley and Pecos Pueblo at its center. The human balance between Indian and non-Indian populations would shift quickly and within thirty years tilt entirely in the direction of the Hispanos who came to San José del Vado. And yet the ecological balance of land use would not change much for the next 130 years. The Hispanos replaced the Pueblos but did not alter the Indian systems of using, organizing, and owning the land. A much more disruptive force, however, was the alien, protean legal systems imposed, willy-nilly, on the already changing valley land system. Pedro Bautista Pino came in 1803 with Spanish land law. Domingo Fernández came in 1824 with Mexican land law. Donaciano Vigil came in 1854 with New Mexico territorial law. Manuel Varela and Thomas B. Catron came in 1877 with the federal version of prestatehood New Mexico law. Francis C. Wilson came in 1914 with the first poststatehood version of state and federal law. John Collier came in 1924 with a very different, strictly federal version of the law. Finally, in the 1950s, Pecos Pueblo returned with its own version of federal law applicable to the tribe's ancient homelands. Each of the different legal positions would have brought to the upper Pecos Valley land-use systems much different from those actually developed between 1803 and today. By and large the growth of the Pecos Pueblo grant proceeded oblivious to the monumental legal debates that swirled around it during the period. But the debates delineated the nature and extent of the ongoing New Mexican battle over land. The fight began at Pecos when Pedro Bautista Pino broke into Pecos Pueblo's natural circle and, on 14 March 1803, officially established San José del Vado.

Sixteen days later Governor Chacón formally endorsed Pino's actions in the margin of the alcalde's report. That completed the transaction. In 1812 Pino recalled the event. After putting the Spanish settlers in possession of their suertes, his

> heart at that moment, as never before, was overcome with joy.
> Parents and little children surrounded me, all of them expressing,
> even to the point of tears, their gratitude for having given them
> lands for their subsistence.

By 1829, only eighteen years after that communal expression of joy, Hispanic settlers would move sixteen miles upriver into the heart of the Pecos Pueblo grant and its water-rich ciénaga. In the process they dispossessed the few remaining Pecos Pueblo Indians of their most valuable land. "How great," pueblo leaders then lamented,

> must be the pain in our hearts on seeing ourselves violently despoiled
> of our rightful ownership, all the more when this violent
> despoilment was executed while they threatened us with the illegal
> pretext of removing us from our pueblo and distributing us among
> the other [pueblos] of the territory.

To say the least, the settlement of San José del Vado and all it implied brought powerful and mixed emotions to the upper Pecos Valley between 1800 and 1830.[6]

Alcalde Pino brought much more than mixed emotions to the Pecos Pueblo world, of course. For one, when he arrived at San José del Vado he brought the nineteenth century and all its ensuing problems. Elsewhere in northern New Mexico the first thirty years of the century saw relentless non-Indian pressure on Pueblo land and water. That acquisitive drive resulted partly from a Hispanic population explosion and partly from the pacification of warlike nomadic tribes which had previously made life in the outlying areas precarious at best. Settled life near remote pueblos like Pecos and Taos now became possible.[7] San José del Vado was small in 1803, located sixteen miles downstream from Pecos Pueblo. The new town did not itself pose much of a threat to the pueblo. Pecos officials had approved the entire San Miguel del Vado grant in 1794. By the late 1820s, when they actively began to complain about non-Indian encroachments on their own lands, Pecos Pueblo leaders now wanted the non-Indians in their grant to be removed to the "lower Pecos," around San José, where the Hispanos could live without bothering the Indians. Even on its own deathbed Pecos Pueblo did not regard non-Indian settlement at San José as part of its problem. But the pressure began there, with Pedro Bautista Pino's help.

In addition, Pino's entrance onto the Pecos Pueblo scene marked the appearance of a family of aggressive, educated, and skillful speculators and businessmen. In the last decades of the eighteenth century and the first decades of the nineteenth, an increasingly stratified New Mexico society began to emerge. At the top stood a small class of wealthy merchants, acute in commerce, rich in cattle, and always interested in land, particularly valuable and vulnerable Pueblo land. Pedro Bautista Pino belonged to the first generation of that new class. Between 1803 and 1854 three generations of his family—the father, Pedro Bautista; the son, Juan Estevan; and the grandchildren, Manuel Doroteo and Justo Pastor—personally presided over and in some cases caused the complete dismantling of the living Pecos Pueblo and the delivery of its ample land and water into foreign hands.[8]

Finally, Pedro Bautista Pino carried with him to San José del Vado the complex repertoire of Spanish colonial land law as developed over the previous three centuries and applied to Hispanos and Indians, settlers and natives, land and water. That law, as applied in northern New Mexico, provided the basic means to force Pecos Pueblo out of its ancestral home. In particular, as New Mexico's only delegate to Spain, Pedro Bautista Pino, between 1812 and 1813, played an important role in adding to that ancient Spanish legal repertoire. While ultimately rejected for application in New Mexico, Pino's legal contribution actually broke the dwindling pueblo's hold on its land.

In the beginning, before the arrival of the Spanish in New Mexico and at Pecos in the sixteenth century, indigenous Pueblos had little sense of property ownership in the European sense as it came to be applied to the vast expanse of their ancestral, upper Pecos Valley home. Communal living and irrigated farming, both of which predated the Spanish incursion, produced the most intense Pueblo land uses and yielded an Indian sense of private property most akin to modern "ownership." But as Indian land uses became less intense and farther away from the center of the pueblo, any idea of private property, something owned by one to the exclusion of others, simply petered out in the long Pecos vistas. The Pueblo world view did provide certain spatial limits to the Indian universe. The points Pedro Bautista Pino noted in 1803 circumscribed Pecos Pueblo's world. In the Pueblo fashion, those external points were mirrored in coterminous, discrete worlds made up of the pueblo's fields, the pueblo's building complex, and the rooms within it. The closer to the center of the Pecos universe, the harder the boundaries became and the more the subdivisions resembled "private property." But at the outer limits of the Pecos universe, the Indians did not measure the natural boundaries circumscribing their world. Instead, they gauged their lives by them.[9]

By 1803 Pecos Pueblo had already lived under Spanish rule for almost three hundred years. Pedro Bautista Pino carried with him three centuries of legal history, asking and sometimes answering the question of who the Pueblos were and what the nature and extent of their claim to property was. The Hispanos asked the questions for the indigenous Pueblos. Hispanos answered for them. But by the turn of the eighteenth century nothing had taken firmer hold among the northern New Mexico pueblos, including Pecos, than the Hispanic answer to the Hispanic question of who the Pueblos were and what lands the pueblos owned, on which terms.[10]

By the mid-sixteenth century, every Hispano knew that the so-called civilized Indians, like the Pueblos generally and Pecos specifically, had the prerequisite capacity to own property. Until then theologians and lawyers had vigorously debated whether the sedentary indigenous peoples discovered in the Americas could own anything. Those who asserted that native peoples in the Americas did not have that capacity advocated breaking up existing communities and dispersing the less-than-human inhabitants among civilized people (*gente de razón*). In an eerie fashion, precisely the same theory and solution would reappear twice again in the specific Pecos Pueblo context, once in 1826, when Mexico held sovereignty over New Mexico, and again in 1880, when the United States ruled. But once the 1560 debate in Valladolid between the pro-Indian de las Casas and the anti-Indian Sepúlveda had ended with a decision in favor of the native Indians, the Spanish empire committed itself to honoring antecedent Pueblo ownership of lands as an exception to what the crown acquired by discovery. Indian lands, like those of Pecos Pueblo, thus represented "acquired property," which no Hispano could claim on the basis of discovery alone.[11]

To the extent that Spain recognized these preexisting rights, it showed the best side of its humanistic and catholic drive toward discovery. But to the extent that the definition of rights so recognized made sense in terms of Spanish, not Indian, conceptions of property ownership, this Spanish recognition showed the basically imperialist roots from which it had sprung. When Spain finally decided that New World Indians had preexisting rights to the lands they occupied at the time of the Spanish arrival, the crown assumed that those rights conformed to an alien Spanish concept of real property ownership.

At its theoretical center, Spanish land law was constructed between the poles of private use and public ownership. The public owned everything except that property which a private entity—a person, a town, or a pueblo—actually used. As one historian of ancient Spanish property law put it,

> The principle behind the idea of public ownership in Castile was that
> no individual had the right to appropriate for himself and
> monopolize a part of the resources of nature that were produced
> without the intervention of man. The only thing that the individual
> had the right to call his own was that which he had produced from
> Nature through his own personal efforts in the form of crops, flocks,
> or manufactured goods. Exploitable land, therefore, should
> theoretically remain at the disposition of anyone who wished to
> benefit from it . . . An individual who wished to use a piece of idle
> land simply occupied and used it without the intervention of any
> authority other than his own. The use might be for pasture or
> cultivation but possession of the land was dependent on the act of
> using it. When the individual no longer wished to use it, he
> abandoned it, after which anyone else who wished to use it could
> occupy it anew without the former owner having any claim over it.[12]

These fundamental underpinnings produced Spanish civil law's basic concern with use as the basis of title; with adverse possession as an honorable, not bastardized, way of acquiring title; and with abandonment and forfeiture as a way of losing title. These fundamental Spanish concerns also produced an esoteric legal language to express them. Genuinely private lands were *bienes raíces* ("real property"). Lands not put to intensive individual use remained *realengas* ("crown lands") or *tierras baldías* ("unappropriated public lands"). Individuals or com-

munities could appropriate either, usually by *merced* ("land grant") from
the crown. These arcane terms all became part of the legal arsenal
which non-Indians used in their assault on the lands of Pecos Pueblo
in the 1820s. But they reflect the fundamental discomfort Spanish
culture felt with "private" land, whether Indian or non-Indian, that
was not used. [13]

An additional term of Spanish land law added another dimension to
the public-private, unused-used, ownerless-owned dichotomies that
informed the ensuing Pecos debate. As early as 1731 in New Mexico,
and probably earlier in the Valley of Mexico, officials began using the
term *sobrantes* ("surpluses," "extras") to describe unused Pueblo Indian
lands. The term implied that the lands so described had owners and
that the owners did not need them. As an idea, sobrantes fit neatly
between the polar opposites that otherwise informed Spanish conceptions of land ownership. As applied, the idea became a critical vehicle
for attempting to take unused Pueblo land and give it to non-Indians,
who would put it to productive use. In central Mexico the notion
caused endless litigation. In New Mexico it did the same, particularly
at Pecos in the 1820s. [14]

One final Spanish legal process—the *repartimiento*—completed the
complex real property system brought to Pecos Pueblo in the nineteenth
century. Initially used to describe a form of forced Indian labor, repartimiento came to define in Pedro Bautista Pino's time the public
division of irrigation water between competing private claimants. Spanish colonial law had always regarded water as a public commodity,
subject to public control and approved private use. Land, on the other
hand, had gained a more secure private status by the nineteenth century.
Water was subject to the repartimiento process but land was not, at
least until the very end of the Spanish regime. [15]

Rather than clarifying the ambiguous relationship between bienes
raices, realengas, baldíos, and sobrantes, codified Spanish law, such as
it was, only further muddied the distinctions between private and
public property. For example, the magnificent *Recopilación de las leyes
de los reinos de las Indias* stated that

> the Indians shall be given all the land with an excess [con sobra] that
> belongs to them, both as to individuals and communities, and
> especially those lands where they may have made irrigation ditches
> [acequias] or any other improvement such that with their personal

industry, they have enriched. This is to apply particularly with
respect to water and irrigation. And for no reason can these lands be
sold or taken away from them.[16]

In this one passage the statute emphasized the oldest Spanish marriage
of use and ownership as the measure of indigenous Indian title, suggested that the Indians should receive the benefit of the doubt (con
sobra) in determining the land they had used, and finally intimated as
well that someone (presumably the crown) might grant the indigenous
Indians additional public land.

Another factor in the Spanish treatment of Indian ownership further
confused the issue of how much land indigenous pueblos like Pecos
were assumed to own. Besides defining the nature and extent of acquired
Pueblo Indian rights, Spanish law tried to protect those rights as well.
Early on the Spanish crown made it clear that the pueblos were both
wards and vassals of the state. As vassals, they could own real property;
but the crown tried to protect them, as its official wards, from disposing
of it.[17] Within a short time, the distinction disappeared between what
New Mexico pueblos owned and what the crown did to protect them
from losing it. Ironically, in Hispanic eyes New Mexico pueblos came
to own only what non-Indians could not acquire.

The Spanish urge to treat the pueblos as wards and to enact prophylactic measures to protect their property came in two separate forms.
First, Spanish law sharply circumscribed the manner in which pueblos
could sell their land to non-Indians. A specific provision of the *Recopilación* required that for the sale to have legal validity, Indian real
property had to be sold at a public auction (*pregón*), with at least thirty
days advance notice of the sale. Later commentators generalized on this
particular requirement and read it to mean that, at least, valid sales
of pueblo land required public approval and official supervision.[18]

Spanish law tried to achieve the same protective ends prescriptively,
not by directing legislation at the pueblos but by banning certain non-
Indian activity that might encroach on their lands. Non-Indians could
not live in pueblos, although many did in New Mexico and, indeed,
the first settlers at San Miguel del Vado, in 1794, were ordered to stay
in Pecos Pueblo and await further instructions there. More importantly,
Spanish law was laced with provisions designed to keep a healthy
distance between Indian pueblos and permanent non-Indian settlements.

Early on this second impulse found its way into the *Recopilación*'s definition of the necessary distance between the two. For example, in one place the *Recopilación* provided that

> the sites where pueblos and *reducciones* ["forced settlements"] are to be formed should have ample water, lands, woodlands, access routes, and farmlands and an *ejido* ["commons"] one league long where the Indians can have their livestock without having them intermingle with others belonging to Spaniards.

In another place, the *Recopilación* also provided that

> cattle ranches [estancias de ganado mayor] may not be situated within a league and a half of existing Indian communities and sheep ranches [estancias de ganado menor] within a half-league; and in new communities a boundary [termino] twice as long may be made.[19]

Obviously the distances between Indians and non-Indians varied from ranch to ranch and, indeed, from law to law. In the crowded Valley of Mexico, Indian towns left each other insufficient space to meet the spread the formal law required. In New Mexico the pueblos of Pojoaque and Nambé lay so close together that neither could claim the full measure of their right to land, not because of non-Indians but because of each other.[20] Whatever the particular circumstance or the varying measure, however, the purpose of these distances was to protect Indian property rights, not to define them.

In New Mexico in general, and at Pecos in particular, the distinction got lost between property protection and property ownership, between the pueblo's league as a prophylactic measure designed to separate Pueblos and Hispanic and the pueblo's league as the actual measure of pueblo-owned territory. By the second half of the eighteenth century, New Mexico practice made it clear that local officials, citizens, and the Pueblos themselves all believed that New Mexico pueblos, including Pecos, each "owned" four square leagues, usually measured from the cross at the center of the pueblo cemetery.

In addition, by the same time, all agreed that New Mexico pueblos did not own this arbitrary league on the basis of any aboriginal possession of their homelands, predating Spanish arrival. Instead, claimed the pueblos themselves, they owned their four square leagues based on grants from the Spanish crown itself, made in 1689. Late in the nineteenth century, a United States handwriting expert proved these "1689 grants" to be clumsy and relatively modern forgeries. Nevertheless by the time of Pedro Bautista Pino's March 1803 visit to the upper Pecos River valley, all New Mexicans knew and asserted that pueblos like Pecos "owned" their leagues, based on grants from the king of Spain.[21]

It made no difference that Pecos Pueblo's league was wrenched out of that long Spanish tradition which measured property rights by actual use rather than abstract paper title. It made no difference that, before the Spanish arrival in the sixteenth century, Pecos Pueblo never limited its land claim to one league in each direction from its center. It made no difference that Pecos Pueblo on its own, initially at least, never attempted to establish any league as its external boundary, in order to wall itself in and others out. Instead, Pecos Pueblo's league defined its land ownership only when it became necessary for the pueblo to defend itself against non-Indian encroachments on its lands and waters.

Thus Pedro Bautista Pino brought Pecos Pueblo's league to it when he came to San José del Vado in marzo loco, in 1803.

It took another decade for the pueblo's league and all the assumptions attached to it, to reach Pecos Pueblo from San José del Vado. Some later said that individual non-Indians moved onto the Pecos Pueblo grant well before 1815. But the actual movement of formal, non-Indian land grants to the borders of Pecos Pueblo's league began in a very halting way in 1813 and picked up speed only in 1816. In the interim, between 1803 and 1813, Pedro Bautista Pino went to Spain as the New Mexico territory's only delegate ever to the European Spanish *cortes*, a first-time, quasi-representative body designed to provide some measure of reform for the faltering Spanish crown and empire. Local wags later described Pino's jaunt as useless, mockingly saying, "don Pedro Pino fue, don Pedro Pino vino" ("don Pedro Pino went, don Pedro Pino came"), as a way of suggesting that nothing had come of his trip.[22] In fact, during his years in Spain, Pino helped contribute to a vastly important change in the Spanish legal view of state authority over Pueblo Indian land. That new law got lost in the chaotic shuffle of Spanish reorganization and then Mexican Independence, in 1821. But it returned between 1823 and 1829, as a Mexican law, to haunt, to plague, and ultimately to destroy Pecos Pueblo as a living entity.[23]

European politics produced the background against which Pecos Pueblo's fate was determined in Cádiz, Spain. The usurpation of the Spanish crown by a Bonaparte, in 1808, led directly to the formation of a Spanish cortes, in 1810. Previous Spanish regimes had also called the peculiar institution into session, but the 1810 cortes had several new twists. For one, it was openly more representative than any previous cortes. That representation included for the first time delegates from Spain's overseas empire, among them Pedro Bautista Pino, as the delegate from the New Mexico province of the Mexican colony.[24]

The 1810 summons to the Spanish cortes called for twenty delegates from Mexico. A complicated procedure, including a series of indirect elections, provided the means for representative selection. The process began in the province of New Mexico on 11 August 1810; Pino soon emerged as the winner. Getting to the continent proved another matter. Of the twenty Mexican delegates only fifteen ever arrived in Spain, but Pedro Bautista Pino was one of them.[25]

The Mexican delegates to the 1810–13 Spanish cortes brought a new and unified American point of view with them. They saw the cortes as a chance to win by democratic means reforms which the ultramarine colonies wanted for their own prosperity, reforms they would ultimately win through rebellion. Those reforms included removal of a wide range of restraints the mother country had imposed on Mexico. The delegates wanted freedom from restrictive trade and mining regulations. They wanted more local control over their own affairs. They asked for policies that would foster the development of indigenous industry and agriculture.

In particular, the Mexican delegates pushed in the Spanish cortes for laws that would free up for development and agricultural production otherwise fallow lands in the New World. They aimed specifically at those otherwise protected communal lands of indigenous pueblos, like the Ciénaga de Pecos, that were "going to waste" and could not be used by non-Indians under existing Spanish law.[26]

There was nothing irregular or new about this focus on fallow communal lands. For years before, liberal Spanish theoreticians had expressed concern about the value of antiquated communal landholdings. In an age when the concept of individualism was on the rise, pueblo commons, especially unused pueblo commons, looked like real anachronisms. In the years after final Mexican independence from Spain, in 1821, the spirit of John Locke infused Mexican political debate with the same anticommunal, proindividual bias.[27] For the moment, in Cádiz, Spain, in late 1812, the Mexican delegates to the cortes favored a law, first drafted by the Overseas Committee on 12 March 1812, which would authorize local Mexican governments to allot unused pueblo communal agricultural land such as the Ciénaga de Pecos be-

tween needy, individual Indians and non-Indians. The proposal spelled
the end of the sacrosanct pueblo league.

On 9 November 1812, the plan, pushed by the Mexican delegates
led by Pino among others, succeeded. On that date the cortes enacted
a proposal authorizing a process by which sobrante pueblo lands could
be unfrozen and put to productive agricultural use by individual,
enterprising, needy Indians and non-Indians:

> if the common lands are very numerous in respect to the population
> of the pueblo to which they belong, the lands will be divided up to
> half of these lands at the most. It should be understood that in any
> of these divisions [repartimientos] the legislatures [las diputaciones
> provinciales] will designate the parcel of land that belongs to each
> individual according to the particular circumstances of that
> individual and of each pueblo.[28]

A few months later, the cortes passed another act calling for the
creation of quasi-representative local governments throughout the province of New Mexico. By the act of 4 January 1813, the cortes created
a New Mexico *Diputación Territorial* ("territorial legislature"), to be made
up of eight local citizens who would provide advice and consent to the
gefe político ("governor") on all New Mexican matters, including land.[29]

The sobrantes act of 1812 provided the legal basis for a direct assault
not on Pecos Pueblo's boundaries but on the pueblo itself. The diputación act of 1813 provided the actual means. New Mexico's cortes
delegate had backed both proposals effectively. In his *Noticias históricas
y estadísticas de la antigua provincia de Nuevo México,* published in Spain,
in 1812, Pino described for his peninsular Spanish audience the potential riches of Sonora, Sinaloa, and New Mexico, as seen in their
skins, furs, wool, cattle, ores, wine, lumber, and future agricultural
produce. The province of New Mexico, he argued, could profitably
exploit these resources if only Spain would ease restrictions on foreign
trade and open up Indian land. On the floor of the legislature itself,
Pino pushed for new laws that would give land to otherwise unstable
citizens, force them to live in stable communities, and thus create a
land-based middle class to solidify the revolution-prone New Mexico
proletariat.[30] The land for Pino's proposal would come either from the
public domain or from the sobrante land of the pueblos, now available
under the act of 9 November 1812.

Before New Mexicans ever had the chance to try the 1812 act on
failing pueblos like Pecos, mercurial Spanish politics shifted drastically

again. By 1814 the reestablished crown had repealed all the work of the 1810–13 cortes. But the act would resurface under Spain, in 1820, and become a critical part of the Mexican law of New Mexico, after 1821. Pedro Bautista Pino's legal legacy would return then, with a vengeance, to Pecos Pueblo.[31] In the meantime, if non-Indians wanted valuable pueblo land, they could not just go into the pueblo's league and get it by using the 1812 act. Instead they were left with the time-honored practice of chipping away, in supposed innocence, at the pueblo's sacred boundaries.[32]

At Pecos that process began seriously in 1813. At that time, Francisco Trujillo, for himself and on behalf of Diego Padilla and Bartólome Márquez, petioned New Mexico's Governor Manrique for some land near Pecos Pueblo. The applicants stated that

> [f]inding ourselves without land in this city [Santa Fe] and knowing that unoccupied and uncultivated public domain [realengas] is found in several tracts of land in the stopping place [paraje] they call "Las Ruedas," located in the vicinity of Pecos Pueblo, which lands are not now owned by either purchase or grant . . . We beseech you that these lands do not encroach on, not at all, the boundary of the league that is directed to be set aside to each pueblo of Indians as the alcalde of Pecos knows full well, nor will this grant harm in any manner or any known way prejudice the settlers of the San Miguel del Bado grant or any other third person.[33]

Note that this first Los Trigos grant application identified the land desired only by naming one place, Las Ruedas. Except for the bald assertion that the land infringed on neither San Miguel del Vado's nor Pecos Pueblo's land, the application did not tell where the proposed grant lay. But that was nothing new in New Mexico land grants. Nor was the applicants' lament that they had no land. Traditionally land grant applicants opened by bemoaning the fact that they were starving where they lived for lack of tillable land. In the case of Santa Fe, where the three petitioners resided, the complaint rang true. By the beginning of the nineteenth century, the erratic, water-short Santa Fe River provided much less than the more dependable Pecos River. Los Trigos, sandwiched somewhere between the San Miguel del Vado grant to the south and the Pecos Pueblo grant to the north, promised much more.

But nothing happened with this 1813 application. A year later the persistent applicants returned and renewed their request. On 26 May 1814 the same three men requested

> an existing place, situated in the stopping place [paraje] they call Los
> Trigos, as far as El Gusano, independent of the league of Pecos
> Pueblo, in order that we can locate our animal farms [estancias]
> without damage to either these [Pueblos] or any other third
> person . . .[34]

This second Los Trigos application replaced Las Ruedas as the proposed
grant's focal point with a spot that gave its name to the grant itself.
Trujillo, Márquez, and Padilla now stated that the land they requested
lay between San Miguel del Vado's northern boundary, at El Gusano,
and Pecos Pueblo's southern one, a league distant from the pueblo
complex itself. Finally, for the first time the applicants suggested, in
an aside that would set lawyers dancing in the century to come, that
they only wanted the land for animal pasture and not necessarily for
either homes or irrigated farms.

Governor Manrique received this second Los Trigos petition and
immediately forwarded it to the *ayuntamiento* ("town council") of Santa
Fe for that quasi-municipal body's consideration. He did so, the governor explicitly stated, because the Spanish act of 4 January 1813
required him to consult with local authorities. There was no talk here
of consulting any territory-wide body, because no diputación yet existed. Nor did Manrique or anyone else mention the applicability of
the 9 November 1812 sobrante act; this petition sought unoccupied
public lands (realengas), not unused pueblo land (sobrantes).[35]

But Manrique's referral to the Santa Fe ayuntamiento did bring a
new body into land grant affairs. Previously New Mexico's governor,
assisted by local alcaldes, had handled grant petitions. Now democracy,
New Mexico style, entered the scene. The Santa Fe ayuntamiento was
supposed to bring public input into land grant affairs. Instead, at least
here, the process brought only private speculation.

Of the ten members of the Santa Fe ayuntamiento in 1814 at least
six turned out to be land speculators, who themselves became interested
in land in and around the Pecos Pueblo grant. At least two of those
six played critical judicial roles in the assault on Pecos Pueblo lands
that would follow the establishment of the Los Trigos grant.

Indeed between 1814 and 1829 the connection between the Pecos
Pueblo grant and members of the 1814 ayuntamiento and other local
politicians became so entwined that the situation requires a program
in order to keep the players straight.

First, the members of the 1814 ayuntamiento of Santa Fe:

Juan Estevan Pino: the son of Pedro Bautista Pino. Between 1818 and 1830 Pino speculated wildly in New Mexico land grants. His interests ranged from Angostura in the south to Tesuque in the north and from Santa Fe on the west to what would become the Texas border on the east. In the process Juan Estevan Pino bought and sold Spanish land, Pueblo land, and land that lay somewhere in between. His own people accused him of being such a relentless businessman that "he would devour them." Juan Estevan Pino was to deal Pecos Pueblo its final, staggering blow, in the fall of 1830.[36]

Juan de Dios Peña: a "retired" military man from the Santa Fe garrison. In 1815, one year after he approved the Los Trigos grant, just south of the Pecos Pueblo grant, Peña himself applied for and received an ill-defined grant just north of the Pecos Pueblo grant. That 1815 grant, which would become the Alejandro Valle grant under American rule, badly overlapped Pecos Pueblo's northern boundary. In the end the Peña grant lopped valuable acreage off of the Pecos Pueblo claim. In addition, at the same time Peña was buying, selling, and otherwise adjudicating land claimed by both Taos Pueblo and settlers at Arroyo Seco, almost ninety miles north of Santa Fe and across the mountains from Pecos. There is no evidence that Peña ever lived in either place. In the 1820s he joined Pino and others on the new Diputación Territorial.[37]

Juan Ortiz II: with Juan de Dios Peña one of the original applicants for what became the Alejandro Valle grant, just north of the Pecos Pueblo grant. Unlike Peña, Ortiz moved to Pecos and directly into the grant itself. By 1850 he held a large tract just below the Ciénaga de Pecos.[38]

Matías Ortiz: also served as *alcalde constitucional* of Santa Fe, an official position connected with the governor's office. In that role Ortiz twice visited Pecos Pueblo in 1815, once to establish the Los Trigos grant settlers south of the pueblo's league, the second time to settle the applicants in the Alejandro Valle grant, just north of Pecos. Both times Ortiz erred in favor of the non-Indian settlers. In each case his measurement of Pecos Pueblo's league shortchanged the Indians and further restricted their boundaries. In 1824 Matías Ortiz, again acting as an official of the territory of New Mexico, entered the Pecos Pueblo grant itself and allotted unused tracts of pueblo land to non-Indians. For his services this time he received some Pecos Pueblo land himself. By 1833 Ortiz appeared as a member of the ayuntamiento of Santa

Cruz de la Cañada, north of Santa Fe. Throughout the period records identify him as a local merchant.[39]

José Francisco Ortiz: perhaps a relative of Juan Ortiz II, this Ortiz is himself mentioned as one of the grantees of the Alejandro Valle grant, in Matías Ortiz's 30 June 1815 act of possession for that grant. In 1824 José Francisco went to Pecos with Matías and parceled out part of the ciénaga to non-Indians. Like Matías, he was paid in Pecos Pueblo land for his services.[40]

Felipe Sandoval: in 1815 official protector of the Indians as well as ayuntamiento member. As special protector, Sandoval was charged with stopping encroachments on Indian land. During his tenure the ayuntamiento of Santa Fe approved both the Los Trigos and Alejandro Valle grants. Sandoval's checkered career had begun early. He is reported to have been one of the instigators of the aborted 1805 San Miguel del Vado revolt against the central government in Santa Fe.[41]

The other four members of the ten-man Santa Fe ayuntamiento which considered the Los Trigos grant application in May 1814 included another Ortiz, a Delgado, a Montoya, and a Gallegos. Some of these men were prominent local merchants, but none emerged as distinctive figures on the Pecos or general land scene.[42] The majority of the 1814 Santa Fe ayuntamiento members, however, did have a direct interest in the Pecos Pueblo grant over the years. From the beginning the Santa Fe politicians sometimes caused, often marked, and always measured the Pecos Pueblo's route to extinction.

Two other prominent Santa Feans in 1814, one directly connected to the Los Trigos grant but not to the Santa Fe ayuntamiento, the other not connected to the grant but subsequently connected to the local governing body, also played critical roles in the Pecos Pueblo drama over the next two decades. They complete the cast of prominent characters who played bit parts in 1814 but who stepped forward to stage center by 1825:

Diego Padilla: one of the three applicants for the Los Trigos grant, just south of the Pecos Pueblo grant. Padilla served as sexton for the Catholic church in Santa Fe. He never established a permanent home at Los Trigos. He may have used the grant for a few years after receiving it in 1815. By the 1820s he and his sons had abandoned the Los Trigos grant in favor of more promising land upriver, in the Pecos Pueblo grant. Padilla and his sons bargained with, cajoled, and threatened Pecos Pueblo survivors to secure their holdings within the Indian grant.

In the process they fought with other non-Indian claimants to Pecos Pueblo's lands. They bequeathed a legacy of bitterness and mistrust to Pecos that neither Indians nor Spanish have ever quite shaken.[43]

Domingo Fernández: a skillful, manipulative, educated, and corrupt native Santa Fean, fully the equal of Juan Estevan Pino and equally as influential in the ultimate fate of the Pecos Pueblo grant. Fernández did not belong to the ayuntamiento of Santa Fe in 1814, but within the decade he became a member and influenced land affairs from that position. Between 1821 and 1831 he waged a campaign for the lands of the abandoned pueblo of San Cristóbal and the lands of the nearly abandoned Pecos Pueblo grant. New Mexico had rarely seen such weapons as those with which Fernández fought; the 1812 act of the Spanish cortes, elegantly written legal papers, appeals to Mexico City. To New Mexico land speculation Fernández brought a sophistication that neither Pino could match.[44]

In the spring of 1814, the Santa Fe ayuntamiento proceeded to consider the Los Trigos grant application forwarded to it by the governor as it would have considered any other petition for land. On 30 July 1814, the ayuntamiento recommended approval of the requested grant to the three petitioners, including Padilla, but only insofar as the Los Trigos grant would not conflict with the previous alleged grant to Pecos Pueblo or with the non-Indian San Miguel del Vado grant. On 22 June 1815, almost a year later, New Mexico's Governor Maynez endorsed the recommendation of the ayuntamiento but added an important, additional limitation. On the back of the ayuntamiento decision, Maynez wrote that while the grantees had the right to pasture their stock on any of the lands covered by the grant, any other people who chose to could appropriate for themselves lands within the Los Trigos grant which Trujillo, Márquez, and Padilla did not cultivate and fence.[45]

The 1815 conditions attached by Maynez to the Los Trigos grant made it resemble a community grant, like San Miguel del Vado, to which new settlers had to be welcomed, rather than a private grant to the three applicants only. The Maynez conditions and the final application itself both gave the Los Trigos grant the look of a strictly grazing grant rather than a more general one for settlement.[46] For the moment the approved Los Trigos grant remained somewhere on the southern edge of the Pecos Pueblo grant, awaiting location in the field to determine its boundaries.

In the normal course of land grant affairs, the sequence of prerequisite governmental approvals would have culminated in an almost immediate formal delivery of actual possession of the land to the three original applicants. In fact, the Los Trigos act of possession did not come until October 1815, nearly six months after Maynez approved the grant on his own terms.

In the meantime, non-Indian settlers formally started to move down on the Pecos Pueblo grant from the north, using what now is known as the Alejandro Valle grant. The Benedictine monastery just north of the present village of Pecos now occupies that grant. Just above it the Pecos River disappears into a canyon. Just below it the river debouches into the Ciénaga de Pecos. But precious little about the original Alejandro Valle grant application indicated exactly where it lay.

The process that gave birth to the grant began on 28 March 1815, when Santa Fe ayuntamiento members Juan de Dios Peña and Juan Ortiz II, together with a third man, the less politically well-connected but ultimaely more troublesome Juan de Aguilar, petitioned Governor Maynez for yet another grant in the vicinity of the Pecos Pueblo. The three applicants stated to Maynez that

> We have registered a place that today is barren and unsettled, a place that is located in the environs of Pecos Pueblo, to its west, outside of the property of the pueblo as both the protector of the Indians and the alcalde of this jurisdiction will tell you. This application will result in damage to neither the Indians of this republic nor to other third persons.[47]

No natural monuments mentioned here located the proposed grant on the ground. The petition merely stated that the desired tract lay somewhere near the Pecos Pueblo (correctly) and that the tract lay to the west of it (incorrectly). Despite the petition's vagueness, on the very same day that ayuntamiento members Peña and Ortiz applied for the grant, fellow ayuntamiento member Felipe Sandoval, now as official protector of the Indians, certified to Governor Maynez that "the cited place [sitio] is independent of the league of farmland [labor] of this pueblo, at a regular distance and very separate from it, so that you may accede to this request and make this grant."[48] Here Protector Sandoval added a farmland qualification to the pueblo's league that no formal Spanish law required. By 1815 Pecos Pueblo farmland did not include the Ciénaga de Pecos, abandoned by the pueblo years before. The Alejandro Valle grant could have included part of the Ciénaga de Pecos without giving the lie to Sandoval's 1815 word. The close political connections between Protector Sandoval and the applicants Peña and Ortiz may explain the protector's casual treatment of Pecos Pueblo's league. But, as a matter of fact, in August 1814 Sandoval had measured the pueblo's league in response to an earlier application for the same place from Peña, Ortiz, and Aguilar.

At that time, Peña and friends had told Governor Manrique that they needed the land to maintain themselves and their families in Santa Fe, where they lived. They said that settlement of the place would "serve as a defensive outpost against the enemy Apaches and barbarians." This first petition did not identify the proposed boundaries of the tract applied for any better than the second one, filed the next year. But the 1814 application had provided grounds for Governor Manrique to order an inspection of the site of the proposed grant.

In August 1814 Peña, Sandoval, and the local alcalde Juan Antonio Anaya had gone to Pecos. "We proceeded," Sandoval later reported, "to measure to the satisfaction of the native principal men of the pueblo the league which from time immemorial His Majesty (God save him!) has granted to them to the four points of the hemisphere." Sandoval did not say where he began his measurement of Pecos Pueblo's league or where the measurement had ended or, most crucial of all, where the proposed grant lay in relation to the beginning and ending places. These were boundaries by consent, not location, and Sandoval swore that Pecos Pueblo had consented. More than that no one knew.[49]

There the matter lay until the next year. In March 1815, and in response to Peña's second request for the same tract, Sandoval reported again that the proposed grant would not infringe on Pecos Pueblo land. At least when Sandoval told the new governor, Maynez, that the land Peña and his friends now requested lay outside the pueblo's league, he had an 1814 measurement to go on. This time fellow ayuntamiento member Matías Ortiz joined Sandoval and also told Governor Maynez that no harm would come to Pecos Pueblo from the grant.

The cautious Maynez, however, would not buy these automatic guarantees from his ayuntamiento lieutenants, perhaps because he knew how tightly Sandoval and Matías Ortiz's interests meshed with those of the applicants Peña and Ortiz. On 29 March 1815 Maynez instructed Alcalde Ortiz to put the three petitioners in possession of the land they had applied for, but limited the grant to that land which they in fact could bring under cultivation. Three months later, on 30 June 1815, Ortiz went from Santa Fe to Pecos and, for the first time, actually

placed non-Indians in possession of land that directly adjoined the
Pecos Pueblo grant, this time on its north side:

> I, Matias Ortiz, the alcalde mayor of the city of Santa Fe, stopped to
> put in possession dn. Juan de Dios Peña retired ensign as principal
> applicant for this grant and at the same time to Francisco Ortiz and
> to Juan de Aguilar, as representatives of other ensigns, and having
> arrived at Pecos Pueblo, I measured the league upriver [de río a río]
> beginning at the cross at the cemetery, and having given to the
> Indians their due league in the surplus lands [sobrantes], I took Juan
> de Dios by the hand and at the same time took his companions as
> partners in this possession and I went with them to the land, putting
> them in official possession together with other individuals who
> entered at the same time and in the name of His Majesty (May God
> Protect Him!) I delivered possession to them and at the same time I
> delivered the individual plots of land [suertes] that belonged to each
> individual, I made them see that others [who might come] should
> receive individual plots as well.

Ortiz started his shot of Pecos Pueblo's league at the cemetery, well
south of the pueblo complex. Pecos's spurious seventeenth-century
Spanish grant had directed the measurement to begin at the corner of
the pueblo, considerably to the north. In beginning where he did,
Alcalde Ortiz removed land from the northern end of the Pecos Pueblo
grant, the part where the rich agricultural land lay. But no one could
tell from Ortiz's 1815 description where exactly the common boundary
between the Alejandro Valle and Pecos Pueblo grants lay. Matías Ortiz
suggested only that he had located that common boundary in the
sobrantes of Pecos, those previously cultivated and now neither used
nor needed lands in the Ciénaga de Pecos, in the grant's northeast
quadrant. Even if accurate surveying had not come to Pecos yet, the
Spanish notion of sobrantes had arrived, with all that it implied.[50]

So had Spanish-style private property. Just as Pedro Bautista Pino
had brought suertes to San José del Vado, in 1803, now in 1815 Matías
Ortiz brought individually owned farming plots to the Alejandro Valle
grant, wherever it was. When Ortiz allotted to Peña, Juan de Aguilar,
and Francisco Ortiz their own suertes, he met Maynez's condition that
each petitioner take only that land which he could use. But when Ortiz
also made it clear that under the terms of the grant others could come
and carve additional suertes out of the remaining, unallotted portions
of the grant, he guaranteed that pressure from the north on Pecos
Pueblo's borders would increase after 1815.

Before that pressure resulted in trouble between the pueblo and its new neighbors to the north, Matías Ortiz installed non-Indian settlers on the pueblo's ill-defined southern boundary as well. On 20 October 1815, less than four months after he had installed his fellow ayuntamiento members in the Alejandro Valle grant, Ortiz returned to the Pecos area. On this trip he went to the site of the Los Trigos grant, immediately south of the Pecos Pueblo grant, to place Márquez, Trujillo, and Padilla in possession of that land. Again Alcalde Ortiz reported to Governor Maynez:

> Without prejudice to the Indians of the pueblo I stopped at Pecos Pueblo and I measured a rope [cordel] of 50 varas in length and I handed it over to the Indians so they could measure the boundaries and rope to their own satisfaction and, having measured 100 rope lengths to all their satisfaction I located for them and showed them their boundaries so that all would recognize them and this grant might be settled forever.[51]

While the starting point would call Ortiz's league measurement into question at the Alejandro Valle grant site, the length of his measuring rope caused subsequent problems at Los Trigos. By 1815 pueblos wanted to use a longer rope and to begin earlier in the morning, in order to lengthen their league. Non-Indians, huddled on their borders, wanted to use a shorter rope and a later starting time in order to cut down on the reach of Indian land they could not encroach on.[52] At Pecos within a few years a battle would erupt not only about where to begin the measurement of the pueblo's league, but also about the proper length of the rope to measure it with. For the moment Alcalde Ortiz's October 1815 act of possession for the Los Trigos settlers meant that Pecos Pueblo was now hemmed in by non-Indian settlements on both the north and the south, where the Pecos River came into and exited from the Pecos Pueblo grant. Theoretically those new neighbors posed no threat to the grant itself as an entity. Non-Indians still could not acquire Pecos Pueblo land. They could only reduce that Indian land by squeezing its boundaries from both sides, thus reducing its area.

The Alejandro Valle site, north of the Pecos Pueblo, and the Los Trigos site, south of it, each was settled slowly. Juan de Dios Peña, the ayuntamiento member and "principal petitioner" for the northern grant, probably never settled in Pecos at all. By 1817 he was in Taos and by 1826 he had sold his interest in the grant to a fellow ayuntamiento member, Juan Estevan Pino.[53] The Alejandro Valle grant was off and running in a speculative race. It did not stand still long enough for a real non-Indian community to form immediately. But by 1818–19, settlement of the grant north of Pecos would apply enough pressure on the Pecos Pueblo remnants to fuel the first Indian/non-Indian litigation over Pecos land.

In the meantime settlement at the Los Trigos site began even more slowly. Years afterwards witnesses swore that by 1816 the original applicants Trujillo, Márquez, and Padilla had built small summer shacks (*jacales*), not permanent homes, in the bends of the river ten miles below the Pecos ciénaga. By 1821 they had small gardens there and some stock as well. But, the witnesses later continued, Plains Indian attacks on the site made more permanent development impossible at the Los Trigos site. By 1826 Comanches had driven off the three original grantees. No new Los Trigos settlers took their place until 1842.[54]

Elsewhere in New Mexico in the first quarter of the nineteenth century, similar non-Indian communities on the borders of various pueblo grants had achieved the critical mass provided by real settlement to cause them to spill over onto the lands of more vital pueblos than was Pecos in 1815. For example, in 1815 Taos Pueblo officials protested to the same Governor Maynez who had approved the Alejandro Valle and Los Trigos grants. Non-Indians, they said, had settled within their league. The pueblo wanted them out. When the local Taos alcalde went to check, he found that over many years non-Indians had seized 1,700 varas of Taos Pueblo's 5,000 vara league to the west of the pueblo and 3,950 varas of the pueblo's 5,000 varas along the southern boundary. The non-Indian Taos settlers resisted vociferously and raised a bewildering array of legal justifications for their presence, including the assertion that the lands where they lived were sobrantes of Taos Pueblo, even if within the pueblo's league, and were therefore appropriatable by them. Governor Maynez ruled that Taos Pueblo's league was inviolate and that the law required the non-Indians to get out; in fact they never did. But in principle Maynez's declarations meant that under existing Spanish law the pueblos' borders should remain intact against the kind of incessant chipping away that characterized non-Indian settlement around them.[55]

At Pecos the boundary issue came to a head in 1818. On 17 August of that year, Juan de Aguilar, one of Juan de Dios Peña's copetitioners

for the 1815 grant north of Pecos Pueblo, filed a curious protest with
the new governor, Melgares. Pecos Pueblo leaders felt that Aguilar had
taken up residence within the Indian grant, although he claimed that
the site lay within his grant and outside that of the pueblo. In a move
that became typical of Pecos Pueblo in the desperate decade to come,
Indian leaders went to the alcalde at San Miguel del Vado and complained about Aguilar. Alcalde Vicente Villanueva came upriver at the
pueblo's request, reported Aguilar to Melgares, and measured Pecos
Pueblo's league. Apparently he found that Aguilar's claim was indeed
located within Pecos Pueblo's lands.

Now in his appeal to Melgares, Aguilar claimed that Alcalde Villanueva had erred in two ways in measuring Pecos Pueblo's league. First,
he had used a one-hundred-vara measuring rope instead of a fifty-vara
rope. Second, Villaneuva had begun his league measurement at the
north edge of the pueblo complex, rather than at the cross in the
cemetery, near the church, well south of the Indian buildings. In fact,
although he did not say so, Aguilar knew that Matías Ortiz had used
the shorter rope and the more southerly starting place when he located
the common boundary between the Alejandro Valle and Pecos Pueblo
grants in 1815. Using Ortiz's system, the pueblo's league would not
have reached Aguilar's settlement. Using Villanueva's alternative, it
did. If Villanueva was right, Aguilar would have to move, according
to the law laid down in Governor Maynez's 1815 Taos Pueblo decree.

The point raised by Aguilar's appeal involved the proper location of
Pecos Pueblo's northern boundary. But the area in debate between
Aguilar and Pecos Pueblo, between the alcaldes of Santa Fe and San
Miguel del Vado, encompassed extraordinarily valuable land on the
very northern edge of the Pecos league. There the Pecos River, lifeblood
of both Spanish and Indian communities, hurtled down from the mountains, swung momentarily and violently to the east from its otherwise
southerly course and then, less than three-quarters of a mile later,
swung back to the south as it debouched for the first time in the wide-
open fields of the ciénaga itself. Subsequent Hispanic residents dubbed
that rich but hidden stretch of east-running river and the land beside
it *El Rincón,* or "the nook." In 1818 Pecos Pueblo said that the ciénaga
and the rincón belonged to the pueblo. Aguilar admitted that the
ciénaga did, but then claimed that the rincón fell within the Alejandro
Valle grant, outside the Pueblo grant. The 1818 debate turned on the

precise method of measuring Pecos Pueblo's league. The almost ludicrous precision of the questions presented by Aguilar indicates the
importance of the issue to both Indian and non-Indian claimants.

On 19 August 1818 Governor Melgares forwarded Aguilar's complaint to the alcalde of San Miguel del Vado and asked for his response.
Answering the same day, Villanueva defended his measurement. He
had made it, he told Melgares, because officials of Pecos Pueblo had
asked him to do so. Once at the pueblo, he had prepared to measure
Pecos's league by

> taking the first [measurement] from the edge of the pueblo with a
> measuring rope [cordel] of 100 varas, which I had moistened and
> stretched in order to untwist it and I gave it [this treatment] because
> it had shrunk while rolled up and stored.

The care with which Alcalde Villanueva prepared his measuring instrument closely followed formal surveying instructions specified as
early as 1567 in the New World and two centuries of practice in New
Mexico. Still, to ensure acceptance of his cordel, Villanueva arranged
a joist to which he could attach it and stretch it prior to measurement.
Aguilar and his sons had checked the length of his rope, Villanueva
said, and "four of them (among them the complainant and his sons)
having taken the cordel some distance, stretched it again, so much to
their satisfaction that they broke it." Thus, both the alcalde and the
Hispanic settlers measured the cordel to make sure that it was one
hundred varas long. Everyone had agreed the cordel measured what it
was supposed to.

In the process no one had objected to the use of a one-hundred-vara
cordel. Villanueva asserted that

> No harm has resulted from using the 100 vara cordel and its use is
> fair. If it must be that the smaller one [50 varas] has to be used the
> pueblo will be prejudiced because of the many ups and downs [tierra
> arrugada y doblada] that make up this rugged country.

Villanueva had never heard of the technical surveying term, but here
he asserted Peocs Pueblo's right to a plane table survey, one that did
not allow vertical changes to affect horizontal distance. Matías Ortiz
had used a fifty-vara cordel to measure the pueblo's league twice in
1815. As early as 1567, formal Spanish regulations had required the
shorter cordel. But, argued Villanueva, a fifty-vara rope would not
reach as far in one hundred measures as a one-hundred-vara rope would

in fifty, because of the Pecos terrain. Perhaps the difference did not amount to much. But the debate itself measured the intensity of pressure on Pecos Pueblo land and the sincere effort of the San Miguel del Vado alcalde to be fair to the Pecos natives.

As to the second point of Aguilar's appeal, complaining that Villanueva had chosen the wrong place to begin the shot of Pecos's league, Villanueva explained his choice of the northern edge of the pueblo rather than cross in the church cemetery, to the south, by once again referring to special conditions in the Pecos area. Curiously, the suspect 1689 so-called Cruzate grant to Pecos Pueblo called on the league measurement to begin at the corners of the pueblo, as Villanueva had done. Rather than relying on that document, however, Villanueva told Governor Melgares that

> It is true that it has been customary (and I have done so myself) to begin at the cemetery cross. This has been done not because of a set rule but rather because all the pueblos, except this one, have the church more or less in the center. This Pecos Pueblo, to the contrary, has the church more than 100 varas away from one end of the pueblo in the opposite direction from the part the natives are defending. Therefore, I deem it just that it be begun in all directions, from the pueblo as center.

As a final justification for beginning where he had and for using his one-hundred-vara cordel, Villanueva told Governor Melgares that he had measured Pecos Pueblo's league twice before using those techniques. The prosettler surveyor Matías Ortiz had twice before used the more distant starting place and the shorter measuring rope. As of 1818 the Pecos Pueblo grant's northern boundary hung in this delicate balance.[56]

No record survives indicating a decision on Aguilar's 1818 appeal. But other Pecos settlers posed a greater threat to the pueblo than did Aguilar. In 1818 at least one non-Indian house, perhaps already abandoned, encroached even further on Pecos Pueblo's northern boundary than did Aguilar's settlement.[57] The measurement business itself became dangerous. Vicente Villanueva was found dead near Los Trigos around 1822, killed, swore the Hispanic *vecinos* ("neighbors," "settlers"), by hostile Apaches, from the east.[58] If population figures are to be believed, in 1820 there were only fifty-eight residents of Pecos Pueblo left, down by more than half from the number reported in 1803, the year Pedro Bautista Pino came to San José del Vado, and by more than 90 percent from the Indian population of a century before.[59] Even accounting for the notorious variances in demographic data for the period, the drift of Pecos affairs was clear. The non-Indian Pecos world was on the rise. Pecos Pueblo's world was waning.

In the meantime chaos on the national Mexican scene continued. Beginning in 1821 Mexico began its break with Spain, a process which started with Agustín de Iturbide's *Plan of Iguala* and ended in 1824, with the enactment of a new, national Mexican constitution. The curious result of this chaos was the establishment in New Mexico of a new sovereignty and the reestablishment of some of the old Spanish laws.[60] In particular, Mexican sovereignty brought to Pecos the act of 9 November 1812 of the Spanish cortes, an act which had had no force under Spanish rule since 1814 and which now suddenly became effective as Mexican law. Under Spain, Juan de Aguilar and the other non-Indians eyeing Pecos Pueblo lands had had to quibble about where the boundaries of the pueblo's league lay, as their only way of approaching pueblo lands. Under the resurrected act of 9 November 1812, they could now try to move right in.

Between 1820 and 1830, that is exactly what they attempted to do.

TWO

The Death of Pecos Pueblo
under Mexican Rule

How great must be the pain in our hearts on seeing ourselves
violently despoiled of our rightful ownership, all the more when this
violent despoilment was executed while they threatened us with the
illegal pretext of removing us from our pueblo and distributing us
among the other pueblos of the territory. Please, your excellency, see
if by chance the natives of our pueblo for whom we speak are denied
the property and shelter of the laws of our liberal system. Indeed,
sir, has the right of ownership and security that every citizen enjoys
in his possessions been abolished?

—Rafael Aguilar and José Cota

Nineteen years after Pedro Bautista Pino stopped at San José del Vado,
on his way back to Santa Fe from San Miguel, and distributed river
lands to the first non-Indians in the Upper Pecos Valley, Domingo
Fernández repeated the journey. In the summer of 1822, the thirty-
six-year-old Santa Fe merchant, politician, and archivist went to San
Miguel del Vado on business. On his return to Santa Fe, he stopped
not at San José, as Pino had done, but at Los Trigos, founded in 1815
along the Pecos River just south of the Pecos Pueblo grant. There he
camped for the night.

He noticed one small house, belonging to the grantees Márquez and
Padilla, in the northern portion of the Los Trigos grant. He remarked
on Padilla's stock, grazing on the grant and cared for by Padilla's sons.
They told him about the settlement of Trujillo, the third Los Trigos
grantee, just downriver, at El Gusano. Fernández himself already knew
of the death of San Miguel del Vado's alcalde, Vicente Villanueva, the
official who in 1818 had measured Pecos Pueblo's league in favor of
the dwindling pueblo. Fernández attributed Villanueva's death to ma-

31

rauding Apaches. More cynical observers suspected non-Indian Pecoseños, seeking revenge for Villanueva's pro-Indian land rulings.[1]

In any case, between Pino's visit, in March 1803, and Fernández's
trip, in July 1822, Pecos Pueblo had declined even further. From the
fifty-two male and seventy-three female Indians in residence in 1804,
Pecos Pueblo in 1821 had only twenty-six male and twenty-eight female
inhabitants.[2] Presumably the amount of land controlled by the pueblo
had dwindled proportionately. The increasing non-Indian population
needed all the unused land they could find. In the summer of 1822,
Domingo Fernández prepared to move against Pecos Pueblo.

Less than a year before Fernández's visit to Los Trigos and Pecos,
the government of New Mexico had finally sworn its allegiance to the
revolutionary government in Mexico City. On 24 February 1821, Iturbide had announced his *Plan of Iguala,* with its guarantee that any
difference between Mexican Indians and others had disappeared. In
August of that year Spain relinquished control over Mexico, including
New Mexico, to the new nation. A month later a triumphant Iturbide
entered Mexico City for a short term as head of a new, permanent
nation. New Mexico acknowledged the new regime in September 1821.[3]

The chaos involved in establishing the new sovereignty and the
length of time news of the situation took to reach Mexico's far northern
frontier could not mask for long the fundamental change in Pueblo
Indian status that the revolution had wrought. Under Spain, New
Mexico pueblos had enjoyed wardship status. Now, under an independent Mexico, their people became full citizens, with the right to own
and dispose of real property without government protection or inter-
ference. After 1821, the government provided no special attorney to
defend the pueblos' interests. They operated their own municipal governments, paid taxes, and served in the militia along with non-Indian
citizens. The Pueblo people themselves understood this. They defended
their land themselves, as owners, not as Indians with a special status.[4]

Of course, this fundamental shift in the status of Pueblo Indians
and their lands did not become clear overnight; it took ten years for
New Mexico to clarify the new vision. The process took place in the
context of intricate, passionate attempts by non-Indians to gain legal
access to the rich, irrigable, unused land within the Pecos Pueblo
grant. Domingo Fernández and Juan Esteban Pino were the chief competitors in these struggles. But when the situation was resolved for the
time being, in 1830, it became obvious that Pecos Pueblo had won

the right to be declared the outright owner of its land, as the new Mexican law indeed declared it to be, only to lose its homelands by selling them away, as the new Mexican law also declared the pueblo could do.

The first direct assault on Pecos Pueblo's irrigable land began contemporaneously with, although apparently incidentally to, the Mexican drive for independence from Spain. On 10 February 1821, two weeks before Iturbide even announced his *Plan of Iguala,* Esteban Baca, a Santa Fe promoter, and some thirty other residents of La Ciénaga and Cienaguilla, south of Santa Fe, applied to Governor Melgares for part of Pecos Pueblo's farm lands. The petitioners, said Baca, had no land of their own. Only "eight or ten" Indian families still lived there. They had no priest. For years, the Pecos church's "sacred voices" had been silent. Pecos Pueblo, said Baca, was vulnerable because it had no "title" to its lands. The easiest solution, he suggested, would be to move the non-Indians in with the Indians, leaving the Pueblos what land they actually cultivated and granting to the new settlers what land the pueblo could not use. The happy union of "españoles indios," as Baca dubbed the new community, would save the pueblo from extinction. In addition, it would satisfy the national goal of increased agricultural production, a goal long espoused, according to Baca, by different royal orders and decrees.[5]

Baca's 1821 petition introduced several themes that would be repeated over the next decade. The suggestion that Indians and non-Indians should share the same terrain according to the needs of each became familiar by the late 1820s. Baca's appeal to increased national agricultural production reappeared frequently in the next decade as a justification for awarding unused Pueblo agricultural lands to non-Indians.[6] But Baca's application was vague about what title Pecos Pueblo might have to its league. When he referred to lack of title, did he assert that Pecos Pueblo had none, or that the applying non-Indians could acquire none adverse to the Indians? Just what did Esteban Baca and his fellow petitioners seek to acquire in the Pecos Pueblo grant?

Despite the vagaries of the application and simultaneous confusion on the Mexican national scene, Governor Melgares handled Baca's request as previous governors had. On 12 February 1822, Melgares passed the Baca petition on to the alcalde constitucional Juan Rafael Ortiz and instructed him, in a marginal note, to investigate. It took Ortiz almost two months to comply, but when, on 1 April 1821, he finally made his report, his inquiry indicated a new direction in land matters.

Normally, as in previous years, an alcalde's report on an application for New Mexico land discussed the status of the land applied for. The alcalde visited the site and informed the governor of whether it was vacant, if it was claimed by Indian or non-Indian owners, and whether, in the alcalde's opinion, making the grant would prejudice the rights of others. In the case of the 1821 Esteban Baca petition, however, Alcalde Ortiz did not go to the Pecos Pueblo grant to investigate the land applied for. Instead, he "checked around" ("heché averiguación") to see if Baca and his allies really needed the land, as they claimed. Ortiz consulted with the assistant commissioner of La Ciénaga, the commissioners of Cienaguilla, two citizens of Santa Fe, and "Pino." The informants told Ortiz, and Ortiz told Melgares, that most of the applicants already owned land and, presumably, did not need more. However, reported Ortiz, seven of the Baca applicants in fact had no land and the status of an eighth was uncertain.[7]

No one ever stated directly that the property-owning status of the majority of the Baca applicants precluded the petition's approval. Apparently the request died with Ortiz's 1 April 1821 report. The government's investigation into the petition, however, indicated a new concern with Indian land. Where previously the question had turned on whether the land applied for was owned by a pueblo, the issue now became whether non-Indians really needed it, regardless of who owned it. Baca's 1821 petition for Pecos Pueblo's agricultural lands began a process that would accelerate in the decade to come. That Alcalde Ortiz consulted a Pino about the application indicated a family involvement from the outset that would also increase over time.

By September 1823, the move against Pecos Pueblo's irrigable lands had developed further. Some of the liberal reforms of the Spanish cortes, which Pedro Bautista Pino had helped to shape between 1811 and 1813, actually began to take hold in New Mexico by early 1822. Pecos Pueblo formed its own municipal corporation, a sign both of the pueblo's liberated status under Mexican rule and its communal status under Spanish law. The Diputación Territorial, called for by the act of 4 January 1813, was formed and began to meet, in Santa Fe. By April 1822, the seven-member quasi-legislative body was holding regular meetings there. Within a year its membership included three Santa Fe merchants and Pedro Bautista Pino himself, just returned, according to some reports, from his years in Spain. The controversial diputación secretary, Juan Bautista Vigil, and Governor Bartólome Baca completed the original membership.

From the beginning, the new body played a crucial role in New Mexico land affairs. Prior to the formation of the diputación, New Mexico governors ruled alone on grant applications, with the help of local alcaldes; after 1822 they consulted with the new body on land matters. The diputación always expressed a general interest in the production of as much food as possible.[9]

Domingo Fernández himself set a number of precedents when, on 22 April 1822, he applied to the governor for a huge tract of land near present-day Galisteo, between Pecos and Santa Fe. "I Have registered," he reported on that day, "a tract commonly called the pueblo of San Cristóbal where, if the truth be known, one can see the ruins of the pueblo and the walls of a Holy Church [santo templo] all destroyed and almost on the ground."[10] This application demonstrated Fernández's early interest in abandoned and nearly abandoned pueblo lands, the prime examples of which were San Cristóbal and Pecos. Over the next ten years, Fernández alternated between the two grants, first trying to secure one and then, when that effort temporarily failed, turning his attention to the other. In so doing, Fernández had dealings with all the governmental officials and bodies concerned with land grant affairs in New Mexico during the 1820s. Sometimes Fernández approached the local ayuntamiento of Santa Fe. Sometimes, as in his original application, he appealed to the governor himself. Sometimes he concentrated on the diputación. But he always focused on the dead pueblo of San Cristóbal or the dying pueblo of Pecos. In the end, he won the San Cristóbal land and lost any claim to that of Pecos Pueblo. But between 1820 and 1830, he so confused the Pecos Pueblo situation that few understood what was going on. In the process he so demoralized the last Indian inhabitants of the pueblo that they sold their most valuable lands, rather than see them expropriated by the Mexican government or simply stolen by land-hungry non-Indians.

Domingo Fernández's attempt to secure San Cristóbal lands began as a request for a direct land grant from the governor. His application for Pecos lands began differently, in the newly formed diputación. There the question of what to do about underutilized communal pueblo lands had surfaced early. On 1 February 1823, the diputación received a curious request for information from the ayuntamiento of San Lorenzo, near el Paso.[11] It specifically wanted to know if it could partition the lands of a pueblo where only one Indian remained between that remaining Indian and the many non-Indians who needed land ("si se podrán repartir las tierras a los vecinos que se hallan sin propriedad"). The ayuntamiento cited the act of 9 November 1812, of the Spanish cortes, as authority for its proposed action, and wanted to know whether it applied in New Mexico.

Within a month the diputación equivocated, promising to answer later. This request raised the issue of the effect of a Spanish act on Pueblo Indian land ownership under Mexican rule. Esteban Baca's 1821 application for Pecos Pueblo lands had not succeeded. Nothing had happened as yet with Domingo Fernández's application for the already abandoned lands of San Cristóbal Pueblo. But in the fall of 1823, Fernández again raised the question asked by San Lorenzo and sought for the first time a forced partition of vacant Pecos Pueblo land in the water-rich Ciénaga de Pecos.

On 1 September 1823, Fernández, Rafael Benavídez, and thirty-one others, all citizens, soldiers, and retired soldiers of Santa Fe, petitioned the governor of New Mexico for what the applicants called the sobrantes of Pecos Pueblo. Fernández cited no formal law in support of his request, but its terms made it obvious that he had something different in mind from his straightforward attempt to gain the abandoned San Cristóbal Pueblo grant. Here at Pecos, Fernández told Governor Baca, the thirty-three applicants he represented needed land to support themselves. The struggling Mexican nation, he added, also required increased agricultural production. Very few Pueblo Indians resided at Pecos. They neither used nor needed much of their formerly vast irrigated lands. On all these grounds, he concluded, the New Mexico government should take control of the Pecos land situation, determine how much land the pueblo required for its sustenance, apportion that to the pueblo, and then divide the rest among the non-Indian applicants whom Fernández represented.[12]

In this application Fernández did not ask for title to the whole grant on the grounds that it had been abandoned or had never been owned. He never claimed that Pecos Pueblo had no continuing rights to the land, the argument he used with San Cristóbal. Here he simply claimed that the Mexican government of New Mexico had the right and the power with respect to Pueblo Indian land, as it had under Spain with respect to water, to order a repartimiento between Indians and non-Indians.

Governor Baca treated Fernández's request exactly as he would have treated a more traditional application for public land. On 1 September 1823, the same day he received it, Baca sent the application to the alcalde of the jurisdiction of San Miguel del Vado and told him to report on the status of Pecos lands. On 18 September, Manuel Antonio Baca reported for the ayuntamiento of San Miguel del Vado, in remarkably blunt terms. Pecos Pueblo did indeed have surplus lands within its league, but the government could not assign them to others because the surplus lands "are already owned."[13] The San Miguel ayuntamiento clearly implied that Pecos Pueblo, not some non-Indian claimant, was the owner and announced, in effect, that the Pecos sobrantes were not subject to government partition and allocation to non-Indians.

The pro-pueblo stance adopted by the local governmental unit closest to Pecos Pueblo recalled Vicente Villanueva's 1818 rulings on Pecos Pueblo's boundaries. The two surprising decisions together indicate that the pueblo's most ardent advocates were those at the lowest and closest, not highest and farthest, levels of government. Over the next two decades the pueblo continued to receive more sympathetic attention from its local non-Indian representatives than it ever did from the central government, in Santa Fe.

Governor Baca kept the unfavorable report for the time being. He later stated that he did not forward it immediately to the diputación because he was awaiting its report on the condition of the Pecos church. But Domingo Fernández and Rafael Benavídez responded immediately. On 21 September 1823, the two wrote to the governor and disingenuously intimated that the ayuntamiento of San Miguel had supported their application in its 18 September report. They told Baca that Pecos Pueblo consisted of only ten married and five single men. They repeated their finding that there were sobrante lands at the pueblo and said that the San Miguel del Vado ayuntamiento had agreed, which it technically had. But the two applicants said nothing about the ayuntamiento's ruling that non-Indians could not take the land, even if it was surplus. Instead, Fernández and Benavídez stated that neither they nor the others they represented wanted to harm the Pecos Pueblo Indians. Indeed, the Indians had said that they would accept Fernández and his friends; the governor could help by insisting that the Indians there keep their word.[14]

Nothing happened through the fall and early winter of 1823. In December 1823, Juan Estevan Pino, Pedro Bautista's son, applied to Governor Baca for a grant to a 318,000 acre tract of land at the confluence of the Pecos and Gallinas rivers, downstream from both the pueblo and San Miguel del Vado.[15] Baca immediately forwarded this application to the diputación. For the first time the quasi-legislative body entered directly into New Mexico land affairs. At its 20 December 1823 meeting the diputación approved the huge grant to Pino and expressed its concern about the sluggish state of agriculture in New Mexico, brought on by the prejudice against making grants of the public lands ("pues de la preocupación de no señalar propriedades en los terrenos comunes resultaba todo o la mayor parte del retraso de la agricultura de esta provincia"). The diputación would soon consider whether its concern with privatizing public land should apply to unused Pueblo Indian land as well. For the moment, the diputación's action brought Juan Estevan Pino onto the New Mexico land scene. Pecos would never be the same.

The explicit changes began on 16 February 1824, less than two months after the diputación blessed the grant to Juan Estevan. On that day Governor Baca finally decided to forward the Fernández application to the diputación for its consideration, together with Fernández's letter of 21 September. Baca wrote that although the full report still lacked some details, he was forwarding the report for diputación action anyway, because "the petitioners are being damaged" by the delay.[16]

Meeting the same day, in Santa Fe, the diputación took up three critical matters of business connected with Pueblo lands. Faced with petitions to apportion Santo Domingo Pueblo and San Felipe Pueblo lands to non-Indians and with the pueblos' protests against the proposals, the diputación directed that the affected pueblos be told that the government of New Mexico had the right to take their unused lands and give them to non-Indians. But with respect to the Fernández application, the diputación directed the governor to speak to the Pecos Indians directly and to report back. Finally, the diputación considered two other applications for land at that meeting. One of the applications apparently involved Miguel Rivera and six others, who petitioned for "one sole bend in the river, located adjoining the lands of Miguel Roibal" ("un solo ancón . . . se halla junto a las tierras de Miguel Roibal"). The other involved an application by the Santa Fe parochial sacristan. The land applied for by both Rivera and the sacristan would later be found to lie well within the boundaries of the Pecos Pueblo grant. But the diputación directed that both parties be put in possession of the land they applied for.[17]

The difference between the diputación's treatment of the Fernández application for Pecos Pueblo land and the Rivera applications may only reflect the fact that the location of the Rivera tract was not precisely known. In any case the Pecos Pueblo situation was already confusing; three days after the diputación meeting, it became even more unclear. On 19 February 1824 Miguel and Felipe Sena, sons of the gunsmith of the Santa Fe military company, petitioned the governor for a plot of Pecos Pueblo irrigated land for themselves. The two had not appeared on Domingo Fernández's original 1823 application. Ten years later, Miguel Sena would become an infamous Santa Fe *rico* ("man of wealth"). With their petition the Senas became the fourth non-Indian group competing for Pecos Pueblo lands in the first months of 1824, joining the Fernández and Rivera groups and Diego Padilla.[18]

In March 1824, the Pecos Pueblo situation emerged as a crisis for the first of many times. On 10 March, Governor Baca announced that he wanted the diputación to consider three points at its next meeting: two involved the territory's perennial money problems and the third involved "the lands sought in Pecos, Santo Domingo and San Felipe."[19]

On the appointed day, 12 March 1824, the diputación considered the alcalde José Francisco Ortiz's report on the situation at San Felipe and Santo Domingo pueblos, on the Río Grande. Ortiz had found that land amounting to three-quarters of a league belonging to the two pueblos was not cultivated by either pueblo and had been apportioned among non-Indian farmers. The two pueblos claimed that they used the unfarmed land to pasture their cattle and that the diputación therefore should not award it to the non-Indians. However, the diputación directed Ortiz to confirm the non-Indians in their ownership, once he had determined and had apportioned to the individual pueblos the land they needed.[20]

Surprisingly, the diputación approached the Pecos Pueblo problem quite differently. Governor Baca reported that he had spoken with the pueblo leaders, as he had been instructed at the 16 February 1824 diputación meeting. Pecos Pueblo officials had told him that the pueblo hardly had enough irrigated land for its own subsistence ("que el terreno que tienen de labor apenas les facilitaba la sustencia") and that the pueblo had to work it all, as well as repair the church. For those reasons, they told Baca, the Fernández and Sena petitions could not be granted ("por cuyas razones no se podía dar a los solicitantes"). San Felipe and Santa Domingo pueblos had protested on the same grounds, without effect. But now the diputación, on the basis of Pecos Pueblo's protest, denied the Fernández and Sena applications. According to the minutes, "it was resolved that the petition of the applicants would not lie."[21]

Domingo Fernández's first attempt to secure Pecos Pueblo sobrantes had apparently died. The thirty-two non-Indian land seekers he represented could not legally use Pecos Pueblo as a solution to their land-poor status. But subsequent documents make it clear that non-Indians, including some whom Fernández represented, took possession of Pecos Pueblo lands anyway, probably by the summer of 1824, if not before.

The 12 March 1824 diputación order directly affected only the Fernández group. In May 1824, Diego Padilla, the Los Trigos grantee, allegedly convinced the diputación secretary, Juan Bautista Vigil, to allocate to him and five cronies valuable farmland within the pueblo's league. Padilla, some said, bribed the people of Pecos Pueblo by promising them six oxen or cows. Padilla had certainly failed to consult with the alcalde of San Miguel del Vado, who had assigned the same land to Miguel Rivera and nine of his companions. Despite the ruling of 12 March 1824, the non-Indian invasion of Pecos had progressed by the summer of 1824 to the point where non-Indian claimants had begun to fight among themselves for pueblo land. Indeed, in addition to the Padilla and Rivera groups, some members of the Fernández group later claimed that they had also taken possession of Pecos Pueblo land in the summer of 1824. By the summer of 1826, non-Indians had under cultivation 8,459 varas of land in Pecos, using almost five miles of new irrigation ditch. Clearly they had not done that work overnight.[22]

In the spring of 1824, however, Domingo Fernández's chances for acquiring Pecos Pueblo land looked bleak. Rather than appeal the denial of his application, Fernández tried to resurrect his claim to the entire abandoned San Cristóbal Pueblo grant, a claim that had lain dormant while he was involved with Pecos. On 1 November 1824, less than eight months after the diputación had rejected Fernández's bid for

Pecos, it considered applications for two grants from the public domain: one by Pablo Montoya for land on the Río Colorado, the other by Fernández for the San Cristóbal grant. Fernández had already received approval for his San Cristóbal claim from the Santa Fe ayuntamiento, of which he was a member. Now he appeared before the territorial diputación to win approval there. Surprisingly, the diputación recommended granting Pablo Montoya's request but denied Domingo Fernández's request. His application, ruled the diputación, was for land "in between the Pecos River and the Río del Norte that has been reserved in common for the entire province as much in times of invasion as for the transport of goods in times of peace with the savage tribes."[23] Less than a year before, the same body had granted Juan Estevan Pino's application for public land, in order to make it private and productive. Now the same body denied Fernández's request in order to keep the land common. As of 1 November 1824, neither Pecos nor San Cristóbal would belong to him.

But even without Fernández, the Pecos Pueblo land situation became more complex. On 4 December 1824, Miguel Rivera and his six partners reapplied to the diputación, asking for confirmation of the Pecos land granted to them the previous February. They had gone to take up their land, they said, only to have Diego Padilla and the secretary of the diputación, Juan Bautista Vigil, throw them out. On 13 February 1825 Rivera and his fellows appealed the complex matter to the governor and the diputación. They had heard that Domingo Fernández had reactivated his petition for Pecos Pueblo land, after the rejection of his request for the San Cristóbal tract.[24] Rivera wanted to be sure to reserve a place in the proceedings.

At its 16 February 1825 meeting, the diputación addressed the increasingly troubled Pecos Pueblo situation. The body considered first Rivera's complaint that he and his partners "had been despoiled of the lands on the Pecos River allocated to them by the gefe político, through the alcalde of San Miguel del Bado, on the grounds that the diputación already had given the lands to the citizen Diego Padilla." Obviously a jurisdictional debate was developing, but the diputación wasted little time on that issue. Both sets of claimants were to follow the allocations of the alcalde of San Miguel del Vado, not those of the diputación secretary, Juan Bautista Vigil. However, in addition to his claim through government repartimiento, Padilla apparently also stated that he bought from the pueblo the tract he claimed, which overlapped Rivera's. On that point the diputación ruled that once the central government had taken jurisdiction over a pueblo's unused land, under the law of 9 November 1812 (here specifically cited), the pueblo no longer had the right to sell it to others.[25] This decision in effect used the 1812 law to provide a general rule of forfeiture for nonuse, applicable to pueblo communal land under circumstances to be decided by the government authorities. Once the forfeiture for nonuse had occurred, the general government then acquired the right to redistribute the abandoned land to others, a public right that could not be upset by a so-called private pueblo sale of unused land. Even if Diego Padilla had bought from Pecos Pueblo supposedly abandoned pueblo land that the diputación had previously allocated to Miguel Rivera and his partners, the diputación allocation still controlled.

At its 16 February 1825 meeting, the diputación announced these general principles, but did not apply them to the confused Pecos Pueblo situation. Instead, the body decided that Miguel Rivera and his companions should reapply for the Pecos Pueblo lands, describing again the boundaries of the land previously given to the group ("pidiendo hacer su reclamo nuebamente con expreción de los linderos que contenga la tierra que se le ha donado"). The diputación would consider the matter at its next meeting, on 3 March.[26]

On 1 March 1825, Miguel Rivera and the five other applicants who had joined in the 13 February request complied with the diputación's demand. Their renewed application stated that the land originally allocated to them had been sold by the pueblo to Diego Padilla. Therefore, they requested other tracts in the unused lands of the Pecos Pueblo grant. Rivera asked that it adjoin the land claimed by Padilla. The tract Rivera first applied for lay "near the lands belonging to Miguel Roibal in the Pecos Pueblo." Padilla had taken that. Now, in replacement, Rivera asked for an adjoining tract with the following boundaries:

> on the east, the arroyo that comes down from the mountains and
> waters the river; and beneath, the trail that comes down Tecolote and
> the little house they call Guadalupe's place; on the east the tract
> reaches the mountains and on the west the said river.

This vague description made the tract impossible to locate precisely. Clearly it lay on the east side of the Pecos River, probably directly across from the pueblo itself and perhaps half a mile south of the

Ciénaga de Pecos.[27] But it turned out that Miguel Rivera and his companions were not the only non-Indians to respond to the diputación's 16 February request that petitioners refile for Pecos Pueblo land. On the same day that Miguel Rivera filed his new application, three other groups of non-Indians also applied for Pecos lands.

The new applicants, who all filed 1 March 1825, included some who had never solicited Pecos Pueblo land before. Rafael Benavídez, who in 1823 had belonged to the Domingo Fernández group, now petitioned separately. Two men in the Benavídez group had previously belonged to Fernández's, but two others had not. José María Gallegos, an original Fernández partner, now filed on his own. And Domingo Fernández himself, whom the diputación had rejected outright on 12 March 1824, now reappeared and asked again for Pecos Pueblo's abandoned land.[28] Alliances had shifted and splintered, while interest in Pecos Pueblo land grew.

The four applications presented on 1 March did not reveal much more than that. The Rivera application only vaguely described the Pecos land it sought. The Benavídez application asked for a tract "on this side of Cow Creek," bounded "on the east side by the little springs that are on this side of Cow Creek, on the west by the river, on the north the trail that comes down from Tecolote and on the south the boundary of Diego Padilla."[29] This description sounds suspiciously like the tract the Rivera group had wanted. Neither Domingo Fernández nor José María Gallegos indicated what particular land they wanted, but simply asked the diputación for land in the Pecos Pueblo grant. The 3 March 1825 diputación meeting appeared to be developing toward a general discussion of what to do about Pecos Pueblo and its lands.

A year before Pecos Pueblo officials had told Governor Baca that they needed all their land; on that basis, the diputación had turned down Domingo Fernández. Now, in 1825, Pecos Pueblo opened the March 3 meeting concerned with non-Indian petitions for Pecos lands by flatly asking the diputación to rule that the pueblo had the right to "the league of land that it had in the time of the Spanish government." The result of this would have been that no non-Indian could take possession of Pecos Pueblo lands.

The diputación responded by appointing a committee of two deputies—Matías Ortiz, who had placed the grantees of the Los Trigos and Alejandro Valle grants in possession of land bordering the Pecos

Pueblo grant, in 1815, and José Francisco Ortiz. The two men were
to give full force to section 5 of the law of 9 November 1812, which
authorized the dismantling of communal Indian holdings and the granting of a pueblo's unneeded lands to non-Indians. In its most eloquent
statement of the philosophy underlying the law, the diputación directed
the two men to make the people of Pecos Pueblo understand that under
Mexico, "just as their ancient duties have ceased, so too their ancient
privileges have ended, leaving equal, one to the other, all the additional
citizens who with the Pueblos form the great Mexican family."

For the first time the diputación made clear the process it considered
necessary to implement the repartimiento of Pecos Pueblo lands. The
two men were to go to Pecos and determine what land the pueblo used
and what additional land it needed. That initial step, termed *la re-
partición,* would serve two functions. It would segregate the property
to remain in pueblo ownership, but it would also indicate what land
was available for non-Indian acquisition. This land should then be
given to the poorest citizens ("a los vecinos absolutamente desacom-
odados"). In granting tracts the diputación would give a preference to
those who qualified and who had applied at that session.[30]

Without waiting for the initial report of its committee, the diputación proceeded at its 3 March meeting to consider three of the four
applications for Pecos Pueblo land that had reached it on 1 March.
The body considered first Miguel Rivera's resubmitted application for
land next to that claimed by Diego Padilla, "in the communal lands,
already vacant and public" ("en las tierras de comunidad . . . ya baldías") in Pecos. The diputación granted these lands to Rivera and his
five partners according to the boundaries they had requested in East
Pecos (the ciénaga east of the river). The group had only to show the
diputación's committee which land they claimed and the transaction
would be complete. In the meantime, Rivera and his companions could
take possession of their lands. If Pecos Pueblo had already sold the
land they claimed, their claim would take precedence; once the diputación had declared land within Pecos Pueblo's league to be sobrantes, the pueblo lost all control of it. It became public land, *tierras
baldías,* part of the public domain and subject to diputación control
and disposal.

As its next order of business the diputación granted Rafael Benavídez's petition for Pecos land, "in the form asked and with the boundaries shown." The diputación required only that Benavídez and his five

partners indicate those boundaries to the two commissioners so that they could integrate the tract with other dispositions of the Pecos Pueblo sobrantes. With respect to José María Gallegos's simultaneous application, the diputación ruled that the division between Pecos Pueblo, the Rivera group, and the Benavídez group should take place first. Then Gallegos could return and claim a tract of what land was left over. Finally the diputación disposed of a procedural problem when it ruled that it, not the alcalde of San Miguel del Vado, had control of the allotment of surplus Pecos Pueblo lands.

The 3 March 1825 meeting proved important for what the diputación did and did not do. The confirmation of land to Indians within the Pecos Pueblo grant represented the first clear imposition on non-Indian lands of the 1812 allotment act of the Spanish cortes. The diputación explicitly cited that act as authority for its actions. At the same time, the diputación did not consider Domingo Fernández's reapplication of 1 March 1825. Apparently the additional allotment of Pecos Pueblo sobrantes to non-Indians would have to await the report and decision of the two diputación commissioners, Matías Ortiz and José Francisco Ortiz.[31]

In the meantime, more applicants for Pecos Pueblo land appeared. On 8 March 1825, Luis Benavídez, another retired soldier from Santa Fe, applied for "a small tract in the surplus land of the Indians of Pecos in order to plant a few corn plants and some wheat." He had not been included in any previous petition. The diputación did not even acknowledge this application, but left the matter, for the moment, to its commissioners.[32]

In the first two weeks of March, the two men went to Pecos on behalf of the governor and in conformity with the diputación's instructions. First they went to Pecos Pueblo, announced that they had come to allot its lands, and asked the people of the pueblo if they would be harmed. Subsequent reactions by the Pecos Indians make it extremely unlikely that they protested strongly, if indeed they were ever asked. But Domingo Fernández, biased reporter that he was, later said that Pecos Pueblo's answer was

> to allow them [Pecos Pueblo] the land they had cultivated and had sold, and to partition among them [Hispanos] the rest that remained untilled even though it might be in the middle of cultivated land. The Pueblos said that because they were poor citizens [vecinos] they agreed to share the lands as brothers; that by being in the middle,

they were safe from all damage and injury. This was their choice
without being constrained, forced, or oppressed in any manner
whatsoever.[33]

According to his account, Pecos Pueblo officials and the two commissioners then went to the Ciénaga de Pecos and inspected it.

The two men returned to Santa Fe and reported to the diputación
on 19 March 1825. Ten Indian heads of families, they said, had received
allotments of pueblo lands, as had eleven heads of non-Indian families.
The names of Hispanic recipients corresponded to the six Benavídez
and the five Rivera applicants. But, continued the 19 March report,
there was still more unused land at Pecos. The committee had another
list of seventeen individuals requesting the lands that remained after
the initial allotments ("el terreno que queda sobrante").[34]

The diputación directed the two Ortizes to return to Pecos, to
confirm the location of the already alloted Indian and non-Indian land,
and to grant whatever was left over to the rest of the waiting individuals.
As pay for their work, the commissioners would themselves receive
plots of excess Pecos Pueblo land. Matías Ortiz had been measuring
the Pecos Pueblo grant for more than a decade, first defining and
redefining the boundaries of neighboring grants, and now dividing the
pueblo grant itself. And he had finally won a piece for himself.[35]

Domingo Fernández provided the details of this second apportionment of Pecos Pueblo lands, which took place in the spring of 1825.
The commissioners had returned to Pecos Pueblo to borrow the pueblo's
measuring rope. The Indians, the applicants, and the commissioners
then traveled north from the pueblo for half a league, to the Ciénaga
de Pecos, where they began their measuring.

The ten pueblo families had already selected land on both sides of
the Pecos River, near the Ciénaga's center. The Rivera group had
claimed tracts to the north of the pueblo core; the Benavídez group
had been allotted lands to the south. The commissioners now measured
these already allotted lands, determined how much unallotted land was
left after the first distribution, and then divided the remainder. The
bulk of it they gave to Domingo Fernández and his coapplicants.
Perpendicular to each side of the river the commissioners reserved
corridors one hundred yards wide as public rights-of-way (abrevaderos),
by which animals pastured in the surrounding mountains could get
through the irrigated and fenced fields to water.

On completion of their work the Ortizes returned to Santa Fe and reported once again. The Ciénaga de Pecos had contained the land of ten Indian families and eleven non-Indian families after the first allotments; it now contained the land of thirty additional non-Indian families. Most of the additional settlers came from the Fernández list of 1823. By planting time, in the late spring of 1825, most had taken possession of their new lands.[36]

The changes in use and ownership of the Ciénaga de Pecos, in the northeast quarter of the Pecos Pueblo grant, were fundamental. Owners of the Alejandro Valle grant, immediately to the north, and the Los Trigos grant, immediately to the south, still sat perched on the ill-defined boundaries of the pueblo grant. Ten years had passed since the Spanish government had approved the two non-Indian grants and since Matías Ortiz had first established their boundaries. In the intervening years the owners of these grants had spilled over into the richer Pecos Pueblo grant. Occupants of the Alejandro Valle grant had moved into parts of the rincón area of the ciénaga, that stretch of east-west river-bottom land attached to the central, north-south area of the ciénaga. From the south, Diego Padilla, owner of the Los Trigos grant, had moved into the ciénaga as well, to the consternation of some and the confusion of all.

But in the summer of 1825 the casual intrusions from the north and south had given way to a full-scale invasion. Non-Indians, primarily Roybals and Riveras, held the entire rincón, which the murdered Vicente Villanueva had ruled, only seven years before, to be part of Pecos Pueblo's land. Immediately below the narrow neck of land connecting the rincón and the main ciénaga, the last members of Pecos Pueblo remained in possession of perhaps two hundred acres of bottom land, on both sides of the river. The balance of the Ciénaga de Pecos, perhaps another two hundred acres of irrigable land, now belonged to the Benavídez and Padilla claimants. Thus, although the rest of the Pecos Pueblo grant supposedly still belonged to the pueblo, the water-rich ciénaga was largely gone, expropriated by the government in the name of increased productivity.

The arrangement did have certain benefits for the remaining inhabitants of Pecos Pueblo. The non-Indians set out to construct (or perhaps rebuild) irrigation ditches around the ciénaga that had at least been abandoned for years. By 1826, a long irrigation ditch, arising in the Alejandro Valle grant and then running along the north and northeast side of the river, watered both non-Indian and Indian land. On the river's west side, another long, new irrigation ditch actually arose on Indian land. It served pueblo and non-Indian land there. For the first time in at least fifty years, the inhabitants of Pecos Pueblo had available the means to irrigate their lands.[37]

However, trouble between the parties started almost immediately. The Pecos said that at least five of the non-Indian claimants to Pecos lands had sold their allotments as early as the summer of 1825, "because they have no use for them except to have something to sell." Other non-Indians, they complained, had planted more land than they were entitled to by the direction of Juan Bautista Vigil, diputación secretary. Despite protestations of brotherhood from the non-Indians, the Pecos still felt that their new and unchosen neighbors were "doing us great harm."[38]

Against that brooding background of ill will, a growing non-Indian community emerged within the Pecos Pueblo grant that would never let go. Two Roybal boys, the sons of "citizens [vecinos] from the Cañón de Pecos," were baptized in the Pecos Pueblo church on 16 April 1825. The relationships of each suggest the tightening bonds between non-Indian Pecoseños. José Polonio Roybal was the son of José María Roybal, one of the Roybals consistently listed with the Domingo Fernández faction of Pecos claimants. His mother, Juana Sena, came from a family that had first applied for Pecos sobrantes in 1824 and whose name appeared on many of the lawsuits concerning Pecos land from 1825 to 1830. His godfather, Tomás Maes, litigated land claims with the survivors of Pecos Pueblo until they left. José Polonio's godmother, Bárbara Aguilar, was sister to the Rafael Aguilar who had fought with Pecos Pueblo about its northern boundary as early as 1818.[39] The second Roybal boy baptized that day at Pecos was the son of Miguel Roybal, whose presence within Pecos Pueblo's league preceded that of all other non-Indians, if Miguel Rivera's chronology is followed.[40] A little more than a year later, a daughter was born to Rafael Benavídez, one of the principal lieutenants of Domingo Fernández. In May 1826, church records identify Rafael Benavídez as a Pecos citizen.[41]

Through the summer of 1825 the diputación maintained its position that the excess lands of Pecos Pueblo were subject to the repartimiento process. An application for the sobrante lands of Nambé Pueblo, addressed on 16 July 1825, was ruled on in the same manner as the Pecos petitions of March 1825 had been.[42]

In the fall of 1825, however, the diputación began to waver again.

On 15 September 1825, it denied a non-Indian request for a reparti-miento of the surplus lands of the "ciudadanos naturales" ("native cit-izens") of San Juan Pueblo, near Española.[43] On 17 November 1825, the diputación once again received a complaint from the "naturales" of Pecos, concerning the invasion of their league led by Domingo Fer-nández, Miguel Rivera, and Rafael Benavídez that summer. Instead of rejecting the pueblo's claims, as it had done in March of that year, the diputación now took a more circuitous approach to the problem. It resolved "after reviewing the precedents and the law of Spain on which this diputación is founded," to refer the question of its authority to dispose of surplus Pecos Pueblo land to the national government, in Mexico City, for its interpretation of article 5 of the law of 9 November 1812. In addition, the diputación stated that it had not ordered the allotment of land in pueblos other than Pecos because of "the very small [cortísimo] number of individuals who make up the ancient Pueblo of Pecos." The diputación may have been willing to justify its handling of Pecos on the basis of the pueblo's abandonment, as was true at San Cristóbal, rather than on the basis of a general application of Pedro Bautista Pino's 1812 Spanish law.[44]

Several reasons might account for this apparent caution in the fall of 1825. Genuine concern about the radical implications of its previous rulings might have given the men of this body pause.[45] But in fact a new governor had just arrived in New Mexico that fall. He had taken over as head of a diputación made up entirely of new members. Neither the new governor nor the new diputación members had ruled on the Pecos Pueblo situation before. The increasingly astute Pecos Pueblo leaders may have seized on the naivete of the new organization to raise immediately and once again a point they had already lost: the inviolate nature of their league under Mexican law. The new governor and diputación acted hesitantly, if only for the moment.

At the meeting the following day, 18 November, a new deputy, one Madriaga, pointed out that the minutes and the decision made con-cerning Pecos Pueblo on the previous day had failed to mention that the lands which Pecos Pueblo claimed were the same ones that the diputación itself had already allotted to individual Pecos Indians, with the surplus lands going to the non-Indians who had petitioned them. That previous action should have laid the question of Pecos Pueblo's league to rest.[46]

By early spring of 1826, Pecos Pueblo leaders returned to the ter-

ritorial government to renew their complaint. Their petition, filed by
the Pecos Pueblo leader Rafael Aguilar and dated 12 March 1826,
initiated a proliferation of legal papers that did not begin to subside
until late the next fall. This document was the first written response
by Pecos Pueblo to its treatment by the territorial diputación.

It was not a new story. In almost phonetic Spanish, Aguilar complained of sales by some Pecos non-Indians, and excessive planting by
others that was ordered by Juan Bautista Vigil, former diputación
secretary, who was now seen as their chief non-Indian enemy by Pecos
Pueblo leaders. What had happened to the appeal to Mexico City?
Pecos Pueblo needed all its land. That which it did not plant, it used
for grazing its animals. Besides, Pecos Pueblo owned its lands. If Juan
Bautista Vigil wanted to give lands away, he could grant ownerless
public lands ("las que no tienen dueños") in such places as Mora, Coyote,
Sapello. But the Pueblos, said Aguilar, were sons of God and the
Mexican nation, just like everyone else. They enjoyed "all the laws and
rights of citizens." The New Mexican government could not just come
in, expropriate Pecos Pueblo land without the pueblo's consent or
compensation, and give the land to others.[47]

Here Pecos Pueblo leaders launched a new attack. Previously they
had relied on their status under Spanish law as grounds for their protest.
Now they emphasized their status as property owners, just like any
other Mexican citizen. The implications were clear: the Mexican government could no longer claim to serve as the guardian and ultimate
owner of Pecos Pueblo land. Only Pecos Pueblo itself could dispose of
its land.

On 18 March 1826, the diputación considered Aguilar's petition.
It directed the governor to tell the non-Indians in Pecos that they
could not sell or otherwise alienate the land ("de ninguna manera vendan
o enagenar tales tierras") they had received the year before.[48] The
diputación might have reached that narrow result either because it took
the Pecos complaint to be directed to non-Indian sales, or because it
was trying to bide time, waiting for a decision on the entire matter
from above.

The governor's message to the alcalde of San Miguel del Vado on
21 March 1826, made it clear that the diputación was in fact awaiting
instructions from Mexico City. Governor Narbona reported on what he
described as the 18 March "address" by Pecos Pueblo Indians, concerning
"their ancient common land" that had been given to various non-

Indians. The diputación, Narbona continued, had decided to direct that the non-Indians who had been given possession of pueblo land could not convey it "until the superior government had resolved the issue." He told the alcalde of San Miguel del Vado to pass the word on to Pecos.[49]

On 31 May 1826, Mexico City initiated its first inquiry into the Pecos Pueblo situation. At that time a deputy secretary of state wrote the governor of New Mexico about a folio of documents, dated 30 March, concerning the Pecos Pueblo transaction. In addition to information on Isleta, First Secretary Cámara wanted to know the extent of the Pecos Pueblo lands which had been subject to the diputación's allotment, the distribution that had been made of surplus lands, and the origin and form of what Narbona had called communal property (mancomún), including its antiquity and the outer boundaries that defined it. The secretary's request employed every esoteric term of land law known to Mexican authorities; still, Cámara's letter made it clear that the central government did not know quite what was going on at Pecos.[50]

Governor Narbona tried to provide the information that summer. He directed the alcalde of San Miguel del Vado, José Ramón Alarid to answer Cámara's specific inquiries. On 18 August 1826, Alarid traveled upriver to Pecos, called out the resident non-Indians, and listed the size and owner of each non-Indian tract within the Pecos Pueblo grant. The Pecos citizens cooperated. But when they asked Alarid why he wanted the information, the alcalde "maintained a profound silence and withdrew."[51]

By the next day rumors had reached them that Alarid had gathered the information because the Pecos Pueblo troublemakers had complained again to the central authorities. Fernández responded immediately. On 19 August he wrote to Alarid requesting permission for the non-Indians to present their side of the case in full. Just as promptly, Alcalde Alarid curtly replied that he could not respond to Fernández's complaint because there was no lawsuit before him; he was only gathering information for the governor.[52]

In the face of the new protest by Pecos Pueblo and the renewed expression of interest by the government, Hispanic Pecoseños began to squabble among themselves. On 25 August 1826, Fernández wrote to Governor Narbona, accusing a dissident faction of non-Indians at Pecos of having instigated Pecos Pueblo's new complaints. On the same day, the governor decided not to consider the Fernández petition on the grounds that any decision in the matter already rested with the national government. The small incident did not count for much. But it showed development in Hispanic Pecos of precisely the kind of internal discord that had brought the great and unified Pueblo of Pecos to its knees a couple of centuries before.[53]

The governor, the diputación, and the alcalde of San Miguel del Vado had each rejected Domingo Fernández's effort to explain his view of Pecos Pueblo grant affairs. Desperate in the fall of 1826 to find someone who would listen to his side of the story, Fernández, joined now by Miguel Rivera, Rafael Benavídez, and José Antonio Armijo, wrote one more position paper in defense of non-Indian holdings in the Pecos Pueblo grant, asking only that the governor forward the information to the central government, where the final decision would apparently be made. This report listed the population of Pecos in 1826 as forty-one non-Indian and twelve Indian families. The Indian lands lay at the center of the ciénaga. The Hispanos held only those outlying lands not used by the Pueblos. The Hispanos had brought both the Indian and non-Indian tracts into cultivation. Had it not been for the presence of the non-Indians in Pecos, Pecos Pueblo itself would already have dispersed across the face of the earth. As it was, the Pueblo and Hispanic families were living together in harmony. If the Pecos Indians still felt wronged, then the non-Indians would give them some oxen and tools to make them feel better.[54]

No record shows whether Fernández's description of 9 September 1826 ever reached Mexico City. But Governor Narbona still had not replied to Secretary Cámara's request of the previous May. It was October 1826 before he finally provided the information the central government had wanted.

First Narbona gave the facts as discovered and reported by the alcaldes of San Miguel del Vado. The pueblo lands given to the non-Indians (vecinos) included about a mile and three-quarters of land on each side of the river (a total of 8,400 varas), separated by more than a mile and one-half from the pueblo itself. Pecos Pueblo still retained the half-league between the distributed land and the pueblo, as well as an additional full league in all the other directions. (Narbona disingenuously failed to state that the allotted land included the most valuable and, indeed, the only easily irrigable land in the Pecos Pueblo grant.) The forty-one non-Indian families in possession had themselves cleared the new tract, which the Indians had abandoned "many years ago." There were only nine Pecos Pueblo families left, with a population of less than forty souls. In Narbona's opinion no harm could come to the Indians under those circumstances.

Narbona then justified his opinion by attacking Pueblo culture and customs just as Sepúlveda had argued at the junta de Valladolid more than two hundred years before.[55] In answer to Cámara's query as to the nature of mancomunidades in New Mexico, Narbona made a vituperative condemnation of Pueblo communal ownership of property. Pecos Pueblo, like other New Mexico pueblos owned all its property communally. While individual Indians cultivated particular tracts of land, the tracts still belonged to the entire community. Slavish devotion to ancient custom among the Pecos continued this practice, which produced the backward state of pueblo affairs.

Given his view of the problem, the solution was evident to Narbona.

> I am of the opinion that if each Indian should have given to him the property rights and perfect dominion of the land thought necessary for his maintenance, the Indian pueblos would progress much better and that more than half the lands which are seen to be uncultivated would be made use of.[56]

In other words, the government should do just as the diputación had done and proceed with the division of sobrante Pecos Pueblo land between the Indians and the non-Indians.

The diputación, of course, agreed. At its November meeting, the body approved Narbona's report, on the grounds that the Pueblos would flourish again if the government approved the recommended course.[57] But no response was heard from Mexico City.

The different parties reacted in different ways. Territorial Deputy Juan Estevan Pino, who had already secured a huge grant on the eastern plains, began to speculate in the insecure Pecos situation.[58] On 23 September 1826, Pino bought the rights of one Pedro Ortiz to what would become the Alejandro Valle grant, just north of the Pecos Pueblo grant. Pedro Ortiz appeared nowhere in the original 1815 grant documents; no sale prior to 1826 linked him to the land. But that sale to Pino served to validate both the existence and the boundaries of the Alejandro grant and identified Juan Estevan Pino as its owner.[59] By early 1828 Pino would join the diputación itself (perhaps for the second time) and in that role he played a critical part in the fate of Pecos Pueblo and its protests. In the summer of 1826 Pino reported from

Pecos on the state of affairs there. By early 1830 neighboring Pecos residents identified Juan Estevan Pino as the owner of the land just north of Pecos.[60] Whatever else Pino had purchased in 1826, he had bought his way into the Pecos land controversy.

Domingo Fernández himself helped Pino, by witnessing the 1826 deed from Ortiz to Pino.[61] In 1827 Fernández's prospects for securing the Pecos Pueblo grant for himself grew less likely. As time passed and the decision of the central government appeared imminent, Fernández returned to his claims on the abandoned San Cristóbal Pueblo grant, temporarily suspended in 1824.

On 25 June 1827, he asked the diputación to grant him possession of the "paraje de San Cristóbal." The diputación sent the request to the ayuntamiento of Santa Fe, for its report. The next day the ayuntamiento approved Fernández's petition, as it had in 1824. It took two months for the matter to return to the diputación and then all hell broke loose. Some deputies claimed that the approval of the Santa Fe ayuntamiento completed the grant. Others thought that the diputación should still deny Fernández the San Cristóbal grant, on the same grounds it had used in 1824: making the land private would cut off access and trade between Santa Fe and points east. Deputy Serracino finally proposed a compromise. Fernández and his party might take those parts of the grant they could actually occupy, and the rest would remain common. This solution had been applied to the Los Trigos and Alejandro Valle grants; it was accepted, grudgingly, by the 1827 diputación. But it gave Domingo Fernández considerably less than he wanted.[62]

Early the next spring, while the people of Pecos Pueblo and non-Indians awaited the decision from Mexico City, Domingo Fernández's claim to Pecos became even less likely. The alcalde of San Miguel del Vado, acting on orders from the diputación, had previously told Hispanic claimants to Pecos Pueblo land that they could neither sell nor alienate their lands, pending the decision by Mexico City. In March 1828, he returned and ordered them not to plant at the ciénaga. Some vecinos planted anyway; others sold out. Others simply abandoned their Pecos land.[63]

But no word came from the central government. Pecos life continued, unstable and insecure. Pecos Pueblo declined further. The last formally identified Indian child was baptized in the Pecos church in March 1826. But on 2 June 1828, the priest at San Miguel del Vado came to Pecos and baptized Juan Manuel Aguilar, son of pueblo leader Rafael

Aguilar and his wife, identified in the church books as "Paula India."
The next day the priest baptized a Barela and a Gonzales, from the
Cañón de Pecos. They joined the Ortiz, Rivera, Roybal, and Benavídez
families as Pecos's first non-Indian pioneers.[64]

In a pattern that would become familiar in Pecos history, non-Indians
responded to the pressure of insecurity by fighting among themselves.
On 1 March 1829, thirty-two residents of the Cañón de Pecos signed
a document at the Ciénaga de Pecos, protesting the behavior of their
non-Indian Pecos neighbors. Only four of the petitioners had appeared
on Domingo Fernández's first application, of September 1823; seven
other names appended to the 1829 protest resemble names found on
earlier applications for Pecos Pueblo land. But the twenty-one other
names were new ones. Fernández himself did not join the protest.

The signers of the 1 March petition asked the alcalde to readjust
and reduce non-Indian claims to Pecos Pueblo land. There was not
enough land to go around. Some non-Indians had never broken the
ground allocated to them in 1825. Others had planted one year and
then quit. Still others had treated the land granted to them with such
disrespect ("con tanto desamor") that they had sold it. If the claims of
all these people were disallowed and redistributed, the remaining non-
Indians, those who joined the 1829 petition, would carry out the
original purpose of the 1825 repartimiento. There was no suggestion
that the remaining members of Pecos Pueblo get any land back.[65]

But, as in 1826, Pecos Pueblo seized the opportunity afforded by
the 1829 struggle among the non-Indians and asked once again that
the governor remove all non-Indians from the entire Pecos Pueblo grant.
The pueblo filed its request eight days after the non-Indian petition
reached Santa Fe. Five or six years had passed, said the pueblo's petition,
since non-Indians had taken over Pecos Pueblo lands.

> Consider the extent of the pain that we suffer when we see ourselves
> violently despoiled of our lawful possessions . . . Your Honor, please
> determine if the natives of our pueblo . . . lack the protection and
> shelter of the laws of our liberal nation. If that is so, Your Honor,
> they have been deprived of the right of property and the security
> which all citizens have.

Their solution to the Pecos problem was to return the land to its
rightful owner, the pueblo.[66]

The pueblo's petitions of 1826 and 1829 both directed themselves
to the rights of Pecos Pueblo as the owner of private lands, identical

to those of any other citizen of Mexico. Rafael Aguilar never claimed special privileges for Pecos Pueblo in his appeals.

But in several critical ways the 1829 document did differ from its 1826 counterpart. This time another Pecos Indian, José Cota, joined Aguilar on behalf of his people, an addition that would make a great difference to the ultimate fate of the failing pueblo. And the current diputación was made up of entirely different members from those who had decided in 1825 and 1826 that the law of 9 November 1812 could be applied to sobrante lands of New Mexico pueblos and that it should be applied to Pecos. Finally, one member of the 1829 diputación was Juan Estevan Pino, the speculator who at least since 1826 had demonstrated a clear interest in Pecos-area land.

Instead of rejecting Pecos Pueblo's protest of 9 March 1829, on the grounds that the diputación already had decided the issue, the 1829 diputación decided to reconsider the problem. Two previous diputaciones had resolved it differently in 1824 and in 1825–26. The diputación had always reserved to itself the question of dividing up particular Pueblo lands, even if the law of 1812 did apply. On this occasion the diputación turned to a new technique; on 16 March it formed a subcommittee to recommend a solution to the issues raised by the 1 March 1829 non-Indian complaint and the 9 March pueblo petition. Deputies Arce, Baca, and (Juan Estevan) Pino would serve.[67]

Within a week their recommendation was ready. In an unequivocal, two-point answer to the questions raised by the March 1829 petitions, the diputación subcommittee ruled

1) That all the lands which they claim belong to the natives of the pueblo of Pecos.
2) That the settlers who have possession of them be advised by the alcalde of that district that they have acquired no right of possession because said rights were given to lands that have owners.

On 24 March 1829, the full diputación considered and adopted this subcommittee ruling. To clarify any remaining ambiguity, the diputación added a third point: The ruling applied only to those lands that the government had forcibly allotted; it did not apply to those lands that Pecos Pueblo itself might have sold. As a result, only the lands "given," as the diputación phrased it, were to be returned to Pecos Pueblo but not those that had been sold by "them."[68]

This decision was a clear defeat for those Pecos non-Indians whose claim to pueblo land arose only from the forced allotments previously ordered by the diputación. It was also a victory for Pecos Pueblo. That victory, however, was based not on any special status of the pueblo, but instead on the fact that Pecos Pueblo was simply the owner of private property. Thus, the government could not appropriate it on the grounds that it was not being used well; but it could certainly be sold as private property.

As a practical matter, the diputación left the enforcement of its decree to the alcalde of San Miguel del Vado. Unsympathetic local officials in the recent past had nullified pueblo court victories in principle by refusing to enforce them in fact. Although San Miguel del Vado alcaldes had always proved sympathetic to the pueblo's cause in the past, Vicente Villanueva's fate had shown that such sympathy could bring serious personal trouble. In the spring of 1829 there was a real question as to whether the alcalde of San Miguel del Vado would journey upriver to Pecos and evict most of the non-Indians there.

Word of the decision did not reach the settlers until May 1829. On 7 May 1829, Domingo Fernández and twenty-one others, including eleven of the thirty-two who had signed the 9 March petition, announced that they would appeal. On 12 June 1829, the diputación itself docketed Fernández's petition asking for the restitution of Pecos Pueblo land already given to them "by virtue of the law of 9 November 1812," along with other documents. On the same day the full diputación remanded Fernández's appeal to Juan Estevan Pino's subcommittee.[69]

Finally the two real estate speculators would meet officially. They had worked together for at least a decade, often sitting on the same governmental bodies. They had involved themselves in each other's real estate transactions over the years, in Tesuque, at Pecos, and elsewhere. By the 1830s they would share a claim to the San Cristóbal grant. It was reasonable to suppose that Pino would help his friend Fernández now, in June 1829.

However, only one day after the diputación sent Fernández's appeal to the subcommittee, it recommended that Fernández's papers be returned to him, "in order that he may appeal to any tribunal he may please." The full diputación agreed.[70]

Apparently Fernández did appeal, to the same Mexico City authorities who supposedly already had under consideration the 1826 Pecos Pueblo appeal, which raised precisely the same points from the opposite perspective. No answer ever came to New Mexico concerning either appeal.

The split between Juan Estevan Pino and Domingo Fernández, between the diputación and the Pecos non-Indians, most probably reflected a difference about how best to dismantle Pecos Pueblo and to allocate its valuable land and water resources among non-Indians.

Domingo Fernández had favored the position that the government had the right to allocate unused Pecos Pueblo land to non-Indians as if it were public land, or as he would have put it, "as if it had no owners." Pino, on the other hand, had bought his way into the Pecos area, purchasing in 1826 what would become the Alejandro Valle grant, north of Pecos. In its 1829 rulings the diputación rejected Fernández's approach and approved Pino's.

Pecos Pueblo's apparent victory brought no relief from the Fernández faction during 1829 and 1830. While some Pecos settlers headed east to small valleys formed by tributaries to the Pecos River, most non-Indian Pecoseños stayed and waited.[71]

Pecos Pueblo and its leaders, Rafael Aguilar and José Cota, also waited. Two more planting seasons passed. At best, the situation did not worsen for the pueblo, but years later reports surfaced about increased non-Indian harassment of the Indians still using the Ciénaga de Pecos. In the fall of 1830 one Pecos Pueblo leader finally adopted the Pino solution to the problem of communal pueblo lands.

On 22 September 1830, José Cota, the Pecos Indian who had joined Rafael Aguilar in filing the protest that led to the 24 March diputación ruling, returned to Santa Fe. There he met Miguel Roybal, one of the first non-Indians in the Pecos Pueblo grant and now the deputy justice of Pecos. Roybal was joined by the diputación members José Ignacio Ortiz, Rafael Sarracino, Santiago Abréu, and Juan Estevan Pino, as head.

Cota and Pino had come to do business. Signing with an X, Cota deeded to Pino "all the land known by the name of the ciénaga of Pecos" ("todo el terreno conocido con el nombre de ciénaga del Pueblo de Pecos"). Cota guaranteed that he was acting for the entire Pecos Pueblo ("todos en unión"). In exchange, Pino promised eleven cows and calves ("bacas paridas") and three bulls, which the pueblo members could select from Pino's herds. Cota made Pino promise that he would fence the land he had bought, and Pino guaranteed that he would put his animals ("sus bueyes y bestias") inside the fence during the growing season, so that they would not harm Indian crops. Roybal, Ortiz, Sarracino, and Abréu sealed the transaction.[72]

Seven years of bitter, actively contested litigation over the Pecos Pueblo ciénaga had terminated in a private real estate deal that signaled the end of Pecos Pueblo. The pueblo had successfully resisted for almost a decade the effort to disperse its communal lands; in so doing the pueblo had shown itself capable of sophisticated maneuvering in the arcane world of Spanish and Mexican land law. But in the processs of winning the battle against expropriation of its unused communal lands, it lost the war to maintain its own land base. Pecos Pueblo surrendered when it sold its most valuable asset to Juan Estevan Pino.

Nothing about the transaction is unique in the context of Pueblo–non-Indian affairs of the period. Three years before, San Ildefonso Pueblo had sold to a Spanish vecino almost fifteen hundred varas of valuable land along the Río Grande. Around the same time, Nambé Pueblo began its second series of transfers of Indian grant land to non-Indian families.[73]

In mid-1831, a number of non-Indians banded together and applied for three thousand varas of land between Santa Domingo and San Felipe pueblos. The petitioners had first applied for the land in 1824, but then the 1829 Pecos Pueblo decision had intervened. When the non-Indians tried again in 1831, the diputación, instead of rejecting the application on the Pecos Pueblo principle, took the old course and sent the request to the ayuntamiento of Cochití and Sandía, so that local officials could report. Diputación archives contain no response.[74]

While the debate about the government's power forcibly to partition and allot unused Pueblo Indian land apparently continued, authorities protected the one-league boundary of other pueblos against straightforward non-Indian trespass. Pecos Pueblo's league had hardly been mentioned since San Miguel del Vado's alcalde, Vicente Villanueva, had shot it in 1818. But the general principle survived.[75]

Pecos Pueblo's sale of its ciénaga to Juan Estevan Pino involved neither a forced partition of pueblo land nor an unwanted encroachment on its league boundaries. But the sale did exacerbate some land-use trends in the upper Pecos Valley that would increase over time.

Between the sale of the ciénaga, in late 1830, and 1840, Pecos Pueblo declined further and then disappeared as a living force at Pecos. After the sale, and in marked contrast to the previous decade, protests from Pecos Pueblo no longer lace official records; indeed, the pueblo itself disappears from the formal documents. In 1832 officials still referred to Pecos Pueblo as an entity. By 1839 romantic reporters found it deserted.[76]

What actually happened in the interim has to be pieced together from documentary fragments, oral history, and myth. Clearly the decline and fall of Pecos Pueblo was not caused solely by the sale of the ciénaga to Juan Estevan Pino, in 1830; the pueblo had not used the ciénaga since 1776 and had survived without it. Years later, Pecos Pueblo survivors would recall that the problem was not so much the simple existence of a growing non-Indian community in the nearby ciénaga as what those settlers did to get rid of the remaining members of the pueblo. Hispanic Pecoseños, according to the Indians, killed the pueblo's few remaining animals and poisoned its water holes between 1830 and 1840. Life became increasingly isolated and intolerable for the Indians.

Individual Pecos Indians had drifted away from the pueblo to other homes in the first three decades of the nineteenth century, and some newcomers had arrived to replace them. But the pueblo itself finally decided in 1837 to formally abandon its ancestral home and move to Jémez Pueblo, whose members spoke a language closest to that of Pecos. The move was definitely planned. The Pecos survivors left the painting in their church, but carried with them their native sacred objects.[77]

But the people who departed left behind several satellite communities, including a few families at Glorietta and at least one in East Pecos. They left behind Mariano Ruiz, an enigmatic figure in local history, who himself supposedly came from Jémez to Pecos in 1837, the year the pueblo formally moved to Jémez. For years thereafter Ruiz refused on two grounds to cooperate with any of the non-Indian factions that remained in the upper Pecos Valley. First, Ruiz claimed to be a Pecos Pueblo Indian himself. Second, he claimed that his Pecos fellows had left him in charge of the part of the land grant they had not sold to Juan Estevan Pino. To prove the arrangement, Ruiz and his progeny claimed that the pueblo had left them a buffalo-skin map of the land as proof of their guardianship.[78]

No proof of such a transaction has ever appeared. But neither was there any proof that the pueblo had disposed of the balance of its eighteen-thousand-acre land grant, once the sale of the perhaps one thousand acres in the ciénaga had been accounted for. The members of Pecos Pueblo may have abandoned their home in 1837, but except for the sale to Juan Estevan Pino, they had not sold their land.

Between 1831 and 1840 the sale to Pino left Hispanic Pecos relatively free to grow in its own ways, including some formal attention to the central authorites in Santa Fe. For example, on 14 April 1831, thirty-six Hispanos applied for land in the Cañón de Pecos, about five miles upriver from the ciénaga, at a place still called *El Macho*. The diputación forwarded the application to the alcalde of San Miguel del Vado, so that he could report on the availability of land there and on the wisdom of granting it. He approved, and on 11 November the diputación concurred. Another non-Indian community had formally established itself in the upper Pecos Valley.[79]

From 1830 to 1840, outsiders drifted into Pecos, some of whom took up residence there. Families began formally buying and selling Pecos real property among themselves. By 1834 local non-Indian residents evidently felt sufficiently established to build a church for themselves on the site of the present St. Anthony's on the Pecos, on the west side of the river and well within the main area of the ciénaga. The lack of formal Catholic approval for the church apparently made little difference to the growing community. As time went on and it became more sure of itself, its presence became less visible in the formal documents of the day.[80]

It was at this time that Juan Estevan Pino and his two sons, Manuel Doroteo and Justo Pastor, emerged as preeminent figures on the Pecos scene. It was a time in New Mexico when the hierarchies that had begun to emerge around the turn of the century intensified, with a rich merchant class at the top and an increasingly isolated, almost stagnant farming and ranching class at the bottom. The bulk of non-Indian Pecos were at the lower end of that hierarchy; the Pino family was near its top.[81]

From his Santa Fe base, Pino and his sons operated a variety of business ventures. Between 1830 and 1840, the family continued its land maneuvering, engaged in the mercantile trade, and ranched; by 1835 they had nine hundred cattle and eighty thousand sheep in their herds. Some of these animals they may have pastured at the Ciénaga de Pecos, but until 1837, the vast majority were kept on the 318,000 acre Rancho Hacienda de San Juan Bautista grant, which Juan Estevan had acquired in 1823. Then Plains Indians began to attack the Pinos, their herdsmen, and their animals. Around 1837 the Pinos moved their whole operation to the Pecos ciénaga.[82]

Juan Estevan Pino, at fifty-two, suddenly achieved a prominence in the Pecos area he had not previously enjoyed. He quickly emerged as Pecos's spokesman in the outside world. The documents reflect little formal interest in the grant between 1830 and 1837, but with Pino's arrival that changed. Land transactions between non-Indians achieved a formality not previously seen. Juan Estevan took it on himself to gain church recognition for the chapel that "the new inhabitants of Pecos," as he called them, had built for themselves in 1834. On 29 December 1837, the Archdiocese of Durango formally granted Pino, together with the settlers of the Cañón de Pecos ("mancomunado con los pobladores del Cañón de Pecos'), permission to build a church (which already existed) and to use it to celebrate mass (which had already been done for over three years). On 10 September 1845 and 18 October 1850, the archdiocese renewed the license.[83]

By the first license renewal in 1845, Juan Estevan Pino had died. Around 1839, he passed away in Santa Fe. In the short period between 1840 and the beginning of American sovereignty, in 1846, and complete United States governance, in 1848, Pino's two sons carried on with their father's business. From the early days of their stewardship, Justo Pastor and Manuel Doroteo revealed a penchant for their father's power without much of his astuteness. As his share of Juan Estevan's estate, Justo Pastor apparently took over the land grant just north of the Pecos Pueblo grant that Juan Estevan claimed to have bought in 1826. But prior to 1846, Justo Pastor showed more interest in horse racing wagers than in managing his inherited property. While Juan Estevan had filed endless property documents and powers of attorney, Justo Pastor sued to collect on bets.[84] Manuel Doroteo took over the ranch in the heart of the Ciénaga de Pecos and quickly won a reputation as a political intimate of Governor Armijo, a skillful, controversial, and sometimes corrupt New Mexico political boss in the period just prior to the American takeover. One less than sympathetic observer connected with the 1841 Texas invasion of New Mexico described an encounter with Manuel Doroteo at San Miguel del Vado:

> Several Mexican officers called at our quarters during this eventful
> afternoon [after the Texans had been captured by the New Mexicans,

in the fall of 1841], among them a prissy, bloated, sallow-faced
wretch named Manuel Pino. He rode a beautiful and spirited black
horse, of which he was so proud that he was continually galloping
and fretting him about the square and spurring him to the execution
of such curvettings as would most induce a rattling of his sword . . .
In short this brute Manuel Pino took such particular pains on all
occasions to impress us with a belief in his prowess and bravery that
we finally became thoroughly convinced of his being an arrant
coward and after circumstances fully justified our opinions.[85]

Even accounting for the author's obvious prejudice, this portrait of
Manuel Doroteo Pino hardly suggests a poor Pecos farmer, working
the land and going to mass.

Between 1841 and 1846, no document connects either of Pino's
sons to the Pecos Pueblo grant. Indeed, the few documents that do
survive from the six years between 1840 and the arrival of the American
army, in 1846, suggest that in the period Pecos simply slipped farther
away from the abstract concerns that had dominated the history of the
land from 1821 to 1830. Pecos continued to grow towards the isolated,
concrete, communal land-based society that characterized rural New
Mexican society elsewhere in the territory at that time. This increasing,
intimate isolation involved no concern with the abstract boundary
disputes that had dominated the earlier history of Pecos Pueblo and
its league in the nineteenth century. Nor was there much respect for
the elegant procedures that the Spanish government had followed to
create and identify the owners of private property on both borders of
the Pecos Pueblo grant.

To the south, for example, by the 1840s the Los Trigos grant had
been abandoned by the original three grantees, Márquez, Trujillo, and
Padilla, the victims, their successor later claimed, of the kind of Plains
Indian attacks which had made Juan Estevan Pino's 1823 grant un-
inhabitable. In 1841 the alcalde of San Miguel del Vado had traveled
upriver, found the Los Trigos grant uninhabited, and had installed
twenty-five new families on the grant. Those families had no legal
connection to the original, 1814 grantees; but they were living there.
When asked, they said that the boundary of their Los Trigos grant
extended all the way to the Arroyo de Pecos, almost to the ruin of
Pecos Pueblo itself. Alcalde Matías Ortiz had identified three other
official owners in 1814 and had established the common boundary
between the pueblo and the non-Indian grant two and a half miles

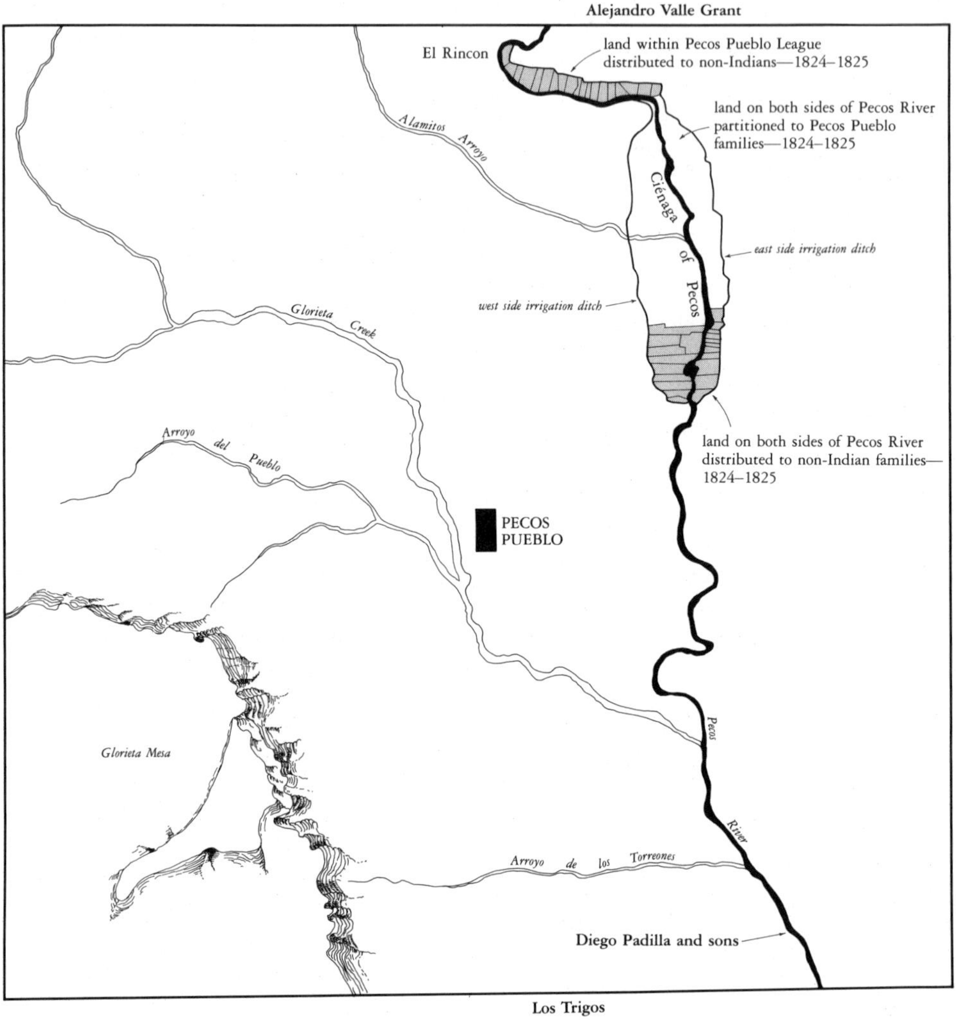

El Rincon

land within Pecos Pueblo League distributed to non-Indians—1824–1825

land on both sides of Pecos River partitioned to Pecos Pueblo families—1824–1825

Alamitos Arroyo

Ciénaga of Pecos

east side irrigation ditch

Glorieta Creek

west side irrigation ditch

Arroyo del Pueblo

land on both sides of Pecos River distributed to non-Indian families—1824–1825

PECOS PUEBLO

Glorieta Mesa

Pecos

River

Arroyo de los Torreones

Diego Padilla and sons

Los Trigos

MAP 3. The Pecos Pueblo Grant in 1825 Under Mexican Rule

By the end of 1825, the New Mexico *diputación teritorial* had begun to exercise the unsure muscle of a new sovereignty on unused lands of local Pueblos. The new government in New Mexico apportioned the water-rich *ciénaga* between forty-one non-Indian families and ten remaining Pecos Pueblo families. As is shown in Map 3, the Indian families were sandwiched between the non-Indian ones, who were assigned lands above and below. Subsequent reports indicated that Pueblos and non-Indians did not share the common *ciénaga* well. By 1829 the *diputación* had reversed itself and decided that non-Indians could not acquire Pueblo land by unilateral government decision, but the short-lived 1825 apportionment of Pecos Pueblo land had set a pattern that dominates Pecos land use today.

south of the pueblo itself. Much had changed in slightly less than thirty years.[86]

The story of the grant north of Pecos was similar. No one knew quite who owned it, where its boundaries lay, or even whether it in fact existed or not. Justo Pastor Pino could not say. The rincón appendage to the Pecos Pueblo ciénaga might belong to the Pecos Pueblo grant, or to the Alejandro Valle grant, or to both, or to neither. The non-Indian residents of the area knew that they were Hispanic Pecos's oldest settlers, even if they could not connect themselves by any clear, abstract legal claim to the land on which their homes stood.

Farther inside the Pecos Pueblo grant, in the ciénaga itself, the village of Pecos continued to grow with equally strong instincts and equally weak formal credentials. The Pinos tract, at the center of the ciénaga, the area left to the pueblo after the forced allotments of the 1820s, remained intact on both sides of the river. But to the north and south, a traditional Hispanic community had formed. Houses huddled together facing the north- and south-running irrigation ditches. Behind them, to the east and west, an expanse of open land rolled on as far as the eye could see.

A mile and a half below the ciénaga, Pecos Pueblo lay in ruins. Many curiosity seekers visited it and provided reports during the period, including the New Orleans journalist who described Manuel Doroteo Pino as "that brute":

> The 17th of October [1841], the day on which we started from San
> Miguel, was warm and showery . . . About sundown, footsore and
> completely exhausted after a hurried march of thirty miles over a
> rough and hilly road, we reached the old mission of Pecos—in
> former times a mission and a fortress, but now uninhabitable, and
> fast crumbling to decay. Salezar [*sic*] drove us into an enclosure
> amidst the ruins, and there herded up for the night in quarters not
> even fit for mules . . .[87]

By 1846 the inhabitants of Pecos Pueblo had long since left their ancestral home. Later stories suggest that they secured formal permission before leaving, but no record survives. On the eve of American acquisition of New Mexico, the formal owners of the Pecos Pueblo grant had disappeared. One set of non-Indian claimants to the land traced their title to the controversial forced allotments of unused pueblo land by the Mexican territorial government. Another set of non-Indian owners, the Pinos, claimed to have bought their land from the pueblo itself. Spanish law had clearly forbidden such purchases, but Mexican law had probably changed matters. In any event, the pueblo itself, scattered and gone, still owned the balance of the Pecos Pueblo grant. Chaos reigned on the local land ownership scene. Into that chaos marched Steven Watts Kearny, bearing the American flag and American sovereignty.

THREE

The Pecos Paper Chase

De la tierra fuí formado
La tierra me da de comer
La tierra me ha sostenido
Y al fin yo tierra he de ser

—Penitente Alabado

There are some considerations higher than the merits of the equities of any particular case. . . .The faith and credit which are due to [the government's] public acts ought not to be lightly impugned. And when so solemn an instrument as a Patent, signed by the highest officer of the Nation . . . is duly and regularly given out as evidence of title . . . it ought to be regarded as sacred.

—Frank Springer

June 1849. Santa Fe, New Mexico. James S. Calhoun arrives by way of Kansas and Georgia to take over the civil reins of government in recently conquered New Mexico. Washington officials have named him governor and ex oficio superintendent of Indian affairs. But they really have no idea what Calhoun is to do or whom he is to deal with. Indeed, they hardly know what he is to take charge of. New Mexico would not be organized as a formal territory until 30 September 1850. In the interim, a tentative government, organized by the conquering American military, awaits its orders. Calhoun finds himself completely at a loss. He cannot even locate a house in Santa Fe to live in.[1]

Across the mountains, in Pecos, Hispanic life continued, for the moment oblivious both to the Indian community that once resided there and to the new sovereign that had just arrived. Pecoseños continued to move down from the north and up from the south, squeezing into the ciénaga of Pecos. Manuel Doroteo Pino and Justo Pastor Pino

were buying, selling, and trading Pecos land, with the help of literate
Pecoseños like Manuel Varela. Others traded river-bottom land back
and forth among themselves. Deeds of the era invariably describe tracts
lying on both sides of the river as bounded by public land. But just
who the public is and where the dividing line between public and
private land might have lain, no one knows.[2] The main public concern
involving Pecos was what the newly arrived Archbishop Lamy would
decide to do with the cantankerous, powerful, and alcoholic priest
ensconced in the Pecos parish church.[3]

The conquering American general, Stephen Watts Kearny, had already moved on to California, leaving behind a handful of military
men with little New Mexico experience to direct civil affairs. One of
them, however, was a young lieutenant, John N. Ward, who spoke
fluent Spanish and perhaps Apache as well. Five months after Calhoun
arrived, Ward negotiated a treaty between the United States and Navajo
leaders. Around the time Calhoun finally departed, Ward was the head
of the Indian office in Santa Fe, where he kept a daily record of Pueblo
contacts. No one ever mentioned Pecos to him. But Ward had begun
a career in New Mexico Indian affairs that over the next thirty years
would come to have a critical impact on the lands of the already
abandoned Pecos Pueblo.[4]

Calhoun lived for only three years from his arrival in 1849. But
before he died he established the Anglo-American title to the so-called
Pecos Pueblo grant. From that start, the United States surveyor general
for New Mexico, William Pelham, and the United States Congress
constructed a patent to the grant. On the basis of the patent, a number
of men prominent in New Mexico history became claimants to Pecos
land: John Ward, David J. Miller, Frank Chapman, Andres Dold,
George Roberts, James Seymour, Pascual Smith, Henry Kelley, and
even 'Tex' Austin.

All these men, spread from New Mexico to New York, shared a
vociferous, if insecure, belief in the efficacy of the United States Pecos
Pueblo patent. They also shared a common dislike for those Hispanic
settlers who were prospering and increasing in the richest part of the
Pecos Pueblo lands, indifferent to official patent recognition.

Between 1848 and 1899 the two groups interested in the Pecos
Pueblo grant sometimes came close to outright war. The Pecos Pueblo
survivors at Jémez themselves occasionally appeared, like the shadows
of some long-forgotten ancestors, a hazy reminder to the active con-

testants that they might be fighting the right battle but the wrong war. No one could bring the sides together because the natures of their respective claims to that one eighteen-thousand-acre tract of land differed so fundamentally.

The United States government created American title to the Pecos Pueblo grant. It did so in good faith and to discharge obligations, to international law and to a conquered people, which it purported to take seriously. But federal officials entered a field they did not understand and which they made no serious effort to comprehend when they began to consider the Pecos Pueblo grant and other claims to New Mexico land originating under the state's antecedent sovereigns, Spain and Mexico. As a result, good faith gave way to bad practice; the government met its obligations to the ultimate satisfaction of no one.[5]

The government's formal obligations grew out of the Treaty of Guadalupe Hidalgo, which in 1848 brought an end to the war that Congress had declared on Mexico in April 1846. By that treaty, the United States won for itself sovereignty over a vast expanse of territory, including that portion of New Mexico where Pecos Pueblo's ancestral lands lay. But articles 8 and 9 of the treaty provided that

> property of every kind belonging to Mexicans established there [in New Mexico] shall be inviolably respected. The present owners, the heirs of these and all Mexicans who may hereafter acquire said property by contract, shall enjoy with respect to it guarantees equally ample as if the same belonged to citizens of the United States.

The Mexican government had previously declared all Indians Mexican citizens. Therefore, the treaty of Guadalupe Hidalgo obligated the United States to honor Pecos Pueblo land rights, if not because the Pueblos were Indians, then at least because they were conquered Mexicans.[6]

There were, of course, a few complications. Texas had secured its independence from Mexico prior to the Treaty of Guadalupe Hidalgo and was perhaps independent of its constraints. Residents of eastern New Mexico had seriously claimed for years that the boundary of the Republic of Texas ran east to the Río Grande, so that they included Pecos Pueblo's lands.[7]

But even if the Pecos Pueblo grant had come into the United States by way of the Republic of Texas, and not directly from Mexico, the U.S. government's obligations would still have been the same. Principles of international law accepted by the United States Supreme Court as early as 1833 required any conquering sovereign to protect and acknowledge existing private property rights in territory acquired by it.[8] Either way, the United States legally had to respect the property rights of Pecos Pueblo.

In theory that principle should have been easy to apply. As the new sovereign, the United States simply replaced the Mexican government that had preceded it. To the extent that Mexican law had incorporated previous Spanish law, those principles too might prove relevant. Thus the line extended back all the way to customary Pueblo law itself. If the preceding sovereign had created rights and the intermediate sovereign had not altered them, then the succeeding sovereign had to honor them. That obligation came with a corollary sovereign right: all land belonged to the succeeding sovereign, to be dealt with as it chose, except for land which it or its predecessors had granted to private interests.

But did the treaty and the general principles of international law mean that the United States had obligated itself simply to respect property rights existing at the time of the treaty's making? Or did they imply a complete readjudication of preexisting property claims by the new sovereign? Was the treaty self-executing or not? If it was, so that the United States did not have to formally pass on preexisting acquired rights to land, how could the new government know when it should treat land as public domain and when as acquired property?

Surprisingly enough, at the time no one asked these serious questions. Instead, the United States took the position that the Treaty of Guadalupe Hidalgo was not self-executing with respect to property rights that might have been acquired by citizens under Spain or Mexico. The federal government presumed that, as sovereign, it owned all the territory acquired from Mexico. Then it set into motion a procedure by which claimants under the law of New Mexico's antecedent sovereigns could establish their claim against the all-inclusive claims of the new sovereign.

This was the adversary system, the American way. It required intricate procedures, which, however, changed in their rigor and formality over the years.[9] It required that American courts apply Spanish and Mexican law to the claims presented, in order to determine their validity in the new courts under the old laws. With respect to the Pueblo Indians, the federal government was to serve in general as guardian of their rights and interests. But when it came to a Pueblo Indian land claim originating under Spain and Mexico (if not before), should the government advance the Indian cause, as its guardian role would suggest, or should it resist the antecedent sovereign claim to otherwise public domain, as its role of successor to the public domain would suggest?

The promised American adjudication of Spanish, Mexican, and Indian land claims in the Southwest created a new, confused set of relationships between the citizens of New Mexico and their recently acquired sovereign. Under the treaty, Mexican citizens were allowed one year in which to accept American sovereignty or move to land still owned by Mexico. Fully one-half of the residents of San Miguel del Vado elected to give up their homes and the United States and move to Mexico. On the other hand, Pueblo Indians welcomed the new sovereign and its promise of fairer dealings than had been true under Mexico. General Kearny had been in Santa Fe for less than two days when a delegation of Pueblo Indians met with him and demanded that the new American government do something to restore the lands stolen from them by Spanish and Mexican settlers.[10]

The men Kearny left behind were more intent on holding what they had gained than on redressing Pueblo injuries suffered under Mexico. Still, they took the time to draft a general set of laws, the so-called Kearny Code, to provide for some formal interim rule until more definite provisions could be made for the new territory. The code called for the convention of a local legislature to specify and implement the code's general provisions. Since no higher body had authorized either the code or its legislature, lawyers argued for years about what authority the provisional legislature might have to carry out anything.[11]

Among other subsequently debated acts, the interim Kearny legislature tried to alter, or at least to define, the formal status of New Mexico pueblos. At its 1847 session that body enacted a bill which made each New Mexico pueblo a corporate body, with the power to sue and be sued as such. The pueblos themselves accepted the designation as corporations and went to court at the first possible moment. Shortly after New Mexico gained territorial status, by an 1850 act of Congress, the official territorial legislature confirmed the earlier incorporation of the pueblos. Congress rejected neither the 1847 act nor its 1851 confirmation. Under existing federal law, involuntary pueblo incorporation became final. By 1851 federal officials knew that Pecos Pueblo was a corporation, even if they had no idea what it owned.[12]

Calhoun had by then been in New Mexico for two years. The gov-

ernment had initially instructed him simply to find out what was going
on there. He heard immediately from the incorporated Pueblo Indians,
who demanded that the new government protect Indian land and restore
what Hispanic interlopers had previously stolen. In his first report to
Indian Commissioner Medill, Calhoun wrote that

> the Pueblos complain of many encroachments upon their boundaries
> and hope the US government will restore them their ancient rights.
> In New Mexico a better population than these Pueblos cannot be
> found and they must be treated with great delicacy. The slightest
> disappointment in their expectations, no matter how created, they
> regard as a deliberate deceit practiced on them. [13]

Calhoun's praise diminished as his frustration with New Mexico and
the Pueblos grew. Less than two weeks after his initial report, Calhoun
noted that "there is scarcely a day that passes that a deputation from
some one or more of the Pueblos does not come to me . . ."[14] Only
two months later, Calhoun reported that he had been "incessantly
annoyed by complaining representations made to me by deputations
from the Pueblos . . ."[15]

What Calhoun knew of Pueblo Indian land tenure did not come
from Pueblo property documents. The Kearny Code had established
New Mexico's first public recording system for private land transfers,
and an enterprising Hispanic politician, who would later settle in Pecos,
had been appointed the first registrar. But until 1856 no law required
the public filing of land documents. In the interim no Pueblo documents had reached the voluntary Kearny docket books. And the formal
archives of the previous Spanish and Mexican governments were in
complete disarray. [16]

But Pueblo officials were quick to tell him themselves. As early as
October 1849, Calhoun wrote to Washington that the "Pueblos hold
their lands in common, the boundaries of which they say are distinc-
tively defined by original grants, now in existence." Three days later,
Calhoun amplified that statement: "To understand the condition of
these people it must not be forgotten, they hold possession of the lands
which they occupy and till by Special Grants from the government of
Mexico or Spain—the extent of these grants are [sic] not well understood
here." Again, in late March 1850, Calhoun repeated this information,
making clear that his source was the Pueblos themselves:

The Pueblo lands are held under Spanish and Mexican grants . . .

> The Pueblos claim that this whole territory originally belonged to
> them and that their Supreme Government was in Santa Fe; but after
> the Conquest, this place was taken from them and their limits fixed
> by the authority of the conquering Government.

No one before or since has said much of a centralized, pre-Spanish
Pueblo government. But throughout the nineteenth century, talk of
Pueblo grants was constant. Throughout his tenure Calhoun repeated
the same homily so frequently that by the time he departed Santa Fe,
in April 1852, the idea that the Pueblo Indians held title under grants
from the United States's antecedent sovereigns had become an im-
mutable historical fact.[17]

Calhoun was less assertive about the extent of those Pueblo grants.
"In relation to the extent of the territory belonging to each Pueblo,"
he wrote in March 1850, "nothing is definitely known . . . The general
opinion is not one of the Pueblos have a square of less than eight miles
and a half on each side." Calhoun's Pueblo informants clearly did not
limit their claims to the standard pueblo league, which yields a square
of only 5.2 miles on each side. And those informants must have understood that there were already numerous non-Indian residents, at Nambé
and Pecos for example, well within the pueblo squares, no matter how
they were measured. They certainly did not specify to Calhoun what
mix there might be of communal and private ownership within the
squares.[18]

But the Pueblos were primarily and vociferously concerned with
Hispanic encroachments on their homelands. They mentioned no specific pueblo; no one said anything about Pecos, for example. As far as
Calhoun knew, the problem was universal. He reported the constant
flow of jeremiads to Washington.[19]

There they elicited no response. The federal bureaucracy had dispatched Calhoun without instructions and sent him no further guide-
lines. By April 1851, Calhoun began to express his frustration:

> Here I have been for nearly two years . . . without the guidance of
> law or special instructions, groping my way in the dark under the
> most adverse and critical circumstances . . . I am without the
> slightest advice as to the purposes of the Government in reference to
> the Indians in this Territory . . .[20]

Calhoun attempted to make recommendations, but they all went
unheeded. Chief among them was his constant call for a formal, quasi-
judicial commission to investigate Pueblo land claims and alleged

Hispanic encroachments on them. As early as 20 November 1849, Calhoun recommended to his Washington superiors

> a commission to examine the tenure by which the respective parties [Pueblo Indians and Hispanic settlers on their lands] hold possession of their lands, with instructions to report all the facts in reference to the complaints made, which would relieve the present anxiety of the Indians and throw such light on the subject as would show a proper course to be pursued . . .[21]

Calhoun had made the same recommendation before; his aides would repeat it later. But more than ninety years would pass until the formation of the Pueblo Lands Board, in 1924.

In the intervening years, the relatively recent Pecos migration to Jémez would become an ancient historical event. By the time the Pueblo Lands Board finally arrived, the 1850 merits of their claim, which might have favored the restoration of at least some land to the Pecos Indians, would shift to denying them the recovery of any land at all. But if it would take ninety years for the federal government to take its guardianship of the Pueblos seriously, it would also take that long to realize that Calhoun was talking about two problems, not one. While the Pueblos complained about the loss of land belonging to them, the government worried about defining in the first instance what had been theirs. Before they could lose it, the Pueblos must have had the land under Mexican law. So the government focused on grant confirmation and the Pueblos on trespass. Everyone finally realized that dealing with the former did not solve the latter.

In the meantime, Calhoun did what he could with an impossible situation. At the request of Washington officials, he attempted to map the territory claimed by the pueblos in New Mexico and Arizona. The resulting map, dated 19 March 1850, showed the rough locations of the Río Grande pueblos, but did not even indicate the existence of Pecos Pueblo.[22] Indeed, there is no evidence in his correspondence that Calhoun had even heard of Pecos Pueblo until just prior to his final departure from Santa Fe, although he had traveled frequently to Las Vegas and Anton Chico and would have passed by the then well-known Pecos ruins en route.[23]

Calhoun also negotiated treaties with some of the pueblos, not including Pecos. The drafts, never approved by higher government officials, pledged the United States to "adjust and settle in the most practicable manner, the boundaries of each Pueblo which shall never be diminished but may be enlarged . . ."[24] Calhoun also struggled with the military over concurrent powers in the new territory; took a healthy, though controversial, part in local politics and the battle for formal status for New Mexico; argued with Washington officialdom over the payment of his office's minor expenses; and fought for the appointment of additional Indian agents to help cover the immense new territory.[25]

In that final effort, at least, Calhoun enjoyed some success. By 1851 Abraham R. Wooley had been hired as one of those new agents. By September of that year, Wooley had employed a remarkable former soldier, John N. Ward, as an interpreter. Before the close of 1851 another new agent, John Grenier, had reported for duty.[26]

Calhoun finally had the staff to investigate the Pueblo land situation. First he dispatched Grenier to report on the pueblos of the Río Abajo. Once he had finished, he turned to the pueblos of the Río Arriba. On 25 March 1852, Grenier filed his Río Arriba report with Superintendent Calhoun, who would remain in New Mexico for less than two weeks, before leaving en route to his eastern home. For the first time, Calhoun formally learned of Pecos Pueblo.

Grenier's March 1852 report began with a recitation of the usual Pueblo complaint:

> Since my last report on the conditions of the Pueblo Indians . . . I have visited the Pueblos on the Rio Arriba. The Taos, Picuris, San Juan, Santa Clara, San Ildefonso, Pojoaque, Nambe and Tesuque Pueblos have all been erected within or near the valley of the Rio del Norte north of Santa Fe . . . They respectfully ask that documents relating to the ownership of their lands may be translated, and investigated—their boundaries fixed—so that they may be protected against the depredations of their Mexican neighbors.[27]

Grenier's report then went on to describe each pueblo he found in the Río Arriba country.

For the first time in the history of United States involvement in the affairs of New Mexico pueblos, the government mentioned Pecos specifically:

> Much has been said about the ruins of the Pueblo of Pecos and speculation has been rife as to the old Aztec ruins, "the sacred fire," "Montezuma," "worshipping the rising sun," etc. etc. The Pueblo of Pecos is about 25 miles east of Santa Fe and was the only one of all the Pueblos that kept what was called the "Sacred Fire of Montezuma" continually burning. Like Taos, it was one of the oldest Pueblos and the one that can make as much pretension to being an

Aztec building as the other. The smouldering fire that was kept alive
in the *Estuffa* was not worshipped by the Pecos Indians.[28]

There is no suggestion here of restoring the Pecos lands to their Indian
owners, no mention of the Hispanic settlers living and farming on the
Pecos grant lands, let alone any discussion of ejecting them from their
homes. Instead, Grenier simply drew on the popular press of the day
for his Pecos report. Pecos Pueblo had already passed into the spectral
world of myth.[29]

In other areas Grenier's original 1852 report and subsequent work
proved more meticulous. For example, he procured for Superintendent
Calhoun the first compilation of Spanish and Mexican laws purportedly
governing the status of the pueblos and their lands, although it proved
to be a collection of arbitrary selections from arbitrary sources. Galván's
Ordenanzas de tierras y aguas, a scholarly and comprehensive treatise on
Spanish and Mexican land and water law, would not be published until
1863, in Paris. But even Grenier's initial efforts lead to the realization
that the problem of non-Indian acquisition of land and water resources
that were once a part of the Pueblo heritage antedated American acquisition of the territory.[30]

Grenier became acting superintendent of Indian affairs when Governor Calhoun departed in April 1852. By June of that year the acting
superintendent formalized the agency's continuous and growing dependence on John Ward by appointing him interpreter to Grenier
himself and by delegating to him the responsibility for the entire agency
when Grenier was absent from Santa Fe.[31] But the problems that had
faced Calhoun continued to face first Grenier and then Calhoun's permanent replacement, William Carr Lane.

New Mexico Indian officials had no idea how to address Pueblo
complaints about what had happened to their land when the territory
still belonged to Mexico. Indeed, they did not even know how to treat
the pueblos under United States law. In the February 1851 appropriations act that provided Calhoun with the money he needed to hire
assistants, Congress had extended to the new Territory of New Mexico
existing federal law governing relations with Indians. Section 7 of
chapter XIV of the general appropriations act for the year ending 30
June 1852 stated simply

that all the laws now in force regulating trade and intercourse with
the Indian tribes, or such provisions of the same as may be applicable

shall be, and the same hereby are, extended over the Indian tribes in the Territories of New Mexico and Utah.[32]

In one form or another the Non-Intercourse Act had been on United States law books since 1790. Congress had reworked and readopted it in 1834. In general the act asserted unique federal guardianship and control over Indian relations. Specifically it forbade any non-Indian to acquire Indian property of any kind without specific federal permission. No matter what protection Spanish and Mexican law had promised the pueblos, the 1851 federal law prohibited non-Indian acquisition of Pueblo land and water after 1851—if in fact it applied to the pueblos at all.[33] Were they "Indian tribes" within the meaning of the act?

From the outset, the Indian agents themselves assumed they were not. They could not have been ignorant of the act, since in addition to extending the 1834 act, it had secured the money that brought them to New Mexico in the first place. Although the agents dealt with the Pueblo, Navajo, and Apache Indians together, they always assumed that the pueblos were not entitled to the same federal protection as the so-called wild tribes. The pueblos held their land by Spanish grant, not by war and treaty. They were civilized, not savage; citizens of Mexico, not enemies of the state. They were not considered the kind of tribe to which the 1834 act referred.

John Ward's own treatment of a Pueblo land question in the fall of 1852, only a year and a half after the passage of the 1851 act, made this clear. In his official day book entry for 16 October 1852 Ward reported that

> The Gov. of Santa Clara with another Ind. from the same Pueblo came in to see the Supt. about some land belonging to one of the pueblos that sometime ago left the said pueblo in consequence of his disobedience to the authorities thereof and now it appears he wants to sell the land which he lived on previous to his leaving the pueblo. Mr. Grenier in the absence of the Gov.r told them that they must have a council composed of three Governors from other Pueblos and to lay the case before them, and whatever they decide on the parties must bide by in order to put an end to this question.[34]

"This question" could have been that of the ability of individual Indians to convey the part of the pueblo where they lived and farmed, or that of the ability of a pueblo to sell any land without federal consent. Ward and Grenier clearly did not believe that the 1851 act applied to Pueblo land affairs. If it had, it would have answered either version of the

Santa Clara question immediately: no sale by either an individual Pueblo Indian or the pueblo itself had any validity without federal approval.

A week later a Santa Clara Indian returned to report to Ward that

The council which Mr. Grenier ordered to take place on Thursday last had come off . . . and that the Governors of San Juan, San Ildefonso, and Santa Clara were the principals of the council and that they had decided that the Pueblos lands is a general gift to the people of said Pueblo by the Spanish government, and that if any individual thinks proper to disobey the orders of the authorities of said pueblo and leave in consequence thereof, in such case the individual so doing has no right to sell any of the land which he might have had in his charge or either has a right to sell the improvements thereon and if he or they insist in leaving the Pueblo as in this case, they may leave and suffer by the consequence.[35]

Over the next decade other officials would respond differently to the same question. For the moment, it was clear that federal law did not provide the exclusive answer to Pueblo land questions.

But the United States also addressed directly the question of Pueblo land titles. In 1854 the government created an independent agency, as it had in other newly acquired territories, to determine the validity of claims to land arising under New Mexico's antecedent sovereigns and protected by the Treaty of Guadalupe Hidalgo. After considerable debate, on 22 July 1854 Congress enacted a law establishing the office of Surveyor General of New Mexico. The statute imposed various duties on that new office, among them ascertaining "the origin, nature, character and extent of all claims to land under the laws, customs, and usages of Spain and Mexico." For each claim, the act directed the surveyor general for New Mexico to recommend first to the secretary of the interior and then to Congress whether the new sovereign should honor the claim, thus segregating the land from the public domain, or reject it, in which case the claimed land would join that to be opened to public settlement or otherwise dealt with under American public land law. Thus the determination under Spanish and Mexican law was necessary primarily so that the United States could deal in its own way with its own public domain. Under the 1854 act, if Congress confirmed a claim, a survey would then follow, to delineate the boundaries of the tract and, finally, a patent would issue. In the patent, the sovereign United States would relinquish forever its claim as succeeding sovereign to the claimed land. But, said the act in language that lawyers would argue over for the next century, the confirmation and patent would not affect other rights to the land, if any. It would simply eliminate whatever interest the United States might have.[36]

To the knowledgeable eye in 1854, it must have appeared that the Surveyor General's Office would not cause the Pecos Pueblo grant much trouble. Clearly the land belonged to someone other than the United States. It had been acquired property under both Spain and Mexico. It had a long and complicated history, which made it uncertain just who owned it in 1854. But confirmation and patent by the United States should not have anything to do with that.[37]

Less than a week after Congress created the position, the government selected William Pelham, a former Arkansas surveyor general, to fill it. Pelham was not a lawyer. He did not speak or read Spanish. He knew nothing of Spanish and Mexican law or legal history. He requested information, but no one would send him any. The New Mexico archives he was about to inherit were in total disarray. And yet the 1854 act expressly directed William Pelham and his successors to recommend to Congress the confirmation or rejection of preexisting claims to New Mexico land—such as the Pecos Pueblo grant.[38]

Pelham's superiors did not help much. In late August 1854, the commissioner of the General Land Office, John Wilson, instructed Pelham, then still in Washington, about what to do when he arrived in New Mexico. In general, Pelham should deal with private land claims in New Mexico as if the United States were Mexico:

> It is obligatory on the government of the United States to deal with
> private land titles and the Pueblos precisely as Mexico would have
> done had the sovereignty not changed. We are bound to recognize all
> the titles as she would have done, to go that far and no farther.

In addition, continued Wilson, Pelham should pay particular, immediate attention to the Pueblo Indians:

> You shall also make a report in regard to all the Pueblos showing the
> extent and locality of each, stating the number of inhabitants in the
> said pueblo respectively and the nature of their title to the land.[39]

With those instructions Pelham finally arrived in Santa Fe on 28 December 1854. Nothing in his tenure as surveyor general of Arkansas had prepared him for what he found in New Mexico. In some accounts of his first six months in office, Pelham struggled, as Calhoun had before him, with the frustrating physical necessities of life in Santa Fe.

In other accounts Pelham was assiduously "familiarizing himself with
Spanish and Mexican law and . . . collecting the [Spanish and Mexican]
archive documents relating to land grants."[40] Like any good bureaucrat,
Pelham actually took on only the former task and delegated the latter.

Pelham's calls to the people of New Mexico for documents in their
possession yielded poor results, particularly among the Pueblo Indians
who, Pelham learned, were afraid to part with their land papers.[41]
When he called on the civil governor to ask for the official archives
relating to private land claims, Governor David Merriwether showed
him to an unlabeled mass of papers, put up in bundles the size of large
boxes, and invited Pelham to take a look. Merriwether refused to go
through the papers himself, separating land documents from other
Spanish and Mexican records, because it was too much work. But he
let Pelham take the bundles to his own office to do the work. Two
aides sorted through the documents until late July 1855.[42]

With those land papers finally in hand, Pelham apparently turned
his immediate attention to the land claims of the Pueblo Indians.
Wilson had previously instructed Pelham to keep a docket book in-
dexing private claims and summarizing their disposition. Initially Pelham kept one book for all such claims, both Pueblo and non-Indian.
One of the earliest entries records a claim for the Pecos Pueblo grant
as filed on 14 September 1855. As evidence of the claim two documents
were registered with the surveyor general: the handwritten Spanish
version of the 1689 Cruzate grant to Pecos Pueblo and the 1829 report
of the Pino committee appointed by the diputación to investigate
alleged encroachment by Hispanic settlers on Pecos lands. On the same
date, according to the docket, English translations of the two documents were also filed.[43]

The docket noted only that the grant claimants were the "inhabitants
of Pecos Pueblo" as of 1855.[44] The last resident members of Pecos
Pueblo departed for Jémez in 1837, almost twenty years before. Grenier
had officially called the pueblo "a ruin," in 1852. Apparently Pelham
believed differently. On 30 September 1855, only two weeks after the
Spanish Pecos documents were filed, Pelham made the following report
to the commissioner of the General Land Office:

"Pueblos"

The grants made by the government of Spain to the Pueblos of Silla
[sic], Santa Ana, San Juan, Jemez and Pecos have been filed,

examined and approved by this office. The population of the above Pueblos as ascertained by the Indian agent is as follows:

Silla	124 inhabitants
Santa Ana	399 inhabitants
San Juan	668 inhabitants
Jemez	365 inhabitants
Pecos	10 inhabitants

The grants to the Pueblos not above enumerated have not come into this office yet. So soon as they are filed and the surveys of their lands made, I will forward the map required by your instructions showing the locality and extent of each Pueblo.[45]

By the next fall Pelham would learn that most of the thirteen other pueblos whose titles he was charged to rule on could produce no written Spanish grants, fraudulent or otherwise. The Pecos document had probably worked its way into the official archives as a result of the pueblo's last effort to save itself in the late 1820s. But Donaciano Vigil, an influential and knowledgeable native Hispano who in 1854 had bought from an Anglo speculator the greater part of the grant's irrigated land east of the river, swore in June 1856 that he had studied and been in charge of all land documents under both Mexican and early American sovereignty. In his years of work he had never seen "title deeds of grants made to Indian Pueblos of New Mexico there."[46] Those documents listed in 1855 as docketed in the Pecos claim before the surveyor general were nowhere to be found. The docket noted that an English translation of the so-called Spanish paper B, the 1829 committee report ordering the restoration of Pecos lands to the pueblo, was filed on 14 September 1855. But the Pecos file itself shows that no one in the Surveyor General's Office translated the document until 1883. At that time, David J. Miller, a surveyor general's clerk, who had already bought and sold part of the Pecos Pueblo grant himself, did the translating.[47]

The confusion in 1855 was probably more sloppiness than collusion, but it was very real. Nevertheless, in September 1855 Pelham decided to recommend that Congress confirm the Pecos Pueblo grant to the Indian inhabitants of Pecos Pueblo, according to the four-square-league Cruzate boundaries and his own population statistics. Only later did he and his successors learn to proceed with more caution.

It took Pelham another year to forward this recommendation to the secretary of the interior and thence to Congress. In the interim he had examined the titles to ten additional New Mexico pueblos; he now

.recommended them for confirmation as well. Pelham also submitted for confirmation three non-Indian private grants, including the Preston Beck grant in San Miguel County and the Tierra Amarilla grant in Rio Arriba County. More than a century of bitter debate would result.[48]

Pelham's report of 30 September 1856 to the commissioner of the General Land Office included the factual basis for his recommendation that Congress approve the eleven pueblo grants. For each pueblo that had furnished one, Pelham reproduced the alleged 1689 Cruzate grant and an official translation of it. For those five pueblos that could not produce one, Pelham included the sworn statements of the *cacique* (traditional head) and a war captain of each pueblo, all to the effect that the pueblos had possessed grant documents but had lost them.[49] But Donaciano Vigil swore again that all recognized that the pueblos were entitled to four square leagues, with or without documents. Finally, Pelham added to his report what little he knew of Spanish and Mexican law, to support the pueblos' claims.

Pelham referred to a royal decree of the Spanish crown dated 15 October 1713, castigating settlers in the Indies for encroaching on native lands, native children, and the native way of life. The 1713 decree restated the *Recopilación*'s requirement that the Indians be given "locations with sufficient water, timber, land, entrances and exits, for cultivation . . . and a common of one league where they can pasture their cattle without being mixed with those of the Spaniards."[50] The 1713 decree suggested that the pueblos were to receive a league in common land in addition to other lands. In fact, formal Spanish law required sometimes less and sometimes more land for Indians in the New World.

Such ambiguities did not concern Pelham. The 1689 documents confirmed the Pueblo testimony of 1855. The 1713 decree seemed to support both. Why should Pelham, with a year's experience in New Mexico, a year of constant affirmation by the Pueblos themselves that the Cruzate documents measured their claim to land, doubt the validity of the documents?

By 1856 Pecos Pueblo had been abandoned for twenty years. A burgeoning Hispanic settlement continued to grow on lands the government was about to regrant to the long-since departed pueblo. Critics of the surveyor general would later complain that the Hispanic residents of Pecos never had notice or heard about what the surveyor general

was about to recommend. Clearly some of the largest non-Indian claimants of land in the Pecos Pueblo grant knew, but they did not seem
to care.[51] What seemed to count in Pelham's mind was the continuing,
general Pueblo complaint that Hispanic encroachers were stealing Indian
lands. In his only personal comment about the Pueblo claims he forwarded to Washington in the fall of 1856, Pelham echoed Calhoun:

> The Pueblo Indians are constantly encroached upon by Mexican
> citizens, and in many instances the Indians are despoiled of their best
> lands; I therefore respectfully recommend that these claims be
> confirmed by Congress as speedily as possible, and that an
> appropriation be made to survey the lands in order that their
> boundaries may be permanently fixed . . .[52]

Perhaps Pelham really believed that confirming the Pueblo grants
and surveying their outer boundaries would somehow cure the problem
of non-Indians who had lived within those boundaries for centuries,
as at Chamita (in the San Juan Pueblo grant), or who had built urban
plazas on Indian land, as at Taos.[53] At those places there were conflicts
where Indians and non-Indians met. At Pecos there were not even
enough Indians to generate such a struggle. Non-Indians were living
on the grant. But Pecos Pueblo was about to get the clearest title the
United States could give.

Technically the statute creating the office of Surveyor General for
New Mexico required that first the secretary of the interior and then
Congress itself were to review Pelham's recommendations of which
grants to confirm in which way. Neither the executive nor the legislative
body could really do so, however, because so little was known about
New Mexico or the Pueblo situation in 1856. As a result, the secretary
of the interior's so-called review of Pelham's 1856 report consisted
simply of repeating the report verbatim.[54] Similarly, Congress, re-
sponding to Pelham's plea for prompt action, confirmed without question the grant to Pecos Pueblo on 22 December 1858.[55] In the years
to come Congress would act more and more slowly and with greater
and greater caution in assessing private land claims from New Mexico.
In 1860 the Senate Committee on Private Land Claims actually mod-
ified several of the surveyor general's recommendations.[56] By 1868 the
same committee would claim that a congressional confirmation perfected land titles but did not cut off the rights of other parties, such
as the Hispano residents of Pecos, not named in the confirmation to

the Indians of Pecos Pueblo.[57] By 1870 committee members would say that the situation was so confused they could not act.[58] But in 1858 Congress immediately sent the confirmed Pecos Pueblo grant back to New Mexico.

There the General Land Office charged Pelham with the responsibility for surveying the confirmed Pecos Pueblo grant according to its four-square-league definition. Pelham was an engineer, not a lawyer; the surveying job should have been more to his taste. But as with everything else in the Territory of New Mexico, matters were not so simple. Just as the grant confirmation required Pelham to bring Spanish and Mexican law to American jurisprudence, so surveying the Pecos league became a problem of how to translate Spanish and Mexican measures into those which American surveyors could use. Everyone knew that the Spanish league contained five thousand varas. But how long was the vara?

Others had previously tried to define it for American use. Texas surveyors, for example, had struggled with the Mexican vara for the better part of a decade, with perplexing results, until Stephen Austin adopted the length of 33 1/3 inches. Californians fought over the issue for so long that the United States Supreme Court finally had to rule on the question, deciding that the California vara measured slightly more than 33 inches.[59] Even the second New Mexico Territorial Legislature, meeting in 1851, attempted to solve the problem when it passed "An Act for the Adoption, Definition, and Establishment of Standard Weights and Measures for the Territory of New Mexico." The territorial legislature based the act on the work of a committee established by Colonel Monroe, in 1850, to supervise the transition from Mexican and Spanish to Anglo-American weights and measures. Section 2 of the act recognized this when it stated that

> The *fanega*, the *almud*, the *vara* and the *cuartilla* are hereby made
> legal weights and measures of the Territory of New Mexico approved
> in the year 1850 by a commission appointed and authorized by
> Colonel Monroe.

Unfortunately, no record of the Monroe Commission work survives. The legislature proceeded to give equivalent American measures for all the Spanish and Mexican units except the vara, about which it said nothing.[60]

This once again left the job to Pelham. As usual, his immediate supervisors could not help much. In appointing him, Land Commissioner John Wilson had told Pelham that

> In a report of the 14th November 1851 from the Surveyor General of
> California it is stated that all the grants of lots or lands in California
> made either by the Spanish government or that of Mexico refer to the
> 'vara' of Mexico as the measure of length that by common consent in
> California that measured is considered as exactly equivalent to thirty-
> three American inches,—that Officer then enclosed to us a copy of a
> document he had obtained as being an abstract of a treaty made by
> the Mexican government from which it would seem that another
> length is given to the *vara* and by J. H. Alexander (of Baltimore)
> *Dictionary of Weights and Measures* the *vara* is stated to be equal to
> .92741 of the American yard. This office, however, has sanctioned
> the recognition in California of the Mexican *vara* as being equivalent
> to thirty-three American inches. You will carefully compare the daa
> furnished in the Table herewith and in the foregoing with the
> Spanish measurements in use in New Mexico and report whether they
> are identical, or if varied in any aspect by law or usage, you will
> make a report of all particulars.[61]

Wilson's request posed theoretical problems for Pelham from the outset.[62] Was he to determine the equivalent length of the Mexican vara in use in 1848, the Spanish vara in effect at the time the alleged Cruzate grants were made in 1689, or some possible New Mexican variation of the two? No New Mexico or general texts specified the length of the vara in use there. The only physical evidence Pelham had were the Pueblo vara measuring sticks in use in the territory at the time of American takeover. They were remarkably uniform, but still varied from 32.3 inches to 33.3 inches in length.[63] Commissioner Wilson had called on Pelham for a finer determination than that.

In the end Pelham could do no better than to accept the California definition of 33 inches. In his report Pelham told Wilson that he had encountered terrible difficulty in determining a consistent vara length in New Mexico for lack of both formal definition and genuine consensus. As a result the California measure would have to do. Apparently the General Land Office agreed.[64] Measuring the Pecos Pueblo grant now simply meant converting the 5,000 vara league into feet (13,750) and from there into the miles (2) and chains (48) and inches (33 1/3) with which nineteenth-century American surveyors worked.

Finding a surveyor who would do the Pecos work proved more difficult for Pelham. He frequently complained that the small fees the government was willing to pay guaranteed that no competent surveyor would take the job. Nonetheless, he managed to contract with John W. Garretson, on 10 June 1859, to survey the external boundaries of Pecos Pueblo's league.[65]

Garretson proceeded to do so, with the tools of his day: a Burt's compass to figure direction, a sixty-six-foot chain to figure length, and long poles to control for the elevation changes between shots. This was to be a plane table survey, despite the marked shifts in elevation over the grant's rough terrain. In the contract itself Pelham specified how Garretson was to lay the league out. But he also appointed an Indian as chainman on the survey crew in an attempt, by the method so familiar to previous Spanish and Mexican surveyors, to gain some Indian approval of the work.[66]

Despite advances in surveying technology, Garretson's methods did not differ much from efforts of the Mexican period. Like Alcalde Villanueva in 1818, Garretson began at the southeast corner of the pueblo ruins, went from there to the ruin's northeast corner, and then began a run due north for one league (as he understood the term), where he stopped at what would be the midpoint of the grant's northern boundary. From there he intended to survey a league to the east and a league to the west, in order to establish the northeast and northwest corners of the Pecos Pueblo grant.

Garretson's baseline run essentially duplicated the earlier surveys made by Alcalde Ortiz, in 1815, when he put the original Alejandro Valle grant settlers in possession and by Alcalde Villanueva, in 1818, when he attempted to adjudicate the boundary dispute between the Hispanic settlers to the north and the remaining members of the pueblo. But Ortiz and Villanueva had not so much established boundaries as determined whether the settlers were encroaching on pueblo land. They left no signs of their work. Garretson was trying to locate and mark the boundaries themselves.

The results were curiously ambiguous. In the "Field Notes of Survey" he later prepared, Garretson simply stated that from his starting place he ran due north one league. In the process he never crossed the Pecos river, indicating that the line he drew lay west of the river and its violent shift in the rincón area. Where Garretson ended up in relation to the river is impossible to guess, since a previous decision of the General Land Office had indicated that rivers were not to be meandered, and the subsequent plat map of his survey did not indicate the river's course. Garretson did state that he "set a stone with a mound of rocks for point on line due north of SE corner of the Pecos Pueblo," one league from it. But rock mounds have a curious way of disappearing; no one was ever able to find the one Garretson claimed to have made.[67]

From that mound, Garretson proceeded to lay out the pueblo's league. The one-league limitation had always been artificial by any Pecos Pueblo standard. The Spanish tradition, imported from central Mexico, suggested that the Indian league had been laid out in a number of different configurations, including circles drawn from a pueblo's center or squares based on four points extended in each of the cardinal directions from a pueblo's center and then simply connected.[68] But Garretson took his midpoint on the grant's northern boundary and from there established its northeast and northwest corners. With those two points to guide him, it was a simple matter to create the remaining two corners.

Reduced to a map, the resulting description of the Pecos Pueblo grant was absurd in its arbitrariness, vague in its exact location, but symmetrical in its abstract form. For example, the Pecos grant's western boundary ran up the east side of towering Rowe Mesa and carved out a section of the flat land on top. The Pecos Indians certainly had no ecological or historical reason to include part of the mesa while leaving the rest out.

By 1859 the Spanish Pecos Pueblo league had become the Garretson survey league. In a literal sense it conformed to the Cruzate grant instructions, that the Pecos league should measure

> on the north one league and on the east one league and on the west
> one league and on the south one league, and these four lines to be
> measured from the four corners of the pueblo, leaving out the temple
> which is situated to the south of said pueblo . . .

It was regular on paper, even if it ignored the terrain. Besides extending over some of Rowe Mesa, it ran partway up the mountain range to the east; it ran on a line to the south and ended in the middle of a flat piñon barren; on the north it reached the ridge between the Pecos River and an expanse of irrigated fields farther north. For the moment the Garretson survey gave the government what it needed to adjudicate the Pecos Pueblo claim: an acceptable survey enclosing 18,768 acres in a perfect square.

The government approved the Garretson survey of the Pecos Pueblo grant four years later, on 26 September 1863. The Civil War occasioned the delay. On 1 November 1864, President Abraham Lincoln, through his secretary of the interior, Edward D. Neil, completed the process by issuing a patent to the Pecos Pueblo, identified elsewhere as the inhabitants of the pueblo.

The patent recited the filing of the Pecos Pueblo claim with the surveyor general, its approval by him, its confirmation by the Congress of the United States, and the deposit in the General Land Office of the approved plat of the Garretson survey. Then the Pecos Pueblo grant patent scrupulously reiterated the long list of bearings and distances which made up the land's written legal description. Finally, the patent ended with a passage that would provide lawyers for the next hundred years with a basis for endless litigation:

> Now the United States of America, in consideration of the premises and in conformity with the act of Congress aforesaid, does give and grant unto the said Pueblo of Pecos, in the county of San Miguel aforesaid, and to the successors and assigns of the said Pueblo of Pecos, the tract of land above described and embraced in said survey but with the stipulation as expressed in said act of Congress "That this confirmation shall only be construed as a relinquishment of all title and claim of the United States to any of said lands and *shall not affect any adverse valid rights, should such exist.* [emphasis added][69]

What was the Pueblo of Pecos to which the patent referred? Was it the corporate body created by local legislative act with the power to sue and be sued? If so, then the land belonged to a formal corporation that had the power to act for all its members. Or was the Pueblo of Pecos an unincorporated association of individuals, holding the grant as cotenants? If so, then all the members of the association would have to join together to convey land belonging to the association. The pueblo's governor could not do so in his corporate capacity.[70]

In either case, what land within the grant belonged to individual Indians and what land belonged to the community as a whole, in some form or other? The general opinion in the mid-1850s was that individual pueblo members owned the relatively small irrigated tracts traditionally worked by individual families within a pueblo's grant. The pueblo itself owned only the unallotted common lands. On the other hand, it was possible that the individual tracts had not been fully privatized and that they still somehow belonged to the pueblo, even if used by individual members.[71]

Aside from such points, however, the Pecos Pueblo patent seemed to concede that there might already in 1864 exist adverse claims to the entire 18,738 acre tract the government had just patented to the pueblo of Pecos. The document itself said that it would not affect "any adverse valid rights, should such exist." Would such rights include the claims of individual Indians to supposedly privatized family tracts within the pueblo's grant? And what about the claims of non-Indian families who had bought one of those privatized pueblo tracts, sometimes centuries before, and who had moved in to build homes and raise generations of descendants? What about Spanish grants, like the Alejandro Valle grant, to the north of the Pecos Pueblo grant, and the Los Trigos grant, to the south of it, whose boundaries might overlap those of Pecos?

And who could decide the question of conflicting land claims if they arose? Could a territorial court in effect alter a congressional determination that the land belonged to the Pecos Pueblo Indians? Could any judicial body challenge the work of Congress?

Finally, a question wove its way through all the other patent ambiguities: What exactly was the status of the Pueblo Indians' claim to 18,768 acres? Did it necessitate clarifying the question of Pueblo Indian status under Spanish and Mexican law? Independent of that problem, what was their status under American law? The patent itself stated that the document ended all title and claim of the United States to the entire Pecos Pueblo grant. But what of the United States government's potential role as guardian of the Pueblo Indians? The patent clearly relinquished the government's claim as sovereign successor to all the lands formerly conceded by Spain and Mexico. Did it also relinquish the sovereign's duty to protect the Indians?

The status of the land was similarly ambiguous. The patent stated that it granted rights to the "Pueblo of Pecos . . . and to the successors and assigns of the said Pueblo of Pecos." Did this mean successors and assigns in the sense that the pueblo could take whatever rights the patent conferred and simply sell them? In 1852 John Ward had at least thought that the question was one for Pueblo, not federal, consideration.

For the next seventy years courts, legislatures, and state and federal agencies would struggle to answer these questions, in varying ways that themselves would change over the years. For the pueblo of Pecos, wherever and whatever it was, as of 1 November 1864 it had a formal paper from the United States government that recognized its title to its ancestral home, disregarding the pragmatic history of the area. The patent finally gave the Pecos Pueblo survivors at Jémez the chance to realize something from their former home. In the American legal system the patent was all-important.[72]

One copy of the Pecos Pueblo patent was filed with the General Land Office. A second copy was filed with the surveyor general, in Santa Fe. A third copy was finally filed in the San Miguel County courthouse in 1890.[73] A fourth copy was delivered to Juan Antonio Toya, also known an Antonio Toya, who in 1864 resided at Jémez Pueblo, but who had allegedly been the last resident governor of Pecos Pueblo.[74]

Toya and his Pecos heirs at Jémez eventually lost the American piece of paper. But in November 1864, they did not want to go home. They wanted to sell.

Earlier that year Pecos leaders at Jémez had gone to the superintendent of Indian affairs, Michael Steck, to ask permission to dispose of the 18,768 acres they had not quite won. The Pecos Pueblo claimants, all residents of Jémez, numbered seven men and twenty-five women and children, clearly too few, by the Indians' own admission, to make returning to Pecos attractive. The only way they could realize anything from the grant was by selling it. Because the Pecos Pueblo grant included several hundred acres of good farmland "and one of the best water powers in the Territory," Steck thought that its sale might bring ten thousand dollars or more. He promised to ask the Indian commissioner in Washington about the permission the Pecos Indians sought.[75]

If Steck ever made such a query, there is no formal response on file. But Toya and the Pecos survivors had their American paper and were in the market with it at just the time that interest was increasing in large tracts of New Mexico land. If federal officials would not answer Steck's question, the territorial courts and legislature would. All the answers they gave denied that Pueblo land had any special status; its marketability thereby increased. The chances that the Pecos Pueblo survivors would ever recover any part of their ancestral home diminished every day. But in 1864 they wanted money, not land.

FOUR

John Ward Markets the Pecos Pueblo Grant

Reposing confidence in the friendship, capacity, honesty, and integrity of their friend, John Ward, they [the Pecos Pueblo at Jemez] name and empower him, as their legal and sole attorney, so that he may legally represent them and defend their rights and interest.

—Juan Antonio Tolla et al.

The undersigned having purchased the Pecos Grant from the grantees, the remnants of the original Pecos population, hereby notifies the public not to make any more settlements on said grant; and to all persons who have heretofore settled thereon to apply to him for arrangements for their present occupation.

Frank Chapman

With their United States patent in hand as of late 1864, the Pecos Pueblo survivors at Jémez readied themselves to sell their ancestral home for perhaps the second time. From the outset local New Mexico territorial officials supported that inclination by considering all Pueblo lands as freely alienable as any private lands. They reasoned that federal law, which forbade non-Indian entries on Indian land, did not apply to the Pueblos, since the Pueblos were citizens, not Indians, and because they now held their land by patent, not by treaty and government reservation.[1] The Pecos survivors were probably pleased by this view. Other pueblos, still struggling to stay alive, could not have been as sanguine about their own prospects.

Federal Indian officials in New Mexico, who thought themselves charged with looking after the Pueblos' best interests regardless of local treatment, despaired. On 2 August 1867, one official wrote Washington that

In the latter part of June last . . . I received a letter from your office enclosing one from Hon. S. B. Elkins, district attorney for New Mexico, requesting that the department here should furnish him with the names of all persons residing upon and occupying lands belonging to the Pueblo Indians.

Agreeably to said request, on the following day I started for the Pueblos of Tesuque, San Ildefonse [sic] Nambe and Pojoaque, and succeeded in obtaining a list of over two hundred names of all persons residing upon and occupying lands belonging to the Pueblo Indians, most of whom were indicted and brought before the District Court.

Some 30 suits were commenced by United States Attorney Elkins. The case tried was one against Benino Ortiz to recover the penalty of $1,000 for settling on Indian lands. This case, it was supposed, would settle and decide all the other cases. In that case a demurrer was entered by the defendant's counsel (Hon. Kirby Benedict, late chief justice of New Mexico) to the effect that the Republic of Mexico recognized them as citizens and that the United States had not made any special allusion to the Pueblo Indians upon the acquisition of New Mexico on the subject. The chief justice of New Mexico, Hon. John P. Slough, sustained the demurrer. Now, sir, this decision, however wise and well meant, is bound to have a bad effect.

Up to this time we have had 7,000 honest and industrious Indians, living quietly in their villages, cultivating the soil for their sustenance, with very little aid from the government or any other source whatever, and in every respect self-supporting; and the very fact of throwing open the doors, as it were, for such individuals as may think it proper to take advantage of these people, of whom there is no lack, will, in the course of years, reduce them to poverty and ruin . . . This is bound to be the inevitable result unless the decision of the Court is over-ruled and the appeal of the District Attorney sustained thereby allowing these Indians to retain the full possession of their peaceable homes, as they have had from time immemorial.[2]

The United States Supreme Court eventually affirmed the principle of the decision complained about in the letter, in May 1877.[3] But the letter is significant for the cast of characters it introduced. The U.S. attorney for the Pueblos was Steven B. Elkins, a long-time crony of land grant baron Thomas B. Catron. By 1870 he was himself a principal owner of the two-million-acre Maxwell Land Grant. By May 1877, he was one of the principal spokesmen for the opposite position before the United States States Supreme Court, arguing for the right of non-Indians to acquire Pueblo land.[4] Defending the right of non-Indians to be on Pueblo land was Kirby Benedict, a retired territorial judge who, ten years before, had upheld the right of the pueblos to defend their own lands and who frequently spent the night at a non-Indian hostel on the Pecos Pueblo grant.[5] And finally, what a magnificent nineteenth-century tale of woe, destruction, and outrage, told by a nineteenth-century Indian hero, devoted to the Pueblo cause, battling against the forces of darkness that threatened to eradicate them.

The author: John N. Ward, the same scrivener who in 1852 had reported on his own office's ambiguous attitude toward federal interest in Pueblo land.

On 24 August 1868, well before the United States Supreme Court made the ruling he requested, John N. Ward, the outraged proponent of federal protection for Pueblo lands, himself purchased paper title to the northern quarter of the Pecos Pueblo grant from Pecos survivors at Jémez. At the same time he secured a power of attorney allowing him to sell the balance of the confirmed, surveyed, and patented Pecos Pueblo grant.[6] In the process he helped Pecos Pueblo take the first major step under American rule in converting a historical land claim into a salable document, bypassing recovery of the land itself. Twentieth-century critics have suggested that Pecos could have been recovered for the pueblo had the government only moved quickly enough.[7] The fact is that the government, through Ward, did move quickly, to do precisely what the Pecos survivors wanted at that time: to sell their land grant.

The Pecos Pueblo survivors "reposed confidence in the friendship, capacity, honesty and integrity of their friend."[8] Ward had won that confidence after nearly twenty years in New Mexico Indian work. The federal census of 1870 recorded that Ward, then forty-eight years old, had been born to parents who were both Spanish citizens, in 1822. Ward had married Jesus Charmonante Ward, forty-four years old in 1870, and herself born a citizen of Mexico. The two were living at the time with their three New Mexican daughters, Jesus's mother (from Mexico), and an Indian servant (from the Navajo nation). Ward gave his 1870 occupation as "late Indian agent."[9]

Between 1850 and 1870 Ward had provided that quasi-official, protean connection between New Mexico Indians and the government officialdom that sought to understand them and to serve national politics at the same time by dispatching an endless sequence of Indian agents to New Mexico. As each agent found himself ignorant of the land and the people, he would be forced to turn to Ward as a source of information. In the twenty-year process, Ward came to know the Pecos ruins and the Pecos survivors at Jémez, and ultimately to the decision that the sale of the ancestral Pecos lands was the best solution, for himself and the Indians, to Pecos Pueblo's claim.

Apparently Ward's experience in New Mexico began with the United States Army. Before 1850 Ward was reported as far west as Canyon de Chelly, in the Navajo country, and as far east as Anton Chico and Las Vegas, each time as brevet first lieutenant, Third Infantry, United States Army.[10] Just when Ward switched from the military to the civil branch of government is unknown.[11] Ward himself told various newspaper reporters in 1868 that he had spent twenty years as an agent for the Civil Indian Agency, seventeen of them in New Mexico.[12] But according to military records he was in New Mexico as early as 1849, as a soldier. At least from 1 September 1851 Ward was employed in various capacities by the agency.

Sometimes government Indian officials labeled him an interpreter for an official Indian agent. At other times they called him a clerk in the office of the superintendent of Indian affairs, at Santa Fe. When the territorial government sought an ambassador to the New Mexico pueblos, it settled on Ward as its "special agent."[13]

A major component of all his jobs was travel. Throughout the 1850s the government dispatched Ward to the Navajo country whenever a crisis arose. Between 1855 and 1858 Ward reported to his superiors in Santa Fe from Jémez, Cebolleta, Cubero, Isleta, Fort Defiance, Fort Wingate, and the Rio Arriba. During this period he made no particular mention of the Pecos Pueblo, but he certainly passed close by and visited the survivors' adopted pueblo of Jémez.[14]

Ward proved especially adept at early New Mexico politics on behalf of the pueblos. For example, territorial officials wanted to tax Pueblo land grants as private land, which made sense under the prevailing view of the status of Pueblo land. But Ward realized that it would be a disaster for the pueblos, who could not hope to pay the real estate taxes. Unable to convince federal officials in Washington to take a more active hand, Ward himself struck a bargain for his Pueblo clients with New Mexico politicians. If the territory would exempt Pueblo lands from taxes, then members of the pueblos would not vote in any public election other than acequia elections. This entirely informal arrangement continued for more than twenty-five years and saved the pueblos from wholesale losses of their grants in the interim.[15]

His proven effectiveness won Ward high praise from superiors in the Indian agency. Some agents called him "daring and intrepid." Others said that Ward "is well acquainted with the [Indians] and has more influence with them than anyone that can be sent here." However, the growing praise neither won him a fixed position in the Indian service during the 1850s nor a salary of more than five hundred dollars a year.[16]

The 1860s brought increased problems with the Navajo nation, eventually resulting in the forced removal to the Bosque Redondo, a move bitterly criticized by Ward. But the Navajo problems only increased Ward's power and prestige. By 1860 he had already been appointed acting Indian agent, at Fort Defiance, for the Navajo nation. Except for a brief repeat period in May 1861 as Pueblo agent, Ward served until 1865 with the Navajo Agency of the Bureau of Indian Affairs. His prestige and salary increased. More officials took note of his work among the increasingly hostile Navajos and the rest of New Mexico's Indians, a group of whom Ward escorted to Washington, D.C., in 1863, a year before the Pueblo patents were issued.[17]

But Ward faced problems as well, not the least of which was liquor. By August 1863 he found himself embroiled in an agency effort to brand him an incorrigible drunk. Although Ward survived the accusation that he could not be trusted with money, from 1863 on he received increasing criticism because of his drinking. By 1864 the BIA solved the problem of Ward's drunkenness on the Navajo reservation by calling him back to Santa Fe because of Navajo hostility.[18]

There Ward continued to work at various jobs in the Indian service, now at fifteen hundred dollars per year. By 1866 he had survived another agency attempt to remove him and, in the process, had won the appointment first as "special agent to assist the Pueblo agent" and then as "special Pueblo agent."[19] Because Congress had never recognized an agent for the Pueblos in an appropriation act, funding for the post in Ward's time came from within the local budget allocation. In later years the status of "special Pueblo agent" would cause problems.[20] In late 1866 Ward was finally preparing, under his own name, the official government reports on the status of Indian pueblos.

By that time he had had extensive contact with Jémez Pueblo, where the Pecos survivors lived, as early as 1858 and as late as 1864. On 31

March 1864 he had filed with the Central Indian Agency (CIA) an extensive analysis of a land dispute between Jémez Pueblo and Santo Domingo Pueblo. Fifteen years before he had traveled between Las Vegas and Santa Fe and would have at least seen the Pecos Pueblo ruins. The Pecos survivors at Jémez called him their friend.[21] But it was not until the summer of 1867 that Ward made public his feelings about Pecos in particular and the New Mexico pueblos in general.

In June, July, and August of that year Ward, as special agent for all the pueblos, wrote three separate reports for New Mexico Super-intendent of Indian Affairs A. B. Norton. All three reports explicitly criticized government inaction in protecting Pueblo lands. In addition the August 1867 report detailed the worsening territorial legal situation, which in effect sanctioned Hispano settlement within Pueblo grants. The July 1867 report provided the most accurate survey of Pueblo land inventories and populations then available.[22]

Ward's Pueblo census differed markedly from that of Pelham's 1855 report. Pelham had listed ten inhabitants of Pecos Pueblo as of 1855. Congress had said that the Pecos Pueblo to which it confirmed the grant meant the inhabitants and Indians of the pueblo. Ward listed no Pecos Pueblo Indian inhabitants after 1809.[23] The truth lay some-where in between. As to the status of the pueblo itself, Ward was closer to the truth:

> The Pueblo of Pecos is now a mass of ruins. The few original inhabitants were compelled to abandon the Village about eight years previous to our government's taking possession of the country in 1846. They left in consequence of their reduced circumstances and numbers and the encroachments of Mexican citizens in general, although in 1790 the number of inhabitants of this pueblo does not seem from the census to have been large; yet agreeable to the tradition of the Pueblo Indians themselves in ancient times, this was considered to be decidely the greatest of all [the pueblos] . . .[24]

In the balance of his census report, Ward projected the eventual eradication of the Pueblo race:

> I have now in my possession a list of the names of about 40 ruins of ancient pueblos which are to be found within a circle of about 40 miles of this place. Besides, the pesent pueblos of Picuris, Pojoaque, Nambe and Zia are in a ruinous condition, and the inhabitants thereof are fast decreasing. Hence they too, like their ancestors, will soon be blotted from the face of the earth.[25]

Apparently Ward viewed the situation as hopeless. Even if there had been a solution, Ward thought the government would be unwilling to implement it.

Ward's own life was also becoming somewhat desperate. In May 1867, two weeks before he submitted the first of his formal reports, Ward was accused by Territorial Governor Mitchell of having been continuously drunk for the previous six months; Mitchell wanted Ward removed. The CIA investigated the accusation in July 1867 and vindicated Ward in August of that year: "he is the right man in the right place and should be made a full agent." In October 1867, Ward wrote a long letter in his own defense.[26]

For both Ward and the pueblos the status quo continued. Ward kept his job as special agent for the Pueblos through 1868, and the government did nothing to prevent the further destruction of the pueblos that Ward had predicted.

The Pecos Pueblo survivors remained at Jémez Pueblo, with the United States patent to their ancestral lands and absolutely nothing to show for it. Several factors could have brought them together with Ward. Of all government-connected Anglo New Mexicans, the Pecos Indians at Jémez would probably have known and trusted Ward the most. They called him their friend. Given what Ward was writing in public, it is likely that he told them the government would do nothing about retrieving their lands, even if they had wanted them back. It would have made sense to entrust Ward with their claim. Ward needed the money as a hedge against the impermanence of his government salary. Besides, in New Mexico at the time, "land, not commerce, is the thing" and, on paper at least, a United States patent was the best evidence of land ownership, even if its holder had never set foot on the property. Other pueblos, notably Nambé, had recently sold large portions of their patented lands.[27] Pecos should also be able to.

The mechanics of the transaction proved simple. On 24 August 1868, while Ward was still special agent to the Pueblos, eleven Indians at Jémez Pueblo, eight men and three women, sold to Ward the northern forty-five hundred acres of the patented Pecos Pueblo grant.[28] Ward was neither the first nor the last nineteenth-century Indian agent who dealt in Indian land. The choice of lands sold to Ward, for ten dollars, probably reflected Ward's and the Indians' realization that the northern part of the grant had come under intensive Hispano settlement that no court would end regardless of what Ward's paper said. On the same day they deeded Ward the occupied northern portion of their grant, the eleven Pecos survivors executed to Ward a power of attorney over the balance of the Pecos Pueblo grant.[29]

The power of attorney did not convey any title to Ward. It only authorized him to act for Pecos Pueblo concerning the grant. In his official capacity as special agent, Ward's job was already to protect the best interests of all the pueblos, including Pecos.[30] But the power of attorney gave Ward the added legal authorization to act himself in such a way as to bind all the Pecos survivors who had commissioned him to act for them.

Some of the confusion between Ward's role as special agent to the Pueblos and as private attorney for the Pecos survivors was expressed in the language creating the power of attorney:

> Reposing confidence in the friendship, capacity, honesty, and
> integrity of their friend, John Ward, they name and empower him,
> as their legal and sole attorney, so that he may legally represent them
> and defend their rights and interest; and with this they give him full
> power and authority to work in such manner as he may be able, to
> obtain some relief in connection with their land known as the Grant
> of the Pueblo of Pecos and which was donated to their ancestors by
> the King of Spain and which has recently been confirmed to them by
> their present government of the United States and secured by means
> of a Grant which they have in their keeping and which makes them
> justly, legally and conclusively the owners of said lands.
>
> And be it also known that whatever contract the said John Ward,
> as their attorney foresaid, enters into with the government or
> presently in some particular or particulars, touching their land at
> Pecos, is duly approved and by them confirmed; so they give and
> confirm this with their sane judgment and full consent.
>
> The many hardships which they now suffer make them urge of
> their said attorney that he may do everything possible to aid them in
> their cause to such extent as he may be able under the terms
> aforesaid.[31]

The relationship created by the document was clear enough: Ward could act as legal representative of Pecos Pueblo, even though the New Mexico courts had just held that existing federal law covering Indians did not apply to the pueblos. The 1868 power of attorney made Ward the private guardian of Pecos Pueblo survivors' interests when local courts had ruled that federal law did not entitle them to a public guardian.

But what might Ward do with this private power as protector of the Indian interest in the Pecos Pueblo grant? He might have done nothing, leaving the patent and at least the relatively unoccupied southern three quarters of the patented lands legally in the pueblo's hands. After all, adverse decisions of the state courts merely held that the pueblos held title to land as anybody else might. And anybody else who held a patent to land would have rejoiced at the strength of his title against the whole world.[32]

But the simultaneous 1868 deed for the northern quarter of the grant indicated that Ward and the Pecos survivors knew of long-standing "encroachments" on former pueblo land that would probably increase unless something were done. With his power of attorney Ward could have attempted to stop further encroachment by posting notices of the pueblo's ownership and by making at least marginal use of the unoccupied portions of the grant, as the next owner of the title would do, in the 1870s. In this way Ward could have asserted and protected the pueblo's claim to the tract. Or Ward could have arranged to have some of the pueblo members return to the remaining fourteen thousand relatively unoccupied acres of their ancestral land.

But the possibility of actual return apparently never occurred to either Ward or the Pecos survivors at Jémez in 1868. Human factors explain part of the reason. At the time there were only about twenty Pecos Indians at Jémez, hardly enough to start the pueblo anew. In addition, many of them had themselves elected to leave the pueblo forty years before.

Ecological factors explain another aspect of their reluctance to return. Ward's deed, covering the northern quarter of the grant, included that land where the area's principal agricultural water resources lay. With the 1868 deed the Pecos survivors had already relinquished to a third party and without condition their claim to the ciénaga, a claim that they had probably already sold, to Juan Estevan Pino, in 1830. The Pecos arroyo, which in days long past might have provided some irrigation water to the pueblo, in 1867 provided only intermittent flows, hardly sufficient to support even marginal crops. On fourteen thousand acres of dry land, what hope for survival and increase would a small band of returning Pecos Pueblo Indians have had? Finally, Ward's assessment of the territorial legal situation, communicated to the survivors, would have led anyone to believe that there was no hope of restoration.

As a result, when the Pecos survivors at Jémez gave Ward their 1868 power of attorney, they probably meant for Ward to dispose of their Pecos holdings in the manner most advantageous to them. They had talked to Superintendent Steck as early as 1864 about selling it. The Pecos survivors expressed an interest in at least a "contract . . . with the government," in their authorization to Ward.

That phrase could have implied two possibilities, both of which would resurface at other pueblos in the next century. The first, and least likely, possibility was some form of public ownership of Pecos land, in trust for the Pecos members at Jémez. By 1911 many surviving pueblos considered this an attractive alternative to further non-Indian encroachments on what was left of their lands.[33] In 1867 no one mentioned it. The second possibility was an exchange of the remaining Pecos land for additional acreage at Jémez. This land could be removed from the public domain near Jémez and joined to Jémez Pueblo. In the event that the government would not contract with Ward, the power of attorney authorized him to do whatever else was possible, including selling the patented grant to private parties.

John Ward publicly thought that Pecos's chances of anything better than a private sale were poor, as he wrote in his August 1867 report. Privately he indicated this belief by selling half of his quarter of the Pecos Pueblo grant, on 7 October 1870. David J. Miller was the buyer. Miller's purchase bore out current popular opinion that government officials publically charged with the adjudication of private land claims in the Southwest quickly became privately interested as well. When Special Agent Ward sold part of his quarter, he sold it to the translator and chief clerk of the surveyor general for New Mexico, the federal official charged with assembling and reviewing private land claims, including those of Indians.

David J. Miller was born in Alabama, in 1831, of parents native to eastern Maryland. The end of the Civil War brought him to Santa Fe, to seek his fortune along with other disgruntled southern sympathizers. There he took a job with his fellow southerner, Pelham. In 1880 he listed his profession as government clerk, his age as forty-nine, and his marital status as single.

Miller's official job was to translate from Spanish into English the numerous documents that came into the Surveyor General's Office.[34] Miller's official position gave him knowledge of the confused New Mexico land situation and allowed him to profit by it.

His 1870 purchase of half of John Ward's quarter interest in the

Pecos Pueblo grant marked the beginning of a personal interest in the grant not reflected in his official position as translator and clerk. For example, in the spring of 1877 Miller accompanied a contract United States surveyor to the Pecos area to check the location of the northern boundary of the Pecos Pueblo grant as it adjoined the southern boundary of the confirmed but not yet surveyed or patented Alejandro Valle grant. It was an unusual trip for a government clerk, but not for the (by then) former owner of a half-interest in the northern four thousand acres of the grant whose northern boundary would be affected by the location of the adjoining grant's southern boundary.

That surveying effort suggested what was happening to the Pecos Pueblo grant in the two decades after Garretson first located the grant's northern boundary, in 1859. By the spring of 1876 the surveyor general for New Mexico, H. M. Atkinson, had recommended the Alejandro Valle grant to Congress and Congress had confirmed it, subject to a survey. On 15 April 1876, Atkinson contracted with the surveyors Sawyer and McBroom to survey the non-Indian grant, directing them to begin at the grant's southwest corner, "at the point of rocks to the south of the tract where the principal house stands."[35]

Sawyer and McBroom did so. The "point of rocks" where they began lay somewhere on Garretson's northern Pecos Pueblo grant boundary. But when the two surveyors went to connect their survey of the Alejandro Valle grant with the northern boundary of the adjoining Pecos Pueblo grant, they could not find Garretson's earlier rock pile, marking the pueblo's northern boundary. As a result, Sawyer and McBroom left the marker they had built to indicate the southern boundary of the Alejandro Valle grant and called it the northern boundary of the Pecos Pueblo grant. To check the accuracy of that derivative determination of the Indian grant's northern boundary, Sawyer and McBroom measured back from the southwest corner of the Alejandro Valle grant, going due south the full "Pueblo league." By this method they claimed to have arrived at the "southeast corner of the old Temple which was the initial point in the Pueblo survey."[36] For the first time under any sovereign the Pecos Pueblo grant had been fixed by reference to another land claim.

Surveyor General Atkinson worried about that reversal, since Pecos Pueblo clearly had the preexisting claim. If anything, the Alejandro Valle grant should be located with respect to Pecos Pueblo, not vice versa. After receiving Sawyer and McBroom's initial survey, Atkinson directed them to return to Pecos to check the correctness of their connection of the two grants. Of the two surveyors, only Sawyer went this time, but he took David J. Miller and another of the surveyor general's employees with him. Sawyer, Miller, and the third participant all agreed that the spot Sawyer and McBroom had previously located as the southern boundary of the Alejandro Valle grant was in fact the Pecos Pueblo grant's northern boundary.[37]

Before the Alejandro Valle grant could be patented on the basis of this survey, however, George W. Julian, a reformer from the East, replaced Atkinson as surveyor general. Julian refused to accept the northern boundary of the preexisting Pecos claim as nothing more concrete than the southern boundary of the subsequent Alejandro Valle grant. If anything, Julian thought the reverse should be true. On 21 February 1887 he instructed Charles R. Ratliff, another United States surveyor, to resurvey the northern boundary of the Pecos Pueblo grant and to make the southern boundary of the Alejandro Valle grant conform to that, reversing the process followed by Sawyer and McBroom.[38]

Ratliff went to work in May of that year, without Miller's help. Ratliff began at the southeast corner of the pueblo ruins and ran north from there for the required league. He marked the end point, looked for any previously erected markers, and found none. The next day he ran another line north from the pueblo and ended up at a slightly different spot, indicating that even in those days surveying was still more an art than a science. Ratliff halved the difference between his two surveys and marked that spot as Pecos Pueblo's northern boundary.

Then he looked for the Sawyer-McBroom survey monument of the Alejandro Valle grant's southern boundary, the one Miller had sworn fairly marked Pecos's northern limit. Ratliff finally found the 1877 monument almost one thousand feet south of the boundary he had just set for the pueblo's grant. In his field notes Ratliff reported that

> I remove the corner previously established by Sawyer and McBroom
> for the point and replace it as the center of the Grant of the Pueblo
> of Pecos, as established by me. Then I mark "P" on the side facing
> the Indian grant and mark "A.V. SW cor." on the side facing the
> Alexander Valle grant and raise a monument along side.[39]

That quiet note ended the century-long dispute over the physical location of the Pecos Pueblo grant's northern boundary. Of course, by then the question of the exact location of the boundary was irrelevant to any living Pecos Pueblo concern. Real estate speculators and competing claimants now had the only interest in the boundaries. Members of Pecos Pueblo had accompanied Alcalde Villanueva in his 1818 effort to locate the grant's northern boundary. David J. Miller accompanied the surveyor in the 1870s.

Miller appeared again in 1883. At that time, for no apparent reason germane to his work at the Surveyor General's Office, he searched through the Pecos documents filed there in 1855 and discovered that no one had ever translated the pro-Indian 1829 report of the Pino subcommittee that had ordered all non-Indian settlers off the pueblo's given league. Miller pulled the document, translated it on 8 August 1883, and returned the original and the translation to the archives that day.[40]

Miller had sold his share of the Pecos Pueblo grant in 1873. By 1883 the grant was being offered for sale in the markets of New York. Miller may have taken a look at the long-buried Pecos documents to see if he could find anything that might strengthen a chain of title he was already a part of. But Miller's 1883 translation never appeared in any of the nineteenth-century courts where the Pecos title was litigated.

By 1883 Miller's private interests had carried him well beyond his public position with the surveyor general. By then he had become corresponding secretary of the resurrected Historical Society of New Mexico. Its prestigious governing board, drawn from each of the territory's counties, gave Miller broad access to New Mexicans interested in land. Miller also used his position to gather further information about New Mexico's people and land. In a typical historical society appeal, Miller asked the public for "old manuscripts and narratives, old letters and journals, and old pamphlets and files of newspapers relative to the early family, genealogy and settlement of New Mexico." "The field," Miller had begun the advertisement, "is broad and exceedingly interesting."[41]

Miller's historical work often touched on the pueblos. Particularly between 1874 and 1882, he aided the researches of Mr. Lewis H. Morgan, of Rochester, New York. Morgan, a lawyer, was among the first to take a serious anthropological interest in New Mexico's pueblos; Miller acted as his representative in New Mexico. For example, in the fall of 1877, Miller recorded the results of a three-day excursion to Taos Pueblo. Before departing, Miller had prepared a detailed list of questions he wanted to ask the pueblo's residents concerning every aspect of their life. Their answers were confusing; some members told

Miller one thing, while others denied it. Still, Miller was interested enough to take every subsequent opportunity to investigate Pueblo life.[42]

In his day book entry for 5 December 1877, Miller wrote that

> two intelligent Indians from the Pueblos of Jemez and Zia were at Santa Fe, and I took occasion to interview them. One of them, Juan Jose, was a native of Zia. The other, Jose Miguel, was a native of the Pueblo of Pecos, whose inhabitants, a remnant of about 50, in or about the year 1837, abandoned the pueblo and went to live, and yet live, at Jemez. I arranged for the interview at my offices where they came and were reasonably communicative. What they said is substantially set forth in the following.[43]

In answer to Miller's questions, Juan Jose and Jose Miguel told him about the Pueblos' social and religious organization. As the surveyor general's translator and chief clerk, David Miller worked with land; his questions naturally tended to focus on that subject. Time and again Pueblo Indians, including a Pecos survivor, explained to Miller that no pueblo could sell land to anyone not a member of its community, "an alien," as they told Miller. "It is not allowed in any of the pueblos that a white person in any way acquire property . . ."[44]

Miller's anthropological interest was probably genuine. But he apparently had no sense of the irony or of the tension between an academic interest in the Pueblos as interesting human beings and a more practical interest in exploiting their lands. Thus Miller recommended to Mr. Morgan two of the most infamous non-Indian exploiters of Taos Pueblo lands as good, knowledgeable informants on Taos Pueblo mores.[45] And a Pecos Pueblo survivor had told Miller that no white man could buy a pueblo's property, when Miller had already bought and sold a part of the Pecos Pueblo grant.

David Miller might genuinely have believed that the Pecos Pueblo grant had been abandoned, as he himself said, and therefore no longer belonged to the pueblo, despite the United States patent to the Indians. But Miller was probably more sophisticated that that. In addition to his interest in the Pecos Pueblo grant, Miller had purchased a 14,249 acre interest in the vast Pablo Montoya grant and another 5,000 varas of land lying directly in the eventual path of the railroad line from Kansas to California. In 1883 he bought into several other speculative tracts as well.[46]

By then Miller had sold his half-interest in John Ward's quarter-interest in the Pecos Pueblo grant.[47] There are numerous possible reasons for his doing so. Formally there is the possibility that Miller had merely lent Ward $210 in 1869 and had secured repayment by Ward's deed to him. When Ward repaid the loan, in 1873, Miller would simply have conveyed it back to Ward. Or Miller may have come to see the futility of his Indian title to the primarily non-Indian northern portion of the grant. Or Miller and Ward may have joined together to produce a single title to the entire Pecos Pueblo grant, so that it could be sold as a single entity to one willing buyer.

Ward had in fact found a willing buyer, in April 1872, for the fourteen thousand acres that Pecos Pueblo still had complete title to. On 12 April 1872, many more so-called remnants of the Pecos "tribe of Indians" than had signed the deed to Ward, four years before, now signed a deed to Frank Chapman, excepting the quarter of the grant they had already sold to Ward. The parties agreed on a sale price of four thousand dollars, to be paid in full on delivery of the title documents.[48]

Completion of the deal took the better part of an additional year. On 25 February 1873, four Pecos elders from Jémez, including Miller's informant, Jose Miguel Vigil, traveled to Las Vegas, New Mexico, perhaps with Ward. They delivered the 1872 deed to Chapman and received thirteen hundred dollars.[49] The previous day the four had gone before the San Miguel County probate judge to state that

> Las Vegas, N.M. Feb. 24, 1873: We, Juan Antonio Tolla, Jose Miguel Vigil, Juan Pedro Vigil and Pablo Toya, the eldest of the Pueblo of Pecos, and as their agents, state and confess, that we came to Las Vegas and to Mr. F. Chapman with the view to sell our interest in the Pecos grant and the interest of our constituents. Not having received any benefit of [sic] said lands and seeing that people are taking up tracts of land on our grant, we consider it proper and as our own benefit to try and sell said grant. We, the Pueblo of Pecos, are reduced to a small number and most of us are old, and have never received any benefit from our grant since it has been confirmed to us by Congress. We, therefore, took the step to see whether we could sell said land grant as according to our patent, we believe we have such right and privilege . . .[50]

No court formally approved the sale. No one determined that the self-styled four Pecos elders were in fact who they said they were. Nothing indicated that the other Pecos Indians at Jémez approved of the action or that anyone outside of the survivors at Jémez condoned the sale. Nothing guaranteed that the four men who made the sale were legally entitled to do so. Clearly no treaty or convention of the United States confirmed the sale of Pecos Pueblo land, as the 1834 Non-Intercourse Act required for Indian land, if it applied. At best, the elders' statement to the San Miguel County probate judge conformed to the long-obsolete Spanish law requiring that sales of Indian land be made in public.

None of these issues were pressing in Las Vegas in 1873. Frank Chapman, however, was concerned about the quarter-interest that John Ward and David Miller still held. But on 10 March 1873, three weeks after the Pecos sale was confirmed to Chapman, Ward purchased back from Miller the interest he had sold him in 1869. On the same day Ward sold to Chapman the outstanding northern quarter of the Pecos Pueblo grant he then held.[51] For that Chapman paid Ward $1,300, $1,290 more than Ward had paid the Pecos survivors for his interest four years before, much more per acre than Chapman had paid the Indians for the remaining three-quarters of the grant, and almost as much as Ward's annual salary in his best years as a public servant.[52]

The final transaction united the patent title to the Pecos Pueblo grant in Frank Chapman and purported to eliminate the claims of the Pecos survivors at Jémez once and for all. Twenty-three years had passed since Governor Calhoun first complained of non-Indian acquisition of Pueblo land. In response the government, in 1854, had established a mechanism for determining and locating Pueblo lands. In 1855 the surveyor general had acted on the Pecos claim. In 1858 Congress had confirmed it. In 1859 the United States had surveyed it. In 1864 the president had patented it to the "Indians of the [Pecos] Pueblo." This sequence of events amounted to a relatively swift government response to pleas that Pueblo lands be protected. In the case of the Pecos Pueblo grant, however, it produced not protection for the Indians but marketability for the grant's new owner: Frank Chapman.

Chapman immediately took the position that he now owned the Pecos Pueblo grant outright. On 15 March 1873, the same day that he recorded the Miller, Ward, and Pecos deeds in the county courthouse, Chapman published in the Las Vegas *Gazette* the following notice in English and Spanish:

> The undersigned having purchased the Pecos grant from the
> grantees, the remnants of the original Pecos population, hereby
> notifies the public not to make any more settlements on the grant;
> and to all persons who have heretofore settled thereon to apply to
> him for arrangements for their present occupation.[53]

No evidence indicates that any Hispanic residents of the growing village of Pecos, in the northern reaches of the grant, made any arrangements with Chapman. But the notice effectively halted the southward expansion of the Pecos Spanish community at its 1873 limits. From then on the northern seven thousand acres of the Pecos Pueblo grant belonged to the Hispanos and the southern eleven thousand acres belonged to the succession of speculators who followed Frank Chapman. His 1873 notice asserted, for the first time under American sovereignty, an effective Pueblo title to the grant. Typically, however, a non-Indian businessman pressed that Indian title on his own behalf.

Otherwise, Frank Chapman was the local area's ideal Pecos Pueblo grant owner. He knew David Miller because both shared a real estate interest in the Pablo Montoya grant. He knew important members of the Jémez community then living in Las Vegas. John Ward knew him from frequent trips to Las Vegas, where Chapman was a dry-goods merchant of long standing on the Las Vegas Old Town Plaza.[54]

In 1859, at the age of nineteen, Chapman had arrived in Las Vegas from Illinois, in the company of a midwestern doctor in search of curative waters. He took a job as a clerk in the growing general merchandise store owned by Andres Dold, located in a large building that still stands on the west side of the Las Vegas plaza.[55] Dold was ambitious, Chapman industrious. The two men got along well, so well in fact that by the mid 1860s, Dold had turned the operation of the enterprise over to Chapman and had left Las Vegas for the East Coast, in search of more lucrative enterprises.

In 1865 Chapman changed the name of the business to *Frank Chapman & Co., General Merchandise,* from *A. Dold & Co.* As far as the growing Las Vegas community was concerned, the entire business belonged to Chapman. It sold such unusual Christmas items as "filigree jewelry from the Lucan factory" and a "superior article of French kid gloves for the Ladies," as well as ordinary general merchandise.[56] Chapman often posed as a high-spirited bachelor at the various Odd Fellow Balls he helped sponsor. The Las Vegas *Optic* of 13 December 1879 reported that "Frank Chapman was conspicuous among gay revelers on the dance floor and his broad face fairly beamed with good will toward man and woman as he whirled in rhythmic circles to the lascivious pleasings of the fiddle."[57]

Chapman's life was somewhat more complicated. There was the question of Chapman's ongong relationship to the absent Dold. After all, Chapman had built his financial success on a foundation laid by Dold. On 22 November 1873, five months after Chapman bought the Pecos Pueblo grant, Chapman and Dold formalized their relationship in a partnership agreement that was not made public until after Chapman's death, in 1880.[58]

On the subject of the general merchandise business, the agreement was straightforward: Chapman and Dold would each share equally the business's profits and losses. But the agreement also made Dold half-owner of the recently acquired Pecos Pueblo grant, a status that would not surface until 1880.

The agreement documented another little-known aspect of Chapman's life: his own participation in the New Mexico real estate market. Between 1860 and 1880, Chapman acquired thirty-six tracts of land, one of which was the Pecos Pueblo grant. The other purchases included much of the private land around the Montezuma Hot Springs (outside Las Vegas), several lots in the town itself, a mine site in southern New Mexico, and part of a land grant in eastern New Mexico. Sometimes Chapman bought for himself; at other times he was joined by co-owners, usually a part of that small class of Anglo real estate speculators who grew and prospered along with Las Vegas. Chapman almost always bought land, usually from Spanish-surnamed people, and only rarely sold it.[59]

He obviously bought for investment. Except for the notices he published in 1873, he took little active interest in his Pecos Pueblo grant. Occasionally he sold Pecos stumpage rights to timber cutters hauling ties for the advancing railroad.[60] At other times, Chapman mentioned the possibility of subdividing some of the grant and selling lots to purchasers at a new town he would call Levy.[61] But nothing ever came of those plans.

For the rest of his dealings with the Pecos Pueblo grant, Chapman depended on very sporadic visits, the last one in the fall of 1879. The trip took one day from Las Vegas. On his return, Chapman found his time filled with Christmas preparations. On the last day of 1879, Chapman told an *Optic* reporter that he would appear at the town's New Year's Eve masquerade ball as

> Robespierre of French revolution fame. He will be powdered, gloved, brushed and buttoned. There will not be a crease in his bright blue coat. He will wear trousers, white stockings, frilled shirt and shoes with silver buckles.[62]

Picture if you can, a more different portrait than the four Pecos elders who had presented themselves to Chapman six months before, to sell him their Indian land grant.

Frank Chapman did appear as Robespierre at the masquerade ball. On the way home from the dance, at the age of forty, he collapsed and died of gastritis. "Frank Chapman was his own worst enemy," read his eulogy in the *Optic*. Even without enemies, Chapman's death left the problem of a vast and largely hidden estate.[63]

Only six days after Chapman's death, Andres Dold returned to Las Vegas from New York. He immediately began the complicated business of discovering and arranging Chapman's estate.[64] In the process, the Pecos Pueblo grant met its first, but by no means last, East Coast connection and prepared to make its journey there. Before it got started, however, the United States Supreme Court blessed the Pecos Pueblo grant's merchantability and gave it an encouraging send-off.

FIVE

The *Joseph* Decision:
Pecos and the Supreme Court

A short two leagues from "La Glorieta," beneath the shadow of the ancient "Pecos Church" is a small tract of land, partially and rudely enclosed. It is virgin soil, unbroken save by a little cluster of small, oblong mounds. These are the graves of soldiers—soldiers slain in battle, and in defence of you and your constituents . . . The slain heroes who died for you and your country lie buried as described. At Kuzlowski's they rest. Not unhonored, though neglected . . . Ought not their graves to be decently enclosed, and, over them the plainly inscribed monument be erected?

—Jonathan P. Slough

If the defendant is on the lands of the Pueblo without the consent of the inhabitants, he may be ejected, or punished civilly by a suit for trespass, according to the laws regulating such matters in the Territory. If he is there with their consent or license, we know of no injury which the United States suffers thereby, nor any statute which he violates in this regard.

—Justice Samuel F. Miller

As Andres Dold readied the Pecos Pueblo grant for its trip to New York, several developments continued on the land itself.

For one, time tightened the still relatively recent and precarious Hispanic hold on Pecos. In 1877 East Pecos's founder, Donaciano Vigil, who had arrived in Pecos only in 1854, died. He left a will by which he divided among his numerous sons the Pecos land claimed by him. It did not matter that the will created a written claim to Pecos Pueblo land hopelessly at odds with the sale of the Indian claim to Ward, Miller, Chapman, and Dold. Donaciano Vigil claimed through Juan

111

Estevan Pino and Preston Beck, Jr. His will rooted another Hispano Pecos generation more firmly on the grant.

At the same time, the already twice-sold claim of the Pecos Indians grew weaker. They had sold the ciénaga in 1830. They had sold the entire grant in 1867. In the 1870s and 1880s they returned to Pecos once again and sold small parts of the grant yet a third time, to people they identified in the documents as "nuestros hermanos," the growing Hispano community there. Most importantly, the courts finally denied any responsibility for the looming chaos that these contradictory developments portended.

Between 1864 and 1880 the courts freed Pueblo land that had been confirmed and patented by the United States from any continuing federal interest in its alienability. The cases focused on Indian status, not Indian land directly, and addressed a question of ethnography, not geography: Who were the Pueblo Indians of New Mexico, and by what rights and limitations did they hold their patented lands? Pecos lay at the heart of the emerging debate.

The question had arisen early in the legal life of the territory of New Mexico. Calhoun was repeatedly confronted by it. He recommended determining what land the Pueblos owned, surveying the tracts, and then deciding what to do about non-Indians residing within them. By 1864, and the issuance of a federal patent to each pueblo, the government had completed the first two steps in the Calhoun program. It now should have been time to determine the status of the thousands of non-Indians, including residents of towns like Española, Taos, and Pecos, living within the patented Pueblo lands.

As early as 1852, New Mexico Indian agents had implicitly decided against applying existing federal Indian laws, extended to New Mexico in 1851, to the pueblos, which would have prohibited non-Indians from settling on their lands. In the mid-1860s, the question arose again, this time accompanied by the government surveys and patents. On 13 December 1866, A. B. Norton, superintendent of Indian affairs for New Mexico, introduced in the Territorial Legislature of New Mexico, at its request, his "annual report on Indian affairs in this Territory."

> I recommend that by Act of Congress the sale of lands granted to
> these Pueblo Indians be absolutely forbidden, and that all sales
> heretofore made be declared null and void and that all Mexicans or

> Americans occupying, claiming or cultivating said lands be required
> to abandon and give up the same to these Pueblos, the only rightful
> and legitimate owners thereof, and that some provision be made in
> said Act for reimbursing the amount actually paid by those
> purchasing said lands under the supposition and impression that the
> Indians had a legitimate right to sell the same. I make this
> recommendation because on many of these Pueblos, they have sold
> most of their best lands or they are occupied by those not having a
> shadow of title . . .[1]

Norton also implied that federal protection of confirmed and patented
Pueblo land would require a new act of Congress. But the news of his
recommendation to Congress cannot have pleased the members of the
Territorial Assembly. Manuel Varela represented San Miguel County
there in 1866.[2] In 1862 he had purchased most of the irrigated land
in the ciénaga of Pecos, west of the river and well within the Indian
grant's boundary. Now Norton was suggesting that Congress pass a
law forcing him to give it up. Fortunately for him, Norton's 1866
recommendation did not have much effect on federal officials in Washington. Commissioner of Indian Affairs D. N. Cooley "mutilated" and
suppressed it. Within the Indian bureau, in Washington and New
Mexico, tensions mounted.[3]

In December 1867, George Hebert, owner of a Santa Fe Trail trading
post and hostel, just west of the Pecos Pueblo grant's western boundary,
wrote to the acting commissioner of Indian affairs, Charles E. Mix.
Hebert informed the commissioner that in October of that year he had
applied "for an agency, without pay, to take charge of Indian lands
belonging to the deserted Pueblo of Pecos." "Daily encroachments,"
Hebert told Mix, "are being made upon these lands."[4] By early 1868,
non-Indians from Pecos, including a Martin Kozlowski, who had moved
into the Pecos Pueblo church itself, complained that "certain persons
have attempted to dispossess [non-Indians] under the pretense that the
Pecos grant belongs to the Pueblo Indians or the United States government." Specifically, complained Kozlowski, "Mr. George Hebert,
of Glorieta, claims the charge of the said land under instructions contained in a private letter to him from the late A. B. Norton." For the
moment the government told Hebert to stop interfering.[5]

Eventually, the Pecoseños Varela and Kozlowski would end up as
defendants in a lawsuit that reached the United States Supreme Court

in 1877. Ten years before, activist government officials in New Mexico had realized that neither the territorial assembly nor Congress would act decisively enough. So they set out to determine the Pueblo land question through the courts and under existing law.

In the summer of 1866, John Ward had helped to prepare the first legal assault on non-Indian claimants to patented Pueblo lands by gathering a list of over two hundred names of settlers. He turned the list over to United States District Attorney Stephen B. Elkins. In July 1867, Elkins filed thirty suits against non-Indian claimants to Pueblo land, none of which involved Pecos, and actually tried one against a resident of the old Hispanic town of Peña Blanca, located within the Cochiti Pueblo grant and with an even more complex history than that of Pecos.[6]

In that 1867 suit Elkins, on behalf of the United States and using exclusively federal law, accused Beniño Ortiz of illegally settling on Cochiti Pueblo land. Local territorial law might decide the relative property rights of private land owners, but Elkins wanted to determine once and for all the status of the pueblos under federal law. From the limited selection of congressional enactments, Elkins chose the so-called Non-Intercourse Act of 1834, as extended to New Mexico in 1851. The 1834 act read in part:

> if any person shall make a settlement on any lands belonging,
> secured or granted by treaty with the United States, to any tribe, or
> shall survey, or attempt to survey, such lands, to designate the
> boundaries by marking trees or otherwise, such offender shall forfeit
> and pay the sum of one thousand dollars. And it shall, moreover, be
> lawful for the president of the United States to take such measures
> and employ such military force as he may judge necessary to remove
> from the aforesaid lands any such person.[7]

Congress had extended the 1834 statute to New Mexico, in an appropriation act of 1851:

> all the laws now in force regulating trade and intercourse with the
> Indian tribes, or such provisions of the same as may be applicable,
> shall be and the same hereby are extended over the Indian tribes of
> New Mexico and Utah.[8]

Congress had limited the 1834 act to

> all that part of the United States west of Mississippi, and not within
> the States of Missouri and Louisiana or the Territory of Arkansas; and
> also that part of the United States east of the Mississippi river, and

not within any state to which the Indian title has not been
extinguished.

United States District Attorney Elkins claimed from Ortiz only the
prescribed one thousand dollar fine for settling on Indian land. Both
the 1834 and earlier statutes on which the 1851 statute was based
contained prohibitions much stronger and more direct that the provision under which Elkins elected to proceed. The 1790 act had provided that "No purchases, grants or seizures of lands from Indian tribes
shall be of any validity unless made by treaty or convention entered
into pursuant to the Constitution." The 1834 act amended that only
slightly: "No purchase, grant, lease, or other conveyance of lands thereto
from any Indian, nation or tribe of Indians shall be of any validity in
law or equity unless the same be made by treaty or convention . . ."
Obviously Congress had meant to deny the validity of any non-Indian
holding of Indian land. But instead of trying to evict non-Indian
encroachers, Elkins elected simply to sue each of them for the one
thousand dollar penalty provided by the statute.[9]

Elkins's choice had a definite effect. In the short run, it allowed the
New Mexico courts to treat the Indian land suits as involving fines
rather than lands. As a result the courts could apply the more stringent
common-law standards for the proof necessary to exact a fine rather
than for that necessary to establish a good title. In the long run, Elkins's
choice avoided a direct decision on Pueblo land tenure. He could have
maintained that the pueblos owned the land claimed by the non-
Indians. Instead he said that under the terms of a particular statute
the non-Indians owed money; what became the determinative nineteenth-century legal case on Pueblo Indian lands began as a mundane
suit for the collection of a debt.

The outlandish, creative attorney for the defendant, the former territorial supreme court justice Kirby Benedict, denied that his client,
Beniño Ortiz, owed anything.[10] He claimed that even though his client
was a non-Indian, and even though he was on Cochiti Pueblo land,
the statute under which the suit was brought did not apply to New
Mexico pueblos or their lands.

The presiding judge, John N. Slough, had led the Union army in
the battle of Glorieta Pass, parts of which were waged well within the
western boundary of the Pecos Pueblo grant. He had billeted his troops
at Martin Kozlowski's hostel in the heart of the abandoned Indian
pueblo. After leaving New Mexico with the Union army, he returned

in late 1865 to replace Kirby Benedict on the territorial supreme
court.[11] On 3 December 1865, he spoke to the legislative assembly of
the territory of New Mexico as follows:

> Gentlemen—A short two leagues from "La Glorieta," beneath the
> shadow of the ancient "Pecos Church" is a small tract of land,
> partially and rudely enclosed. It is virgin soil, unbroken save by a
> little cluster of small, oblong mounds. These are the graves of
> soldiers—soldiers slain in battle, and in defence of you and your
> constituents . . . The slain heroes who died for you and your country
> lie buried as described. At Kuzlowski's they rest.[12]

Slough was not a man impassioned by the Pecos Pueblo cause.

What Slough lacked in detailed knowledge of New Mexico history,
he made up for in administrative speed. In his July 1867 term he
disposed of 250 pending United States cases, according to the Santa
Fe *New Mexican*. Nearly half of them involved "indictments concerning
violations of the revenue law."[13]

One of the revenue law violations cleared that summer was Elkins's
suit to recover for the United States the one thousand dollars the
government said was owed by non-Indians living within Pueblo grants.
In those days, lawyers simply stood up in the lower courts and argued
their points orally; nobody wrote briefs, and judges decided quickly.[14]
In the Pueblo lands case, Slough needed no evidence of facts to reach
Kirby Benedict's demurrer. The law alone determined the answer to
the question Benedict posed.

Under those circumstances, it is surprizing that Slough wrote a
district court opinion. In fact he wrote a lengthy one, which the Santa
Fe *New Mexican* printed in its entirety on 3 August 1867.[15] Two years
later, when the territorial supreme court reviewed Slough's initial decision, in *United States v. Lucero,* it appended Slough's lower court
opinion to its own affirmation.[16] The Supreme Court apparently did
so partly because of the importance of the case, and partly because
Slough himself had been killed in a Santa Fe hotel lobby brawl in late
1867.[17] As a last tribute, the Supreme Court printed his most important
decision.

Through the nineteenth century Slough's legacy gained weight and
power as court after court reached the same result he had, often using
language from Slough's decision without acknowledging it. In the years
to come, Slough's anthropological categorization of the Pueblo Indians,

based on less than two years in New Mexico, became more and more fixed as objective fact.

Slough began his 1867 opinion, as would later nineteenth-century courts, with a question forced on him by Kirby Benedict's procedural maneuvering: Did the 1834 Non-Intercourse Act, as extended to New Mexico in 1851, apply to the Pueblo Indians? Posed in that way, the question became one of interpreting a federal statute, not one of deciding who the Pueblos were and by what rights and obligations they held their land. Slough and all the courts that considered the issue after him eventually reached that second, much more comprehensive question, but only by way of the narrow confines of particular statutes.

Slough first examined federal law to determine what tribes of Indians Congress had intended to include. By its own explicit terms, the 1834 act regulated affairs in Indian country. The act also stated that that included everything west of the Mississippi. But, argued Slough, Congress had enacted that law when New Mexico was unknown; all of New Mexico was not Indian country just because it fell on the far side of the river. The 1851 act did not illuminate the problem. Slough finally decided that Congress, by the 1834 and 1851 acts, had intended to regulate affairs between white settlers and Indians "beyond the settlements or on the frontiers." New Mexico Pueblo Indians lived in settlements and among white settlers, not beyond them. Therefore, the federal non-intercourse acts did not apply to the Pueblos. Non-Indians living on their lands thus did not have to pay for residing there.

But there were several weak points in Slough's logic. For one, his conclusions about what was and was not Indian country were open to serious doubt. The 1834 act had addressed the unsettled West. But earlier versions of it had concerned the long-settled East, indicating that relative population densities had not been of much concern to Congress.[18] Slough avoided that problem by deciding that the acts applied only to tribal Indians who lived "beyond the settlements or on the frontiers." Such a vision neatly divided the world into civilization, on one side, and whatever was uncivilized and presumably tribal Indian, on the other. The federal acts, held Slough, regulated affairs between Indians and non-Indians only when the two met at some defined boundary line between civilization and non-civilization.

The 1834 act itself belied that interpretation. It was intended only to protect Indians and their claims to land, not non-Indians and theirs. The act's prohibitions ran entirely against non-Indians, in favor of Indians. In fact, it even authorized the president to call out the army to defend Indian lands.[19]

Slough's 1867 decision had the opposite effect. In his view, under federal law non-Indians could encroach on Pueblo lands with impugnity. Slough reached that conclusion by irrelevantly damning the Pueblos with faint praise:

> For centuries the Pueblo Indians have lived in villages, in fixed communities, each having its own municipal or local government. As far as their history can be traced, they have been a pastoral and agricultural people, raising flocks and cultivating the soil. Since the introduction of the Spanish Catholic missionary into the country, they have mainly been taught not only the Spanish language but the religion of the Christian church. In every Pueblo is erected a church, dedicated to the worship of God, according to the form of the Roman Catholic church, and in nearly all is to be found a priest of this church who is recognized as their spiritual guide and advisor. They manufacture nearly all their blankets, clothing, agricultural and culinary implements, etc. Integrity and virtue among them is fostered and encouraged. They are as intelligent as most nations or people drprived of means or facilities for education. Their names, their customs and their habits are similar to those of the people in whose midst they reside, or in the midst of whom their pueblos are situated. The criminal records of the courts of the territory scarcely contain the name of a Pueblo Indian. In short, they are a peaceable, intelligent, industrious, honest and virtuous people. They are Indians only in features and complexion, and a few of their habits; in all other respects they are superior to all but a few of the civilized Indian tribes of this country; and the equal of the most civilized thereof.[20]

For his anthropological authority, Slough offered only "judicial notice," a source that raised the judge's personal opinion to the more elevated status of court-mandated truth. Slough himself asserted that no books existed on the subject.[21] More than a decade would pass before Adolph Bandelier would bring a trained anthropological eye to New Mexico's Pueblos, and even then the facts would be skewed. What Anglos knew about Pueblo land and culture in 1867 confirmed Slough's view.[22]

Only John Ward and other dissidents within the New Mexico Indian agency took written offense at Slough's decision. Ward argued strongly for appealing the decision, because otherwise the adverse district court decision would "open the doors, as it were, for such individuals as may think it proper to take advantage of these [Pueblo] people."[23] On 23 November 1867, the United States attorney general instructed Elkins to appeal the Slough decision, first to the territorial supreme court. "Should the decision there affirm the ruling below, you will take the proper steps for bringing up the respective cases for adjudication by the Supreme Court of the United States."[24] Clearly the attorney general was not relying on the territorial supreme court for relief.

Indeed, territorial politics permeated the court that in 1869 reviewed Slough's 1867 decision. Chief Justice Watts and Associate Justice Joab Houghton both had strong personal and political ties biasing them toward Slough's point of view.[25] Even good taste could not constrain Watts's approach to the subject of the Pueblos in particular and Indians in general. In his 1869 opinion, reviewing and upholding Slough's earlier decision, Watts began, as Slough had, by deciding which Indians the Non-Intercourse Act concerned:

> Who and what are the Indians for whom said laws were passed, and
> upon whom were they intended to operate? They were wandering
> savages, given to murder, robbery and theft, living on the game of
> the mountains, the forest and the plains, unaccustomed to the
> cultivation of the soil, and unwilling to follow the pursuits of
> civilized man. Providence made this world for the use of the man
> who had the energy to pull off his coat, roll up his sleeves, and go to
> work on the land . . . Land was intended and designed by
> providence for the use of mankind, and the game it produced was
> intended for those too lazy and indolent to cultivate the soil, and the
> soil was intended for the use and benefit of that honest man who had
> the fortitude and industry to reclaim it from its wild, barren and
> desolate condition and make it bloom with the products of an
> enlightened civilization . . . Let us now look at the Pueblo Indians
> of New Mexico and see if there is anything in their past history or
> present condition which renders applicable to them a set of laws
> designed and intended to regulate the trade and intercourse of
> civilized man with the wandering tribes of savages . . .[26]

Watts's homily on man, land, and work sounds strange coming from one of New Mexico's earliest land speculators.[27] But his perspective guaranteed that Pueblo Indians could not win existing federal protection except by losing that intricately organized culture they had long maintained. Watts widened further the distinction between civilized and uncivilized Indians by maintaining that Pueblo Indians had held full citizenship under Mexico. As for Spanish and Mexican treatment of so-called savage Indians, Watts suggested that New Mexico's antecedent sovereigns "would have as soon have thought of legislating upon what time the wolf should be admitted into their sheep fold, the bear into the cornfields, the fox into their hen roosts, or the skunk into their parlors."[28] The United States, Watts continued, had recognized the Pueblos' acceptability according to that nineteenth-century scale of values which only yielded judgments running from better to worse, by granting them fee simple patents for their lands, just like any other claimant under the Treaty of Guadalupe Hidalgo. Watts, writing in *United States v. Lucero,* agreed with Slough: the Pueblo Indians were too civilized to receive federal protection of their lands.

Again, only the Indian agency protested this analysis. Agent after agent wrote to Washington superiors predicting the disastrous effect the territorial supreme court's decision would have. The 1867 report of the commissioner on Indian affairs reproduced in full Judge Slough's district court opinion. Elkins reported on the territorial supreme court's 1869 affirmation of that decision. His superiors had expected that result and instructed Elkins to appeal the *Lucero* decision to the United States Supreme Court. Instead, as was to become typical of subsequent Pueblo attorneys, Elkins resigned on 17 September 1870.[29]

But individual Pueblo agents refused to let the matter rest. In August 1871, Pueblo Agent Arny urged "the importance of some action in relation to their [the Pueblos'] lands occupied by citizens, and the question of the citizenship . . . which has caused much trouble . . ."[30] New Mexico Superintendent Pope himself reported in 1872 that

> The question of citizenship [of the Pueblo Indians] has not yet been satisfactorily settled, and every year renders it more difficult to solve. The Courts of this Territory have decided upon several occasions that the Pueblo Indians are citizens of the United States . . . but it is doubtful if this action will be sustained till their status is finally fixed by the Supreme Court of the United States. A decision on this matter, which I trust will be obtained this year, will facilitate the settlement of other questions regarding the affairs of these Indians, more or less dependent upon that citizenship.[31]

The commissioner of Indian affairs commented in the same year that the Pueblos were

> a remarkable people, noted for their sobriety, industry and docility. They have few wants and are simple in their habits and moral in their lives. They are indeed scarcely to be considered Indians in the

sense traditionally attached to that word, and, but for their residence upon reservations patented to these bands in confirmation of ancient Spanish grants and their continued tribal organizations, might be regarded as part of the ordinary population of the country.[32]

Although this sounded like the Slough and Watts view of the Pueblos, minus invective, the commissioner himself directed the United States attorney to start proceedings in the courts again and this time finally resolve the question of the Pueblos.

The job fell to the new United States attorney, T. B. Catron. By 1872 Catron had started to rise in territorial politics;[33] he was said to use his official position to advance his private political causes. In 1872 Catron had been accused of bringing a number of federal indictments and using them to encourage various voters to help Elkins, who was running for territorial representative to Congress.[34] In 1873 U.S. attorney Catron raised the Pueblo issue once again, on instructions from Washington, by filing no less than 204 suits against non-Indians residing within different Pueblo grants.[35] As in Elkins's 1867 suit, each of these suits claimed that the non-Indians had violated the 1834 and 1851 non-intercourse acts and owed the United States one thousand dollars as a result. In 1867 Elkins had begun with the Cochiti Pueblo grant. In 1873 Catron selected from the 204 pending suits charges involving two other Pueblo grants: the very much alive Taos Pueblo grant and the abandoned lands of the Pecos Pueblo grant. Once again, local politics informed his choices.

On 24 January 1873 Catron filed his first challenge to the right of non-Indians to occupy Pueblo lands. In this first suit Catron named that Pecos resident Martin Kozlowski as the sole defendant and the Pecos Pueblo grant as the land encroached on. On 28 January 1873 Deputy United States Marshall Tomas Romero brought a copy of Catron's complaint to Kozlowski at Pecos.[36]

It is still a mystery why Catron elected to begin a case that was expected to go to the United States Supreme Court in the most moribund of New Mexico's twenty confirmed Pueblo Indian land grants. Catron may have been trying to block the first Pecos Pueblo deal with Frank Chapman, which John Ward was trying to assemble between August 1872 and February 1873. Catron may also have been interested in clearing the Pecos Pueblo grant of all Indian claims to it, so that the railroad would have secure title to its right-of-way through the grant and also so that the tract of land itself would appear freely salable on world markets.[37] Finally, Catron and Martin Kozlowski had crossed political paths before. Catron may have selected him out of spite.[38]

If local politics motivated Catron's choice of Kozlowski, it is difficult to understand why he failed to sue an even more famous non-Indian Pecos Pueblo grant claimant, Donaciano Vigil. The aged Vigil had opposed Catron politically from time to time, and claimed an important part of the Pecos Pueblo grant. In 1876 Vigil would testify that Catron's own claim to the Nambé Pueblo Gaspar Ortiz grant was based on a forged document.[39] In January 1873, Catron limited the Pecos suit to Kozlowski.

The complaint stated that Kozlowski "owed to . . . and detained from" the United States the one thousand dollars because on 10 January, two weeks before the complaint was filed, Kozlowski had settled on five acres of land belonging to the "Pueblo tribe of Indians of the Pueblo of Pecos."[40] In fact, Kozlowski had arrived in the Pecos Pueblo grant long before 10 January 1873. And he claimed much more land than five acres.

Martin Kozlowski, a native of Warsaw, Poland, had emigrated in 1853 to the United States with his English wife. In that year he enlisted in the First Dragoons of the United States Army and served five years, fighting Indians. In 1858 he mustered out and settled in Pecos at a site well south of the Hispano village that was pushing down from the north, and well north of Las Ruedas, the growing Los Trigos grant settlement that was pushing up from the south. In fact, the site chosen by Kozlowski lay close to the center of the Pecos Pueblo grant, next to the pueblo ruins, near the Arroyo de Pecos, the water source that had sustained the pueblo in its last days, and along the route of the Santa Fe Trail. There he ran a way station and hostel.[41]

His actions had not gone unchallenged before 1873; George Hebert had inquired since 1867 into his right to live on Pecos Pueblo land. But everyone knew that Kozlowski was there. Kirby Benedict had stayed there on his trips to court in Las Vegas.[42] Territorial Supreme Court Justice Slough had billeted his Union troops at Kozlowski's, in 1862. According to Kozlowski, "When they camped on my place and while they made my tavern their hospital for over two months after their battle in the canyon [the battle of Glorieta Pass], they never robbed me of anything, not even a chicken."[43]

Now Kozlowski had a problem. No known document from anyone purported to grant him title to the Pecos Pueblo tract he claimed. On

24 June 1861, Kozlowski transferred to his wife, Elena, his supposed rights in a house and a portion of land located in the "arroyo of Pecos," near the pueblo ruins. The deed alleged that the land involved was bought from one Johan Piser.[44] But no deed from Piser appears anywhere. Neither the census, nor the records of San Miguel county, nor Pecos oral tradition indicate the existence of any landowner named Piser in Pecos before Kozlowski's arrival. In 1879 Kozlowski said he had bought the bulk of his Pecos Pueblo holdings from a Julius Mahan, again apparently a product of his imagination. As early as 1862, he had dealings with the Beck family, whose connections to the Pecos Pueblo grant were recorded. But Kozlowski did not buy land from them, he borrowed money.[45] Kozlowski, in short, appeared to be one of those non-Indian claimants to Pueblo land who had settled there, as Norton warned in 1866, "without having a shadow of title."

The area of land claimed by Kozlowski proved as ephemeral as the source from which it had come. In 1861 Kozlowski formally declared that his tract of Pecos Pueblo land consisted of a long, narrow strip on both sides of the Pecos arroyo.[46] In 1862 he told the visiting Union troops that he owned 600 acres in the grant.[47] By 1879 he had reduced his claim to 160 acres, coincidentally scaling it to a territorial law passed that winter which purported to allow New Mexico settlers to lay claim to federal land under territorial law. Numerous Hispanos claimed large, undefined amounts of Pecos land under the same statute.[48]

Curiously enough, however, Kozlowski's 160 acre claim materialized in the form of an 1879 mortgage deed from Kozlowski and his wife to Frank Chapman, the man who, on paper at least, already owned the entire Pecos Pueblo grant. On 20 June 1879, Kozlowski borrowed two hundred dollars from the Las Vegas merchant. To guarantee repayment, he promised Chapman a ranch which Chapman technically already owned. Kozlowski described his holding as

> that pice [*sic*] of land lying . . . in the Pecos Grant known as the
> ranch of Martin Kozlowski on the Arroyo de Pecos and in a southerly
> direction near the Pecos church containing 160 acres of land, this
> being the land conveyed to said Martin Kozlowski by Julius Mahan
> by his deed dated [blank] including all the houses and improvements
> in said lands and the said parties of the first part agree to transfer all
> documents they have relating to said land to said Frank Chapman in
> better description and in better showing of the said premises
> conveyed as foresaid . . .[49]

If Kozlowski ever gave Chapman the deeds he promised, on which he based both his claim and his mortgage, they never appeared among Frank Chapman's papers.[50] Immediately after purchasing the entire Pecos Pueblo grant, Chapman had called on grant residents to make arrangements with him. Kozlowski's 1879 mortgage might have been intended to fill that request.

Kozlowski's life became more mysterious as time went on; even his identity proved troublesome. Adolph Bandelier, visiting Pecos in 1880, identified the hostel keepers as Mr. and Mrs. Andrew Kozlowski.[51] The *New Mexican* of 15 March 1881 identified him as Joseph Kasloski:

> Joseph Kasloski, whose term of imprisonment has expired, has just been set at liberty. The costs in the case amounted to $109, which amount was raised by Mess. [*sic*] Wm. Breeden and W. Scott Morse, who also furnished $3.50 to defray the expenses of the released man to his home. Kasloski is the man who owned a ranch on the Pecos upon which the old Pecos church, one of the most interesting relics of New Mexico, stands. Thinking that the church was his property, he destroyed the records of its antiquity, tore down its beams and used its adobes for building purposes. It is also related in this connection that Kasloski's son, while engaged in the same work of Vandalison [*sic*] was struck and killed by lightning. Two or three years ago, the father became insane and killed his only remaining son, for which crime he was tried, convicted and sentenced to two years imprisonment. He has just served out his sentence as above stated and is now probably at his old home. Kasloski was birth a Pole.[52]

The 1880 federal census recorded a Martin Kaslowski as a resident of the San Miguel County jail.[53] The same census recorded three living sons and a daughter still at home, with Helen Kosloski, in Pecos. A fourth living son, Jose, had married Eutemia Ruiz, daughter of the Pecos grant claimant Mariano Ruiz, and reported his family separately.[54] Seven years before, in January 1873, the federal process server bearing the United States complaint had delivered it to Martin Kaslowski.

Three days after he had filed suit against Kozlowski, on 27 January 1873, Catron filed another suit against a non-Indian claimant to Pecos Pueblo lands, Manuel Varela.[55] By the mid-1860s Varela represented San Miguel County in the New Mexico Territorial Assembly. There he had argued with Catron and with the local Indian agents seeking to enforce the non-intercourse acts.[56] As in the case of Martin Kozlowski, the complaint against Varela did not elucidate much. It said only that

Manuel Varela occupied five acres of land within the Pecos Pueblo grant, alleging that he had begun that occupation only ten days before Catron filed suit against him, and that as a result Varela also owed the United States one thousand dollars.

In fact, Varela had arrived in the Pecos area around 1848, in the earliest and most confused days of American sovereignty. In July of that year he witnessed a deed conveying Pecos real estate from Juan Estevan Pino's two sons to their wives. By 1854 Manuel Varela was serving as San Miguel County justice of the peace. In that office he prepared and witnessed numerous local Pecos property transactions. He helped Alejandro Valle secure the grant just to the north of Pecos. In May 1877 he witnessed Donaciano Vigil's important will.[57]

But on his own, Manuel Varela emerged as a significant Pecos-area landowner only in the mid-1850s. On 29 September 1855, he purchased from Jesús López a small, ill-defined tract of land in Pecos that, according to the deed, was bounded on all four sides by the lands of Manuel Doroteo Pino.[58] Subsequent events would show that the surrounding Pino tract consisted of the pueblo's former ciénaga lands, west of the river. On 22 December 1857, for fifty-six bushels of corn, Varela purchased 175 yards of land along the Pecos River, in a settlement about four miles upstream from the Pecos grant's northern boundary, in a place called La Posada.[59] In 1879 Varela filed, in the San Miguel County courthouse, along with numerous other Pecos residents, a claim for 160 acres of public domain somewhere south and east of the Santa Barbara divide, but not within either Pecos Pueblo or San Miguel del Vado grant land.[60]

None of these small, often ill-defined acquisitions placed Manuel Varela in the heart of the Pecos Pueblo grant. But between 1861 and 1862 he and a partner, Jesús María Baca y Salazar, purchased from the estate of Preston Beck, Jr., Beck's claim to the Pecos Pueblo grant irrigated land lying west of the river. This purchase eliminated any Pino claim to the land. It followed by eight years Donaciano Vigil's purchase of the eastern half of the same tract, and made Manuel Varela the grant's second most substantial Hispano claimant after Vigil.[61]

By late 1862 Manuel Varela lived in West Pecos, near the first church, at the site of the present St. Anthony's on the Pecos. He resided just west of the ancient West Pecos acequia, in a large, fortress-like house built around an open quadrangle. By 1880 his wife and nine children, three girls and six boys, lived there with him.[62] Just to the north of his house he would have seen Juan Estevan Pino's church and the few, scattered houses of Hispano families that had left the hidden rincón area and moved with Manuel Varela into the open fields of west Pecos. To the east he would have been able to look across the irrigated fields and the river and see scattered shacks and the more substantial structures of Donaciano Vigil, to the north, and the Valencia family, to the south. South along the river, there would have been only open space. Kozlowski's ranch lay two miles away, across an intervening ridge.

No one knew exactly how much Pecos Pueblo land Manuel Varela actually claimed. When the Pueblo Lands Board arrived, seventy years later, its investigators found his heirs in possession of slightly more than twenty-six irrigated acres and almost two hundred dry acres. But the irrigated acreage originally claimed by Varela might have changed by purchase and sale subsequent to his death in 1884. The Pueblo Lands Board, bent as it was on finding an owner for every bit of Pecos Pueblo non-irrigated land, certainly inflated Manuel Varela's claim.[63]

But on the same day that Deputy United States Marshall Romero brought Catron's complaint to Martin Kozlowski, he walked up the Pecos River and handed a similar document to Manuel Varela. That set the stage for a lawsuit that would eventually reach the United States Supreme Court. The decision there would change the course of Hispano-Pueblo relations for years to come. In the winter of 1873, Martin Kozlowski and Manuel Varela did what they could to avoid paying the one thousand dollars the United States said each man owed for settling on the Pecos Pueblo grant. They hired a lawyer.

Joab Houghton, "that learned fountain of justice," as his enemies called him, was their choice. A jack-of-all-trades, Houghton had sat on the 1869 territorial supreme court which had reviewed and upheld Slough's 1867 decision in the first Pueblo lands suit. He knew Donaciano Vigil and Preston Beck, Jr., as well as the intricacies of New Mexico land and politics.[64]

On 10 February 1873, less than two weeks after Varela and Kozlowski were served with the complaints, Houghton demurred on behalf of his Pecos clients, just as Kirby Benedict had done in the first Pueblo lands case, seven years before. Houghton's pleading said that Varela and Kozlowski did not even have to answer the complaint's allegations that they were non-Indians occupying land patented to Pecos Pueblo, because the Non-Intercourse Act applied to neither Pecos nor the Pueblos.

To buttress his argument Houghton raised three points. Two of them

were familiar: there never was a tribe of Pecos Pueblo Indians as contemplated by the statute; the United States had patented the land
involved to citizens of first Mexico and then the United States. The
Pecos Pueblo grant was not Indian country under the statute.

The third ground for dismissal set out by Houghton, however, was
new:

> the lands described in said petition belong to the Pueblo of Pecos, a
> town in the County of San Miguel and the Territory of New Mexico,
> . . . owned and occupied by a community of citizens of the United
> States by right . . ., lately citizens of the Republic of Mexico who,
> with the soil upon which they live, the sovereignty held over them
> by that government, together with all their rights and privileges as
> such citizens, guaranteed to them by treaty, were transferred to the
> government of the United States by the said government of Mexico.[65]

Here was an intriguing, original idea. Houghton suggested that the
Hispanos who had moved onto the Pecos Pueblo grant had taken over
not only the land but the pueblo governmental framework as well.
Just as Pecos had once belonged in common to the Pueblo Indians, it
now belonged to the Hispano residents of the valley. The race had
changed, argued Houghton, but the nature of land ownership had not.

Twenty-three years later, Hispanic Pecos's one effort to make this
idea formal reality failed. In fact, however, non-Indian Pecos land use
survived in Houghton's terms well into the twentieth century. While
other Hispano land grants fell before the imposition of Anglo-American
law, Pecos survived as a community land grant precisely because it was
not legally a community grant, but a Pueblo Indian grant.[66]

The district court before which Houghton placed these theoretical
possibilities never dealt with their implications. On the same day that
Houghton filed identical demurrers for both Varela and Kozlowski,
United States Attorney Catron responded. He simply asserted that the
complaints he had filed did meet the prerequisites of the 1834 Non-
Intercourse Act, as applied to New Mexico in 1851.[67] New Mexico
Territorial Chief Justice Joseph Palen, sitting initially as district judge
in Santa Fe, wasted no time on elaborate reasoning and fine points in
rendering his decision. On 10 February 1873, the same day that Houghton
demurred and Catron responded, Palen ruled in favor of Houghton
and the non-Indians. In less than one working day court proceedings
had again attempted to settle the Pueblo Indian land question.[68]

Three weeks later, Catron announced that he would appeal the two

Pecos Pueblo grant cases to the territorial supreme court, presumably en route to the United States Supreme Court itself. However, that first appellate court would not sit until January 1874. In the meantime, Catron did more than just wait. On 13 June and 30 June 1873, he filed two additional land suits, identical to the earlier suits but this time involving the Taos Pueblo grant.[69] While there may have been some uncertainty about Catron's political motives in selecting defendants for the Pecos Pueblo land litigation, his choice of Taos Pueblo and of Juan Santistevan and Antonio Joseph as defendants left no room for doubt. Both men had speculated in Taos Pueblo land, and each had recently offended Catron politically, in 1871 and 1872. In 1873 Catron was looking for revenge.

Catron was a Republican, Santistevan a prominent Taos County Democrat. Santistevan had resided since 1843 on the Antonio Martinez grant, which overlapped the Taso Pueblo grant. He had taken part in local politics since the mid-1850s. Although he called himself a merchant, he held the highly political job of Taos County probate judge for two terms, from 1863 to 1865 and from 1867 to 1869. During that period he also served as a Democratic member of the Taos County Commission for one year. Since 1865 he had held the lucrative position of United States postmaster.[70] As one of the county's leading Democrats, it appeared that Santistevan might keep the job as long as the Democrats retained their hold on Taos County.

But Catron's Republican party had almost broken that hold in 1871–72. In the fall 1871 elections, four Republican candidates for the territorial senate had ousted the four Democratic incumbents. The four Democrats had challenged the election at the 1872 legislative meeting. They also had led a walkout from the legislature, setting up a body of their own, and leaving Catron to support the Republican faction.[71]

Catron attacked a more prominent Taos County resident through his choice of a second defendant in the Taos Pueblo litigation, Antonio Joseph, the man who ultimately would lend his name to the final decision in the nineteenth-century Pueblo land litigation. Joseph was an educated Portuguese-American who moved easily between Taos County and the more urbane world of St. Louis.[72] He speculated almost as heavily as Catron did in New Mexico land grants. In 1872, when Joseph had just begun, he purchased several large tracts near Taos Pueblo and began in earnest to acquire undivided interests in the Ojo Caliente grant. Like Catron, Joseph became increasingly controversial for the questionable means he used.[73] At the least, the two competitors for New Mexico land must have viewed each other with a wary eye.

Joseph's contacts with powerful local figures extended beyond land matters. He joined other speculators on the board of the New Mexico Historical Society, for which David Miller served as secretary.[74] He actively participated in Taos County and territorial politics. In 1871 he ran on the Democratic ticket for Taos County probate judge and lost to the Republican challenger. Joseph did not challenge the results in his own election, but he certainly had encouraged the four other Taos County Democrats to challenge the election of the Republican legislators at the 1872 session of the territorial assembly and then to walk out, to Thomas Catron's great chagrin.[75] For his support, Joseph found himself a defendant in the 1873 Pueblo land litigation.

The Taos County defendants immediately hired lawyers of their own. William Breeden, a one-time law partner of Catron's, appeared to defend Juan Santistevan.[76] R. H. Tompkins, a long-time political figure in New Mexico, repesented Antonio Joseph.[77] In July 1873 the two new lawyers took the same course that Houghton had followed for Varela and Kozlowski, earlier that year, before the same district judge who had heard Houghton's demurrer. Predictably, the result did not change. On 22 July 1873, Chief Judge Joseph G. Palen ruled that Catron's complaint against the non-Indians Joseph and Santistevan did not state a cause of action under the 1834 and 1851 non-intercourse acts. Catron immediately filed a notice of appeal to the territorial supreme court.[78]

The process joined the defendants from Pecos and those from Taos before the territorial supreme court, sitting at its January 1874 term. Technically each case stood on its own. The Kozlowski and Santistevan appeals reached the territorial supreme court on writs of error; the Varela and Joseph cases reached the court on much more straightforward appeals. Beneath these arcane differences of pleading and practice, however, the four cases shared that familiar question: What was the status of the Pueblo Indians and their lands under federal law?[79]

By mid-October 1873, the territorial supreme court had consolidated the four cases for hearing, scheduled in January 1874. The justices directed each party to file briefs. On behalf of the Pecos defendants, Joab Houghton submitted a one-page, type-set document, itself a curiosity at a time when most New Mexico court documents were handwritten. Houghton simply wrote in the names of his Pecos clients.

Houghton's 1874 brief on behalf of Kozlowski and Varela began with the same tautological maneuver that Judge Slough had used in 1867, although Houghton did not mention *United States v. Lucero*.[80] Houghton simply suggested that "the statute imposing a penalty upon persons settling on Indian lands clearly intends such Indians as are not citizens but under the wardship of the Government."[81] Once again, the possibility that citizenship and wardship were not mutually exclusive did not arise. He certainly did not cite the 1851 decision of the California supreme court that found the two ideas compatible.[82]

Houghton simply suggested that the territory of New Mexico's Pueblo Indians also had held citizenship under the Mexican Republic, before the area became part of the United States. He had new authority for that proposition: Mariano Galvan's *Ordenanzas de tierras y aguas*.[83]

But Houghton argued that the United States Supreme Court had already decided that Pueblo Indians could "take, hold, and dispose" of their property, as any other citizen could. But in *United States v. Ritchie*, the Supreme Court had upheld the right of an individual, emancipated California Pueblo Indian first to obtain a Mexican grant in his own name and then to sell it himself. This was a far cry from the New Mexico situation, where the pueblos held some type of communal ownership not based on a new grant so much as on recognition by the previous sovereign of long-existing rights. In *Ritchie*, the Supreme Court itself had recognized this:

> It is conceded that the lands in question do not belong to the class called Pueblo lands, in respect to which we do not intend to express any opinion, either as to the power of the authorities to grant or the Indians to convey.

The *Ritchie* decision thus explicitly stated it did not apply to such a situation as that of Pecos Pueblo.[84]

On behalf of the two Taos defendants, William Breeden took a more sensible approach and went straight to the statute under which the suits had been brought.[85] Confirmed New Mexico Pueblo grants like Pecos and Taos, argued Breeden, were not Indian country under the 1834 and 1851 statutes, because they had not been created by treaty. The pueblos themselves were not tribes under the statutes, because they had no tribal governments recognized and approved by the federal government. In fact, suggested Breeden, Pueblo communities were

> similar to those of the Shakers and other people living in
> communities in other parts of the United States, and are not Indians
> in contemplation of the statute under which the suit is brought.[86]

Because the statutes did not determine the status of the pueblos, the Fourteenth Amendment to the Constitution did: it prohibited any restriction on the pueblos' ability to sell. If they could sell, then the United States could not protect them from buyers, or from trespassers like Varela and Kozlowski. If, concluded Breeden, Joseph, Santistevan, Varela, or Kozlowski were

> intruders upon the lands of the Pueblos, and a right of action exists
> against them, such right of action is in the pueblo and the intruders
> are not subject to a penalty to the United States, nor liable in any
> way under the statute upon which the suit is brought.[87]

The United States Supreme Court would later pick up various threads from these themes, introduced by William Breeden in 1874, and weave them into its 1877 decision in *United States v. Joseph*. For the moment, the territorial supreme court only had to consider the arguments of United States Attorney Catron and render its decision.

Catron responded to the defendants' arguments with a one-page, printed form similar to that used by Houghton, with the name of the individual defendant written in. Both Catron and Houghton appear to have prepared for trial and appeal on behalf of any defendants that might present themselves, and seemingly only later learned who they would be.[88]

Catron cursorily suggested five grounds for overturning Palen's district court decision. The first three simply stated that the complaint conformed to the statute. Nothing more could be demanded, particularly in view of the fact that Congress reserved the power to decide whether Indians fell under federal protection. Catron's fourth point relied on a case as foreign to Pueblo history as Houghton's *Ritchie* case, to prove that Spain, Mexico, and the United States had all forbidden the alienation of Indian land. As a final argument, Catron added as an afterthought, and in his own hand, that "each Pueblo of Indians is a separate tribe or community of Indians who [*sic*] hold all of their lands in common."[89]

Just what point Catron was making in this reference was unclear even then, but it played a major part in subsequent, diametrically

opposed court treatment of Pueblo Indian grants and non-Indian community grants.[90] Hispanic Pecos, for a while at least, proved the residual
beneficiary of its illegitimate beginnings on Indian land.

But in 1874 nobody would infer these distinctions from the spare
arguments Catron made to the territorial supreme court. It heard an
afternoon's oral arguments on 18 January 1874 and then issued two
opinions in the four cases before it, each of which denied Pueblo lands
the federal protection of existing law, although by slightly different
means. Neither 1874 opinion shares the style of Judge Watts's decision
in *United States v. Lucero,* nor do they refer to it, even though the court
could simply have said that the issue had already been decided in 1867,
without adding anything. Instead, Judges Johnston and Bristol gave
two different narrow, legalistically argued opinions.

Johnston formally reviewed Juan Santistevan's case.[91] He elaborated
on a grammatical nicety suggested by Breeden, using two thousand
words of exegesis to show that the 1834 act, as extended to New
Mexico in 1851, only protected lands secured to Indian tribes by treaty.
Because the Pueblos held their lands by United States patent, the acts
could not apply.

Then Johnston added two more points. Congress had enacted the
Non-Intercourse Act under the authority of the Constitution's commerce clause. Therefore the act regulated dealings between Indians and
non-Indians, technically a question of commerce, by giving the government exclusive authority to do so. The act said nothing about the
right of Indians to protect their own lands. Because the government
owned the title to Indian land, subject to the tribe's right of occupancy,
the 1834 act protected government rights in Indian land. But the
Pueblos themselves held title to their grants, under patent from the
United States. They were citizens as well. Because the United States
had no property interest in the lands of private citizens, the 1834 act
obviously could not apply.

Johnston's neat argument had the virtue of internal consistency. But
nearly contemporaneous courts, considering analogous problems, would
reach the opposite conclusion on each of the three points on which the
argument was based. Those courts rejected Johnston's narrow, syn-
tactical reading of the 1834 act and instead found that the act applied
to Indian land held under treaty or by any other means, including the
straightforward fee simple patents under which the pueblos held their
land. The courts also held that the 1834 act was based not on the

commerce clause alone, as Johnston believed, but on the property clause as well. In the case of the pueblos, the government's proprietary interest in patented land came not as an owner, but as the guardian of land owned by Indians.[92] Johnston's argument was faulty on both grounds.

Territorial Supreme Court Justice Bristol issued a separate opinion in the four Pueblo land cases. He formally reviewed only Antonio Joseph's case, although what he said applied to all non-Indians settled on Pueblo lands.[93]

Bristol relied neither on Watts's enthnocentric world view nor on Johnston's grammar. Instead he focused on what he considered to be the political meaning of an Indian tribe in the 1834 act:

> Indian tribes are distinct, independent, domestic nations, having and maintaining distinct tribal organizations, capable of maintaining the relations of peace and war . . . and who, as such independent political communities hold only treaty relations with the United States, very much on the footing of quasi-foreign nations."[94]

But New Mexico Pueblos were not independent, domestic nations; they were simply Hispanic towns. They held their land as any other Spanish or Mexican town did, under a patent that did nothing more than confirm their Spanish and Mexican rights to the land. The pueblos could not be independent nations in the sense of the statutory term *Indian tribe.* The act did not apply.

Over the years the courts would gradually alter the notion of Indian tribes as "quasi-foreign nations," until almost nothing was left of the distinction that Bristol thought made such a difference in the 1874 Pueblo litigation.[95] But at that time, on either his terms or Johnston's, no federal statute protected Pueblo lands. Varela and Kozlowski remained secure in Pecos. Santistevan and Joseph kept up their speculation in Taos County.

This time, however, Catron could not let the matter rest there, as his predecessor, Elkins, had in 1869. On 24 January 1874, the same day on which the territorial supreme court announced its decision, Catron appealed the cases of Antonio Joseph and Juan Santistevan to the United States Supreme Court. Also that same day, Joseph's attorney, R. H. Tompkins, accepted service of a notice directing his client to appear at the October 1876 term of the nation's highest court.[96]

At that point the Pecoseños Varela and Kozlowski technically dropped out of the proceedings that led to the May 1877 Supreme Court decision in *United States v. Joseph.* So did Catron, who passed the case on to his

superiors in the solicitor general's office in Washington, D.C. The New
Mexico lawyers Houghton, Breeden, and Tompkins passed their case
on to the Washington lawyers W. A. Evarts and Stephen B. Elkins.
As United States attorney, Elkins had lost the Pueblo case in the 1866–
69 litigation. That case had not reached the United States Supreme
Court, because Elkins had not perfected the appeal there. In 1877 he
was back on the case, this time representing the opposite side, in a
successor suit before the court.[97]

Solicitor General Philips wasted no time in his opening brief for the
pueblos. All things being equal, he argued, no Indians lost their status
as such until Congress, exercising its plenary control over Indian affairs,
specifically said they did. Neither Pueblo citizenship nor Pueblo fee
simple title amounted to a specific declaration that Pueblo Indians were
not technically Indians under federal law. Therefore the 1834 and 1851
acts applied.

The government's argument picked up a subsidiary theme only suggested by Catron and expanded on it. The question of whether New
Mexico's Pueblos were technically Indians depended not on whether
Congress had ever defined them as such but on whether Congress had
ever said they were *not*. To lawyers, Philips's suggestion made a critical
difference: until Congress stated that Pueblos were not technically
Indians, emancipated them, in other words, the Pueblos were Indians
under the 1834 and 1851 acts. This approach gained more and more
cogency among Indian advocates as time went on, until by the twentieth
century it became the pivotal point in Pueblo land litigation.[98] For the
moment the argument represented a novel government tack.

In their own three-page brief, the attorneys Evarts and Elkins presented in abbreviated form every argument that had been made before
the territorial supreme court. The 1834 act protected the Indians' quasi-
independence and "excluded occasions of war between them and the
United States." In other words, the non-intercourse acts only applied
to regions

> in which the government's title to the land is maintained and the
> Indian title of occupancy has not been extinguished. This certainly
> does not cover the case of these little communities of civilized
> Indians, planted here and there as dependencies upon the Spanish
> settlements and occupying little patches of land like this Taos patent
> of five miles square.

Besides, Pueblo Indians had been citizens under Mexican law, as the

Ritchie decision proved. Congress had patented the land to the pueblos "as in ordinary cases to private individuals," so that the patent itself determined the status of the Pueblos as citizens and their lands as private lands. "All sources," concluded Evarts and Elkins, "concur in excluding the Pueblo Indians from any such quasi-international relations as belong to the Indian tribes proper to which the Acts pertain."[99]

The Supreme Court considered the short briefs filed in *United States v. Joseph* that spring. On 20 April 1877 Elkins and Evarts, for the non-Indians, and Solicitor General Philips, for the Pueblos, argued the case before the court itself. It took the justices an astonishingly short three weeks to decide the case and to issue a written opinion. On 7 May 1877 the Supreme Court released its decision and opinion. By 9 May 1877, New Mexicans had reason to believe that pueblos would not bother their non-Indian neighbors again.

Associate Justice Samuel F. Miller, author of the *Joseph* opinion, borrowed freely not only from arguments made to his court, but from gratuitous statements and suggestions regarding the pueblos made in previous decisions not technically before him. For example,

> The character and history of these people are not obscure but occupy a well-known page in the history of Mexico from the conquest of the country by Cortez to the cession of this part of it to the United States by the Treaty of Guadalupe Hidalgo. The subject is tempting and full of interest, but we have only space for a few well-considered sentences of the opinion of the chief justice of the court whose judgment we are reviewing.[100]

Nearly one thousand words follow, taken directly from the deceased Judge Slough's first, groping 1867 district court description of the Pueblo Indians in *United States v. Lucero.*[101] There is none of Judge Watts's polemic in Miller's opinion, nor of the narrow interpretation of Judges Bristol and Johnston, which formed the actual basis of the decision under review by the Supreme Court in 1877. Instead, Miller returned to Judge Slough's belief that the Pueblos were too civilized to warrant federal protection. He used Slough's naive anthropology to substantiate it.

In another section of his *Joseph* opinion, Miller recalled William Breeden's suggestion to the New Mexico Territorial Supreme Court (not repeated before the United States Supreme Court) that the Pueblos were more like Shakers than Indians. As Miller paraphrased it,

> If the Pueblo Indians differ from the other inhabitants of New

Mexico in holding lands in common, and in a certain patriarchal form of domestic life, they only resemble in this regard the Shakers and other communistic societies in this country, and cannot for that reason be classed with the Indian tribes of whom we have been speaking. [102]

Out of that kind of legal scavenging Miller forged the federal government's answer to the questions posed by Pueblo Indian land tenure. "The pueblo or village of Taos," wrote Miller, taking the generic term and rendering it literally into English, as if New Mexico pueblos were nothing more than municipalities with a Spanish name, was not an Indian tribe within the meaning of the statute. The 1834 law, as extended to New Mexico in 1851, did not dictate any different result, because in 1834 there were no Indians like the Pueblos other than the Senecas and Oneidas of upstate New York, "to whom it is clear the eleventh section of the statute could have no application." On the other hand, in the New Mexico Territory of 1851 there were plenty of so-called wild Indians, including the "nomadic Apaches, Comanches, Navajos, and other tribes whose incapacity for self government required both for themselves and for the citizens of the country this guardian care of the general government." The 1834 statute could apply to them, but not to the civilized Pueblos.

According to the *Joseph* court, Pueblo Indian land tenure confirmed this view. The 1864 patents issued to the pueblos divested the United States of all claims to Pueblo lands. The patent admitted that "the pueblo Indians . . . hold their lands by a right superior to the United States." The Indian tribes to which Congress had directed the non-intercourse acts did not own their lands; the United States government did, subject only to the Indian right of occupancy and possession. While that right may have been as "sacred as the fee of the whites," it was always subject to plenary congressional control by the owner of the fee title, the United States. This was not so with the Pueblos, since they held the fee title themselves. Thus, concluded Justice Miller's 7 May 1877 decision,

If the defendant is on the lands of the Pueblo without the consent of the inhabitants, he may be ejected or punished civilly by a suit for trespass according to the law regulating such matters in the Territory. If he is there with their consent or license, we know of no injury which the United States suffers by his presence, nor any statute which he violates in that regard. [103]

The Supreme Court obviously meant to leave some means of redress open to the Pueblos, while denying others. The court implied that proceedings under local, territorial law might be adequate; no one in New Mexico tried to use them. The court's analysis suggested that Congress itself could amend the 1834 and 1851 acts at any time to include the New Mexico Pueblos; Congress did not do so until the 1910 enabling act that stated the grounds on which New Mexico would be admitted as a state. The Supreme Court itself specifically stated that it would not decide in the *Joseph* case whether Pueblo Indians were citizens or not.

Various factors could have suggested this cavalier approach to Pueblo land affairs. An 1875 drive for New Mexico statehood had just foundered, primarily because the territory was still so unknown and undeveloped.[104] The Court may have been reluctant to meddle with such a dark situation. In addition, Congress was about to embark on the federal policy of allotment, which was designed to accomplish for tribes covered by the 1834 act what the court just had accomplished for the Pueblos in the *Joseph* case: the termination of tribal holdings and their conversion into individual private ownership, as marketable as any other private land would be.[105]

From a Washington perspective, the Pueblo land holdings were not very significant. Evarts and Elkins had suggested to the *Joseph* court that the pueblos each occupied "little patches of land like this Taos patent of five miles square." The Pueblo grants were all insignificant compared to the Maxwell land grant, which embraced 2,000,000 acres, or 2,680 square miles. During the same term the Supreme Court also decided *Tameling v. United States Freehold and Immigration Co.,* which involved conflicting claims to one 998,000 acre grant.[106] Pueblo claims to 18,000 acres each were insignificant by comparison. In effect the United States was not interested in New Mexico Pueblo land.

This benign neglect left Pueblo land vulnerable to non-Indian exploitation. Calhoun had indicated in 1849 that the problem of non-Indians on Pueblo land predated American sovereignty. No one knew how bad the situation had been in 1846 or how much worse it became immediately thereafter. If the Pecos Pueblo grant situation was typical, one could say that the tentative incursions of the period before American succession intensified and consolidated with the permanent arrival of men like Varela and Kozlowski, in the 1860s. But to the extent that the Indians had abandoned Pecos Pueblo some thirty years before, so that the land looked open, Pecos was unique. The effect of the 1877 *Joseph* decision in general was to confirm some long-existing holdings within Pueblo grants and to open them to future speculation.[107]

That neglect left David Miller, land speculator and surveyor general employee, writing, in the name of Pueblo anthropology, to Dr. Lewis Morgan in Rochester, New York, about Morgan's proposed trip to Taos Pueblo. Miller recommended that Morgan use the Taoseños Juan Santistevan and Antonio Joseph as cultural informants and ambassadors to the Taos Pueblo. Later Morgan described Miller's suggestions as "not very useful."[108]

That neglect left T. B. Catron, United States attorney, that stalwart defender of the Pueblos in 1873 and 1874, free to pursue his own business. That business included an interest in the Gaspar Ortiz grant, which overlay part of the Nambé Pueblo grant. Catron quickly began using the *Joseph* case, which he had lost, to prove the validity of the controversial Gaspar Ortiz claim. By the turn of the century, Catron would still use *Joseph* as an argument preventing the assertion of any federal interest in Pueblo lands.[109]

That neglect left at least three sawmills operating within the Pecos Pueblo grant. Camps in the mountains around Pecos provided the logs from which the mills made crossties. From Pecos, the ties went down the new railroad line to support newer tracks.[110]

That neglect left Martin Kozlowski and his family under the very eaves of the old Pecos Pueblo church. It left Manuel Varela and his large family free to continue working the rich, irrigated land west of the Pecos River and well within the Pecos Pueblo grant.

Finally, the benign federal neglect that the *Joseph* decision announced left Donaciano Vigil, one of New Mexico's most remarkable native politicians, growing older and weaker by the year but still working the Pecos Pueblo irrigated land east of the river. Unlike Kozlowski and Varela, Vigil had never been a defendant in the lawsuits that led to the May 1877 *Joseph* decision. But Vigil's claim to Pecos Pueblo land hung in that balance as well. When word from Washington reached New Mexico that non-Indians were safe (for the moment) on Pueblo Indian land, Donaciano Vigil once more landed on his feet, as he had so many times before in the chaotic history of New Mexico.

Left, Frank Springer, rancher, paleontologist, and lawyer. As New Mexico's most famous land grant lawyer in the 1880s, Springer represented the New York owners of Pecos Pueblo Grant in San Miguel County litigation. (Courtesy Museum of New Mexico.)

Right, Taos County land speculator and politician Antonio Joseph, who got in a political squabble with United States Attorney T. B. Catron in the mid 1870s and ended up as the principal defendant in the famous *Joseph* litigation. (Courtesy Museum of New Mexico.)

Left, Land baron T. B. Catron, who in his role as United States attorney directed what became the *Joseph* litigation. (Courtesy Museum of New Mexico.) Right, This, the only surviving portrait of Donaciano Vigil, comes from an 1867 Santa Fe photographic gallery print. Contemporary accounts indicate that Vigil was a large man, perhaps 6'2" tall, possessed of great physical strength. (Courtesy Museum of New Mexico.)

OPPOSITE PAGE: Top, With his distinctive hand, Donaciano Vigil first witnessed the signatures of Justo Pastor Pino and his wife, Gertrudis Rascon, on the deed transferring the Grant just north of the Pecos Pueblo to Alejandro Valle. Then, acting in a different capacity, Vigil filed the deed as an official land document. This facsimile was made from a copy which Donaciano Vigil retained in his private papers. (Facsimile by author.) Lower left, Herbert J. Hagerman, patrician head of the Pueblo Lands Board in the 1920s and 1930s. (Courtesy Museum of New Mexico.) Lower right, "Smooth" Stephen B. Elkins, the New Mexico attorney who brought the first legal challenge to non-Indians residing within the boundaries of congressionally confirmed Pueblo Indian land grants. He then defended the non-Indians when the case reached the United States Supreme Court in 1876. (Courtesy Museum of New Mexico.)

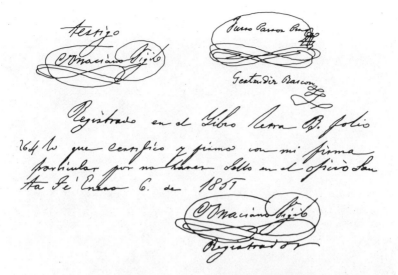

This 1953 aerial photograph shows the *ciénaga* of Pecos and the surrounding uplands in the northeast quarter of the Pecos Pueblo Grant twenty years after the Pueblo Lands Board had finished its work. (Courtesy Soil Conservation Service.)

SIX

Donaciano Vigil's Pecos

Declaro tener dos ranchos de terreno que constan sus tamaños por los documentos que me dan autoridad y derecho sobre ellos, uno en el lugar que llaman El Gusano y el otro en Pecos donde resido. De este ultimo por fin y muerte de mi finada esposa dividí una porción del en darle a cada uno de mis hijos una parte como legítima por parte materna, a cuatro les repartí ciento y tres varas a cada uno y a Antonio por ser el primogénito y verlo cargado de una numerosa familia, convine en dejarle una porción grande de terreno bajo la condición de que no había de tener parte en lo demás del Rancho de Pecos . . .

—Donaciano Vigil's Last Will and Testament

En que es suspendido este mundo? De la voluntad de Dios.
    Y en que es suspendido nuestro pueblo? Del río de Pecos.

—Traditional Pecos *adivinanza*

On 7 May 1877, the United States Supreme Court announced its decision in *United States v. Joseph*. The nation's highest court ruled that non-Indians could hold Pueblo Indian land in New Mexico without offending general federal law otherwise prohibiting it. Exactly one week later, Donaciano Vigil, East Pecos's founding father, sat down to arrange the affairs of his long and prosperous life. Although the *Joseph* case took its name from Antonio Joseph, a famous speculator in Taos Pueblo land, the litigation had begun in Donaciano Vigil's own Pecos. Now that the new sovereign's highest court had apparently blessed his presence on Pueblo land, the seventy-five-year-old Vigil called his most trusted Pecos friends to his home and asked them to witness his second and last will. Six months later, on 11 August 1877, Donaciano Vigil, "one of the most unusual men ever to live in New Mexico," died.[1]

Don Donaciano had executed his first will in 1842.[2] He still resided in Santa Fe at that time. He had not yet begun his rise to power in the service of New Mexico's last Mexican governor, Manuel Armijo, a power he would use to attain much more in the beginning years of American sovereignty. By May 1877 his estate had increased tremendously. It had come to include the Los Trigos grant, just south of the Pecos Pueblo grant, and most of the irrigated land on the east side of the Pecos River, well within the Pecos Pueblo grant itself. The residents of Hispanic Pecos who witnessed his final will had done well for themselves as well. Manuel Varela, the only witness who could sign his name in 1877, had endured the chaos of the *Joseph* litigation as an actual defendant in the early phases of the suit. Alejandro Valle, who could only sign with an X, had survived the American system of adjudicating Mexican and Spanish claims so well that he was now owner of the land grant that adjoined the Pecos Pueblo grant on the north.[3] The other two witnesses had persevered as Pecos ranchers and farmers. But Donaciano Vigil had bested them all. In his last will and testament he celebrated that triumph.

The will followed a traditional New Mexico Spanish-language form.[4] Vigil stated that he wrote the May 1877 will now, at the start of the Pecos growing season, because he had been beseiged for years by chronic illness and feared death. He directed his soul to God and his body to earth, asking that his funeral be the most humble possible, without any commotion that would attract public attention. He told of his marriage and the ten children born to it; five sons had survived.

Then Donaciano Vigil began describing and directing the division of his worldly goods. He cataloged an amazingly specific list of farm tools and equipment necessary to the operation of a Pecos ranch in the 1870s. An iron bar, twelve pounds of steel, a thirty-pound "little" kettle, a big iron skillet, one large saw and two small ones, two large planes and two jack planes, two small turning chisels, one $1^1/2$ inch auger and other smaller augers, two curved cutting tools, one joiner, one wood rasp, and a large chain, among other things, made up his list of tools. A wagon, two plows "of American make" and four common plows of local construction, a yoke, two saddles, some bridles, and a riding outfit comprised part of his livestock equipment. Donaciano Vigil also listed "a certain number" of cattle, oxen, cows, yearlings, calves old enough for branding, one mare with colt, two burros, three pigs, and interests in numerous other herds let out on *partido* ("share-ranching") contract to friends and Pecos neighbors.

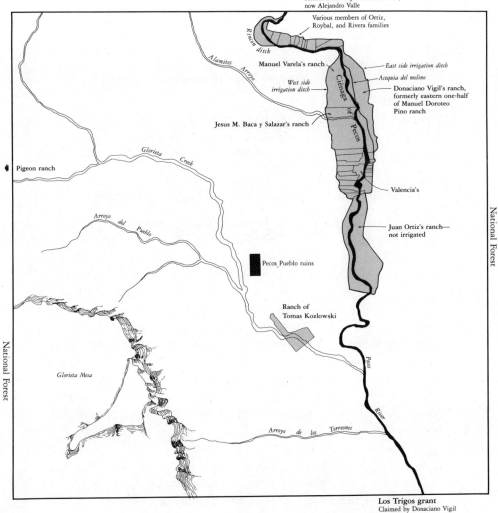

Former ranch of Justo Pastor Pino,
now Alejandro Valle

Various members of Ortiz,
Roybal, and Rivera families

Rincon ditch

Alamitos Arroyo

Manuel Varela's ranch

East side irrigation ditch

Acequia del molino

West side irrigation ditch

Ciénaga of Pecos

Donaciano Vigil's ranch,
formerly eastern one-half
of Manuel Doroteo
Pino ranch

Jesus M. Baca y Salazar's ranch

Glorieta Creek

Pigeon ranch

Valencia's

Arroyo del Pueblo

Juan Ortiz's ranch—
not irrigated

Pecos Pueblo ruins

Ranch of
Tomas Kozlowski

Pecos River

Glorieta Mesa

Arroyo de los Torreones

National Forest

National Forest

Los Trigos grant
Claimed by Donaciano Vigil

MAP 4. The Pecos Pueblo Grant on the Eve of the 1877 *Joseph* Decision

By 1876 non-Indians had made claims to the entire Pecos Pueblo Grant,
based on three separate and conflicting sources of title.

The shaded area of Map 4 in the *ciénaga* of Pecos represents lands
claimed by virtue of an 1830 Pueblo sale of the *ciénaga* to Hispanic
politician and speculator Juan Estavan Pino. Donaciano Vigil, east of the
Pecos River, and Manuel Varela and Jesus M. Baca y Salazar, west of the
river, had obtained most of the land covered by the 1830 sale.

The shaded areas outside the *ciénaga* of Pecos represent lands simply
squatted on by non-Indians.

The unshaded areas of Map 4 indicate portions of the Pecos Pueblo
Grant sold by the Pueblo survivors at Jemez in 1872 and not included in
any previous transactions.

And Donaciano Vigil's final will provided for the division of his real property among his heirs. As for his residence and other Pecos improvements, Vigil wrote:

> Item: I declare as my goods my house of residence [la casa de mi morada] one part in good condition and the other reduced to ruins, threatening to fall down, three rooms in this condition and seven in order. In addition, two separate rooms for storing wheat, stables, a log cabin, a walled corral, another cabin and another building of upright logs [*jacal*] that my son, Epitacio, has the use and benefit of.

The ten-room house and the various buildings surrounding it were located toward the northern end of the irrigated land east of the Pecos River and became, after Donaciano's death, the *plaza de los Vigiles*. Vigil's descendants still live there.[5]

All the Vigil houses were located just above the main East Pecos irrigation ditch, which began in the Alejandro Valle grant, almost five miles north and west of Donaciano Vigil's residence. Vigil himself had built a second irrigation ditch, the Acequia del Molino, entirely within the longer *acequia madre,* to drive the wheels of his grain mill.[6] In his will he described the ditch, confirming that Pecos irrigators below him had the right to use the water once it had passed the mill. In addition, Vigil indicated that he had permitted the use of mill water for a sawmill in a nearby arroyo. That use, he directed, should continue after his death as well.

With respect to the tools, buildings, and other constructed works that would have supported a large northern New Mexico farm in the middle of the nineteenth century, Donaciano Vigil spoke in his will with real particularity. Yet about his most valued possession, the land, he spoke only vaguely:

> Item: I declare I have two ranches consisting of the size indicated by the documents that give me authority and right over them, one in the place called El Gusano and the other in Pecos where I reside. Of this last one [Pecos] on the death of my deceased wife, I divided a portion of it, giving to each one of my sons a part as their maternal share, to each of four [of them] I gave one hundred and three varas, and to Antonio, as the first born and seeing him burdened with a large family, I agreed to give him a larger portion of land on the condition that he would take no further part in the Pecos ranch at the end and on my death.

Pecos legend, developed long after 1877, extended the reach of

Donaciano Vigil's claim to Pecos-area land. His only formal biographer asserted in the 1960s that Vigil acquired 27,000 acres in the Pecos Pueblo and Los Trigos grants prior to his death. By his will, according to Father Stanley's erroneous report, Donaciano Vigil gave to each of his children 353.5 acres and to each of the Pecos residents who worked in his fields 118.5 acres.[7] In the 1970s Vigil descendants still claimed that Donaciano Vigil had once owned the entire 18,763 acre Pecos Pueblo grant and the entire 9,646 acre Los Trigos grant. After the Civil War, they said, Vigil wrote to President Lincoln and asked him what to do about the *peones,* or *esclavos,* who worked for him but owned no land. Lincoln replied, Pecos legend now has it, that Vigil should give each peon his freedom and a small tract of land—the Hispano equivalent of 40 acres and a mule. Donaciano Vigil had followed the president's suggestion. That beneficent gesture explains the presence of other families in Pecos today.[8]

In fact, Donaciano Vigil's claim to the Los Trigos grant and his presence in Pecos in the first place were products of Anglo aggression and Hispanic politics. The two forces overwhelmed most native New Mexicans, but Donaciano Vigil turned them both to his advantage. The "affable, intelligent, pro-American" Vigil always kept his balance during those years of frequently changing sovereigns.[9]

Throughout the period, Vigil maintained a constant focus on New Mexico land, both for himself and for his friends. In the process he contributed significantly to the creation of New Mexico's largest and most controversial land grants, under the regime of the Mexican governor Amijo; to the preservation of those sometimes fantastic claims to land under the provisional Kearny Code in the earliest territorial days; and finally to their approval by the New Mexico surveyor general and subsequent confirmation by the Congress of the United States. Vigil created and then attempted to solidify his own claims to New Mexico land, not only in Pecos and El Gusano (Los Trigos), but elsewhere as well. In so doing, he became an important member of that "territorial machine" that existed long before the more famous "Santa Fe ring."[10]

In developing his claim to the Pecos Pueblo grant, Donaciano Vigil demonstrated how that organization worked to acquire interests in New Mexico land, even Pueblo Indian land. In his early and almost constant appearances before the New Mexico Surveyor General, Vigil and his coterie of land-minded friends lobbied for the confirmation of Mexican and Spanish grants for their own benefit and to the ultimate detriment of less-skilled New Mexico natives. Finally, in his claim before the surveyor general to the entire Los Trigos grant, Vigil applied everything he had learned from his Pecos Pueblo grant maneuvering. In this way his general land career sheds light on a critical period in New Mexico's history that is often completely obscured by the subsequent, more spectacular dealings of T. B. Catron, Stephen B. Elkins, Max Frost, and their well-documented fellows. Donaciano Vigil and his less well known friends made the bed that the more famous Santa Fe Ring then lay down in.

Yet, beneath it all, Donaciano Vigil remained true to the rich culture from which he had come. His devotion to the essence of the Catholic faith apparently never wavered, although he railed against the church's own political maneuvering. He publically espoused the liberal ideas of his times, in a genuine effort to help his own people survive in a chaotically changing world.[11] This other side of Donaciano Vigil was also reflected in his interest in land; in the way he used Pecos Pueblo land, not in the means by which he acquired it.

Donaciano Vigil built his Pecos Pueblo grant holdings on Juan Estevan Pino's much earlier foundations. In 1855 Donaciano Vigil told Surveyor General Pelham that he had known Pino in 1825 and knew the "Rancho Hacienda de San Juan Bautista del Ojito del Río de las Gallinas," which Pino had acquired in that year. At the time Vigil did not mention the extent of his acquaintance with Pino's other land-holdings, stretching from Angustura on the south to Tesuque on the north and from Santa Fe on the west to the Llano Estacado on the east. But a second Pecos resident, Bernardo Varela, brother to *Joseph* defendant Manuel Varela and a friend of Donaciano Vigil, told the surveyor general that he had worked for Pino at Pino's various ranches since 1830.[12] By the time of the American arrival in New Mexico, in 1846, Juan Estevan Pino's interests had passed to his two sons, Manuel Doroteo Pino and Justo Pastor Pino, and had focused, in their hands, on the Alejandro Valle grant and its Pecos River neighbor immediately to the south, the Pecos Pueblo grant. The two sons had apparently split their Pecos-area interests in half. Justo Pastor settled on the land purchased by his father to the north of the Pecos Pueblo grant. Manuel Doroteo moved south, into the Indian grant itself, and took possession of the abandoned but not forgotten ciénaga in the grant's northern reaches.[13] In the meantime, other settlers simply moved onto the also abandoned grazing grant of their father, Juan Estevan Pino, near the eastern plains.[14]

From that point on the affairs of the two Pino sons and their claim to Pecos and other lands became increasingly intertwined with those of Donaciano Vigil. On 2 January 1851, Justo Pastor Pino sold his inherited grant, north of Pecos, to Alejandro Valle, the man who witnessed Donaciano Vigil's 1877 will with his X.[15] In 1851 Vigil witnessed the deed from Pino to Valle and then recorded it in his official capacity as secretary and ex oficio registrar of lands, under the Kearny Code.[16] Curious aspects of the document raise real questions about its authenticity. But a subsequent document, dated 31 May 1852, nearly eighteen months later, confirmed the sale from Justo Pastor Pino and his wife to the same Valle. This time the deed gave a clearer description of the land sold, represented Justo Pastor Pino to be Juan Estevan's only heir (which he was not), and stated the amount of money Valle paid Pino for the grant: 5,275 pesos, or about $1,200.[17]

Enter Alejandro Valle onto the increasingly complex Pecos land scene in the 1850s, a scene staged in much earlier speculation in land around the Pecos Pueblo that now had begun to produce a second and different generation directed by Donaciano Vigil.

With his 1852 purchase, Alejandro Valle joined *Joseph* defendant Martin Kozlowski as the principal non-Hispanic claimant to land in and around the Pecos Pueblo grant. Like Kozlowski, Valle had established a trading post on the Santa Fe Trail as it cut across the Pecos Pueblo grant toward Glorieta and Santa Fe. He ran the prosperous business under his real last name, Pigeon. He had come from St. Louis in the 1840s and simply settled, like Kozlowski, on abandoned Indian land. Thereafter, he adopted the name Valle and speculated in both Missouri and New Mexico real estate.[18] With his purchase from Justo Pastor Pino, he established himself on the north edge of the Pecos Pueblo grant lands as well.

The appendage of his mark to Donaciano Vigil's 1877 will showed that Valle could not write, but that he knew Vigil. A joint complaint in the mid-1860s from the two men about Comanche damage to their sheep herds, which grazed together in the mountains east of Pecos, showed that Vigil and Valle worked together. The survival of so many of Valle's private papers among Vigil's documents suggests that the two men had established a working relationship much earlier. And Vigil's help in the 1851–52 Pino-Valle transaction indicates Vigil's interest in Pecos-area land much earlier than his formal biographer has acknowledged.[19] Indeed, in one instance a Vigil claim to land belonged, on paper at least, in part to Valle and perhaps others as well. Whatever interest Donaciano Vigil had in the Los Trigos grant, on the Pecos Pueblo grant's south border, an interest he asserted as early as 1850 and that by 1856 would amount to the entire grant, he shared with Alejandro Valle.[20] It was as if the two men had conspired to absorb the Pecos Pueblo grant, one acquiring land to the north and the other to the south.

However that may be, Valle, with $1,200 and Vigil's paperwork, had relieved Justo Pastor Pino of his claim to land just north of the Pecos Pueblo grant. Juan Estevan Pino's other surviving son, Manuel Doroteo Pino, had abandoned altogether the pretense of avoiding Indian land, and had moved into the heart of the pueblo's ciénaga. A little more than a year after Justo Pastor sold out to Valle, Manuel Doroteo also used his Pecos land to raise capital.

On 14 June 1853, he and his wife, Josefa Ortiz, mortgaged the place they called the *Manuel Pino Ranch at Pecos* to Hugh N. Smith, as trustee for Preston Beck, Jr. The mortgage deed described the ranch as consisting of about three hundred acres and bounded on the east and west by "public land," on the north by Manuel Barela [*sic*] and Blas Ortega, and on the south by Vicente Quintana and Pablo Moya. The deed did not even mention the fact that the tract lay wholly within the Pecos Pueblo grant. In fact, subsequent transactions would show that the mortgaged land lay on both sides of the Pecos River, in the ciénaga. The 14 June 1853 deed from Pino to Beck only guaranteed payment of $2,460 one year from the date of the deed.

On 18 June 1853, Manuel Pino and his wife signed a second mortgage deed to Smith (as Beck's trustee), pledging as additional security for the loan their half-interest, shared with brother Justo Pastor, in the abandoned but not forgotten Ojito de las Gallinas grant. On the same day Justo Pastor mortgaged his half-share. The note would fall due on 14 June 1854.[21]

Thus between 1851 and 1853 the Pino brothers used their Pecos-area land and their father's eastern New Mexico land grant claim to raise nearly $4,000.[22] They may have needed that large amount of cash to keep their Pecos stock operation going. But, at the same time, they were also making a bold move to maintain the paper claim to their father's much larger Ojito de las Gallinas tract, by bringing suit to eject more than one hundred families who had settled on the eastern grant after the Pinos had departed for Pecos, in the 1840s. Their case began in San Miguel County, in 1851. Procedural maneuvering had delayed trial at the county seat, Las Vegas. Then, in 1853, the Pinos had moved the case to Santa Fe, claiming that they could not get a fair trial in their own county. Finally, in June 1854, the case would be ready for trial in Santa Fe.[23]

Essentially, the Pino brothers sought to use the New Mexico territorial courts to establish their claim to the grant their father had applied for when Spain still ruled, and which he had received under Mexican hegemony. With the advent of the United States and territorial status for New Mexico, land suddenly became more valuable. Interest in long-dormant land claims increased, together with rumors that the Americans intended to confiscate preexisting claims through sympathetic officials like Vigil.[24] But Congress did not establish the office of Surveyor General for New Mexico until 22 July 1854. It was another year before William Pelham arrived, charged with the duty imposed by the Treaty of Guadalupe Hidalgo of determining claims to land originating under New Mexico's antecedent sovereigns. In the meantime, the Pinos had done what they could by taking their case to the local courts. Ironically, if the Pinos did so to avoid pro-Americans like Donaciano Vigil, they ended up delivering themselves and their lands into his hands.

But first they hired the Santa Fe lawyer Hugh N. Smith to prosecute their claim to the Ojito de las Gallinas grant against such men as Alexander Hatch, an Anglo who had come to settle there only after the Pinos had left. In 1851 Smith was already an old hand at New Mexico politics, increasingly the politics of land. He had represented Donaciano Vigil in other business. He took care of his friends and himself.[25] He accepted the Pinos' case and arranged for the mortgages and loans that paid his fees.

The man who lent the money, Preston Beck, Jr., became the owner of the Pino claim to both the Pecos Pueblo land and the Ojito de las Gallinas tract. Eventually, Beck brought Donaciano Vigil to Pecos. Most of the sketchy details of Beck's life surfaced after Beck and John Gorman killed each other in a bowie-knife duel, fought on the Santa Fe Plaza, in 1858. A pitched battle ensued over Beck's estate, involving Beck's Missouri family members and even a putative illegitimate daughter, in Santa Fe, who filed suit in the 1860s claiming a share of her deceased father's estate.[26]

That latter contest elicited the testimony of Francisca Salazar Manderfield, the wife of a prominent Santa Fean and the alleged mother of Beck's daughter. She provided most of the details of Beck's life. She described Donaciano Vigil's acquaintance and business compatriot as a man with many northern New Mexico business interests but without an established home there. Sometimes Preston Beck, Jr., lived out of one hotel room, sometimes out of another. For the last two years of his life, however, he had lived with her as man and wife. That arrangement had produced the daughter who now claimed a share of her deceased father's estate.

The four-way battle over rights to Preston Beck's estate provided a glimpse of his equally complicated economic life. The various formal inventories filed in court detailed Beck's partnership in a Santa Fe mercantile house, some individual property holdings, and an extensive network of outstanding loans. The loans indicated that Preston Beck, Jr., was as much banker as merchant and was certainly no stranger to the complex world of higher finance. Beck's financial web had already drawn in Pecos's Martin Kozlowski, who claimed the abandoned pueblo's church itself.[27]

Prior to his death, in 1858, Beck had already completed the transaction that would bring Vigil to the Pecos Pueblo lands east of the river. The Pino brothers, awaiting the outcome of the litigation intended to secure their claim to the Ojito de las Gallinas grant, neglected to pay back the money they had borrowed from Beck to finance the suit. The note, and the lands that secured it, fell due on 14 June 1854.

On 29 August 1854 the Pinos' own lawyer, Hugh N. Smith, the same man who also represented Beck and Vigil, began foreclosure proceedings against his own clients. To secure payment of the notes the Pinos would not or could not repay, Smith filed for their interest in the Pecos Pueblo grant and what would shortly be called the Preston Beck Jr. grant. At the subsequent foreclosure sale, held 30 September 1854, in the Santa Fe Plaza, Preston Beck, Jr., purchased both the Pecos tract and the eastern plains grant for $100.

On 12 December 1854, Smith formalized the transaction by executing his deed as trustee for the tract to Beck.[28] By mid-December 1854, Preston Beck, Jr., owned paper title to three hundred acres of the richest agricultural land on both sides of the Pecos River, well within the Indian land grant. Shortly thereafter the surveyor general and Congress would confirm that grant to Pecos Pueblo itself, subject to the rights of any third parties.

Donaciano Vigil became one of those unnamed third parties, on 26 December 1854. On that day he purchased from Preston Beck, Jr., the eastern half of the Pecos Pueblo tract that Beck himself just had taken from Manuel Pino that fall.[29] For the $1,500 sale price, Donaciano Vigil formally established a claim to the Pecos Pueblo grant. His was no innocent claim to Pueblo land. His interest was not born of mistake, ignorance, good faith, and long use, as non-Indian interests in Pueblo land were said to be elsewhere.[30] Rather, the Pecos Pueblo grant land came to Donaciano Vigil from legal and financial dealings supposedly characteristic only of much more sophisticated environments than mid-nineteenth-century New Mexico. After 1854 Donaciano Vigil would acquire other interests in the Pecos Pueblo grant, in more traditional ways.[31]

In a straightforward sense, Vigil's purchase from Beck fell into an emerging general pattern. Under the Spanish and Mexican regimes, non-Indians had been moving for years onto Pueblo Indian land. Old abandoned pueblo sites, including Cuyamungue and Galisteo (San Cristóbal), had long since been taken over by Hispanos. No one had complained. One of Donaciano Vigil's long-time political and personal associates from the Mexican period, Domingo Fernández, had acquired the abandoned San Cristóbal grant, southeast of Santa Fe, without the slightest complaint from the formal authorities. Pueblo Agent John Ward, who himself dealt in Pecos Pueblo land, offered to show confused Washington bureaucrats the ruins of more than forty abandoned Indian Pueblos around Santa Fe. In that kind of atmosphere, no one would protest about Donaciano Vigil's acquisition of the already sold and abandoned Pecos Pueblo lands.[32]

The timing of Vigil's purchase fell into a different general pattern. Whatever the extent of non-Indian encroachment on Pueblo lands had been prior to the arrival of the Americans, in 1846, it increased thereafter. Over the next eighty years officials would consistently remark that non-Indian takeovers of Pueblo lands had multiplied enormously during the 1850s. Eight months before Donaciano Vigil purchased the Pecos land, the pueblo of Nambé formally assembled and sold a portion of its land to local Hispanic residents.[33]

Apparently Donaciano Vigil had no cause to worry. In 1855 he moved from Santa Fe to Pecos and, according to his biographer, retired from politics and started to farm.

If anyone in the early days of American sovereignty knew, however, that there might be legal problems with the non-Indian acquisition of Pueblo lands, Donaciano Vigil certainly did. Of all native New Mexicans whose position survived the arrival of the United States, Vigil had an intimate knowledge of the Spanish and Mexican law of real property that the United States inherited with New Mexico, including the law of Pueblo Indian land. He had served as secretary to the Mexican governor Manuel Armijo, in the 1840s, when Armijo made his largest, most significant, and most controversial New Mexico land grants. Vigil said he used the job to study the history of New Mexico land.[34] General Kearny named Vigil secretary of the newly won territory and ex oficio the first registrar of land documents in the history of New Mexico under any sovereign. For Armijo, Vigil made and learned about land documents. For Kearny, he controlled them. Long before the United States surveyor general arrived to pass on land claims originating under New Mexico's antecedent sovereigns, Donaciano Vigil became intimate with that form of real property ownership which American law required and which New Mexico custom hardly recognized: paper title.[35]

In the years after American succession, Vigil continually used the expertise he acquired under Armijo and Kearny to speak before a variety of forums on Spanish and Mexican law and documents. Prior to 1854 and the establishment of the Office of the Surveyor General for New Mexico, Vigil appeared in various local courts and testified both on the law of the antecedent sovereigns and on the validity of various documents stemming from that earlier period. For example, he had tried to testify on behalf of the Pino brothers in their first local court battle to secure title to their father's Ojito de las Gallinas grant, although the trial court had not let him say much in their behalf.[36] While the appeals dragged on, Vigil took part of the Pinos' land instead.

With the arrival of the American surveyor general, Donaciano Vigil found a forum where he was indispensable. For lack of any contradictory information, American officials would let him say what he liked. Donaciano Vigil frequently provided the confused surveyor general not only with what information and documents he needed to assess land claims, but also with all the information he received, of any kind.

Sometimes, particularly in the early days of the surveyor general's land adjudications, William Pelham and his clerks depended simply on grant documents previously certified by Donaciano Vigil as Armijo's secretary or Kearny's registrar of land titles. In several cases, the documents had particular and increasingly controversial importance because they provided the principal evidence of those fantastic claims to millions of acres of land based on Armijo grants allegedly made in the 1840s. Donaciano Vigil's certificates of authenticity provided one of the bases for the surveyor general's approval of at least 3,425,602 acres of recognized private claims in only five tracts.[37] When the time came to produce those claims, Vigil's written guarantee that the supporting documents had been filed with him in one of his official capacities lent considerable weight to the claims' authenticity.

But Donaciano Vigil's role before the surveyor general did not stop there. Between 1854 and 1857 he testified personally so frequently that it is difficult to believe, as his only biographer states, that Vigil retired from public life with his 1854 Pecos land purchase and became just another local farmer.[38]

Sometimes Vigil's testimony simply involved certifying the authenticity of the official signatures attached to various documents. In most cases he vouched for Governor Manuel Armijo's hand.[39] But in at least two instances, Vigil's testimony on such a seemingly straightforward question suggested political undertones. In the case of the alleged John Scolly grant, encompassing some one hundred thousand acres at the junction of the Mora and Sapello rivers, Vigil certified Governor Armijo's signature of the supposedly official grant documents even though Vigil himself held another document, also bearing Armijo's signature, granting the same land to him.[40] In the matter of the Gaspar Ortiz grant, Vigil denied the authenticity of an Armijo document; he said the governor's signature had been forged. The conflicting testimony involved Vigil in a debate about when steel pen points had first arrived in New Mexico and whether Armijo ever had used one. Vigil swore he never had. Joab Houghton, the Santa Fe lawyer who had been involved in the early stages of the *Joseph* litigation, said that Armijo had. The esoteric debate, which the surveyor general had to decide, involved the date on which American traders first introduced metal writing implements into New Mexico. Vigil and Houghton had previously worked closely together, but they disagreed on the issue of New Mexico statehood.[41]

Less frequently, Donaciano Vigil appeared before the surveyor general to authenticate and explain papers previously executed by him in different official capacities. On 3 December 1856, Vigil testified about the nearly one-million-acre Sangre de Cristo grant, in northern New Mexico and southern Colorado. Vigil certified all the papers necessary for Charles Beaubien to establish his claim to that vast holding. He vouched for the 1843 grant papers as "acting secretary of the department of New Mexico." He said that, on 10 April 1848, he had registered those grant documents as "actual gobernador." Finally, he testified that, as "registrar of land title of the New Mexico Territory," he had filed, on 10 June 1848, an administrator's deed from the estate of Luis Lee, one of the two original grantees, to the claimant, Charles Beaubien. For each document Vigil also provided the explanatory background information.[42] But the three documents themselves, each attested to by Vigil, established what appeared to be a perfect chain of paper transactions. The record appeared to bring a previous Mexican title into American sovereignty in the name of Charles Beaubien.

Contemporaneous history, related by Vigil, makes the Sangre de Cristo grant look much less solid. Subsequent revelations, arising well after the surveyor general and Congress had approved the grant, made its genuineness even more suspect.[43] But in 1856, Donaciano Vigil provided the Sangre de Cristo grant with the appearance of legitimacy needed to reassure a bewildered Surveyor General. Vigil and Houghton also performed the same service for other grants.

In other instances Vigil supplied the surveyor general with all the information available to that American official concerning the history of New Mexico and the applicable laws of the antecedent sovereigns. For example, in the case of the Anton Chico grant, Vigil explained in detail how and when word of Mexico's 1821 independence from Spain had reached the northern borderlands, what effect that earlier change in sovereignty had had on New Mexico land policy, and the specific settlement of the Anton Chico area.[44] In another case, Vigil described the process by which the Mexican government had made land grants and suggested that Mexican law had required the procedure. When tracing the supposedly prerequisite procedure failed to yield any document substantiating the New Mexico claim of an acquaintance, Donaciano Vigil retired for two months and then returned to vouch for the authenticity of an original title paper that had not been filed where Vigil had said Mexican law required it to be.[45]

Despite this critical activity concerning non-Indian claims to land, Donaciano Vigil had almost nothing to do with the 1856 confirmation of eighteen grants to pueblos, including the approval of the Pecos Pueblo grant where he lived. However, in a minor way Vigil did substantiate the land story that pueblo members themselves told Surveyor General William Pelham. On 21 June 1856, ten months after Pelham indicated approval of the Pecos Pueblo grant to the pueblo, Donaciano Vigil signed an affidavit for the surveyor general which provided the only non-Indian testimony before that office on the subject of Pueblo land grants and their source. In the affidavit Vigil swore that he had had occasion to study the documents under his charge in both the Armijo and Kearny regimes. He had never seen any grant documents there. But, he continued, the pueblos of Tesuque, Nambé, Santa Clara, and San Ildefonso had always been recognized "as belonging to said Indians by virtue of grants made to them by the Spanish government towards the close of the 17th century."[46]

Ten months before, on 20 August 1855, Vigil had responded to the same question in the same forum, but in a different way. On that occasion a lawyer for a non-Indian claimant to non-Indian land asked Vigil if he ever had seen any of the grants supposedly made to the Pueblo Indians of New Mexico. Vigil replied that he had. "By whom were they signed?" "By the King," answered Vigil. Pressing further, Vigil's interrogator forced him to admit that in fact he had only seen the 1746 grant to Sandia Pueblo and none of the earlier Cruzate grants, under which the rest of the pueblos, including Pecos, claimed. Of course, stated Vigil, one could find the Pueblo grants in the archives, where they were supposed to be.[47] By June 1856, Vigil would say he had never seen a Spanish grant to a New Mexico pueblo and that he knew of none in the archives he had been in charge of since 1840.

Omissions compound the problems of Donaciano Vigil's testimony before the surveyor general, and bring them closer to the Pecos Pueblo grant. They suggest that, as early as 1854, Vigil himself knew that there might have been legal problems with his purchase of the Pecos Pueblo grant land from Preston Beck, Jr. In the Anton Chico case, Vigil explained to the surveyor general that the Spanish *Recopilación* continued to apply in New Mexico even after Mexican independence, in 1821. Of course, that famous code prohibited the alienation of Indian land to non-Indians, except under strictly defined conditions involving explicit government supervision. Vigil had explained to the same body that New Mexico pueblos held title to their lands under grants made by Spain and recognized by Mexico, although he was less

clear on the point of where those grant documents were located. Together these points suggest that Donaciano Vigil suspected that the
law of the antecedent sovereigns might have made illegal precisely the
kind of acquisition he had just made of Pecos Pueblo land.

Surveyor General Pelham may have acted too quickly on the Pecos
Pueblo claim for Donaciano Vigil and his associates to arrange the kind
of prolonged proceedings they initiated in other matters that affected
their interests. Perhaps Vigil counted on the United States government
to change preexisting law, as it had appeared to do in the *Joseph* decision.
Obviously, he did not bank on American courts finally reaching the
results they did in the 1913 *Sandoval* and the 1926 *Candelaria* cases.
Perhaps Vigil was relying on the language in the 1854 act which seemed
to protect the rights of third parties, like himself, against the rights
of those to whom Congress patented private claims, like the pueblo of
Pecos. Perhaps, just in case, Vigil and his sons continued to promote
the rumor that in 1841 the last Indian residents of what became the
Pecos Pueblo grant had applied to Governor Armijo for permission to
sell the grant, before departing for Jémez. Armijo had reportedly assented and the pueblo had sold its land, which Juan Estevan Pino had
bought. Donaciano Vigil had moved into Pecos on this chain of title.
For whatever reason, Donaciano Vigil did not contest the surveyor
general's finding that, after 1854, his home still belonged to Pecos
Pueblo.

Instead, Donaciano Vigil concentrated on other land fronts. After
1846 he became increasingly skilled at the maneuvers required to deal
in New Mexico land. In a sense, he had trained in the service of the
lawyer Hugh N. Smith and the financier Preston Beck, Jr. He acquired
the Pecos Pueblo grant property from them. For them he secured title
to the grant at the confluence of the Pecos and Gallinas rivers, Juan
Estevan Pino's Ojito de las Gallinas tract. The proceedings before the
surveyor general that led to the confirmation of what became the Preston
Beck Jr. grant reveal Donaciano Vigil at his most adaptable.

Before Pelham, Vigil explained the antecedent law that created Pino's
claim to the enormous tract in the first place. He explained how Spain
and Mexico had made the grant. He identified the grant's recipient.
When that initial grantee turned out to be inconvenient for Preston
Beck, Jr.'s cause, Vigil changed his mind and identified a more suitable
recipient. From personal memory he detailed the history of the settlement of the grant, in a way which seemed designed to substantiate

Juan Estevan Pino's claim.[48] When the opposition challenged the accuracy of his account, Vigil provided witnesses from among his Pecos friends.[49] He even tried to bring to the surveyor general's hearing the man he had just helped squeeze out of any interest in the property.[50] The Preston Beck Jr. grant claim was one of the first filed before the surveyor general and was the first decided by him. In the end, Donaciano Vigil, more than anyone else, convinced the confused Pelham, who then convinced an increasingly confused Congress, to confirm the claim to the successor of Juan Estevan Pino (Preston Beck, Jr.), rather than to the families who had settled on the land after the Pinos had ceased to use the tract.

When asked whether he had any interest in the Preston Beck Jr. grant, Donaciano Vigil gave an emphatic *no*.[51] As a matter of direct, personal ownership of the land in question, that may have been true. But, obviously, Vigil and Preston Beck, Jr., shared very particular common interests that revolved around the Pinos and their claims to New Mexico land. Vigil did not explain those common interests to the surveyor general. Nor did he suggest that from the Preston Beck Jr. grant imbroglio would evolve a common tactical scheme to use the surveyor general's adjudications to determine local land battles, a scheme that Donaciano Vigil would soon bring home to his own Pecos-area affairs.

Preston Beck, Jr., Hugh N. Smith, and Donaciano Vigil used the surveyor general to resurrect the earlier claim of Juan Estevan Pino to the Ojito de las Gallinas tract and then to transfer it directly to a subsequent purchaser of that first claim, in this case Preston Beck. In so doing the three tried to bypass the intervening claims of families who had actually settled on the land between the first grant under Mexico and its confirmation under the United States. Donaciano Vigil employed the same technique for himself when, on 17 July 1855, two months after Beck filed his claim, he filed his own claim to the entire Los Trigos grant, which bounded the Pecos Pueblo grant on the south.[52] As in the case of Beck's claim, Donaciano Vigil's petition for confirmation of the Los Trigos grant in his own name involved a conflict between a formal, early government grant and subsequent, Mexican-period occupation of it without apparent formal authority. Like Beck, Vigil aligned himself on the other side of the earlier grant, in an effort to nullify intermediate claims to it and so establish his own subsequently acquired rights.

The complex history that led to Donaciano Vigil's claim to the Los Trigos grant began when the grant was made, in 1814, and ended in Surveyor General Pelham's decision recommending congressional confirmation on 17 September 1857.[53] Two aspects of that story had particular importance for Donaciano Vigil's land ventures. First, from the outset everyone agreed that the southern boundary of Pecos Pueblo's league determined the northern boundary of the Los Trigos grant. Although no one could be sure at the time exactly where either was, Donaciano Vigil pursued in his Los Trigos claim a tract adjoining his Pecos Pueblo holdings. The second, both more important and less obvious aspect of the Los Trigos controversy placed Donaciano Vigil squarely on the side of a technical claim to the land in the face of a growing community's more intensive, competing use of it.

Hugh N. Smith filed Vigil's claim to the Los Trigos grant on 17 July 1855, just after the surveyor general formally began his work, in the name of "Donaciano Vigil, a citizen of the United States and resident of the Territory of New Mexico for himself and the legal representatives of Francisco Trujillo, Diego Padilla, and Bartolome Marquez," the original 1815 grantees.[54] Of the 267 claims eventually filed before the various New Mexico surveyors general, the Los Trigos claim was filed eleventh and decided eighth. The Preston Beck Jr. grant, with which the Los Trigos grant shared so many legal points, was filed second and decided first. By August 1855 Vigil would be testifying in one and himself advocating the other.

Like the Preston Beck grant application, that for the Los Trigos grant represented another of those claims to New Mexico land presented to the surveyor general by men of power already well established in New Mexico. In filing his claim so early, Donaciano Vigil joined such prominent New Mexico survivors of the change in sovereigns as Beck; Manuel Álvarez, former American consul to Mexican New Mexico; Tomás Cabeza de Baca, a leading Las Vegas promoter; Gervacio Nolan; Alejandro Valle; E. W. Eaton; and Charles Beaubien. The list of these initial claimants to large tracts of New Mexico land is virtually a *Who's Who* of the early days of the New Mexico Territory.[55]

Like the Preston Beck Jr. claim, Donaciano Vigil's application for the Los Trigos grant came to the surveyor general as a private claim from one individual, rather than as an application for land belonging to a community. As late as 1887, government officials still referred to the grant as the "Los Trigos *or* Donaciano Vigil Grant."[56] Like Tomás C. de Baca and Preston Beck, Jr., Vigil claimed the entire Los Trigos grant as his private property, despite the fact that a substantial, unrelated community had established itself and had grown up on the place he now claimed as his own.

The Vigil claim, like the Beck claim, had an existing history of previous litigation in other, more traditional forums, before being presented to the surveyor general. The Pinos had gone to the territorial courts in an early effort to establish their claim to what they said had been their father's private property. As early as 23 February 1850, Donaciano Vigil had employed New Mexico attorneys to litigate his claim to the Los Trigos grant in the local courts. No record of any pre-1855 suit survives among San Miguel County documents. In 1861 Donaciano Vigil would reassert the same claim in the local courts, this time using different lawyers.[57] Between these two efforts Vigil, like Beck, had discovered a better place to litigate his right to the Los Trigos grant: the Office of the Surveyor General.

There the conflict pitted Donaciano Vigil's claims, for himself and the three original grant recipients whose interests he said he represented, against the claims of Rafael Gonzales and twenty-four other heads of families who claimed the same land because they had occupied the tract since 1842.[58] What Preston Beck, Jr., was to the "Rancho Hacienda de San Juan Bautista del Ojito del Rio de las Gallinas," Donaciano Vigil was to Los Trigos. What Alexander Hatch was to Beck's claim, Rafael Gonzales was to Vigil's.

Both Beck and Vigil took the same approach in presenting evidence of their claim to the surveyor general. Beck claimed that his grant's original owner, Juan Estevan Pino (whose interests Beck now owned), had settled the land in eastern New Mexico and used it according to the terms of the grant. Rights had vested in him. Then interlopers like Alexander Hatch had arrived. Vigil told the same story about Los Trigos: the Márquez, Padilla, and Trujillo families, whose interests he presumably now owned, in 1815 had settled the area just south of Pecos Pueblo. The families deserted the place only when the attacks of hostile Apaches made further use of the land impossible. But none of the original owners, said Beck and Vigil in each case, had ever abandoned their original grants. No subsequent trespassers could acquire rights there, neither Hatch nor the twenty-five families who had settled the Los Trigos grant after 1842.⁵⁹ As successors to the original grantees, Beck and Vigil each now owned the grant's original rights, despite the claims of others.

Before the surveyor general, Beck used Vigil to substantiate the facts of his theory. In the Los Trigos case the reverse would not work, since Preston Beck, Jr., had arrived in New Mexico too late to know much about what had happened under Mexico. To support his Los Trigos story before the surveyor general, who heard the evidence in July 1857, Donaciano Vigil called the one witness who had as much, if not more, right as he to be called New Mexico's senior native statesman: Domingo Fernández. Fernández, twenty years older than Vigil and his model in many ways, played the role in Vigil's case that Vigil himself had already performed in the Beck case. When formally asked, Domingo Fernández swore to the surveyor general that he had no interest in the Los Trigos grant claimed by Vigil.⁶⁰ Otherwise the interests and careers of the two men were intimately connected. Indeed, when the older Fernández died, Donaciano Vigil helped arrange his estate.⁶¹

Both Vigil and Fernández had shifted successfully for survival under Spain and Mexico. Both had survived the early days of American sovereignty. Both came to the surveyor general with excellent paper qualifications. Indeed, if the two men are to be believed, Domingo Fernández had charge of the Mexican archives of New Mexico from 1825 to 1846, "with some interruption," until Donaciano Vigil took his place. Together the two had complete official control of a commodity that came to have increasing value: written title to land.⁶²

In addition, both Vigil and Fernández showed an increasing interest in abandoned Pueblo Indian land. The unfiled, "Spanish" records of New Mexico, assembled by the surveyor general's staff but not assigned to any particular grant, contain numerous misdesignated Mexican-period documents showing an early (1830s) and abiding interest on the part of Domingo Fernández in the lands of the Pecos Pueblo grant.⁶³ In subsequent years, Donaciano Vigil, rather than Fernández, claimed the Pecos Pueblo grant; Fernández never pressed his claim to Pecos before the surveyor general. Instead, he pursued his more promising claim to the abandoned San Cristóbal Pueblo, in the neighboring Galisteo Basin. In 1827 Fernández had finally secured a Mexican grant to the lands of the latter pueblo. In 1851 he sold the grant to two Anglos for five hundred dollars, and then brought Donaciano Vigil to the surveyor general to vouch for his claim and for those who had bought from him.[64] No one seemed much concerned that San Cristóbal had first appeared on the surveyor general's docket books as a Pueblo Indian grant, like Pecos.[65]

As with Los Trigos, the existence of a settled community, called El Cadijal (Galisteo), in the middle of Domingo Fernández's claim, only slightly complicated his case. Donaciano Vigil supported the Fernández claim despite the presence of the settlers.[66]

In the Los Trigos case before the surveyor general, Vigil and Fernández switched roles. This time Fernández authenticated the original grant documents to Trujillo, Padilla, and Márquez. He told Pelham that he personally had knowledge of matters concerning the Los Trigos land since 1872, the year he acquired the Pueblo Indian San Cristóbal grant. That spring he had spent the night on his way from San Miguel del Vado to Santa Fe. Yes, Fernández affirmed, the three original grantees had settled on the grant shortly after it was made. They had built houses and worked the land. Marauding Apaches did give them trouble, killing there a small Indian boy who had worked for the grantees, tending their flocks. The three original grantees had never abandoned their claim to the land.[67]

Rafael Gonzales and the twenty-four other family heads then residing on the grant countered Fernández's testimony as best they could. They told the surveyor general that no one had lived on the land just south of Pecos Pueblo until they arrived, in 1842. They related that, in that year, the alcalde of San Miguel del Vado, Manuel A. Baca, had allocated the land to them after giving public notice that he intended to do so. Baca had assiduously avoided alloting the small tract that in 1842 showed any sign of previous settlement. Indeed, Donaciano Vigil's own brother, Gregorio Vigil, alcalde of San Miguel del Vado after Baca, had approved the distribution. In other words, various Mexican officials had confirmed the possession of Rafael Gonzales and the twenty-four others then living on the grant.[68] Donaciano Vigil could not now claim it as his own.

On the contrary, argued Vigil in the closing brief his lawyers filed with the surveyor general: the original 1814 grant still stood.[69] No one could claim rights not stemming from it or that were at variance with it. Vigil's opponents disagreed, saying that the original grantees had abandoned whatever rights they might have acquired in 1814, by neglecting to maintain the requisite residence on the land. As a matter of law, the 1814 grant had been for grazing only, was specifically limited to plots of land actually occupied by the original grantees, and, in any case, recognized that other, subsequent settlers could come and take possession of unoccupied parts of the tract, which Rafael Gonzales and his friends had done. Finally, argued the contestants in perhaps their most telling point, the present claimant, Donaciano Vigil, had shown absolutely no transfer to himself from the grant's original recipients, Márquez, Padilla, and Trujillo.[70]

To that challenge Donaciano Vigil offered neither response nor documents. The man who according to all reports was more informed about American custom than any other native New Mexican produced no written evidence before the surveyor general to support his personal claim to the Los Trigos grant.[71]

Vigil kept in his private possession the only two documents that could possibly connect him to the tract. In one, a beautifully written English deed dated 15 July 1850, Catarino and Jesús María Archuleta sold not to Vigil but to his friend, Alejandro Valle, for $14.50, "a piece of tillable land and the ruins of a house" in the settlement of "Las Ruedas, county of San Miguel del Bado." Donaciano Vigil had only recorded the document as part of his official work.[72] The other document was an almost illegible Spanish deed from the same two Archuletas for a slightly different piece of land.[73] Neither document was presented before the surveyor general, perhaps because Donaciano Vigil realized that a claim to the entire Los Trigos grant based on the two obscure Archuleta documents would have aroused the suspicions even of Surveyor General Pelham.

Obviously, no matter who did own the Los Trigos grant, the United States certainly did not. It did represent some kind of valid claim originating under New Mexico's antecedent sovereigns. Under the trying circumstances, Pelham did what he could to aid Vigil's cause. On 15 September 1857, three days after he approved Domingo Fernández's claim to the abandoned pueblo of San Cristóbal, the surveyor general decided that he would recommend confirmation of the Los Trigos claim neither to Donaciano Vigil nor to Rafael Gonzales and the twenty-four other family heads who opposed him. Instead, ruled Pelham, Congress should confirm the Los Trigos claim to the "legal representatives of the original grantees," Márquez, Padilla, and Trujillo, whoever those representatives might be.[74] Vigil was free to prove in some other forum that he had succeeded to the interests of the original grantees. If he could not do so, the real representatives could come forward. Years later that decision would itself cause a fracas in the General Land Office. For the moment the surveyor general had at least rejected Rafael Gonzales's contention that the community he spoke for had a right to the grant under Spanish and Mexican law. The congressional committee which received Pelham's report approved it without question.[75] Congress confirmed the grant in Pelham's form with no more debate.

Ironically, Donaciano Vigil's partially successful maneuvering ultimately deprived both him and the community of settlers of any claim to the unallotted eight thousand acres of the Los Trigos grant. Confirmation by Congress of the grant to the "legal representatives of Francisco Trujillo, Diego Padilla, and Bartolome Marquez," from whom the surveyor general had heard nothing, and who did not live on the grant, opened the door to land speculators in the 1860s, 1870s, and 1880s. They came with the Atchison, Topeka and Santa Fe Railroad, which ran a line through the Los Trigos grant, and found it easy to pick up deeds from various presumptive heirs of the original recipients for undivided interests in the grant, to consolidate those undivided interests, and to offer for sale in a single block a substantial portion of the grant's unallotted common lands. By 1910, what was left of the original Los Trigos indigenous community had been forced into small lots in the village of Rowe, two narrow strips along the railroad track. Donaciano Vigil's grandson, also named Donaciano, lived there, as the local magistrate to the tiny community around him. An ocean of open land, the unoccupied eight thousand acres of the grant surrounded the cluster of homes. That open land, the balance of the grant and the necessary land base to support a self-sustaining, indigenous, community-based economy, had long since passed into alien private ownership.[76] The first Donaciano Vigil had tried to grab it all for himself and had lost it for everyone then connected with it. The western singer Tex Austin and the movie star Greer Garson would prove to be the twentieth-century residual beneficiaries of Vigil's Los Trigos legacy.

Meanwhile, in the Pecos Pueblo grant, the ironies of Donaciano Vigil's land schemes emerged in a different way. Vigil had arrived in Pecos in the wake of mundane, though sophisticated, local political maneuvers. He had not attempted to use his influence or the influence of his friends to gain federal recognition of his presence there. He had not manipulated the newly arrived surveyor general to create, enlarge,

or even confirm his Pecos Pueblo grant holdings. And he did not lose
Pecos for the growing Hispanic community there, in an unsuccessful
effort to claim it all for himself.

Instead, the United States had confirmed and patented the Pecos
Pueblo grant to Pecos Pueblo, and had left Donaciano Vigil out entirely.
That confirmation, combined with the *Joseph* decision, left Vigil entirely
free to contribute to the development of Pecos's lands in the deepest
traditional way.

On the surface, the *Joseph* case decided, for the time being, that
non-Indians could live on Pueblo Indian land without offending federal
trespass law. The Supreme Court eventually reversed itself on that
explicit, controversial point. But the 1877 *Joseph* court also decided,
in a subtler point never altered in the shifting course of subsequent
Pueblo land litigation, that New Mexico pueblos held their land by
"fee simple communal title," even without federal protection.

That English term, drawn from the arcane terminology of common-
law land estates, in effect recognized the indivisible corporate nature
of Pueblo Indian real property ownership. To the sovereign United
States at least, if not to the Pueblos themselves, land grants to pueblos
formed unified tracts whose external boundaries the government would
define, but in whose internal affairs it would not meddle.[77]

Hispanic community land grants might have shared that attribute
as well. But American law quickly encroached on that corporate status
by distinguishing between allotted and unallotted lands within the
community grants by showing an increasing interest in segregating
the two. In the end, the American government ruled that Hispanic
communities, unlike pueblos, had never owned the unallotted, common lands within their community grants.[78] Unoccupied non-Indian
land the government took; unoccupied Pueblo land the government
left alone.

Thus, the *Joseph* decision removed two potentially unsurmountable
obstacles to Donaciano Vigil's development of Indian land. First, the
decision meant that Vigil, his friends, and his heirs were more secure
in the Pecos Pueblo grant, since the United States government would
not prosecute them as interlopers on federally recognized Indian land.
More critically, the decision also removed the Pecos Pueblo grant from
any continuing federal interest in the forms of land ownership within
its boundaries.

Even the federal surveyors had disclaimed any continuing interest in what happened inside the Pecos Pueblo grant. By late 1882, the United States government had brought its system of public surveys to the boundaries of the Pecos Pueblo grant. The surveyor White came from the south in 1879. Taylor and Hollander came from the west in 1880. Cunningham and Warner brought the public land surveys from the mountains to the east of the Pecos Pueblo grant in 1882.[79] But none of them ever entered the grant to determine property boundaries or ownership there.

Spanish Pecos was left to develop according to its own traditions long after surrounding non-Indian communities, based on Spanish grants, had suffered the American imposition of surveying and common-law categories of land ownership. Where American common law insisted on the basic indivisibility of private land ownership, Spanish law emphasized that the same tract of land could share many different forms of ownership—some private, some public, and most mixed.[80]

Donaciano Vigil acknowledged that deep Spanish tradition when, in his 1877 will, he described his landholdings in terms of a single, linear measure of varas along the East Pecos irrigation ditch. That acequia divided the lands of the Pecos community much more surely than any line which might have been imposed from without by the surveyor general.

The community called the irrigated land below and on the river side of the ditch *Los Regadillos*. A foreclosure-sale purchase in 1854 brought Vigil fifty of those acres. Other non-Indians north of him irrigated about seventy-five acres from the same source. Those south of him used the same irrigation ditch to cultivate another eighty acres.[81] From May to October each year, those irrigated tracts were private property. Their crops belonged to each individual farmer, although the lack of sophisticated farming equipment in the nineteenth century required the whole community of farmers to cooperate in harvesting each field. Donaciano Vigil and his sons would go north and south in the spring and fall, to help plant and harvest. In exchange, their Pecos neighbors would come, in time and turn, to the Vigil fields.

After the harvest, from October to the next May's planting, the private irrigated fields were public land. Each tract owner took down his fences, and Donaciano Vigil's animals joined the rest of the community's livestock wandering the entire length of the ciénaga, grazing on the stubble of the fall's harvest while the snow piled up in the surrounding mountains. In so doing, Hispanic Pecos honored the ancient Iberian practice of *derrota de mieses*. Pecoseños called it *los rastrojos*. The mixed concept, tied directly and seasonally to use, was anathema to English common law.[82]

Donaciano Vigil, his children, and his neighbors had equally unfamiliar names for the lands above and outside those along the irrigation ditch, as mentioned in Vigil's will. They called a relatively narrow strip of land just above the ditch *mancomún,* to indicate that the strip was quasi-public and available, with permission, for new family houses.[83] New Vigil families built homes there before and after Donaciano Vigil's death.

Just above what became a fairly dense, village-like cluster of homes were the *eras,* threshing corrals open to all Pecos farmers after the fall harvest. There, near the top of a hill where a breeze always blew, Pecoseños threshed their wheat on a flat, well-trodden, immaculately clean circular dirt track. A post at the center was used to tether the horse that circled patiently, separating wheat from chaff.

Above the eras, toward the rugged mountains that surrounded Vigil's Pecos estate, lay a vast stretch of forested land, part of it the balance of the Pecos Pueblo grant as surveyed by the United States and part of it what would become, after 1896, the Santa Fe National Forest. In the 1870s and 1880s all of it was still open and available to the community for stock grazing, foraging, and wood gathering. In most instances the idea of owning some part of that land as private property was as alien to Donaciano Vigil's world as the idea of claiming individual pieces of air. The mountains were the commons. Vigil and Alejandro Valle used them as such when they grazed their sheep as much as fifteen miles east of Pecos.

In his own lifetime, on his own ranch, Donaciano Vigil honored that intricate, instinctual Hispanic system of land use. His sons and daughters also did so for two generations afterwards. Not until the 1930s did that careful, curious mix of public and private land use begin to collapse in Pecos, despite the presence of outsiders.

But the Hispanic community of Pecos paid a price for that freedom. Federal title to Pecos land did not belong to its residents. Financial interests in other parts of New Mexico, and as far away as New York, were trading in that title, even as Donaciano Vigil was writing his will.

That was a gap Donaciano Vigil never tried to bridge. He left the two Pecos land worlds entirely separate. He devoted most of his career to manipulating the strained, awkward linkage between American sovereignty and native land use. The rest of New Mexico suffered—Pecos did not. There even Donaciano Vigil could not manufacture a plausible connection. In the coming decades it would become increasingly difficult to consider the New York Pecos, the Jemez Pueblo Pecos, and the Hispanic Pecos as common entities.

SEVEN

Pecos Visits New York

The Pecos is the very pride of the country. It presents advantages to
be found in such a degree in no other portions of this Territory.
Among these are genial climate, pure water and fertile soil.

—Las Vegas Optic, 6 June 1880

The *Joseph* decision turned Hispanic Pecos, now in 1880 minus Donaciano Vigil, in on itself. Frank Chapman's death left Pueblo Indian
title to the whole grant, confirmed by Congress and emancipated by
the Supreme Court, in the limbo of the deceased bachelor's estate. The
arrival of the railroad made the East readily accessible to New Mexico
for the first time, and vice versa. The entrepreneur Andres Dold, a
resident of Las Vegas from 1850 to 1871 and a resident of New York
from then until 1880, came back to New Mexico, eager to introduce
New Mexico land to the markets of the East.

Dold arrived in Las Vegas in 1880, in time for the federal census
of that year. Dold was then fifty-four years old, married, a merchant,
and was born in 1826 in Wuerttemberg, to parents who were both
natives of that kingdom in southwest Germany. Mrs. Dold reportedly
came from the same place. But if she was still alive in 1880, she
apparently was not with her husband. Andres Dold's household consisted of himself and two sons: John, twenty years old in 1880, and
Henry, eighteen. Each declared New Mexico as his place of birth.[1]

The Las Vegas *Optic* noted Dold's return to the city in 1880 and
guessed that he had lived there "thirty years ago."[2] Early New Mexico
historians recorded Dold as a plains freighter in 1864, hauling west
from St. Louis with his brother, John, what little goods reached New
Mexico prior to the coming of the railroad.[3] More recent accounts
suggest that the Dold brothers arrived in Las Vegas from the East in
1850, soon emerging as the "leading merchants" on the Old Town

Plaza.[4] An 1854 account reported the brothers' business located in a "nice appearing" two-story building on Las Vegas's Old Town Plaza.[5] Wherever they came from, by the early 1850s the Dold brothers had arrived in Las Vegas, apparently to stay. In 1881 the local paper repeatedly referred to Andres Dold as "one of the patriarchs of New Mexico."[6]

By 1865 Andres Dold had built for himself an enormously successful and, for capital-poor New Mexico, enormously profitable network of businesses, centered in Las Vegas. The books of his company for that year show $35,821.22 worth of merchandise received, presumably for sale in his store, and fifty thousand pounds of wool purchased, presumably for shipment east, where Dold would resell it. At the same time that Dold was building this early, traditional mercantile business, he also involved himself in local real estate. As early as 1860 and as late as 1869, Dold bought and sold tracts of land in San Miguel County. At least once the transaction involved Alexander Hatch, the man who gave the Pinos so much trouble and who, ultimately, gave Pecos to Donaciano Vigil.[7]

In this early development of Andres Dold's business affairs, a second pattern emerged: shifting, but ongoing partnerships with men who shared in, and sometimes fronted for Dold's complex interests. Dold began with his brother, John. By 1861 the two had fallen out and had dissolved that partnership. Thereafter Dold joined Fred Meyer, a fellow German, who worked with Dold for a while and then moved on to Mora, where he opened a store of his own. Finally, on 22 November 1873, Andres Dold and Frank Chapman entered the partnership that would bring the Pecos Pueblo grant into Dold's hands after Chapman's death.[8]

By the time of that formal agreement with Chapman, Dold had left Las Vegas to reside for nearly a decade in New York. In 1887 F. O. Kihlberg, a long-time Dold employee in a variety of capacities, swore that Dold had lived in New York "most of the time" between 1871 and 1880; he visited Las Vegas only occasionally.[9] Each year between 1875 and 1880 Dold listed himself in the New York City directories as a merchant, and resided each year at a different address on the city's prosperous East Side.[10]

No record survives indicating just what kind of merchant Andres Dold was in New York between 1871 and 1880. In the general system of the times, most evolving New Mexican mercantile houses kept at

least one East Coast employee, who would supply the distant home
business with those items of civilized life so hard to come by in New
Mexico and so easy to find in New York.[11] Andres Dold may have
supplied Frank Chapman with those "superior articles of French kid
gloves for Ladies" which "Chapman and Co., General Merchandise"
advertised in the winter of 1879. Even if he had not had contacts in
New York prior to his first arrival in New Mexico, his years in Las
Vegas between 1850 and 1871 would have provided him ample op-
portunities for making them. Several of Las Vegas's leading businessmen
during the time, men who would join Dold in various enterprises on
his return in 1880, had close New York relatives.

The arrival of the railroad in Las Vegas, in 1879, and Frank Chapman's death shortly thereafter, changed things for Andres Dold. The
railroad brought New Mexico to New York. Chapman's death brought
Dold from New York to New Mexico. On 7 January 1880, he got off
the train in Las Vegas to stay.

There he found a town much different from the one he had left ten
years before. The railroad brought new capital and new blood to the
previously traditional New Mexican settlement. The promise of the
railroad had spawned Las Vegas's first bank, in 1876, in a building
rented from Frank Chapman. By 1881 Dold's youngest son, Henry,
would take a job clerking at a second city bank. A new and increasingly
cantankerous local newspaper was founded. New people appeared daily,
some serious about exploiting the promise of Las Vegas's altered future,
others not. By late 1880 the *Optic* praised the arrival of new "capitalists"
and reported on an "opium den . . . in full blast in Las Vegas":

> It is operated by an enterprising Mongolian and it is said that men
> and women congregate to drown their cares and vexations with a
> pipe of the narcotic. This is for the information of those concerned.[12]

Andres Dold simply picked up where he had left off in 1871. By
the end of January 1880, he had reopened the store closed by Frank
Chapman's death less than a month before. "Dold and Co., General
Merchandise" employed Andres's two sons and Frank Chapman's nephew,
as clerks. "Under its present management," predicted the *Optic*, "the
store will soon get back its old patrons and many new ones."[13]

In addition, Dold returned to old real estate. By 5 March 1881 he
had laid the cornerstone for a new building on the Las Vegas plaza.
He began to speculate in mining properties. He even incorporated Las

Vegas's first proposed electric power company. Several of the largest land owners and most powerful citizens in the town and in the whole territory joined him.[14]

However, Dold's immediate task on arriving in Las Vegas, on 7 January 1880, was to arrange the affairs of his deceased partner, Frank Chapman, dead less than a week when Dold returned to town. As usual, Dold moved quickly.

Two days after Chapman's sudden death and three days before Dold arrived, Marcus Brunswick, a long-time associate of Dold, and Chapman's nephew, John, petitioned the San Miguel County court for appointment as the administrators of Frank Chapman's estate. The probate judge approved their appointment the same day.[15] Five days later, one day after Dold's return, there appeared in the county courthouse for the first time two partnership agreements between Chapman and Dold, one dated 22 November 1873, the other dated sometime in February 1879, but both filed 8 January 1880.[16]

The 1873 agreement provided simply that Frank Chapman would continue Andres Dold's previous business under his own name. The two men would share equally the profits and the losses. Although Chapman had acquired numerous tracts of land and the Pecos Pueblo grant prior to this agreement, the document said nothing about the two men sharing their real estate acquisitions. The 1879 agreement, however, added that the two men would share as "equal partners and joint owners all real estate held and possessed by said Chapman . . ." including the Pecos grant.

The second partnership agreement gave Andres Dold his explicit claim to at least half the Pecos Pueblo grant. Why he and Chapman waited until 1879 to formalize the arrangement is nowhere made clear. How they managed it at a time when Chapman was in Las Vegas and Dold in New York is another enigma. No notary sealed the document so that it is impossible to tell where it was signed (if it actually was). A private witness had signed the agreement. But that witness turned out to have as many links as Dold himself to the markets that would control Indian title to the Pecos grant for the next twenty years.

He was the Las Vegas attorney Louis Sulzbacher. In 1873 he had witnessed the receipt of four thousand dollars by twelve Pecos Pueblo elders then residing at Jémez, as partial payment by Frank Chapman for their grant.[17] By 1880 the railroad would bring a small section house on its line through the Pecos Pueblo grant and call the small subdivision near it *Sulzbacher,* in honor of his claim to part of the grant itself. By the next year he would incorporate, with the former surveyor general Guy F. Atkinson, the New Mexico Mining Company, with capital stock of ten million dollars and an executive committee of New Mexico land speculators joined by a New York treasurer. All the while he kept in close contact with his brother, John Sulzbacher, still in New York, who subscribed to and read the *Optic* "regularly" and who himself "traffics in mining stock at No. 61 Broadway." Over the next decades four New York so-called capitalists, all doing business within a few blocks of 61 Broadway, would buy and sell the Pecos Pueblo grant like financiers in the twentieth century would promote grain futures.[18]

But in early 1880, Andres Dold had only to ready the 1879 agreement Sulzbacher had certified, make it available to the financial world he and Sulzbacher knew so intimately, and let it take its own money-making course from there. With the 1879 agreement, Andres Dold could easily make the Pecos Pueblo grant his own.

The formalities took him less than three months. He already owned a half-interest in the grant by virtue of his partnership agreement. On 19 January 1880 the probate judge ordered that Chapman's other half-interest be sold "at private or public sale." On 24 January the administrators told the judge they could find no will for Frank Chapman (an unusual state of affairs for a man who otherwise did such careful business), but that Chapman had left two surviving brothers, one in Chicago, the other in St. Louis, as well as the children of a deceased third brother, who also lived in Chicago. On 3 February 1880, Marcus Brunswick informed the court that he had found a buyer for Chapman's half-interest: Andres Dold himself.

Dold had agreed, Brunswick said, to pay $21,125 for all Chapman's real estate, including the Pecos grant. The court approved.[19] By February 17, less than two months after Dold's return to Las Vegas, Chapman's heirs in Illinois and Missouri signed a deed to Dold confirming the purchase. By mid-February 1880, all of the Pecos Pueblo grant was his, on paper at least.[20]

Like Preston Beck, Jr., twenty-three years before, Dold hardly knew the grant he had just acquired. Occasionally he sent employees to look at it. They told him the grant was "wild land, wood and timber and pasture land."[21] With his long experience in New Mexico, Dold must have known better, must have known that a substantial community already existed in the midst of this "wild land." Indeed, by early 1881 Dold was circulating a notice similar to the one Frank Chapman had published in 1873, without effect, warning trespassers off the grant. The *Optic* of 24 March 1881 reported that

> the owners of the Pecos Pueblo Grant are out with a framing poster printed on cloth, warning all parties concerned not to cut any timber, nor build settlements nor put up improvements of any kind or for any purpose on the grant. This strip of land is 6½ miles square, its center point being the old Pecos church. All buildings thereon and on the town site of Montezuma, known as Baugh's siding on the NM&SP road, are held liable for the price or lease of the grounds upon which the improvements are made. Notice is given that suit will be commenced against all persons having appropriated lots or land without having first contracted for the same with Don Andres Dold, Las Vegas, New Mexico.[22]

No matter that Pecos residents disregarded this notice as they had disregarded Chapman's. What interested Andres Dold, however, was the speculative value of the paper title he now held. San Miguel County land was an extremely active commodity at the time. Santa Fe County Judge L. Bradford Prince, a man who through his own eastern connections would have a critical impact on the Pecos Pueblo grant nearly twenty years later, himself bought and sold land on his trips to Las Vegas to hold court.[23]

There was just enough to connect the Pecos Pueblo grant with the allure of easy fortunes to be made. Pecos grant timber, in increasing demand by the railroads, already provided some income to the grant owners. By midwinter 1881, various railroads would call for huge new timber contracts to support the construction of new lines. By May of that year Dold's factotum F. O. Kihlberg would go to Pecos to check timber supplies on the grant, with the added purpose of finding out exactly what his employer had acquired. Tie camps already existed on the grant; their owners already paid Dold annual rental and stumpage fees. Increasing demand should bring growing revenue.[24]

In addition, there was a rumor of mineral riches beyond imagination on the Pecos Pueblo grant. The 7 May 1881 *Optic* reported that a group of unnamed men had prospectors at work at Pecos. They reported that possiblities were "very bright indeed." Less than a month later, Kihlberg, other Las Vegas associates of Andres Dold, and an "eastern capitalist" ventured to Pecos to "skirmish around an ancient tunnel on the

Pecos Grant." Although no one found anything, the possibilities lingered.[25]

Finally, if nothing else, the Pecos Pueblo grant in Andres Dold's hands represented a relatively large tract of pastoral land.

> The Pecos is the very pride of the country . . . it presents advantages
> to be found in such a degree in no other portions of this Territory.
> Among these are genial climate, pure water and fertile soil . . .[26]

Donaciano Vigil alone had kept upwards of five hundred sheep on the grant. By 1882 Las Vegas would ship more wool east than any other town on the AT&SF line.[27] Pecos might be expected to produce some pastoral income also.

But the potential was definitely limited. Within twenty years excessive sheep grazing and timber cutting on and around the Pecos Pueblo grant caused the federal government to protect the surrounding mountains as the first New Mexico forest reserve. All the talk of mineral wealth at Pecos through the nineteenth century remained just that. Finally, the grant's high elevation produced a cold, unpredictable climate with its first and last killing frosts in September and late May, respectively.[28]

None of that mattered, because what Andres Dold held in the Pecos Pueblo grant was an eighteen-thousand-acre possibility that had real appeal in the financial world of the East, so remote from New Mexico in the 1880s. Complex economic factors produced a viable market for large tracts of New Mexico land in that period. Dold understood such esoteric matters of international finance as differential interest rates. In capital poor New Mexico, for example, borrowed money brought upwards of 25 percent interest charges at the time. In New York the same money cost 7 percent to borrow. London banks charged 3.7 percent. To the Hispanic residents of Pecos and the Pecos residents at Jémez, this would have meant nothing. But the differential interest rates reflected international forces that had a critical effect on the widely differing attitudes toward the land.[29]

That local New Mexico money cost three times as much as New York money and eight times as much as London money indicated a relatively small pool of local capital in high demand. This demand was motivated by a growing perception of economic opportunity, in part based on the large tracts of land with unknown assets, which could be bought and which might yield huge fortunes. At the same time, the high cost of local capital kept local land values depressed. In New Mexico in 1880, it was hard to raise even the $18,768 the Pecos Pueblo grant would have brought at one dollar an acre.

The opposite was true in London and, to a lesser extent, in New York. There the relatively low interest rates indicated a large pool of available capital and relatively few new places to put it to use. For more than a decade, British and European investors in search of markets had poured money into Australian pastoral stock combines, Rocky Mountain mining enterprises, and vast New Mexico land grants. A few New Mexicans, like Stephen B. Elkins, who had begun the *Joseph* litigation in 1867 as United States district attorney for New Mexico, even traveled to New York and Europe to market New Mexico land.[30]

In the summer of 1880, the Pecos Pueblo grant, on paper at least, belonged to Andres Dold, a man from Europe and New York who resided in Las Vegas, and who presumably knew the urban financial world as well as he knew New Mexico. He had only to pay taxes on his newly acquired grant, to continue Frank Chapman's marginal interest in the property, and to wait in Las Vegas for the speculative fervor of New York and London to discover the Pecos Pueblo grant.

In the meantime, the *Las Vegas Optic* did its part. Through the winter of 1880 and the spring of 1881, the newspaper was filled with promotional rhetoric and the rumors of gold strikes all over San Miguel County. Although no one mentioned Pecos directly, it shared in the general prospects.

> No section of the U.S. offers greater advantages to the capitalist than New Mexico. She has gold, silver enough to supply the world, and vast beds of copper and inexhaustible fields of the best coal in the world.[31]

Such paeans were meant for a wider audience than the residents of San Miguel County. Louis Sulzbacher's brother, John, read the *Optic* in New York. The brother of the Las Vegas businessman T. B. Mills, Charles Edgar Mills, who was the commissioner for New Mexico in New York, must have read his brother's new publication, *Mining World,* "the recognized authority on the mines of New Mexico," issued for the first time in March 1881.[32] Judge L. Bradford Prince passed the word on to his family connections in New York and Flushing, Queens. All these men would have a critical impact on Pecos Pueblo grant affairs in the coming years.

But in the spring of 1881, no one had to send out the good word. The world of eastern capitalists pressed in on Las Vegas. Hardly a day passed in which the *Optic* did not note the arrival in town of another easterner or European, intent on assessing the area's self-proclaimed prospects:

> Gilbert Glass, Belgium mining engineer, is in Las Vegas after
> reading of the Tecolotina strike [just west of the city] in Kansas City.
> He was on his way to Colorado but hit Las Vegas instead on hearing
> the news.

In March, "a party of wealthy Pennsylvanians" stopped in town to look around. In May, a "well known Philadelphia mining expert and correspondent of the *Chicago Mining Review*" paid a visit.[33] Apparently Andres Dold had only to wait and the world would come to him.

By 6 July 1881 it had arrived. In a one-sentence notice, published 8 July, the *Optic* observed that "Don Andres Dold has sold the Pecos Grant to J. Whitaker Wright of Philadelphia for a consideration unknown." The *Optic,* usually privy to such affairs, had made no previous reference to a possible sale; no subsequent news item discussed it. No one ever publicly alluded to possible conflicts with the tie cutters, with the Hispanic residents of the village of Pecos, or with the defunct pueblo of Pecos. The deed itself, made in Las Vegas on 6 July 1881, made no mention of them. But Dold did guarantee to Wright title to all 18,768 acres in the Pecos Pueblo grant, excepting only the railroad right-of-way and a few lots in the townsite of Montezuma, which Dold had previously sold.[34]

James Whitaker Wright, in 1881, was a thirty-three-year-old, English-born Philadelphian, who had arrived there in 1879 to set up what soon became a far-reaching business. He had a twenty-year-old wife and an infant daughter.[35] He told the federal census taker that his name was James W. Wright, while the editors of *Gopsill's City Directories: Philadelphia* listed his formal name as J. Whitaker Wright. In the census he declared himself a silver miner; in the directory he was a meteorologist, whatever that might have meant in 1880.

Over the subsequent years, less esoteric self-definitions helped explain just who Wright was and just where his interest lay. By 1882 he declared himself "in mining." From 1883 to 1885, he headed the Security Land, Mining and Improvement Company, a Philadelphia investment firm whose name bespoke its interests and purpose. Between

1885 and 1887, he ran his business under the name of Whitaker Wright & Co. and declared its interests as "cotton, grain and petroleum." By 1888 Wright was back on his own, still in Philadelphia, describing himself in 1888 and 1889 as an individual broker, in 1890 as a "broker of real estate," and finally, in 1891, as a "capitalist."[36]

Wright finally left Philadelphia, to move closer to the natural resources he traded in. By 1891 his address was listed as a post office box in San Francisco. He stayed there until 1895, when he returned to London. He continued his American affiliations from there until in 1905, at the age of fifty-seven, he discontinued his overseas business interests.[37]

Wright clearly did not buy the Pecos Pueblo grant in July 1881 to settle on it and make it his home. There is no indication that he ever visited New Mexico, let alone Pecos, before or after his acquisition of the grant. The general pattern of Wright's life, his career, his economic interest in New Mexico, and his purchase of the Pecos Pueblo grant were all typical of the new era.

Wright was European. As a Londoner, he surely understood those continental market forces that would make investment in obscure New Mexico land attractive to Old World residents with a surplus of capital and no promising places to invest it closer to home. As a mining engineer by training, Wright paid close attention to the verifiable reports from California and Colorado of fantastic mineral resources. He was also aware of the speculative guesses from New Mexico that wealth existed there as well. Despite several spectacular failures, eastern U.S. and European capital markets still responded to the vaguest of possibilities.[38] New Mexico land, purchased at less than one dollar an acre in the territory, brought at least twice that amount in New York and London, as late as 1880.[39]

No document survives to indicate what Wright paid Dold for the grant in the summer of 1881, or where the money came from. Clearly Dold profited from the deal.[40] But Wright did too. He had not bought a place to live or even use; he did not even publish the perfunctory notice Chapman and Dold had issued in 1873 and 1880. Instead, he simply took possession of the Pecos Pueblo grant papers and waited while the commodity, 18,768 acres of New Mexico land, gained in marketable value.

It did not take long, as it had not for Andres Dold. On 31 March 1883, less than two years after Wright had bought the grant, George

D. Roberts, who described himself as in mining, and who did business at 115 Broadway, in the heart of New York's financial district, bought the Pecos Pueblo grant. Again, no record of the purchase price survives.[41]

Roberts held the Pecos Pueblo grant for such a short time that it is impossible to tell what he had in mind when he bought it. However, his purchase did have an important impact on the history of the eastern claim to the land. Most obviously, Roberts brought the Pecos Pueblo grant from Philadelphia to New York, to the center of its financial district. A few blocks away, Louis Sulzbacher's brother traded in mining stocks. Over the years, the various commissioners for New Mexico in New York, the only officials in the city empowered to approve transfers in New Mexico land there, did business at 115–117 Broadway—in the same building complex where Roberts worked.[42] Several subsequent Pecos Pueblo grant owners either had offices in the near vicinity or other, more direct connections.

On 3 June 1884, less than fifteen months after he had bought it, George D. Roberts sold the Pecos Pueblo grant to James M. Seymour, according to the deed a resident of "Orange, Essex County, New Jersey," a small, yet prosperous suburb of New York City.[43] James Madison Seymour was one of New York City's early commuters. Thirty-seven years old in 1884, he lived in New Jersey but did business as a self-styled broker at 3 Exchange Court, near the stock exchange itself. On his trip uptown on 3 June 1884 to pick up the Pecos Pueblo grant deed from Roberts, at the office of the commissioner for the territory of New Mexico, Seymour took along a fellow New Jersey resident and broker at 3 Exchange Court, James W. Fox, to witness the transaction. Again no record survives of what Seymour paid for the grant. But five years later, in the spring of 1889, Fox would himself purchase the Pecos Pueblo grant from Seymour for one dollar an acre.[44]

In the intervening five years, James Madison Seymour made the only serious effort by a New York owner formally to establish exactly what he had bought. He did not visit Pecos or New Mexico to do so, but instead hired two Las Vegas agents who had close connections to Andres Dold and the New Mexico land market. He also employed two New Mexico attorneys, one of them the territory's preeminent land grant lawyer, to secure judicial recognition of his ownership of the entire grant.

One of Seymour's agents in New Mexico was his brother-in-law, San Miguel County resident Gerald Hudley. The other was T. B. Mills,

Las Vegas's most enterprising real estate entrepreneur and brother to a commissioner for the territory of New Mexico in New York, who did business at 115–117 Broadway. Seymour's agents in New Mexico stated that they had the grant, after 1885, "in our hands for sale and to look after and manage for him."[45]

The two agents hired two New Mexico lawyers to study and then formally to repair whatever defects might exist in the title to Seymour's purchase. Their first choice was the Las Vegas attorney J. H. Koogler, an Indiana native who had lived in the city for some time and who had proved himself adept at numerous professions in addition to the law.[46] Seymour's agents also hired Frank Springer to assist them.

Springer had as many callings as Koogler did and was more eminent at all of them. But one aspect of his life must have held a particular attraction for the new owner of the Pecos Pueblo grant. Since early in the 1870s, Springer had served in a variety of corporate capacities for the Maxwell Land Grant Company. That company promoted the allegedly two-million-acre grant in New York and Europe. In 1879 the United States had finally patented that vast acreage and then, in 1882, itself brought suit to cancel the patent, on the grounds that government surveyors had "falsely, fradulently and deceitfully" surveyed the grant to include many more acres than the original grant of 1841 had contained. Frank Springer defended himself and the company in that litigation. In the process he won himself the reputation as New Mexico's finest land grant lawyer.

The Maxwell Land Grant case took five years to bring to a conclusion. Springer himself argued the case before the United States Supreme Court on 8–11 March 1887.[47] Less than two months before, on 20 January 1887, Springer and Koogler had filed suit in Las Vegas, on behalf of Seymour, to quiet title in him to the Pecos Pueblo grant.

The two lawyers were not concerned about the confusing presence of a Hispanic town in the middle of land their client claimed as his own. They were more interested in establishing the formal marketability of the Pueblo Indian land they had bought. In the late 1860s and early 1870s, New Mexico land grants could be, and had been, sold on nothing more than an attorney's certificate that title to the tract was good. By the 1880s, a still eager market now demanded more formal proof of legal title to the commodity offered for sale. In the case of the Pecos Pueblo grant, Seymour, through Mills and Hudley, and Springer and Koogler, moved to eliminate its most obvious title problems.

The chief difficulties they saw centered on the fact that the Pecos Pueblo Indians had once owned the tract. The *Joseph* litigation had established, if only temporarily, that existing federal law did not prohibit the pueblos from selling their land. But the Supreme Court had not specified just how New Mexico pueblos might sell parts or all of their grants: could individual Pueblos sell the tracts traditionally assigned to them; could tribal elders sell for the whole pueblo; or was some more formal mechanism required? No one really knew. The *Joseph* decision itself only compounded the confusion when it suggested that New Mexico pueblos held their land in "fee simple communal title." Did that mean the six Pecos survivors living at Jémez, who had sold to Frank Chapman in 1873, could speak for the title the United States had confirmed in the Pecos Pueblo?

Koogler and Springer set out in January 1887 to get the San Miguel County district court to say just that. The complaint they filed for Seymour listed as defendants all the non-Indian purchasers of the grant, beginning with John Ward and ending with George Roberts. All except Roberts and Wright had died, the complaint alleged, and so Seymour asked the court to take jurisdiction over the "unknown heirs" of each, whoever they might be. Every Pecos Pueblo survivor who had ever signed a known deed conveying the Indian grant was deceased as well, alleged the complaint. So their unknown heirs were also listed, although none received any other notice of the suit than that which appeared in the back pages of the Las Vegas *Optic*. Finally, no mention at all was made of any of the Hispanic residents of Pecos, living and farming in the middle of the grant Seymour claimed in the suit as his own.

Instead, Seymour named as defendants in the suit the pueblo of Pecos itself, in a number of possible forms:

> the unknown heirs of the Pecos Indians, and the unknown heirs of
> the Indians of the Pueblo of Pecos, and the unknown heirs of the
> Indians of Pecos, and the unknown heirs of the Pueblo Indians of
> Pecos, and the Pecos Indians, and the Indians of the Pueblo of Pecos,
> [and] the Pueblo Indians of Pecos . . .

This concern with syntactic permutations indicated a genuine uncertainty about just who the pueblos, including Pecos, were, and about how one sued them. While *Joseph* had freed grants to pueblos from the onus of existing federal prohibition against the private sale of Indian land, the decision only led to a debate about *how* pueblos like Pecos could execute the sales they were allowed to make.

In his suit Seymour tried to avoid controversy by naming the Pecos Pueblo as a defendant in every conceivable form. At worst, the suit might have rid his 18,768 acres of all possible Indian claim to it. At best, it would have provided judicial confirmation that James Madison Seymour had the right to sell in New York, or anywhere else, the New Mexico land grant he said he owned.

Styled as it was, the suit almost guaranteed that no one would actually contest Seymour's claim to total ownership. Twenty years later a subsequent purchaser of the pueblo's interest would try to adjudicate his claim to all 18,768 acres against the claims of Hispanic residents who by then had lived there for more than a century. That hopeless litigation would drag on for almost a decade, to end in a settlement of competing claims. But in 1887, Koogler and Springer tried to move so quickly and with so little notice to other claimants, that no one would contest Seymour's title.

By 15 March 1887, less than two months after the suit had been initiated, Koogler and Springer, on behalf of Seymour, filed with the San Miguel County District Court an affidavit indicating that the *Las Vegas Optic* had published in its back pages a notice to all the defendants named in the suit, directing them to appear in court if they wished to contest Seymour's title to the entire grant. No other notice was given; no defendants appeared.[48]

In line with the practice of the day, the case was assigned to a so-called special master, here the San Miguel County District Court clerk, R. M. Johnson, to take whatever uncontested evidence Seymour might want to offer in support of his claim. Apparently the resident judge, Elisha V. Long, who doubled as chief justice of the territorial supreme court, was not interested in a suit whose aim apparently no one debated. During that same period, Long had to face the bitterly contested issue of just who owned the common lands of the Town of Las Vegas grant and under just what conditions, with regard to its alienation. But no one expected much opposition to Seymour's claim.[49]

Through the spring of 1887 Koogler and Springer gathered the formal evidence necessary to support Seymour's claim to all 18,768 acres. They secured sworn statements from Marcus Brunswick; Henry

Dold, Andres Dold's oldest son; John L. Chapman, Frank Chapman's nephew; and Frank O. Kihlberg, a former Dold employee. Together, the affidavits proved that Seymour had acquired the grant that the Pecos Pueblo survivors had sold to Ward and Chapman, and that the 18,768 acres of "wild land, wood and timber and pasture land," as Kihlberg reported, now belonged to the New Yorker. Although they had some trouble locating the original deeds, Koogler, Springer, and Mills did provide the special master with recorded copies of the various transfers to substantiate their story.[50]

In addition, on 14 May 1887, Koogler submitted to Johnson a detailed version of his view of the status of Pueblo Indian lands in general and the Pecos Pueblo grant in particular.[51] The Koogler brief was long, scholarly, erudite for its day, and ultimately wrong, according to subsequent court decisions. Koogler concluded that New Mexico pueblos belonged to a class of their own, *sui generis,* so that the status of their land was unique as well.

That conclusion, of course, allowed Koogler an expansive field for his analysis of the validity of the original 1868 sale to John Ward and Frank Chapman. Since no analogies applied, the transfer had to be assessed on "general principles." These, in turn, led Koogler to his "primary question": "in whom was the fee simple title to these lands vested originally?" He demonstrated that full title had vested in Pecos Pueblo since before the arrival of the first Spaniards. That preexisting title had always implied the complete right to sell as well. The pueblo had sold. Now Koogler's client, James Madison Seymour, had ultimately bought the grant. It was his. The court should now confirm it to him.

Koogler's line of argument completely overlooked the fact that the members of the Pecos Pueblo were Indians. While the *Joseph* court had decided that a pueblo's lands did not fall within existing federal prohibitions against unauthorized sale of Indian lands, Congress might still assert another guardianship interest in their lands. But no one raised such esoteric points in the San Miguel County District Court in 1887.

Curiously, the court's special master, R. M. Johnson, who was appointed to take the evidence in this uncontested suit, did quite a bit more. In his report to the judge, filed 14 November 1887, Johnson wrote that

the large interests involved in this cause, the great number of
unknown heirs attempted to be made parties to the proceedings, the

peculiar relation which many of them are supposed to have sustained
to, and their rights in, the land in question, together with the fact
that not one of all the parties which the Bill herein makes defendants
to the action appears to defend any interest he may have in the large
tract of nearly 20,000 acres of land which the Complainant seeks by
his proceeding to divest him of the title . . . has made it necessary
for me in the discharge of my duty in the premises, to look into the
whole record of these proceedings . . .

There followed seven pages of the most minute technical objections to
the manner in which possible adverse claimants had been notified of
the suit filed against them. Finally, at the end of a catalogue of complaints, Johnson reached the heart of his problem:

> The tract of land in question was granted to this Pueblo of Pecos,
> then organized and existing by the Kingdom of Spain, in the year
> 1689; but under the law then in force and under which it received
> the said grant of land, said tract was not given to it in absolute
> property with full right of disposition and alienation, but it held the
> same thereunder by a tenure which was of a fiduciary nature and in
> trust for the entire community constituting such body politic,
> municipality and corporation and could only alienate the same or any
> part thereof in accordance with the said trust, by and with the
> consent of the parent government, expressed through its regularly
> constituted authorities, which retained for itself the power and right
> to decide how that trust should be performed and executed.

Johnson cited John Arnold Rockwell's *Spanish and Mexican Law*
(1851), a standard American treatise on Spanish and Mexican real
property law, as his authority. He used it to support his conclusion
that Pecos Pueblo had not conveyed properly the grant which it had
owned and the United States had confirmed. As a result, Seymour did
not own it. But Rockwell's text, like Johnson's interpretation, hopelessly confused two kinds of fiduciary duties—that of Pecos Pueblo to
its members, and that of the current national government to the pueblo
itself. Johnson concluded that the court should not confirm the title
Seymour asked for, despite the fact that no one opposed it.[52]

But on 27 November 1887, two weeks after Johnson filed his adverse
report, the presiding judge apparently decided the issue in favor of
Koogler and Seymour.[53] He signed a formal decree quieting title in
Seymour to the entire grant, despite Johnson's recommendations. The
territorial courts had formally certified that the New Yorker owned the
grant. Seymour could now find other buyers for his land and prove to

them that he owned what he offered to sell, according to the San Miguel County court decree.

However, three weeks later Judge Long, for no apparent reason, reversed himself. On 17 December 1887, he sent an order to the San Miguel County court clerks, directing them to set aside the judgment entered in favor of Seymour, to strike the decree, and to mark on the docket books that the decision of the court confirming the New Yorker in the ownership of his grant was hereinafter "null and void."[54] For less than a month, Seymour had had what he wanted: a judicial stamp of approval on his sole ownership of the Pecos Pueblo grant. Now the court had sent him back to his starting point.

No record survives to explain the court's decision. It is possible that Judge Long had not considered Johnson's report until after the first, pro forma decree had been entered. It is possible that Koogler and Springer had surreptitiously influenced the other county clerks, only to invoke the supervising judge's wrath when he discovered what had been done. It is also possible that Long, recognized as a leading member of the most "intellectual court" of the territorial period, suddenly realized what a complex set of issues Pueblo Indian land ownership involved and honestly reconsidered his earlier approval.

In any event, by 1 January 1888, James Madison Seymour had learned something new: even the courts of New Mexico were not quite sure what he had bought, if anything, when he purchased the Pecos Pueblo grant from George Roberts. His attorneys and agents in New Mexico showed no urgency in pushing the question. On 7 June 1888, they asked the court for permission to withdraw the suit altogether, preferring that course to the possibility of a formal ruling against their client's claim. Judge Long approved.

Hispanic Pecos had never responded clearly to the suit that claimed Pecoseños did not own the land on which their homes stood. They never appeared in court to challenge the Seymour claim. Instead, they flocked to the San Miguel County courthouse, in Las Vegas, in the summer of 1887 to record Mexican-period documents dating as far back as 1830, to prove their ownership of Pecos Pueblo land. Many of the documents involved the Pino family. Some even included Juan Estevan Pino. A few of the deeds dated from very early days, but all of them involved only Hispanic Pecos residents.[55] Not one of the deeds filed in 1887–88 purported to convey the Indian pueblo's land from Pecos Pueblo to the Hispanic Pecos residents. The Pueblo Indian title and the non-Indian title were still completely separate. The Pecos Indians remained at Jémez. The Pecos Hispanos remained in Pecos. The New York owners of the grant remained in New York.

There Seymour had to decide what to do with what his suit had left him. He did not have a court-certified Pecos Pueblo grant title to sell. But at least on paper he still owned 18,768 acres in New Mexico. To sell the insecure commodity must have appeared to be the wisest course. On 6 May 1889, Seymour found another New York buyer for the tract. The new purchaser brought a New York bank with significant New Mexico connections into the chaotic affair.

The new buyer, James W. Fox, was no stranger to Pecos Pueblo grant sales. In 1884 he had witnessed the sale of the tract from George Roberts to Seymour. In the ten years between 1885 and 1895 he moved his self-described mining office around lower Manhattan's financial district. By 1892 he was at 3 Exchange Court, the location of Seymour's office in 1883. Like Seymour, he lived across the Hudson River, in northern New Jersey.[56] Fox and Seymour clearly knew each other when they entered into a sale agreement for the New Mexico grant, in the spring of 1889.

For the title he acquired, Fox paid Seymour one dollar an acre. On 7 May 1889, after owning the grant for twenty-four hours, Fox and his wife sold the Pecos Pueblo grant to the Flushing Bank of Queens for exactly one thousand dollars more than the $18,768.33 the documents stated he had paid Seymour for the tract.[57]

The rapid sequence of transfers in the spring of 1889 probably reflected some intricate financial maneuvering. Unfortunately, records no longer survive to explain the bank's acquisition. The Flushing Bank of Queens might have lent Fox money and then taken the Pecos Pueblo grant title as security. Seymour or Fox might have owed the bank money and repaid an existing obligation with New Mexico land. The bank itself had connections with New Mexico business and real estate. The prominent New Mexico lawyer, politician, and judge L. Bradford Prince had come to New Mexico from Flushing, then still a small town in the shadow of nearby New York. Prince's family remained prominent in Flushing and New York society. L. Bradford Prince had arrived in New Mexico in 1877. But every fall he returned to New York for the annual Episcopal conference there. He used his trips to attract eastern capital to New Mexico, as a way of providing economic development for his adopted state. In early January 1889, Prince was in New York, receiving letters at 39 Nassau Street about New Mexico land grant business from fellow speculator S. B. Elkins. Elkins, also in New York at the time, wrote Prince from No. 1 Broadway, just around the corner. Later that spring the two discussed New Mexico politics. By the fall of 1889, Prince had launched an active campaign for territorial governor. His opponents accused him of "unloading a worthless mine on innocent and confiding New Yorkers" and otherwise misleading East Coast investors about the value of New Mexico property.[58] For whatever obscure purpose, the Flushing Bank of Queens became the owner of the Pecos Pueblo grant on 6 May 1889.

For the next six years the bank simply held onto its papers. Then, in December 1895, another flurry of land transactions returned the title to New Mexico.

First, in New York, on 11 December 1895, the Flushing Bank conveyed its interest in the Pecos Pueblo grant to Mattie G. Smith. In New Mexico, less than two weeks later, she and her husband, Pascual R. Smith, sold to John L. Laub the tract they had just bought. The fact that the Smiths bought the title to the grant in New York and sold it two weeks later in the heart of New Mexico mining country, in McKinley County, indicates a real connection between New York finance and New Mexico mining. The Smiths only transported the grant title to the Southwest. In John Laub they finally found a purchaser with real San Miguel County connections.[59] The Pecos Pueblo grant had found its way home.

John Laub operated out of Las Vegas as a timber cutter and railroad tie contractor. Prior to 1895 he had occasionally contracted with other owners to cut timber on the Pecos Pueblo grant. By January 1896 he owned the grant itself. He later stated that he went on using the property for the next year and a half, cutting more timber and hauling more ties.[60] But, as had been true of the merchant Frank Chapman, there was more than a simple logger in John L. Laub and more than a straightforward purchase in his acquisition of the Pecos Pueblo grant.

For one thing, Laub acknowledged the claims of Hispanos residing on the grant. For example, in 1897 Laub lent money to at least two Hispanic families. In return he took mortgages to property he already owned. Indeed, in 1898 Laub filed two San Miguel County suits to foreclose against Pecos Pueblo grant property he had just bought from the Smiths. Nothing connected with his paper ownership of the entire grant prevented John Laub from doing business with trespassers on his land.[61]

However, the Hispanic town in the middle of the Pueblo grant did not provide the only challenge to Laub's title. Beginning in the middle 1880s the territorial legislature for the first time had authorized the taxation of private real estate. County governments, steeped in the *Joseph* tradition, placed Pueblo grants on their tax rolls. By 21 July 1886, the territory of New Mexico had placed the Pecos Pueblo grant under San Miguel County's name and had assessed a tax against all 18,768 acres within the grant. The fact that a few other Pecos citizens had smaller, private tracts assessed within the same grant did not stop the territory from taxing the entire grant.

But no one paid taxes on the Pecos Pueblo grant as such. On 16 November 1888, the San Miguel County District Court entered judgment against the grant for $253.56. Once again, no one paid. Finally, on 28 March 1889, the sheriff of San Miguel County, Lorenzo Lopez, acting pursuant to court order, sold the Pecos Pueblo grant to James L. Bridge, of Las Animas County, Colorado, for the sum of $253.56, the amount of taxes owed.[62]

That 1889 tax sale added another layer of confusion to the history of the Pecos Pueblo grant. Now the American Pueblo title resided with John Laub, in Las Vegas. The Mexican Pueblo title resided in Pecos. The American tax title resided with Bridge, in Colorado.

James L. Bridge wasted no time before offering for sale parts of whatever it was he had bought. On 3 February 1890, he sold a quarter-interest in the Pecos Pueblo grant to Frank Keeler, a fellow resident of Las Animas County. Keeler kept his share for a few years.

Two months before, on 17 December 1889, Bridge had sold a quarter-interest in the Pecos Pueblo grant to the Coloradan W. M. Mahin. Unlike Keeler, however, Mahin did not keep his $1,000 purchase. Immediately he divided his interest in half, selling one eighth-interest to a Las Animas county neighbor for $600 and the other eighth-interest to another neighbor for $500.[63] In one day Mahin had netted one hundred dollars by trading undivided interests in New Mexico Pueblo Indian land.

By 1890, then, the tax transactions had brought four more owners to the Pecos Pueblo grant—Bridge with his remaining undivided half-interest, Keeler with his quarter-interest, and Blair and Bell with their eighth-interests, purchased from Mahin.

None of the Coloradans did anything further with their interests until John L. Laub began investigating the matter, in the mid-1890s. On 18 January 1895, Laub located James L. Bridge in Colorado and for $400 bought Bridge's remaining half-interest in the Pecos Pueblo grant. (In the end, Bridge received $1,750 for the grant he had bought for $253.56. Of all the traders in Pecos Pueblo grant titles, he realized the greatest relative profit.) Six months later Laub found the two men who held the undivided eighth-interests and bought them out also. Finally, on 2 March 1896, Laub located Frank Keeler, who held the one outstanding quarter-interest in the grant. Laub bought him out too. For his four purchases between January 1895 and March 1896, John Laub paid $950.[64]

Now Laub owned both the United States Indian title and the tax title to the Pecos Pueblo grant. The potential chaos due to the addition of the tax title had been avoided. When, in 1904, the territorial supreme court affirmed that the territory had the power to tax Pueblo lands and that local forced sales of them were valid, John Laub's single hold on the land was strengthened.[65] A year later Congress opened the way for much more serious problems when it quietly struck down any territorial imposition of real property taxes on Pueblo grants and further ruled that sales based on failure to pay those taxes had no validity. For the moment, taxes did not appear to be a probable source of serious problems for the owners of the Pecos Pueblo grant.

However, Hispanic Pecos now tried for the first time to organize and fight back legally against the claims of ownership by complete outsiders. In an unexpected and spectacular move, on 29 May 1894 Pecoseños filed in the records of the San Miguel County courthouse a 20 September 1830 deed from José Cota, acting for Pecos Pueblo, to Juan Estevan Pino. The deed purported to convey to Pino the entire Ciénaga de Pecos, the area of large, irrigated fields on both sides of the Pecos River just as it entered the Pecos Pueblo grant from the north.[66]

The deed, if valid, confirmed the title of all the Vigils and Varelas then residing on the grant, since their presence there could be traced directly through Preston Beck, Jr., to Juan Estevan Pino and through him to Pecos Pueblo itself. Indeed, if pueblos could sell their land, then as the older sale, the pueblo conveyance to Juan Estevan Pino would take precedence over the subsequent conveyance of the same land to John Ward. The recording of the 1830 deed further confused the already tangled trail of Pecos deeds. But its appearance gave the Pecos Hispanos the first real legal basis for their presence there.

Internal inconsistencies cast some doubt on the validity of the 1830 document, however. The long delay between the deed's alleged making and its appearance in the San Miguel County courthouse also makes its authenticity suspect, especially in light of the care Juan Estevan Pino normally took in documenting his real estate acquisitions. Neither the Spanish nor Mexican archives include the document or references to it, even though they otherwise contain numerous Pino real property documents. Spanish forgeries of ancient Pueblo deeds were not unknown at the time. In any event, the Pino deed of 1830 was now filed.

The Pecos Hispanic community did not stop there, however. For the first time in the grant's already complicated and controversial history, Pecos residents took the affirmative and tried to turn the grant's ownership their way. They did so by ingeniously trying to recast the Indian grant where they lived into the form of a Spanish community land grant.

In February 1891, the New Mexico Territorial Legislature authorized Spanish and Mexican community grants, confirmed by Congress as such, to organize formally. Before 1891, control and direction of community grants vested in communities that had no formal, corporate governments. The awkward lack of legal identity made it hard for local *towns,* or *pueblos,* to control their so-called common lands, those parts of the grants that belonged to no private owner. And the vague situation also made it hard for real estate speculators to acquire interests in those undisturbed common lands, since there was no one to sell them. On both counts, there was pressure for determining some formal status for these grants. The 1891 territorial act gave it to them, by allowing them to form municipal bodies to direct public affairs on their land.[67]

Everyone understood that the 1891 act applied to Hispanic pueblos, not Indian ones. Existing Indian pueblos like Taos and San Juan already had formal organizations and, in any case, did not need the legislature of New Mexico Territory to tell them how to organize. As early as 1849, New Mexico had made legal involuntary corporations of the pueblos, anyway.[68] The 1891 act authorized Hispanic communities to do the same thing, if a majority of property holders within the grant approved. Pueblo corporate ownership amounted to "fee simple communal ownership" of the entire Indian grant. No one had ever thought that non-Indian grants, incorporated or not, included for public ownership anything more than the common lands. The allotted holdings within them were private property. The 1891 act did not even attempt to make Indian pueblos of non-Indian community grants; they differed too much.

In the winter of 1896, Hispanic Pecoseños went to the Las Vegas law offices of George Hill Howard and asked him what to do about their title problems. Even then Howard had a reputation as an experienced land attorney; by the turn of the century his career would become more controversial.

In 1896 Howard suggested using the 1891 voluntary incorporation statute, so that grant ownership would be placed in a board of directors, elected by the community. John Laub might claim more acres in the Pecos Pueblo grant, but Pecoseños could at least command more votes. Surely they could control an elected board of directors. As a result of the meeting, on 25 February 1896 Howard presented a petition to the San Miguel County District Court, asking it to call a land grant election at Pecos. If the vote was favorable, then the court should incorporate the Pecos Pueblo grant. Ten petitioners, all from West Pecos, signed the formal court request.

The petition traced the history of the Pecos Pueblo grant through 1825, while it was still in Indian hands. Then, said the petition, between 1825 and 1842 the Pueblo Indians, at different times and by different deeds, sold large portions of the grant to the ancestors of the 1896 Hispanic petitioners. Finally, in 1842, the Pecos Pueblo survivors had gone before the last Mexican governor, Manuel Armijo, and asked for formal, governmental permission to sell their irrigated land, to abandon their ancestral home, and to move to another pueblo. Governor Armijo had approved all these requests. Now, in 1896, the heirs of the original purchasers of the grant from the Indians had come to court to incorporate it. The issue was as simple as that.[69]

The allegations of the 1896 petition were designed to build for Hispanic Pecoseños a case showing that the Mexican government had approved the replacement of the Pecos Pueblo Indians by the Hispanic community there. Such governmental approval would have satisfied any Spanish, Mexican, or United States requirements of government supervision of Indian land sales. Unfortunately, no 1842 document in the Mexican archives of New Mexico substantiated George Hill Howard's tale. While measurement (and protection) of Indian land against Hispanic encroachment continued until 1846, no trace survived of the 1842 events the Pecos petition described.

As the 1891 territorial statute required, Howard and the ten Pecos supplicants went on in their petition to enumerate the 1896 residents of the Pecos Pueblo grant. Their census contained 106 names, 104 Hispanic and 2 others—Martin Koslowsky, of *Joseph* case fame, and George Hebert, a minor character mentioned in Donaciano Vigil's will. The old Pecos Hispanic families accounted for the bulk of the names. The list of families included 14 Vigils, 12 Roybals, 11 Quintanas, 7 Varelas, 4 Pinos, and an assortment of Valencias, Senas, Ortizes, and Luceros. Under the category of "other claimants," the petition listed "Pascual Smith of Silver City" and Mariano Ruiz, a Pecos Pueblo grant resident who opposed the petition.

To give the other, presumably uncommitted Pecos residents notice of the proposed incorporation, the San Miguel County District Court ordered that notices of the petition and election be posted around Pecos. In 1873 and 1881, Frank Chapman and Andres Dold had each posted notices. Now Hispanic Pecoseños got the chance to post a notice of their own. On 28 February, Emirijildo Vigil, Donaciano Vigil's third son, and Hilario Vigil, another relative, walked around the village of Pecos, tacking this notice on the door of the church and store:

PUEBLO OF PECOS GRANT

To Whom It May Concern:

Know Ye that on the 25th day of February, A.D. 1896, Juan Jose Martinez, Valentin Flores, Tiburcio Lucero, Crisantos Lucero, Juan Lucero, Vicente Lucero, Aniceto Deabueno, Pedro Rivera, Agapito Lucero and Marcos Lucero filed their petition in the clerk's office of the District Court in and for the County of San Miguel, Territory of New Mexico, praying that the Honorable Judge of the said court will on the 4th day of May, A.D. 1896, at 10:00 A.M. of said day or as soon thereafter as the matter may be heard, and at the courtroom of the said court at Las Vegas, proceed to hear and determine the matter of said petition, the object of which is, that the tract of land situated in the said county, known as and called the Pueblo of Pecos grant, shall be incorporated and constituted a body politic, under and in accordance with the provisions of an Act of the Territorial Legislature of New Mexico entitled "An Act relating to Community Land Grants and for other purposes," being H.B. 48, approved February 28th, A.D. 1891.

FELIX MARTINEZ
Clerk, District Court, Fourth Judicial District of New Mexico[70]

Pecos citizens did not respond to the notice immediately. But on 24 March 1896, Howard went back to court for the original petitioners, asking the court to call a community-wide election to determine whether Pecos residents wanted to incorporate or not. The court agreed and set 4 May as election day. The judge appointed Francisco Varela, Encarnacion Rivera, and Pedro Rivera as election judges.[71]

Then the local political squabbles began. On 17 April 1896, three of the original petitioners for incorporation, Agapito Lucero, Aniceto Deabueno, and Juan Jose Martinez, none of whom could sign his name, asked to be removed from the original petition, now stating that each opposed incorporation. Nine days later, on 26 April 1896, the original petitioners called a meeting to discuss growing community dissension. By then five more original petitioners had dropped out of the proceedings. By the time George Hill Howard came from Las Vegas to Pecos for the meeting, only Valentin Flores and Pedro Rivera remained of the ten original Pecoseños who had asked the court to incorporate the grant. The others now evidently opposed the project they had begun.

Howard explained this to the Pecos citizens assembled at the local school house at 2:00 P.M., 26 April 1896, only eight days before the election. At that point eighteen additional Pecoseños asked that their names be added to the list of formal petitioners. The new petitioners included five Varelas, three Vigils, three Pinos, and a Roybal. Even the Pecos parish priest, Rev. Maximo Marquez, joined the group, along with Manuel Doroteo Pino, who had lost the major share of the Ciénaga de Pecos to the Vigils and Varelas, forty years before. Clearly local politics was heating up.[72]

Whatever else could be said about the 1896 incorporation effort, it had not unified the local Pecos community. By election day the situation had not improved. The original petition had named 106 heads of household residing on the grant. At the election only 56 voted. Of the 10 original petitioners for incorporation, only 2 even appeared on election day. The final vote reflected a badly divided community. Twenty-seven heads of household voted in favor of incorporating the Pecos

Pueblo grant; 29 voted against. All 6 Varelas voting favored the incorporation. But 4 Vigils voted in favor and 6 voted against. Families separated over the explosive issue. The only unequivocal fact about the 4 May incorporation effort was that it failed.[73]

The failure reflected an age-old problem with both Indian and Hispanic Pecos. As much as anything else, internal strife had contributed to the Indian pueblo's demise.[74] In 1896 Hispanic Pecos's one attempt to present a unified front to the threatening forces from New York, Colorado, and Las Vegas only revealed more clearly the serious divisions within the community itself. After the incorporation election, Pecos sank back into that legal limbo somewhere between John Laub's alien title to the grant and Hispanic Pecos's own claim to the ciénaga, through the connection to Juan Estevan Pino.

At least the Pecos Pueblo survivors at Jémez did not threaten that precarious balance. In the last decade of the nineteenth century, they occasionally returned to Pecos to visit their ancestral home. From time to time they brought with them captured Navajo children that they gave to the Quintanas, among other Pecos families, as presents. These children often worked their way into the community, themselves taking Hispanic names.

The Pecos survivors at Jémez also honored the presence of their Hispanic successors in Pecos when they sold to that community two large tracts of land on the village's western outskirts, in 1892 and 1894.[77] The conveyances represented at least the second, and perhaps the third, time that the Indians from Pecos Pueblo had sold the same tract of land—once to John Ward, once, perhaps, to Juan Estevan Pino, and now to the Hispanic Pecos residents that the Indian Pecos survivors identified simply as "nuestros hermanos."

Pecoseños made the properties mancomún, community property. Others might wonder who the community in fact was, since Pecos had refused to identify itself formally in the 1896 proceedings. But local residents knew who they were and what belonged to them. On the eve of the twentieth century, no one guaranteed their presence there. But no one actively threatened them either.

EIGHT

The Deepening Pecos Confusion, 1900–1920

Colonel Collier asked me to pass on the title [to the Pecos Pueblo grant in 1914] . . . to see whether it was worthwhile buying. He had some very wonderful ideas which, if carried out, would have been remarkable concerning the possibility of its development—a summer resort proposition and also an irrigation scheme which did not prove practical. However, he went over to Vegas and I went with him and he took an option and paid Gross-Kelly $5,000 to bind the bargain. The condition of it was that Gross-Kelly should bring a quiet title suit and endeavor to quiet title to the tract so it would be definite.

—Francis C. Wilson

The twentieth century opened in relative peace for the small but growing Hispanic community half a mile upriver and across a ridge from the site of the deserted pueblo of Pecos. On the west side of the Pecos River various settlers had begun to move their houses and families south from the northern reaches of the grant, an area in dispute between Indians and non-Indians since at least 1818. They followed the example of Manuel Varela, Donaciano Vigil's contemporary and also a beneficiary of Preston Beck's largesse. But at the turn of the century, the new settlers pushed even beyond don Manuel and built houses on the west side of the river, in the heart of the Ciénaga de Pecos. By 1910 Jesus Baca had built a large adobe on the southern edge of the settlement in West Pecos.

East of the river, Hispanos had pushed even farther into the Pecos Pueblo grant. Clemente Valencia had moved well beyond Donaciano Vigil's *rancho,* beyond the Jesus Baca house, west of the river, to the very southern tip of the Pecos bottom land. Juan Ortiz II had moved even farther than that, into the canyon nearly opposite the deserted pueblo ruins, and had established a ranch there.[1]

The Hispano future looked secure and promising enough for the Pecos parish priest, the mildly alcoholic Father Mailluchet, to begin plans for the construction of a larger Pecos church. By 1904 work had begun on what would become St. Anthony's on the Pecos. Local parishioners quarried rock for the new church from the site of the abandoned pueblo. That fall, it rained for almost a month. The Pecos River rose up out of its banks and changed course. When the flood receded, Pecos parishioners gathered the deposited river rock and built it into the new church too.[2]

Pecoseños did not show much concern for the Indian claims or the Indian patent to the Pecos Pueblo land where they lived. The *Seymour* suit, based on a sale by pueblo elders of the whole grant, had been consigned to limbo, as far as Pecoseños knew. In addition, the pueblo survivors had sold bits and pieces of the same land to the Hispanic residents. As for the critical irrigated land at the heart of Hispano life in the area, documents contemporaneously appearing in the San Miguel County courthouse proved that the Hispanic residents' predecessor had purchased the ciénaga from the pueblo leader, in 1830. Even though their own effort to incorporate the grant had failed, who could doubt that Pecoseños had the right to be where they were, living, farming, and increasing?

Certainly not the federal government. The days had passed when the Office of the Surveyor General or the Court of Private Land Claims had ruled on native title to millions of acres of New Mexico land, disallowing some claims, confirming a few others, and generally creating a speculative chaos in New Mexico real estate.[3] Will Tipton, the Las Vegas handwriting and archival expert who did such spectacular work for the Court of Private Land Claims, now labored mundanely for government survey crews in the brushy, flat plains between Taos and Tres Piedras. Donaciano Vigil II, the original Donaciano's grandson, worked as an axman on Tipton's survey crew. In time the second Donaciano Vigil would return to his small house in Rowe, near the AT&SF railroad tracks, as local magistrate for the community that had survived his grandfather's much more grandiose effort to obtain federal title to the entire Los Trigos grant, fifty years before.[4]

What federal problems remained in turn-of-the-century Pecos involved not the Indian land grant but the surrounding mountains. For years Pecoseños had regarded the high country around their homes,

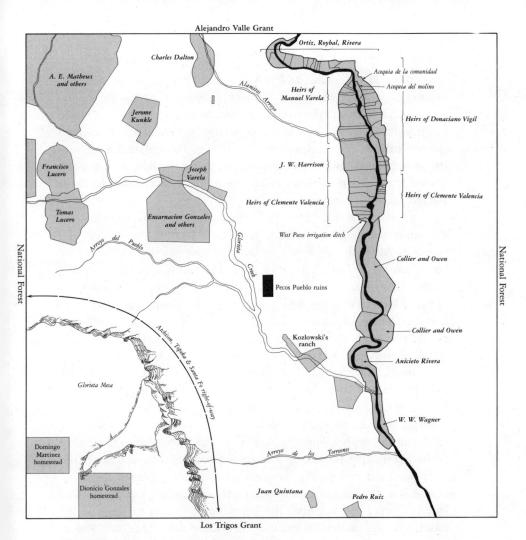

MAP 5. The Pecos Pueblo Grant in 1915.

Combined in Map 5 are the 1912 Jones Survey of the Pecos Pueblo
Grant, made for the Gross-Kelly Company of Las Vegas, New Mexico, and
the 1920 Pecos Valley Hydrographic Survey, made by the New Mexico
State Engineer for the United States District Court in the Hope
Community Ditch Adjudication. The combined surveys show that by 1915
all the river-bottom land on both sides of the Pecos River had been claimed
by owners with no connection to the Las Vegas company's claim to the
entire grant. Inheritance had splintered the ownership of the Donaciano
Vigil and Manuel Varela ranches in the *ciénaga* of Pecos. Anglo speculators
like D. C. Collier had bought up river frontage tracts south of the *ciénaga*.
The Atchison, Topeka & Santa Fe Railroad Company claimed a long right-
of-way through the southwest quarter of the grant.

inaccessible in the winter and rich in natural pasture in the summer, as an extension of their own domain. Then, in 1897, the federal government created in those mountains its first forest reserve and began to administer land use there much more strictly. Local ranchers resented the new rules designed to prevent overgrazing. Trouble smoldered from the outset, never quite cooling down completely.[5] But, at least, the United States seemed to have shifted its attention away from the Pecos Pueblo grant land itself.

As a result, internal Pecos land affairs appeared to have settled into a comprehensible pattern. True, Jesus Baca lost his Pecos ranch and moved to Albuquerque, where he built a house exactly like the one he had left at Pecos. But a horse-race wager had cost him his Pecos Pueblo grant holdings, rather than maneuverings by Anglo and Hispano speculators.[6] Other Pecos ranchers borrowed small amounts of money from Las Vegas businessmen and pledged their homes in the belief that they owned that land. Pecos and its land had entered a new era, an era in which economics, not land titles, moved local affairs.

As usual, however, another current still ran beneath the apparently placid surface of Pecos life. In 1898 John Laub sold the grant to the Las Vegas businessman Henry W. Kelly.[7] With substantial New York connections and a booming New Mexico business, the Kellys were the ideal cultural bridge between New York and New Mexico ownership of the grant. That the family now owned both tax title and legal title to it promised to simplify the confused paper situation of the Pecos Pueblo grant. Writing seventy years later, Henry W. Kelly's son said that his father had acquired the Pecos Pueblo grant to carry on his own timber operations. Of course he mentioned neither Hispanic Pecos, in the heart of the grant, nor the Pecos Pueblo survivors, at Jemez.[8]

In the meantime, however, federal interest in the status and dilemma of New Mexico's Pueblos belatedly increased. James S. Calhoun and John Ward had, from the onset of American sovereignty, prophesied that the Pueblo Indians would disappear unless their landholdings were protected by the United States. But Congress had responded slowly, if at all, and the United States Supreme Court had denied the Pueblos the protections of existing federal law.[9] Now, at the turn of the century, the climate changed.

Beginning in the 1890s, Pueblo agents and Indian service area superintendents began to report on the depressed conditions in existing pueblos and what they saw as the depressing status of the Pueblos themselves.[10] But these views contradicted those earlier expressed by the judiciary. Haltingly, Congress began to act.

Two federal actions near the turn of the century critically affected the Pecos Pueblo grant's twentieth-century fate. By 1905 the territorial imposition of real property taxes on all New Mexico lands, including confirmed and patented Pueblo grants like Pecos, had resulted in sweeping tax sales and purchases like the one John Laub had bought. The application of the territorial tax act to Pueblo land had been challenged, but the territorial courts had upheld their efficacy. In 1905 Congress, exercising at least a power it reserved over territorial affairs, if not Indian affairs, quietly, but succinctly and directly, struck down the territorial law and subsequent decision. Not only did Congress prohibit the future taxation of Pueblo Indian land, but voided as well any previous real property taxes since 1882.[11] One of the bases of Henry Kelly's title to the entire Pecos Pueblo grant was eliminated.

Earlier Congress had taken another serious action in affording Pueblos additional protection by appropriating an annual fee, beginning in 1898, to provide for a special attorney to defend their legal interests.[12] From the beginning, however, it proved hard to find a New Mexico lawyer free of possible interests that conflicted with those of the Pueblo Indians they were to represent.

The first special attorney for the Pueblos, appointed in 1898, for example, was none other than George Hill Howard. In 1894 Howard had represented those Pecos Hispanos who had tried to incorporate the Pecos Pueblo grant. That effort had failed. But Howard had gone on from there to speculate wildly in New Mexico land, including grandiose plans for the Juan Jose Lovato grant, in Rio Arriba County.[13]

In the meantime, he became directly involved with Pueblo affairs, as their special attorney. By the first decade of the twentieth century, the pueblos became embroiled in an increasing number of local court disputes with their non-Indian neighbors. For example, Howard represented Nambe Pueblo in a series of complex suits over the use of water within the Nambe Pueblo grant. Throughout the litigation, he neglected to assert a preferential Indian right to water originating in a source shared by non-Indians. In all fairness that doctrine had not yet been used in Indian water cases. But some would later say that Howard's interests were so connected to those of non-Indian development that he could not or would not assert all possible Pueblo claims.[14]

The problem became more convoluted and complex when Howard's successor as special attorney, Francis C. Wilson, arrived in New Mexico, in 1907. Sent by the Department of the Interior to investigate New Mexico scandals, Wilson remained in the state and contributed to them.[15] Over the succeeding twenty years Wilson would immerse himself in New Mexico land affairs, as special attorney to the Pueblos from 1907 to 1914, as private counsel to several pueblos thereafter, as a lawyer for New Mexico's landed interests, and, ultimately, as an oil and gas entrepreneur himself. Wilson took various positions over the years, with contradictory results. But the constant element underlying his many-sided professional life was the Pecos Pueblo grant.

For the first years of his New Mexico career, Francis C. Wilson worked against the backdrop of the territory's final drive toward statehood status and the ironic effect that had on Indian affairs in general and the Pecos Pueblo grant in particular. New Mexicans had skirmished with Congress over the statehood issue since 1850, with no decisive result. In those preliminary battles neither side had made an issue of the status of Pueblo Indians and their lands or of the territory's definition of them.[16] New Mexico's final series of moves toward statehood, however, coincided with growing federal interest in protecting the Pueblos. As a result, the bargain that New Mexico Territory had to strike, in order finally to gain statehood, included for the first time a new, explicit definition of Pueblo Indians and their lands.

The 1910 enabling act by which Congress granted New Mexico permission to organize as a state specifically required the new state to recognize land "owned or occupied" by the pueblos of New Mexico as "Indian country."[17] A little historical exegesis would have shown that the term *Indian country* came from the various Indian non-intercourse acts, which the territorial courts had said did not apply to the pueblos, a view which the United States Supreme Court had confirmed. Now Congress rejected that view and demanded that New Mexico accept the change as a condition of statehood.

The enabling act also condemned, both more subtly and more directly, the territory's previous legal handling of matters involving the Pueblo Indians. General federal law always had prohibited sale of liquor to recognized Indians. As recently as 1905, the New Mexico Territorial Supreme Court had ruled that those federal prohibitions laws did not apply to sales to the Pueblos.[18] Now, in the 1910 enabling act, Congress explicitly extended the prohibition to them, in defiance of the territory's own view of the legal situation, and invited New Mexico to accept this change or lose its opportunity for statehood. Congress clearly intended to impose on the new state a radically new vision of who the Pueblos were and to what special protections they were entitled.

Curiously, the enabling act's special provisions caused little controversy in New Mexico. In the final political struggle over statehood, a struggle that had underlain territorial politics from the mid-1860s on, no one mentioned, let alone complained about, the proposed Pueblo provisions.[19] The Pueblos themselves, the intended beneficiaries of the new definitions, still opposed statehood, as they always had, on the grounds that it would only make a bad situation worse.[20] As special attorney, Wilson would try to allay their fears and then propose extraordinary measures to protect them against what they viewed in statehood as a palpable ploy to make it easier for non-Indians to acquire what little they had left.

The Hispanic residents of Pecos selected Manuel Varela's third son, Joe, to attend New Mexico's constitutional convention. Citizens called the meeting to draft a state constitution that would conform to the enabling act's Pueblo specifications.[21] Joe Varela probably never suspected that his acceptance of Congress's terms would throw his home town into the worst turmoil it had ever seen.

But on 6 January 1912, New Mexico entered the union as a state, complete with its new and very different general laws about Pueblo Indians. Just what those new laws meant soon became evident, when the U.S. government secured a federal indictment against a non-Indian, Jose Sandoval, who had sold liquor at San Juan Pueblo. The territorial supreme court had said federal law did not apply to liquor sales to Pueblos. The enabling act said it did. Federal Judge William H. Pope agreed with Sandoval's attorney, A. B. Renehan, who argued that Congress could not impose the liquor condition on New Mexico when admitting the territory to the union, since the *Joseph* decision had already established that status under federal law. For Congress to change the law at this late date (1910) meant that New Mexico would enter the union as a state on an unequal footing with the other states. The United States attorney, Stephen B. Davis, had asked Wilson to prosecute the case for him. When the federal district court decided against him, Wilson prepared the basic papers for an appeal and then turned over the case, as was customary at the time, to Department of Justice superiors, in Washington.[22]

The trial and appeal introduced the opposing issues and personalities that would eventually lead to the formation of the Pueblo Lands Board, fourteen years later. The case also raised again the question, already elliptically answered in the *Joseph* case, of the status of New Mexico Pueblo Indians under United States law.

The issues raised by the *Sandoval* appeal involved the most delicate problem of adjusting American federalism to the contorted historical development of the legal status of Pueblo Indians and their lands. Were the Pueblos Indians or not? At this late date what power did Congress still have to say who they were and under what conditions they held their lands?

District Judge Pope had decided that Congress had no such power, not even in the enabling act. Wilson called Pope's opinion "learned and . . . distinguished," but appealed anyway, in his role as special attorney for the Pueblos. The United States Solicitor's Office took the case to the Supreme Court. "There was not a living soul in New Mexico, lawyer or layman," Ralph Emerson Twitchell, Santa Fe attorney and historian, later remarked, "who ever believed Judge Pope would be reversed in the Sandoval case."[23]

But no one in New Mexico counted on the changed national atmosphere. No one realized how skillful lawyers could bend mutually exclusive positions to make them consistent. And no one counted on Supreme Court Justice Willis Van Devanter, a former Interior Department specialist intimate with both Indian law and western property law. In the fifteen-year period between the *Sandoval* case and the 1926 *Candelaria* decision, Van Devanter himself would gradually rewrite Pueblo Indian law.

In the spring of 1912, before the Supreme Court panel that heard the *Sandoval* appeal, the attorney for the non-Indian, A. B. Renehan, ran through all the old arguments. The *Joseph* case, he argued, had decided that Pueblos were not Indians under the Non-Intercourse Act. Spanish and Mexican law had given them full civil rights, including the right to own real property and to sell it without restriction. The Treaty of Guadalupe Hidalgo had guaranteed them. How could Congress now alter those rights and, in the process, force New Mexico to enter statehood on a footing different from that of any other state?[24]

For its part, the government did not deny any of Renehan's historical argument. Instead, the solicitor general directed the court's attention to the purely federal issues involved. Congress, argued the government, had always treated the Pueblos as Indians and, more significantly, had never declared them not to be Indians. As a result, the Pueblos remained Indians and Congress retained power over them, a power it had exercised in the 1910 enabling act.[25]

The *Sandoval* arguments pitted historical fact against theoretical power. But both points of view could be true or false. A unanimous Supreme Court, speaking through Van Devanter, adopted the government view that the case involved simply the *power* of Congress to act as it had in 1910. However, in the process, the court included just enough of Renehan's history to suggest that in addition to affirming Congress's continued power, it was also rejecting the previous view and legal status of the Pueblos in the prestatehood period:

> The people of the Pueblos although sedentary rather than nomadic in their inclinations and disposed to peace and industry, are nevertheless Indians in race, custom and domestic government. Always living in separate and isolated communities, adhering to primitive modes of life, largely influenced by superstition and fetichism, and chiefly governed according to crude customs inherited from their ancestors, they are essentially a simple, uninformed, and inferior people . . .[26]

Had he known of their ways, Justice Van Devanter would have described the Hispanic people of Pecos with the same adjectives. As for the Pueblos, this decision reversed the outcome of the debate between Sepúlveda and Las Casas, in 1550. There champions for the Indians fought to have them declared human. Their victory allowed New Mexico Territorial Justice John Watts to declare that New Mexico Pueblos were too civilized to be relegated to the status of incompetent wards. In 1913, more than 350 years after the sociological debate began, Indian advocates fought to have the Pueblos declared Indians again.

Over the centuries the terms of the debate had proved impossible to fix. At Valladolid Indians had proved their humanity and had won crown protection for their lands. In the *Joseph* decision the court had rewarded their civilization by removing that protection. In the *Sandoval* appeal the Pueblos won back that protection only by proving their inferiority. Just how the three standards related to one another, or, indeed, what right a court had to apply any of them, went unasked.

As a matter of legal theory, what was left of the *Joseph* decision in the aftermath of the *Sandoval* case? The government attorneys who argued the latter appeal made it clear that they did not believe that the Supreme Court had to reject *Joseph* in order to uphold their posi-

tion.[27] But Van Devanter himself recognized that his sociological judgments contradicted those of that earlier case. In his decision he attributed
the difference between the two views to the more recent, supposedly
more scientific research on Pueblos provided by such men as Adolph
Bandelier. The *Joseph* view, wrote Van Devanter, was wrong. That did
not, however, necessarily make the *Joseph* decision wrong, as Van Devanter also implied.

Remember that the narrow legal issue in *Sandoval* was whether
Congress, in 1910, could designate the Pueblos as Indians in the
enabling act. The racial characterization of the Pueblos bore only on
that issue in *Sandoval*. Van Devanter skirted the problem of what that
meant for the earlier, contradictory *Joseph* view when he stated that
those very different racial characterizations bore not on the power of
Congress, but on the much narrower meaning of a particular federal
act, not at issue in *Sandoval*. This judicial legerdemain technically left
open the issue of the extent to which *Sandoval* overruled *Joseph*. The
Supreme Court would not have to face that issue explicitly for another
thirteen years.[28]

In the meantime, the relationship between the two decisions held
disturbing portents for non-Indian residents of the Pecos Pueblo grant.
If *Sandoval* did away with *Joseph,* then, without further qualification,
the decision would also do away with those title transfers beginning
with John Ward and the Pecos remnants at Jemez and leading to the
Gross-Kelly ownership. It might also obviate whatever claim Hispanic
Pecos might make to the grant lands on which the community was
located. No Indian alienation would have any validity. If they chose
to do so, the Pecos descendants at Jemez could return to Pecos and
repossess all of their ancestral tract. On the other hand, if the *Sandoval*
decision simply affirmed federal power over Pueblo lands, then the
decision only meant that Congress still had some role to play in the
ownership of the grant, a power it could exercise as it now saw fit,
subject to whatever rights non-Indians might have acquired or Congress
chose to recognize.

In spite of its implications, lawyers and nonlawyers alike treated the
Sandoval decision with indifference. Some referred to it contemptuously
as "that liquor case." Others regarded it as a decision on the Pueblos'
personal status, not the status of their real property. Most Pecos residents never even heard of it. But if they had, they would not have
inferred that the decision had something to do with the land on which

their own ancestral homes now stood. On his arrival in Albuquerque as the new Indian superintendent, in 1919, Leo Crane found most New Mexicans still "studiously blind to the *Sandoval* decision of 1913." Among the six New Mexicans whom he credited with understanding the fullest implications of Van Devanter's ruling, Crane included "their [the Pueblos'] former counsel Mr. Wilson."[29]

Wilson's understanding came from experience. Time and again he had taken the Pueblo land cause to the territorial and then to the state courts. Time and again he had lost, sometimes because of the antipathy of the territorial courts, sometimes because of the state of the law before the *Sandoval* decision, and sometimes because of the complexity of his own professional life. The controversial litigation over the Pueblo of Laguna's purchase of the Paguate tract owed part of its tortured history to Wilson's comings and goings as Pueblo attorney. His involvement in the Taos Pueblo's Tenorio tract suits left an ambiguous legacy whose effects were still being felt well into the second half of the twentieth century. While Pueblo advocates continued to praise him as "very efficient" well into the chaotic period of the 1920s, the fact remained that Wilson tried and lost the *Sandoval* case. When the Supreme Court reversed the district court decision, changing the course of Pueblo history, including Pecos, Wilson himself later admitted that it took years for him and other New Mexicans to realize what had happened.[30]

But between 1911 and 1913, Francis C. Wilson continued to work for the Pueblos. The prospect of statehood terrified them, even with the enabling act's special provisions. Wilson took a Pueblo delegation to Washington in the winter of 1912/13, to dramatize their concerns. At the congressional hearings, United States Senator T. B. Catron of New Mexico taunted Wilson, mocking his ideas about the Pueblos.[31] But Wilson also developed a more traditional legal strategy to allay the Pueblos' fears of statehood. That strategy led Wilson to the Pojoaque and Pecos Pueblo grants and from there, ironically, to waiting private speculators in Pueblo lands. Thereafter Wilson's private interests in supposedly abandoned Pueblo lands would increasingly diverge from his simultaneous public role as Pueblo defender.

As early as December 1911, less than a month before New Mexico formally became a state, Special Attorney Wilson had begun working with a Department of the Interior inspector, Dorr, to arrange to have each pueblo deed its remaining lands in trust to the United States. Fearing increased invasion of their land and water once their grants became part of the state of New Mexico, the Pueblos, through Wilson, sought to guarantee federal protection by this means. Wilson and Dorr visited each of the pueblos to explain their idea. Dorr later reported that at a 28 February 1912 general meeting in Santa Fe, ten pueblos (including Jemez) voted in favor of the plan and seven (including Pojoaque) voted against it. Of the seven opposed, Dorr and Wilson thought that Nambe and Santa Ana might change their vote. No one even mentioned Pecos Pueblo.[32]

The trusteeship plan was the first federal action to address the Pueblo problem. In addition to reporting to his superiors on the possibility of the pueblos deeding their remaining lands to the federal government, Dorr also suggested "that a determined effort be made in the courts to regain for the [Pueblo] Indians certain large tracts of land which have been at least temporarily lost to them through decisions of the local courts."[33] By the spring of 1912, the government would transfer Dorr from New Mexico to Arizona. In his final report he again supported Wilson's trusteeship proposal, recommended government surveys of non-Indian claims within the Pueblo grants, and suggested for the first time that

> it would probably be necessary to establish some sort of authority
> here to summarize the titles [of adverse non-Indian claimants within
> the Pueblo grants] and determine their validity and extent before any
> surveying party is placed in the field in order that the surveying
> party may not be impeded in its field work by lack of knowledge.[34]

The Bureau of Indian Affairs rejected each of Dorr's final recommendations, although as much as two years later the attorney general told the secretary of the interior that the United States could accept the remaining Pueblo lands in trust if Congress decided to take them.[35] But within two decades, Congress would finally reverse its rejection of two of the three 1912 Dorr and Wilson proposals, calling in 1914 for the surveys and in 1924 for a federal commission to investigate non-Indian claims within confirmed Pueblo grants.

Only the trusteeship proposal was never approved. But, already in the second decade of the twentieth century, the trusteeship possibility would lead Wilson away from the federal protection that plan offered, toward the interest of private speculation in Pueblo land—in particular, Pecos and Pojoaque grant lands.

This aspect of Wilson's career began when Antonio Tapia appeared on behalf of Pojoaque Pueblo at the Wilson-Dorr trusteeship meeting in Santa Fe. The new ethnologists, whose work the Supreme Court had praised in the 1913 *Sandoval* decision, had already declared Pojoaque extinct.[36] Yet when Wilson summoned the pueblos to send representatives to the February 1912 meeting, Tapia came to speak for the supposedly extinct Pojoaque Pueblo grant. On behalf of Pojoaque he voted against the deeding of his pueblo's lands to the United States.[37]

Tapia gave no reason for this opposition then. Dorr and Wilson thought that he would not change his mind. But neither Dorr nor Wilson suspected at the time that from the trusteeship proposal Tapia would get the idea of selling the Pojoaque Pueblo grant himself, to California-based promoters who already had started to move into the Pecos Pueblo grant. The ensuing entanglements would enmesh the "anthropologist" Edgar L. Hewitt, the "archaeological promoter" D. C. Collier, the "real estate promoter" Frank Owen, and the "Pueblo attorney" Francis C. Wilson in a complex web of twisted interests, some historical and some archaeological, some pro-Pueblo culture and some anti-Pueblo land, that would carry the Pojoaque and Pecos Pueblo grants through the 1924 Pueblo Lands Board Act.

After the February 1912 trusteeship meeting, Antonio Tapia was approached by Frank Owen of Santa Fe. Owen represented the Californian D. C. Collier in New Mexico. Francis C. Wilson acted as Collier's attorney. Collier was president of the Panama-California Exposition Company, the organization that mounted the San Diego World's Fair, in 1915. Collier was also an officer in the San Diego branch of the American Institute of Archaeology. In both roles he shaped the 1915 world's fair into an extraordinary celebration of Southwestern and Central American archaeology.[38]

For help as early as 1912, Collier had turned to Edgar L. Hewitt, no stranger to southwestern Pueblos by virtue of his role in founding and heading the School of American Research, no stranger to the Pecos Pueblo grant by virtue of his earlier role as first president of New Mexico Highlands University in Las Vegas, and, finally, no stranger to the Pecos Pueblo grant intrigues by virtue of his acquaintance with fellow Highlands regent, Frank Springer, James Seymour's attorney in the 1880s. The various, contorted New Mexico lines tightened when Antonio Tapia, Frank Owen, Charles Catron, and D. C. Collier, then visiting in Santa Fe, went for a ride in September 1912, possibly at Edgar L. Hewitt's suggestion.[39]

The self-proclaimed last surviving Pojoaque Pueblo Indian (Tapia), the California champion of New Mexico antiquities (Collier) and two Santa Feans (Frank Owen and Charles C. Catron) spent an afternoon haggling over money. Collier's attorney, Francis C. Wilson, had said that the Pojoaque grant could be sold, despite the fact that the enabling act had become effective six months before; the *Sandoval* case was still working its way through the appellate process. Tapia wanted three dollars an acre for his ancestral land, on the grounds that the new state was successfully charging that amount for land belonging to it. Collier and Owen said they would pay only one dollar an acre for the Pojoaque grant, primarily on the grounds that they could buy whatever they wanted of the Pecos Pueblo grant for that reduced sum.[40]

Indeed, two months before Collier and Owen had formally arranged to purchase the Juan Quintana ranch, south of Ciénaga de Pecos, where the village lay, along the Pecos River and just inside the Pecos Pueblo grant. Now the two promoters were negotiating with Juan Ortiz and his wife for the purchase of an even larger tract within the Pecos Pueblo grant, just south of the ciénaga. By early 1913, D. C. Collier and Co. would strike a formal bargain with Ortiz for the purchase of that second much larger tract. True, in the Ortiz deal they would have to offer three thousand dollars for just over three hundred acres of Pecos River bottom land, or ten dollars an acre. But the tract had been traded among Spanish Pecoseños at least since 1853 without any attention to possible Pueblo claims to it.[41] And in early 1913, no one paid much attention to the fact that Gross-Kelly had as well a very different deed to the entire grant, a deed that would bring the pueblo and D. C. Collier attorney Wilson into the middle of the Pecos Pueblo grant imbroglio from yet a third side. For the moment D. C. Collier was using the Pecos Pueblo grant to negotiate a price for the purchase of the Pojoaque Pueblo grant from Antonio Tapia.

After giving the matter some thought, Tapia accepted Collier's offer. Some money and papers exchanged hands. Like Collier's transactions at Pecos, his terms with Tapia called for periodic payments and subsequent papers. But before the transaction could be completed, the situation became further confused, mainly because of Wilson's multiplicity of roles.

At Pojoaque the trouble and misunderstanding started almost immediately. Tapia had signed a number of documents, including one at the direction of the special Pueblo attorney, Francis C. Wilson, which Tapia thought entitled him to annual payments from Collier. But when he appeared at Wilson's office, a year later, to collect the money, Wilson angrily informed him that there would be no further payments until title to the whole Indian grant had been quieted. Everyone involved had to find out how much land Pojoaque Pueblo still owned after the years of Hispanic encroachments and how much Tapia could in fact convey to Collier. Wilson promised Tapia that he would file the Collier suit by early 1914. But Tapia went to another Santa Fe attorney, J. H. Crist, the man who would succeed Wilson as special Pueblo attorney in September 1914, to see what could be done.

The suit Wilson promised was filed on 23 January 1914. *D. C. Collier and Co. v. Petra L. Bouquet et al.* claimed all fourteen thousand acres for Collier and asked the court formally to establish those rights against more than two hundred Indians and non-Indians who also claimed the tract. Curiously, Francis C. Wilson did not sign the complaint as Collier's attorney. Instead, Melvin T. Dunlavy, a young attorney apparently in Wilson's employ, said he represented the California company.[42]

The matter took an even more awkward turn when Crist and two other Santa Fe lawyers filed a twenty-eight-page answer on 18 February 1914, on behalf of Antonio Tapia, the man who had sold the grant, claiming that Collier, who had bought it from him, did not own it. Essentially the answer blamed Wilson for the trouble.

Wilson himself finally appeared, on 7 March 1914. He spoke, however, neither for D. C. Collier and Co. nor for Antonio Tapia. Instead, he answered the complaint his junior associate had filed for the Pueblos on behalf of certain residents of the nearby pueblo of Nambe, who claimed that their Pojoaque lineage entitled them to share the proceeds of the sale to Collier.[43]

At one time or another between 1912 and 1914, Wilson had represented the buyer of the Pojoaque Pueblo grant, the individual Indian who claimed to be able to sell it, and finally, a different faction of Pojoaque Indian heirs, who wanted their own share. In all this maneuvering, Wilson never suggested the obvious implication of the enabling act and the *Sandoval* appeal: no one could buy the Pojoaque Pueblo grant and no one could share in the proceeds of its sale because no Indian could sell it.

That response would come soon enough. In the meantime Wilson had fulfilled his 1912 promise to D. C. Collier and Tapia by arranging for an internal survey of the Pojoaque Pueblo grant, in order to determine just how much land the pueblo still owned and presumably could sell. To do that he turned to a young Las Vegas surveyor named Vincent K. Jones.[44]

Jones was familiar with New Mexico land grant affairs. His father, A. A. Jones, had speculated in New Mexico land and water before departing for Washington, shortly after statehood, as one of New Mexico's first senators. Vincent had helped his father, for instance, when he surveyed the common line between the Mora and Las Vegas grants and prepared plats for his father's fantastic irrigation plans.

When he came to Pojoaque, in 1914, under Francis C. Wilson's direction, he discovered that ten thousand acres of the Pojoaque Pueblo grant's original fourteen thousand acres remained unclaimed by non-Indians and were thus presumably available for acquisition by Collier.[45] Remarkably, part of the experience Vincent Jones brought to the Pojoaque survey he had acquired in a 1913 survey of so-called land ownership within the Pecos Pueblo grant. D. C. Collier had gone to the special attorney for the Pueblos, Francis Wilson, to arrange the purchase of the Pojoaque grant. The Gross Kelly company, which had already purchased all of the Pecos Pueblo grant, including two tracts which D. C. Collier himself claimed, had also turned to Wilson to establish just what that Las Vegas company had bought. In turn, Wilson had turned to Vincent K. Jones to make that initial determination for his private clients.

A year before he arrived at Pojoaque, Jones had attempted to figure out the confused situation of the Pecos Pueblo grant. His 1913 and 1914 surveys of Pecos and Pojoaque represent the first efforts by anyone actually to map interior landholdings within confirmed Pueblo grants. Government officials, in an effort to stop non-Indian encroachments on Pueblo land, had been calling for a survey since at least 1851, without response. Now those long-awaited surveys would finally be made, not to save Pueblo land but to market it.

By October 1913 Jones had finished his Pecos Pueblo grant work for Wilson and the Gross Kelly company. He submitted a map and a written report that showed conflicts with title to the entire grant the company claimed to own. The map showed the buildings of the Hispanic town of Pecos huddled in the center of section 28, on the grant's northeastern border. In orange it delineated Hispanic claims spreading out from there, east and west all the way to the grant borders, until the claims covered nearly all of the ten northern sections of the grant, or 6,400 acres. Claims by Emirijildo Vigil, as administrator of the estate of Donaciano Vigil, accounted for almost 1,000 acres. South of the Hispanic settlement, along the Pecos River, the Jones map of 1913 indicated the D. C. Collier claims adverse to the complete title the Gross Kelly company said it owned, one a tract of 193 acres that Collier had purchased from Juan Ortiz, the other an adjoining 79 acres that Collier purchased from Vincente Quintana. Together with the large Pecos community claim to the Ciénaga de Pecos, through which the river ran, and two smaller claims below the Collier purchases, the Jones map indicated that in 1913 all the Pecos River frontage in the Pueblo Indian grant was claimed by other parties than the Pecos Pueblo Indians and those purchasers who had bought the Indians' patented rights to the entire grant.[46]

Something was obviously wrong with the company's claim to all 18,768 acres of the Pecos Pueblo grant. The Jones map showed only about 9,000 acres within the grant not claimed by someone else, mostly relatively barren, high Sonoran desert plains. Jones would find about the same acreage, of the same type, available without contest in Pojoaque as well. But in neither situation did Francis C. Wilson refrain from claiming the whole Pueblo grant for a subsequent non-Indian purchaser, rather than for the pueblos themselves.

In late January 1914, Wilson's assistant had filed the D. C. Collier suit claiming the entire Pojoaque Pueblo grant. In March of the same year, Wilson had answered his own suit on behalf of certain Nambe Pueblo families who claimed Pojoaque membership. In June 1914 he filed, for the Gross Kelly company, a quiet title suit claiming ownership of the entire Pecos Pueblo grant.

Nine years later, Wilson explained to a congressional committee his involvement on behalf of Gross Kelly in the Pecos Pueblo grant suit. He made it clear that he had actually been working for D. C. Collier, although nominally he represented the Las Vegas company:

Of course Gross-Kelly's title was passed upon by lawyers when they purchased it, no doubt, and very able lawyers. In fact, I am informed that that was the case: and the title came down, they having paid taxes on it for all those years—some 30 years, I think— to 1914 when Col. Collier asked me to pass on the title and to see whether it was worthwhile buying. He had some very wonderful ideas which, if carried out, would have been remarkable concerning the possibility of its development—a summer resort proposition and also an irrigation scheme which did not prove practical. However, he

went over to Vegas and I went with him and he took an option and
paid Gross-Kelly $5,000 to bind the bargain. The condition of it
was that Gross-Kelly should bring a quiet title suit and endeavor to
quiet title to the tract so it would be definite.[47]

Pecoseños had not responded to the similar *Seymour* suit, filed thirty
years before. This time, in the early summer of 1914, Hispanic Pecos
did react. On 26 June, eleven heirs of Jose Mariano Ruiz, including
parts of the Kozlowski and Ruiz families who had merged through
marriage, filed an answer denying the Gross-Kelly claim and stating
that they, not the company, owned large tracts of the Pecos Pueblo
grant. Four days later the Las Vegas attorney O. A. Larrazolo filed
another answer, on behalf of an even larger number of Pecos Pueblo
grant residents, also denying the Gross-Kelly claim.[48] For a moment
it look as though the aborted *Seymour* battle would finally come to a
head, at least between those who had purchased the Pecos Pueblo grant
as a whole and those who had bought it piecemeal.

Then, without explanation, Wilson and the other opposing attorneys
let the Pecos Pueblo grant suit slip into abeyance. For almost two years
nothing happened to resolve the potentially explosive situation. In the
interim the special Pueblo attorney, Wilson, resigned his part-time
governmental position as Indian defender, ran for Congress, lost, and
returned to private practice in Santa Fe.[49]

As a private attorney, Wilson went back to court for Taos Pueblo
in its ongoing struggle over the Tenorio tract, winning part of the
pueblo's claim, losing the balance, and creating confusion that still is
not resolved. On behalf of the pueblo of Laguna, he returned to the
United States Federal District Court in a second effort to win the so-
called Paguate purchase after failing in the state courts. Again he lost
the case and left a situation that would later come to have a profound
affect on Pueblo land tenure in general.[50] And he continued his work
in Pecos, trying to wrest the grant from claimants other than the Gross
Kelly company.

On the federal level, Pueblo Indian affairs continued to change. As
special attorney to the Pueblos, Wilson had backed Dorr's 1911 proposal for a thorough investigation of the general land situation, including archival and survey work. Wilson had succeeded in bringing
Will Tipton back from Taos, where he had worked with Donaciano
Vigil, and had set him the more arduous task of organizing the Spanish
and Mexican archives dealing with Pueblo lands. Tipton's work, Wilson

said, was indispensable to the suits he intended to bring to restore lost lands to the pueblos.[51] His federal superiors authorized Tipton's work, but balked at approving the survey of non-Indian claims within confirmed Pueblo grants. They could not justify the expense, they said, since it was clear that Pueblos could convey their land; to whom and how much was of no interest to the federal government.[52]

Then, between 1913 and 1914, at just the time Vincent Jones began his survey work in Pojoaque and Pecos, the federal government changed its policy and finally set out to determine formally how much land in fact was claimed by non-Indians within confirmed Pueblo grants. The ultimate aim was to provide Special Attorney Wilson with systematic, definite information about non-Indian claims to confirmed Pueblo land, so that he could begin the process of quieting title in the pueblos to their ancestral homes.[53]

Francis C. Joy (U.S. surveyor), A. F. Dunnington (topographer in charge of Indian surveys), and two transitmen began the surveys in the summer of 1914 while the very different Pojoaque and Pecos suits were beginning, also under Wilson's direction.[54] Almost from their outset, the Joy surveys caused controversy. Indians and their non-Indian supporters said that the government surveyors accepted any non-Indian claim, no matter how baseless or ludicrous. The government responded by attaching to each Joy survey map a disclaimer stating that the plat was intended only to indicate, not to confirm, non-Indian claims. Even so, non-Indians regarded the Joy surveys as a vindication of their increasingly vulnerable rights.[55]

The results of the Joy surveys were still drifting in in 1919, five years after they had been begun. For the pueblos mapped, the surveys located approximately three thousand non-Indian claims to patented Pueblo land. But the irrigation statistics gleaned from those mapped claims pointed to an even more fundamental problem. At Nambe Pueblo, where 3,000 of 14,000 acres were under existing ditch, the Indians still held only 280 undisputed acres. At the San Juan Pueblo grant, where there were 4,000 irrigable acres, the pueblo retained 580 acres. So the alarming lists catalogued the loss of irreplaceable Pueblo farming land: at San Ildefonso, only 240 of 1,200 acres were not claimed by non-Indians; Santa Clara still held only 15 percent of the irrigable land within its grant.[56] It was clear that the valuable, irrigable land within Pueblo grants had already by and large escaped Pueblo ownership.

But the Joy surveys never included Pojoaque, Pecos, or Zuni, for that matter. Zuni Pueblo was too far away for the government surveyors; Pojoaque and Pecos were still outside the federal government's concern for its Indian wards. Both pueblos had presumably ceased long ago to exist as Indian country.

Special Attorney Wilson certainly thought so. While the Joy surveys moved slowly ahead, Wilson in 1916 turned his attention back to the Gross-Kelly litigation over the Pecos Pueblo grant. The fight presaged by the 1914 response of Pecoseños to the original complaint had never materialized; Wilson had simply let matters lie. Then, in the first week of January 1916, he published a notice in the *Las Vegas Optic,* as Seymour's attorneys had fifty years before, informing "all unknown claimants of interest" that the Las Vegas company claimed the whole grant. In addition, and at the same time, Wilson named over fifty new defendants and asked the court to add them as parties and to serve them formally with the complaint. Once again no Pecos survivors at Jemez were named, although the "Pueblo of Pecos" remained as a defendant.[57]

This time the non-Indians living on the Pecos grant protested even more strenuously. Some claimants said that the suit had already died, since Wilson had left it dormant for so long. Others said the state courts had no jurisdiction over Pueblo Indian lands, although they did so to save their own claims. Still others further confused the situation by asking that the court allow them to intervene as a third group of defendants. By 1918 Wilson would have to ask for permission to join more claimants and even others would also ask to come in. What had started as a complex land suit was turning into a nightmare. And still no one had thought to ask the Pecos Pueblo survivors at Jemez what they thought about the situation.[58]

By late 1918, the Gross Kelly company and Wilson had begun to take a more conciliatory stance. In that year the company began to issue quitclaim deeds to all non-Indians who claimed tracts in the northern third of the Pecos Pueblo grant—the century-old Hispanic Pecos. Some of the claims recognized in this way by the company dated back to the 1820s, according to the papers. Other claims could be traced to deeds from Pecos Pueblo itself. Since Gross Kelly also claimed the whole grant through Pecos Pueblo, Wilson decided not to push the relative merits of the deeds from the same grantor, the Pecos Indians. Finally, Gross Kelly also recognized those sometimes recent undeniable encroachments on vacant, dry land that enterprising Pe-coseños had simply taken over and tried to make productive.[59]

As a result, the Gross Kelly company significantly scaled down its original total claim and admitted that it owned only that part of the Pecos Pueblo grant not claimed by others. The decision, made on Wilson's advice, reduced the company's claim from all 18,768 acres within the Pecos Pueblo grant to approximately 10,870 acres.[60] But the decision also made possible a compromise solution to an otherwise impossible lawsuit.

On 30 June 1919, the San Miguel County District Court formally confirmed the Gross Kelly company's ownership of more than half the Pecos Pueblo grant. No other claimant now complained. The company had recognized the claims of all who had protested and of some who had not. Pecos Pueblo and its survivors at Jemez were treated as irrelevant to the division of the grant. It appeared that the Pecos Pueblo grant confusion might finally be resolved, under Francis C. Wilson's guiding hand.

There remained some ambiguities in the decree. In its own terms, the company's suit had begun with a request for the court to adjudicate all acreage within the Pecos Pueblo grant. Yet the decree covered only 11,695 acres, divided between Gross Kelly and other non-Indian claim-ants. What had happened to the remaining 7,000 acres? None of the numerous descendants of Donaciano Vigil in East Pecos had ever ap-peared in the suit or were ever mentioned in any of the proceedings. What had happened to their extensive claims, as shown on the Jones survey itself? The decree did mention the heirs of Manuel Varela, but their claims were limited to four acres "and no more." What had happened to the much more extensive claims of his family?

The decree did establish, however, in the clearest terms possible, that as far as the state courts were concerned the pueblo of Pecos had no remaining interest in the land confirmed to it by Congress in 1858 and patented in 1864.

Francis C. Wilson should have known better. The Pojoaque Pueblo grant suit Wilson had brought for Collier had inched along then had failed, with the collapse of the Collier company itself. U.S. Attorney Sumner Burckhardt, one of Wilson's admirers, had then gone to the United States District Court and had managed to have canceled, on two grounds, the original deed from Tapia, on behalf of Pojoaque

Pueblo, to Collier. First, argued Burckhardt, federal law prevented
Pueblos from conveying their land to non-Indians. Second, federal law
also gave federal, not state, courts exclusive jurisdiction over Pueblo
land questions. In 1920 the federal court agreed. Had Wilson recognized either principle, he would have realized that the power of the
San Miguel County District Court to parcel out non-Indian ownership
of the Pecos Pueblo grant in its 1919 decree was dubious and, worse,
that the ability of his client, Gross Kelly Co., to stand on a string of
purchases that began with a pueblo's sale of its own land was suspect.

But by 1919, other Pueblo Indian matters diverted Wilson's attention. In that year Clara True, that controversial, feisty, meddlesome
Pueblo advocate, who had been following Wilson's and the government's activities since at least 1911, reported Wilson's Pecos Pueblo
grant dealings with D. C. Collier to the Philadelphia-based Indian
Rights Association (IRA), for whom she sometimes worked in New
Mexico.[61] The IRA, one of the first eastern organizations to enter Pueblo
affairs, demanded an immediate investigation of Wilson's alleged breach
of trust to his Pueblo clients, on the grounds that he had arranged for
the sale, rather than the protection, of what they called "pojuaoque
Pueblo" lands. The Department of the Interior responded by dispatching an inspector Linnen, one of the "most experienced men in the
service," to Santa Fe to investigate the charges, just as the department
had sent Wilson himself, twelve years before, to pursue earlier allegations of New Mexico land fraud.

Linnen's report, issued in early 1920, was apparently based almost
entirely on Antonio Tapia's 1914 affidavit, attached to his answer to
the Pojoaque quiet title suit. But Linnen's conclusions independently
condemned Wilson for his participation in both the Pecos and Pojoaque
affairs:

> Attention is further invited to the fact that said Francis C. Wilson
> was attorney for and represented C. C. Collier & Co. in the purchase
> of the Pecos Pueblo Grant from the Gross-Kelly Co. of Las Vegas.
>   This whole transaction [Pojoaque and Pecos] shows inconsistencies
> on the part of said Francis C. Wilson, if not indeed conspiracy to
> defraud the Government and the Indians out of their lands. He
> should be prosecuted for the same if the facts will warrant. Said
> Francis C. Wilson, said Frank Owen and said Francis Delgado appear
> to have been joined in a conspiracy to defraud the Indians and
> rightful owners of the Pojoaque Pueblo Land Grant, out of their
> lands.[62]

The Interior Department forwarded Linnen's report to the Justice Department, for prosecution. In turn the Justice Department sent the charges to the U.S. attorney for New Mexico, Sumner Burckhardt, the man who had already undone whatever mischief the original deed from Antonio Tapia to D. C. Collier might have done to the title to the Pojoaque Pueblo grant. Burckhardt reviewed the report, realized that the situation was more complex than either the Tapia affidavit or the report indicated, and avoided the whole explosive issue by finding that the government could not prosecute Wilson because, if nothing else, the statute of limitations had run. The government never filed any formal charges against Wilson.[63]

The range and timing of Francis C. Wilson's roles—from special Pueblo attorney to possible felon—marked the evolution of a new context for Pueblo Indian land affairs in the second decade of the twentieth century. Outside the Pecos Pueblo grant, the federal government was becoming belatedly but increasingly interested in the land plight of the Pueblos. As the meaning of the *Sandoval* decision became clearer and as the disastrous results of the Joy surveys drifted in, the federal government finally began to think seriously about restoring lost land to the pueblos. At the same time, Hispanos, some of whom had resided on formally Pueblo land for centuries, decided that the time had come to strike back. Some applied to the Department of the Interior for patents on tracts shown to belong to them by the Joy surveys. Other non-Indians filed suit in the state courts, seeking to secure judicial determinations that they owned what Pueblo land and shared water they claimed. Still other non-Indians tried to strengthen their claims by fencing new tracts on Pueblo lands. In one instance Pueblo Indians themselves, in a rare show of militancy, tore down those fences.[64]

At the onset of these new non-Indian assertions, federal officials acted defensively. Then, in 1919, the Interior Department appointed Richard H. Hanna to Wilson's former job as special Pueblo attorney and the situation changed. Hanna succeeded in defeating at least two of the non-Indian lawsuits filed in the state courts on purely jurisdictional grounds: only the United States District Court could hear claims involving Pueblo lands. But then Hanna pressed the issue by refiling the suits in the appropriate federal court, suggesting in each that non-Indians had no rights of any kind within confirmed Pueblo grants, no matter how long they had resided there. Hanna had added three more suits to that list by the summer of 1920, each one of which rested on the same fundamental theory: that Pueblo Indian lands were absolutely inviolate.

If this were true, of course, Gross Kelly and the Hispanos then living on the Pecos Pueblo grant might as well have stopped their squabbling. None of them would have any rights, since Congress had confirmed and patented the land to Pecos Pueblo. But no court ever had a chance to decide the basic issues raised by the Hanna suits.

Instead, Congress itself stepped in. While the suits were pending, the House of Representatives Committee on Indian Affairs, chaired by New York Congressman Homer P. Snyder, convened hearings on Sunday, 16 May 1920, at Tesuque Pueblo. For the next four years the Pueblo Indian problem would involve politics, not law. Francis C. Wilson, astonishingly enough, would play a critical role in the developing legislative battle. The Pecos Pueblo grant would pass into and out of legislative focus, raised primarily as a weapon by different factions. The law that finally emerged from the increasingly bitter debate, on 7 June 1924, hardly recognized Pecos as relevant to its purpose. But the attempted final legislative solution had critical and unforeseen effects on the Pecos Pueblo survivors at Jemez Pueblo and on the non-Indians living at Pecos.

In addition, the fall of 1919 brought a disgruntled California and New York social worker to northern New Mexico. There John Collier discovered Taos Pueblo and made the Pueblos his own cause. John Collier would never be the same. Neither would Pueblo Indian land affairs or the Pecos Pueblo grant.[65]

NINE

Congress Faces the Pueblo Dilemma

As I have stated all along, there are so many things in connection
with this entire business that 20 King Solomons can not unravel the
knot.

—Ralph Emerson Twitchell

The complex legislative scene in which John Collier played opened in
May 1920 when a subcommittee of the House Committee on Indian
Affairs started three days of hearings on New Mexico Indians on Sunday,
16 May, at Tesuque Pueblo, just north of Santa Fe. No one had specifically charged the subcommittee with looking into Pueblo land problems; it devoted most of its time to other matters.[1] But the dispute
over Pueblo lands had been intensifying in the new state since the
Sandoval decision. Non-Indians had struck first. By April 1920, under
the leadership of an aggressive U.S. attorney and a cooperative special
attorney, the Pueblos had struck back. The issues were drawn in the
courts, but no judge had passed on them when, in partial response,
the congressional committee arrived to hold its Tesuque hearings.[2] As
far as the committee knew, the Pueblo land problem involved one or
two bothersome lawsuits then pending and a few instances of fence
cutting. But that impression changed when, on the first day, Jose
Ramon Archuleta, of San Juan Pueblo, and Porfirio Mirabal, of Taos,
made brief statements on the Pueblos' view of their land situation.
Archuleta spoke on behalf of Tesuque, Taos, Picuris, Santa Clara,
Cochiti, and San Ildefonso pueblos. The U.S. representative for northern New Mexico, Ben Hernandez, translated Archuleta's remarks. (The
Pueblos later maintained that Hernandez "spoke not for the Indians
but for those opposed to them and his interpretations did not represent
the whole truth.") For the moment in May of 1920, the congressional
subcommittee heard that the New Mexico Pueblos for whom Archuleta

spoke favored the old Wilson trusteeship plan, abandoned since 1912. The Pueblos did not want to become citizens of either New Mexico or the United States. They did want something done about the ongoing loss of Indian land to non-Indians. Then Congressman Hayden asked, "you want the government . . . to examine into the title of these lands and make the people who are not members of your tribe show their title. Is that right?" Archuleta replied:

> What we desire: That the government help us to secure all of the area contained in this land—that is this six square miles I have described . . . We have been informed here recently that our neighbors, Spanish-speaking people who live around here, do not claim that they have grants of the land by either the Spanish or Mexican governments. They live inside of some of our land, and, of course, we want the Government to help us out in that question. It is now in the Courts.[3]

In this, their first formal statement to a congressional committee, the Pueblo representative spoke truthfully about pending court actions. He misidentified the size of the Pueblo league and the claim of each pueblo to one. He spoke only vaguely about what in fact they wanted the government to do for them. But the Pueblos made it clear, as they had since 1848, that the Indians wanted the United States to do something about the non-Indians living among them.

That evening, in Santa Fe, the non-Indians responded. The local attorney A. B. Renehan spoke for them. Where Archuleta and Mirabal were short and vague, Renehan was long and detailed, though ultimately confusing. Renehan used much of his time to lecture the committee on esoteric points of New Mexico history and to chastise the United States Supreme Court for the error of its ways in the *Sandoval* case he had lost. The Supreme Court had characterized the Pueblos as "always living in separate and isolated communities, adhering to primitive modes of life, largely influenced by superstition and fetichism . . . they are essentially a simple, uninformed and inferior people." According to Renehan,

> In every word of that, the Supreme Court of the United States shot as wide of the mark as it is possible for any man to shoot. These Indians drive their automobiles, have the finest grade of livestock, and many of them have the most modern implements of farming. They live in what might be termed elegance and luxury, and there is not one word in that declaration by the Supreme Court of the United

States that will bear investigation . . . They have never been at any
time within historic knowledge uncivilized people.

Renehan continued at length, indirectly implying the existence of proof
that non-Indians had acquired rights within Pueblo grants that the
United States and the Pueblos were bound to recognize.[4] Finally the
subcommittee caught on. Congressman Elston voiced their question
to Renehan:

I assume from the fact that you are taking it up with this
committee—I assume that your argument is driving toward some
kind of curative act or remedial act that will fix such status [of non-
Indians' land within Pueblo grants] and fix a rule to have these titles
again investigated, ascertained, and determined.

Renehan admitted that he wanted such an act, one that would take
the question out of the hands of the courts, where he was afraid the
non-Indians might lose, and place the question in the hands of Congress.[5] For the first time, the Hispanos' intentions were clear: fearful
that the courts might take everything from them, they would resort
to Congress and legislation instead.

These developments ultimately led to the Pueblo Lands Board Act
of 7 June 1924. When subcommittee members in 1920 asked Renehan if he had a specific legislation proposal to recommend, however,
the Santa Fe lawyer had to say he did not. After the close of the
hearings, Renehan did submit to the subcommittee a copy of the
San Juan Pueblo suit against the town of Chamita and "suggestions
for a Congressional act for the Adjustment of Rights to Lands Within
the Pueblo Grants in the States of New Mexico and Arizona."[6] Those
suggestions began the complex process that averted the court decision Renehan so feared, and that culminated in the Pueblo Lands
Board Act.

His suggestions were little better than a rough outline. Renehan's
proposal called for a presidential commission to determine whether
non-Indians within the Pueblo grants had held their land for at least
ten years prior to the declaration of New Mexico's statehood, in 1912.
If they had, then the land belonged to them. If they had not, then
the land would revert to the pueblos. The state would continue to
control water rights. This solution was simple, argued Renehan, and
vastly preferable to a judicial resolution of the problem.

In the courts, the fundamental legal issue would have been whether

Pueblo Indians could ever convey real property and, if not, whether title by possession alone could run against them. A negative answer to both questions would have meant that no conveyance from Pecos Pueblo, no matter how long ago made, would stand and no possession by non-Indians, no matter how long-standing, could eliminate the underlying Indian right to the land.

Over the next four years, different sides would debate each of Renehan's points. In the end each of his suggestions would lose. But those naive suggestions definitely initiated the legislative process that, during the next four years, would occasionally catch the Pecos Pueblo grant in its grip.[7]

Of course, at the outset, no one explicitly limited the Pueblo land problem, or proposed solutions to it, to particular Pueblo grants. San Juan, San Ildefonso, Taos, and Sandia pueblos stood in the front ranks of the pueblos and took the brunt of the non-Indian counterattacks. But by 1922 even Tesuque Pueblo had begun to cut non-Indian fences on its land.[8] Emotional events had begun that obscured the awakening interest of the Pecos Pueblo survivors at Jemez in the ancestral Pecos lands they had left, long before the United States had patented the lands to them in 1864.

In June 1921 Pablo Toya, with the help of the historian Lansing Bloom, wrote from Jemez to the federal land office in Santa Fe. Toya explained that his father had received the United States patent to the Pecos Pueblo grant in 1864, shortly after the federal government had issued it. He had since lost it. Could the General Land Office send him another now?[9]

Toya's letter was much less aggressive than action taken by other Rio Grande pueblos (and the United States) to force the issue of non-Indian claims of confirmed Pueblo land and water. But the letter was striking, coming from a pueblo whose claim neither Indians nor non-Indians had considered to be part of the increasingly volatile problem.

Less than eight months later, on 7 February 1922, the Indian advocate Clara True wrote to the commissioner of Indian affairs, Charles Burke, about the Jemez claim to the Pecos Pueblo grant. At that time True identified herself as the school teacher in Glorieta, just west of Hispanic Pecos. She asked Burke if something could be done to restore the Pecos lands to the Indians, since she had many Pecos descendants in her school.

They also have a large band of descendants at Rowe, a little Santa Fe
station near here. The Ruiz family yet has some old papers written
on skins. The Pecos family, named Ruiz, has of course become
Mexicanized. Pedro, the head of the family is justice of the peace of
my precinct.[10]

No record survives of Burke having responded to True's request. But
apparently the Pecos at Jemez took matters into their own hands,
perhaps with True's assistance. They asked that the special attorney for
the Pueblos, by then the prestigious Ralph Emerson Twitchell, bring
suit, as Hanna had done for the other pueblos, to recover their ancestral
Pecos home for them. Twitchell himself never took the request seriously; he later complained that it was just another of those completely
contradictory demands being made on him by the Pueblos and their
advocates. On the same day that fifty Pecos Indians had stormed into
his office demanding that he file suit to recover the Pecos Pueblo grant
for them, delegations from San Juan and Sandia had arrived to tell him
to postpone critical lawsuits already pending on the lands of those two
grants. How could he proceed?[11]

But by 1922 the Pueblo Indian land battle had switched from the
courts to Congress, from legal theory to legislative politics. The issue
of the legal status of non-Indian claims to confirmed Pueblo land and
shared water had become an explosive one in local politics. In the 1920
and 1921 elections the New Mexico Republican party promised to
resolve the issue by legislation favorable to non-Indian settlers. New
Mexico Congressman Hernandez, the controversial translator of the
May 1920 hearings, had introduced a bill along the lines suggested
by A. B. Renehan in his statement to the subcommittee. New Mexico
Senator T. B. Catron, who had helped to arrange the aborted sale of
the Pojoaque Pueblo grant in 1913, himself introduced a very similar
bill. Each would have recognized non-Indian claims that preexisted
formal New Mexico statehood by at least ten years. Either proposal
would have completely extinguished all Indian claims to the Pecos
Pueblo grant. But Congress passed neither.[12]

Instead, the Department of the Interior, now in early 1922 under
the direction of the New Mexican Albert B. Fall, opposed both bills.
The department called Twitchell and Renehan to Washington, after
Twitchell had drafted a long report giving his analysis of the Pueblo
land situation. In May 1922 the group hammered out an administration

substitute for the previous efforts. Twitchell himself later confessed his belief that in a court of law

> I could go to trial tomorrow and by consistent adherence to and
> demand for an application of the strict rules governing trials of this
> character in ninety cases out of one hundred deprive the settlers of
> rights and lands which are honestly theirs.

Whether this blanket claim might cover the abandoned lands of the Pecos Pueblo grant, Twitchell never said, although it appears doubtful. In the legislative arena, where only differing statutes of limitation were proposed and debated, none of the proposed solutions would have addressed, let alone restored Pecos Pueblo land. Only in court, where the debate centered on whether any statute of limitations had ever run against Pueblo land, did the Pecos survivors at Jemez have the faintest hope. [13]

The so-called Bursum bill, termed an administrative measure by Fall and others, was introduced on 20 July 1922, as Senate Bill 3855, by New Mexico Senator Holm Bursum. It slipped through the Senate without much attention by either committee or the full Senate, on September 12. John Collier heard about it as it passed on to the House, and began in the fall of 1922 to organize opposition to it. [14]

Collier began in New Mexico and quickly reached out to that wider intellectual community to which he had unique access. For expertise in New Mexico, he turned to the purported Pecos and Pojoaque grant expert, the ubiquitous Francis C. Wilson. As Wilson later related the story, he was working "rather informally and for another purpose," on a Pueblo brief in the first week of October 1922, when Collier contacted him from Taos. The two met in Santa Fe and quickly composed a position paper on the Bursum bill and Pueblo Indian land. Collier then went on to California, to raise money for the fight he saw coming. Wilson stayed and "without compensation" oversaw final publication, in mid-October 1922, of the *Blue Book,* the Collier organization's basic argument against the proposed congressional legislation. [15]

The *Blue Book's* basic position, shared by Collier and Wilson at the outset, was expressed by Wilson in his initial reaction to the ten-year limitation period proposed by the Bursum bill:

> The manifest injustice of this provision is demonstrated by the fact
> that the Indians and the government have a valid defense against all

> titles by adverse possession for the reason that the statute of
> limitations cannot run against either; and yet by the provisions of the
> act the defense is destroyed and made unavailable.[16]

Of course, if pueblos could not convey titles to their land, then every
non-Indian claim to confirmed Pueblo land would depend on adverse
possession alone for its superiority. If no adverse possession ran against
the pueblos or their guardian, the United States, then every non-Indian
claim, including all the claims to the Pecos Pueblo grant, could be
defeated. Wilson's basic argument, obviously, was in total contradiction
to work he had done for non-Indians in the Pojoaque and Pecos Pueblo
grant cases.

Initially, Collier spent his time instituting a massive national
publicity campaign against the Bursum bill. The wave of opposition
was so strong that the commissioner of Indian affairs and the secretary of the interior both said they had never seen anything like it.
At the same time, Collier set out to try to organize the pueblos
themselves against the Bursum bill. Later he claimed that the initiative for the first meetings had in fact come from the pueblos, princi-
pally from Santo Domingo, San Felipe, and Cochiti, all major Rio
Grande pueblos. In any event, the Pecos survivors at Jemez were
also included.[17]

On 25 November 1922, representatives from nineteen pueblos, including the Pecos at Jemez, met at Santo Domingo, under the aegis
of John Collier and Francis C. Wilson, both of whom attended. There
the Indians drafted their objections to the Bursum bill. A month earlier,
the eight northern pueblos had met and had agreed to oppose those
parts of the proposed law which would sanction the continued presence
on Indian lands of non-Indians who did not have deeds from Indians,
a position that would not have helped the Pecos claim to their ancestral
home at all.[18] At Santo Domingo, the nineteen assembled pueblos,
including Pecos, went considerably further. The Indians objected to
the provisions of the Bursum bill which would give title to those who
had no color of title at all. They also argued that if compensation was
to be paid, the non-Indian settlers, not the Pueblos, should get the
money, while the Indians should receive their lost lands, a reversal of
the Bursum bill's proposal. Finally, the assembled Indians argued that
the entire issue should be resolved by a special commission, not the
courts. A statement was drafted which concluded as follows:

Now we discover that the Senate has passed a bill called the Bursum
Bill, which will complete our destruction and that Congress and the
American people have been told that we, the Indians, have asked for
this legislation. This, we say, is not true. We have never asked for
this legislation. We were never given the chance of having anything
to say about this bill. We have studied this bill and found that that
bill will deprive us of our happy life by taking away our lands and
waters and will destroy our government and customs . . . S: Pueblo
of Pecos. Jose Romero and Pablo Toya[19]

It was astonishing to find the Pecos descendants maneuvering on the
fringes of a battle most people assumed they had long since given up
for lost.[20]

Instead of becoming a more solid presence in the developing conflict,
Pecos Pueblo became an increasingly symbolic and divisive issue among
the previously unified friends of the Pueblos. The mounting tension
was most evident between John Collier and Francis C. Wilson. The
two collaborated for long enough to defeat the odious Bursum bill,
but not for long enough to recover anything of the Pecos Pueblo grant.
Pecos provided the fuel for strife—and that, in the end, was all.

Signs of the impending split appeared in the late fall of 1922, as
Collier and Wilson turned from defeating the Bursum bill to suggesting
a positive alternative of their own. From the outset, Collier made it
clear to Wilson that he opposed recognizing non-Indian possession of
Pueblo grant land originating prior to the 1848 Treaty of Guadalupe
Hidalgo. The difference between the two men involved that between
recognizing the non-Indian towns of Espanola and Taos, which Wilson
wanted to do, and denying the validity of those non-Indian, almost
urban claims, mostly stemming from the eighteenth century or earlier,
which Collier was willing to do.[21] In that context, Pecos represented
the farthest reaches of a possible Pueblo claim. Collier was willing to
press for the recovery of the Pecos Pueblo grant, while Wilson was
not.

In December 1922, their opponents seized on this flaw in the Pueblo
forces and exploited it. The Santa Fe attorney A. B. Renehan, an
informer for the commissioner of Indian affairs throughout the process,
began the counterattack when he responded to a pro-Pueblo editorial
in the New York *Herald Tribune* by sending a long letter of protest, on
2 December 1922. Among other things, Renehan complained bitterly
and explicitly about Wilson's apparent hypocrisy in his handling of
the Pojoaque and Pecos Pueblo grant litigations in the previous decades

and his much more pro-Indian position in 1922. The editors of the *Tribune* found the letter libelous and did not print it. But Renehan had sent a copy to Commissioner of Indian Affairs Burke, who had forwarded it to Congressman Homer P. Synder, of New York, chairman of the subcommittee that had held the May 1920 hearings, in Tesuque. Snyder then inserted the letter into the *Congressional Record*. By 1 December 1922, the Pecos Pueblo grant had become a symbol of the corruption of the pro-Pueblo forces.[22]

December had begun calmly enough for Wilson. Even Clara True, who had tried to have Wilson indicted for his Pecos and Pojoaque Pueblo maneuverings, asked him to go to Washington as the representative of all the "Indian societies so that something can happen."[23] But matters rapidly became more troublesome. The day after Renehan's letter appeared in the *Congressional Record,* Wilson wrote to the chairman of the Board of Indian Commissioners, George Vaux, to explain his involvement in the Pecos Pueblo grant purchase by D. C. Collier. Then he went on to accuse Renehan of fraudulent involvement in the Juan Jose Lovato grant controversies of the recent past.[24] In typical New Mexico fashion, the conflict had immediately become one of mutual recriminations.

Through December 1922, Wilson stayed in New Mexico, working on an alternative Pueblo bill, while Collier sought support in the East. On 20 December 1922, Wilson wired Collier from Santa Fe, indicating he would mail a revised version of the proposed pro-Pueblo bill that day. He had eliminated any mention of the Pecos Pueblo grant from the proposed bill and told Collier why in his wire:

> It is in my opinion a serious mistake to put in Pueblo of Pecos . . .
> If you insert Pueblo of Pecos you will arouse distrust against the bill
> on the ground that you intend to destroy all titles subsequent to
> 1848 held and occupied in good faith under the status then existing.
> We cannot afford to arouse public opinion against us by a
> meaningless inclusion in the bill such as would be this provision.
> The title is almost 60 years old and has not in any manner ever been
> contested or questioned. I cannot be responsible if it is included and
> I am omitting it from the copy furnished the newspapers today. See
> no reason for including Zuni. But am doing so as per your
> instruction. If you desire to include Pecos, wire me reasons.[25]

Here Wilson indicated a further weakening of the all-inclusive claim Collier had wanted to make for the restoration of Pueblo land and water. Earlier in the fall, some tension had developed between Wilson and Collier over whether the pueblos should recognize claims that preexisted the transfer of sovereignty from Mexico to the United States, in 1848. Now Wilson was worried about Pueblo attempts "to destroy all titles subsequent to 1848 held and occupied in good faith under the status then existing." Wilson referred to *Joseph;* the "status then existing" continued until *Sandoval* in 1913. Wilson's telegram obviously boded ill for the Collier alliance. As for the reasons Wilson wanted Collier to provide, in order to justify inclusion of Pecos in the alternative bill, Wilson himself only had given Collier some of his own reasons when he told Collier of the public mistrust that the inclusion of Pecos would cause.

Of course, by then the Renehan letter had reached the *Congressional Record.* Collier himself had guessed at least some of Wilson's unstated reasons for leaving Pecos out by the time he replied to Wilson's 20 December telegram, two days later:

> Bursum in conversation drops hint you have started action to quiet title in some relation to the Pecos Pueblo Grant in state court. Wire whether for some tactical reason Pecos should be inserted. Address: Cosmos Club.[26]

Misunderstanding confounded confusion: Wilson wanted to drop Pecos because of his previous dealing with the grant and Collier wanted to consider including it for the same reason. This curious exchange of telegrams ended with Wilson's 29 December 1922 wire to Collier:

> Final decree quieting title to Pecos Grant entered some seven years ago. No action now pending or intended. I do not now represent people interested in the grant. Do not advise inclusion in the bill for reasons stated by Jones for his proposed amendments, that is that it is important to avoid any appearance of litigation especially where there can be no dispute, as in the case of Pecos.[27]

Collier and Wilson never resolved the issue of how to treat Pecos in the proposed legislation. But the Pecos grant galvanized a growing tension between pro-Pueblo forces. On the one hand, the so-called radical Pueblo supporters, headed by Collier, believed in the restoration of Pueblo land, like Pecos, lost or abandoned in previous centuries. On the other hand, the more conservative Indian supporters, like Wilson, believed that ancient non-Indian possessions within land formally belonging to the pueblos but lost centuries before should be recognized, as the loss of Pecos to non-Indian Hispanos and Anglos should be. To the delight of the so-called anti-Pueblo forces, the split between Collier and Wilson became more pronounced at the congressional hearing which opened on 15 January 1923, in Washington, D.C. Once again Pecos played a largely symbolic role, emphasizing the differences between Pueblo advocates, providing ammunition for Pueblo opponents, but in no case actually taken seriously as the subject of Indian restoration by anyone but the Indians themselves and the most unrealistic of the Pueblo supporters.

By the time of the hearing, several preliminary maneuvers had already shaped the course of events to come. The Senate had succeeded in recalling the Bursum bill from the House; now it returned to the Senate Committee on Public Lands and Surveys, from which it had issued, months before. On 14 December 1922, Congressman Snyder, chairman of the House Committee on Indian Affairs, introduced his own version of the bill in the House. The Snyder bill increased prerequisite non-Indian possession from ten years to twenty years and deleted the Bursum bill's vague treatment of Spanish and Mexican land grants that might overlap Pueblo grants. Otherwise, the Snyder and Bursum bills did not differ substantially.

At the same time, Collier and Wilson had New Mexico Senator Jones and Congressman Leatherwood introduce in their respective bodies a third proposal, one the Pueblo advocates considered acceptable to the Indian cause. Where the Bursum and Snyder bills would recognize non-Indian claims after a certain period of time, the Jones-Leatherwood bill would not. Instead, the Pueblo proposal authorized a commission to negotiate all non-Indian claims that the Pueblos "in equity and conscience" should recognize. Failing negotiation, the Pueblos and non-Indians would go to court with all legal rights, whatever they might be, intact and unaltered by any congressionally mandated statute of limitations such as suggested by the Bursum and Snyder bills.[28]

The Pecos Pueblo grant did not play an explicit role in defining the differences between the three approaches. But both the Bursum and Snyder bills specifically named the Pecos Pueblo grant as one of the Indian tracts of land to be dealt with by the laws. Either the ten- or twenty-year standard proposed by the two bills would have eliminated all Pecos Pueblo claim to the land confirmed to the Indians. The much vaguer, "equity" standard proposed by the Jones-Leatherwood alternative might have left the possibility of a Pecos claim to its ancestral home. But the late December exchange between Collier and Wilson had resulted in the deletion of the Pecos Pueblo grant from the bill, thus compounding the problem of whether the legislation was meant to include Pecos at all.

The politics became more bitter and more complex. Anti-Pueblo New Mexicans regarded the Collier campaign as "the work of a few neurotic individuals appealing to the Women's Clubs of America." In an even less charitable moment, the same critic wrote the New Mexico sponsor of the Jones-Leatherwood alternative, accusing John Collier and his associates of being

> artists, authors, psychologists, soul mates, Bolshevists, socialists,
> psychotics, rightemists and the whole gamut of national neurotics
> and foreigners who try to corrode the very foundation and decency of
> the government with headquarters at Greenwich Village, New York
> and branches at Taos and Santa Fe, New Mexico.[29]

Such remarks prompted John Collier to complain that New Mexico itself was the worst place for rumors and "fables" that he knew. Among those fables, indicated Collier, was the one relating that he drew a fantastic salary and that the Pueblos, under his direction, claimed every inch of northern New Mexico, including Pecos. True or not from Collier's own point of view, Alfred V. Kidder, who had done years of archeological work at Pecos, and the trustees of Harvard's Peabody Museum signed a telegram opposing the Bursum bill. The commissioner of Indian Affairs in New Mexico saw the loss of Pecos as another part of the Hispanic "harvest" of Pueblo lands. Others cited Pecos as an example of the awful destruction worked by Hispanic encroachment. "The Pueblo Indians," wrote one Bursum bill opponent,

> are in actual want and they are surely dying out. . . . Witness the
> dead Pueblo of Pecos, the lands of which are all claimed by a
> prominent New Mexico business man while the few survivors of that
> once prosperous Indian community and the rightful heirs to the land,
> are starving in the Pueblos of Jemez and Cochiti . . .

The wave of opposition was so strong that the commissioner of Indian affairs and the secretary of the interior both said that they had never seen anything like it.[30]

A special subcommittee of the Senate Committee on Public Lands and Surveys opened hearings on 15 January 1923. Formally convened to consider the merits of the Bursum bill and the Jones-Leatherwood alternative, the subcommittee quickly became a public forum for venting the charges and countercharges that surrounded the Pueblo land question. Once again the Pecos Pueblo grant did not have much to do with opinions about the merits of either bill, although it was significant as an emotional symbol.

The New Mexican Ralph Emerson Twitchell took the brunt of the blame for the looseness of the Bursum bill. After a short introduction by Indian Commissioner Charles Burke, on 15 January, Twitchell took the stand as the bill's principal draftsman. Unable to defend its provisions authorizing recognition of non-Indian claims, in the light of his earlier conclusion that almost none could be justified, Twitchell himself became so exasperated that he used the Pecos example time and again to show how unreasonable his opponents had become.

As special United States attorney he had not pursued Pueblo litigation because Pueblo supporters had given him simultaneous contradictory messages, directing him to abandon the almost completed *Garcia* test suit, for example, while also telling him to sue to recover the Pecos Pueblo grant for the few survivors at Jemez. In response to criticism by Wilson, Twitchell brought up the example of Wilson's quiet title suits for non-Indians claiming the Pojoaque and Pecos Pueblo grants, to show that Wilson was not so pure either. When the subcommittee chairman, Lenroot, politely tried to get Twitchell to change his topic to something closer to the subject of the bills, Twitchell responded, "Mr. Chairman, I appreciate very thoroughly the position which you take, but you are not in my position." Twitchell's reputation was at stake.[31] "Under cross examination by Chairman Lenroot," John Collier wired to the editor of the Santa Fe *New Mexican,* Dana Johnson, "Twitchell collapsed and acknowledged the validity of practically all our criticisms."[32] Twitchell had used Pecos to salvage what he could of his own reputation; by the end of his testimony, everyone agreed that the Bursum bill itself was dead.

A. B. Renehan, who had helped Twitchell and the administration to write the bill, could not resurrect it before the subcommittee. But in order, he said, to illustrate the complexity of the Pueblo land situation, the committee should know about Wilson's treatment, a decade before, of the Pecos and Pojoaque pueblo grants. At Pecos, Wilson had

> brought suit to quiet title to it. Title there claimed, adverse to the
> Pecos Indians, was based on a tax sale for $1,800; I think Gross
> Kelly & Co. afterwards acquired some claim which was to be

transferred to D. C. Collier & Co. . . . D. C. Collier . . . is
chairman of the American exhibit at Buenos Aires. They [he and
Wilson] were not seeking to deprive the Indians of any property
whatsoever and I do not think Mr. Wilson was willfully seeking to
deprive the Indians of any property, but the result was in the Pecos
case, the loss to them of over 15,000 acres of land, and in the
Pojoaque case the loss of another 15,000 acres of land would have
resulted but for the intervention made by me in behalf of Antonio
Montoya, the lieutenant governor of the Pueblo and others. This is
an illustration of another proposition that I am not antagonistic to
the Indians. I want them to have what is theirs . . .[33]

Laced with half-truths as Renehan's statement may have been, it served
its primary function of disarming Collier and his associates.

Renehan did, however, touch on two other subjects that would have
a critical impact on the Pueblo Lands Act as finally passed, over a year
and a half later, and on the adjudication of non-Indian claims within
the Pecos Pueblo grant, in particular. At one point the New Mexican
Jones, the Senate sponsor of the Collier-backed substitute bill, asked
Renehan:

What do you think of the idea of adopting the New Mexico statute
of limitations and applying them to the time when they were in
force in New Mexico; for instance, prior to 1899 allow the statutes to
run without color of title but since that time to conform to the
statute of 1899?

Renehan replied:

That conforms identically to my idea, and an idea that I hope to
express better before I quit, that back to 1899 and prior there might
be a title ripened through adverse possession without color of title
but subsequent to 1899 it should be by color of title.[34]

In fact the two standards eventually adopted in the act of 7 June 1924
for determining when non-Indians had gained title to Pueblo lands
were based on those which Jones suggested and Renehan agreed to
here, for the first time in any formal discussion of the legislation. To
that extent the act as finally adopted embodied a victory for the Renehan
forces. Of course, the adoption of any statute of limitations doomed
all efforts to recover parts of the Pecos Pueblo grant for the Pecos
survivors.

But Renehan's testimony touched for the first time on an even more
arcane aspect of New Mexico land law, developed in two New Mexico

cases which had reached the United States Supreme Court—*Montoya v. Unknown Heirs of Vigil* and *Maxwell Land Grant v. Dawson.* Both cases were mentioned in both House and Senate discussions of proposed Pueblo land legislation. New Mexico lawyers like Wilson, Renehan, Twitchell, and Senator Jones knew the cases well, and the territorial statutes on which they were based. The other committee lawyers were not as familiar with this esoteric subject. Its distinctions between land grant land and other land, between color of title and no color of title, between adverse possession and fee simple title, baffled nonlawyers. But the "Alameda case" (*Montoya*) and the *Maxwell Land Grant* case were critically important to the general Pueblo legislation eventually passed in 1924 and the particular adjudication thereafter of non-Indian claims to the Pecos Pueblo grant.

In 1923 New Mexico lawyers knew that the *Maxwell* case meant that under territorial law and prior to 16 March 1899, a person could defeat the claim of the legal owner of a piece of land by proving exclusive use for ten years. Possession of a deed made no difference. As a matter of fact, the territorial act presumed that prior to 1899 the adverse claimant would have no written claim to the premises. All that counted was the character of the adverse possession: if the claimant had treated the land as his or her own for ten years, and the real owner had not sued, then thereafter he or she could defend against the claims of the real owner on the grounds that the real owner had waited too long. Although the adverse possession guaranteed the claim against that of the true owner, it also limited that claim to the land actually adversely possessed. Under the doctrine as explained in *Maxwell,* an adverse possessor could not occupy the corner of a tract, leaving the rest vacant, and thereby acquire a claim to the entire tract.

That is where *Montoya,* construing New Mexico's other adverse possession statute, differed. Where *Maxwell* gave a claimant a defense, *Montoya* conferred absolute title. Where *Maxwell* limited that defense to land actually occupied by the adverse claimant, *Montoya* conferred title to entire tracts, both occupied and unoccupied. But where *Maxwell* did not require, prior to 1899, some written document on which to base the adverse claim, *Montoya* and the territorial statute it construed did. In practical terms, the application of the *Maxwell* decision to the non-Indian claims in Pueblo grants would guarantee to non-Indians only those small, irrigated tracts which they had fenced, built houses on, and otherwise used. It would not win for non-Indians the expanses of open rangeland behind and above the occupied, private tracts. But application of the *Montoya* decision would accomplish just that. Adoption of either standard meant land loss to the Pueblos. But adoption of the *Maxwell* terms meant much less land loss than adoption of the *Montoya* terms.[35]

None of this was lost on Renehan, who pressed the House committee for adoption of the *Maxwell* standards, as the Bursum bill had in effect tried to do. Francis C. Wilson understood the relevant issues also. But the discretionary and vague Jones-Leatherwood standards, based on "equity and fairness," did not fare well with the congressional committee, which saw the original Wilson-Collier standards as much too loose. As for the Pecos Pueblo grant, it had become a pawn in the government and non-Indian effort to defend against the Collier group's attacks. Time and time again, Wilson found himself disclaiming any interest by the Pueblos in reclaiming Pecos land for the Pecos survivors at Jemez. He was led to explain the Pecos Pueblo grant quiet title suit to the committee, suggesting that his previous work there provided precisely the kind of experience that would be necessary in each of the pueblos, before the damage created by *Sandoval* was undone. He even introduced the results of the investigation that exonerated him from any blame in his handling of the Pecos and Pojoaque Pueblo grant litigations. In the end, Wilson even had to use the Pecos Pueblo grant as an example of land which should never be restored to a pueblo, under any circumstances:

> It is my belief, expressed publically and in writing even last fall that the title to that land never should be disturbed . . . That is the fact as to the Pecos Pueblo grant. It is one of those cases which illustrate our point very clearly, that the people who acquired title to those lands at that time did so in good faith and in the belief that the various cases—the *Joseph* case, the *Lucero* case, and all the Territorial Supreme Court cases—laid down the law; and the lawyers believed so during that period and have advised their clients accordingly.[36]

If *Joseph* and the territorial supreme court cases to which Wilson referred did in fact control the Pueblo land situation, then it was going to be very difficult for the Pueblos to recover much land, since most of it had been lost fifty years before. It would be impossible to recover any Pecos land. John Collier may not have had this possibility in mind at the Senate hearings, but his lawyer and chief advocate certainly did.

As the Senate hearings droned on, Wilson tried to salvage what he could by insisting that no matter what period of non-Indian possession Congress finally recognized, the prerequisite possession measuring and limiting the extent of a non-Indian claim should fall under the *Maxwell,* not the *Montoya,* rule. On all other counts, Wilson admitted defeat for Collier's original position:

> If our bill does not fulfill the needs of the situation, we are willing
> to sit down with the Commissioner of Indian Affairs and the
> Secretary of the Interior and draw one that will, and we want to be
> on record now as saying that it is our purpose here to get something
> constructive, something practical to meet the situation—and we will
> meet the Commissioner of Indian Affairs or the government officials
> in general more than half way to accomplish that result.[37]

Charitable talk from Collier's cohorts, people who had come into the Senate hearings demanding the restoration of all lost Pueblo land, including that of Pecos, and who blamed lax public officials for the situation in the first place. If there were hard-liners at the end of the Senate hearings they were now the government men themselves. The beleaguered secretary of the interior, Albert B. Fall, appeared on the hearing's final day, reaffirmed that he would shortly leave office, and stated that he would fight to the end against the Wilson-Collier version of the Pueblo lands bill.

Shortly after the close of the Senate hearings, the House Committee on Indian Affairs opened hearings, 1 February 1923, on the Snyder version of the Pueblo bill and on the House version of the Jones-Leatherwood substitute. Initially the committee had trouble defining just what the purpose of its hearing was, especially in the wake of the publicity that had attended the Bursum bill. After an executive session to consider the problem, Chairman Snyder announced that the committee would consider the two bills formally before it against the background of arguments presented for and against the Bursum bill. From the outset, then, the committee frankly admitted that it would consider any evidence related to the government's handling of Pueblo affairs. But it also considered itself free to inquire into all aspects of the pro-Pueblo group's affairs.[38]

Most of the House hearings proceeded in the spirit of open antagonism. Committee members questioned Pueblo defender Stella Atwood, head of the Federation of Women's Clubs, concerning the most minute details of that organization. John Collier accused them of trying to "crucify her" in the process. Francis C. Wilson, early on referred to as the "principal witness for the Pueblos," refused to continue his testimony, against the specific request of the committee. Wilson insisted that John Collier testify first as to certain controversial matters.[39] Increasing bitterness characterized the hearing.

Where the Pecos Pueblo grant had played an important emotional role before the Senate committee, no one now argued about the previously touchy subject. Although identified in the Snyder bill as one of the Pueblo grants to be adjudicated under that proposal, the Pecos grant was now relegated to history. A. B. Renehan now stated that

> nobody questions it and the government does not attempt to recognize the Pueblo of Abiquiu or Pecos, and to a very slight extent it recognizes the Pueblo of Pojoaque. There is not an Indian living in that Pecos Pueblo, not one. The three or four full bloods that still exist, if there are any, have emigrated to the Pueblo of Jemez and live there. In the town of Glorieta, on the Santa Fe railway, there is a great number of Pecos mixed blood but they pass as Spanish-Americans; the Indian trace is lost.[40]

Basically the other Pueblo Indians had agreed. In the only formal statement by any of them introduced into the legislative hearings in 1923, the leaders of San Juan Pueblo asked, in the House,

> Is it the wish of the American people that the last remnant of a once happy people perish untimely from the face of the earth? Is it their wish that our graves shall so soon be prepared before the portals of the centuries old cliffs upon whose walls the smoke of the ceremonial fires of our ancestors still cling, and that all our pueblos vanish into the past with the Pueblo of Pecos and others now crumbling into dust?[41]

Whatever legislative standards might once have been proposed to include some of Pecos Pueblo's land and to restore it to the moribund pueblo had apparently slipped out of anyone's consideration.

The House hearings continued on to other substantive questions besides those involving the accuracy of Collier's accusations of improper government handling of Pueblo affairs. Francis C. Wilson wavered around the issue of what time limitations the pueblos would accept for distinguishing between acceptable and unacceptable non-Indian claims to Pueblo grant land. At the outset of the House hearings, he seemed to return to the initial Collier position, announced in the October 1922 *Blue Book* and not espoused since, that the pueblos did not have to recognize any non-Indian encroachments on their lands, as confirmed by Congress. Later in his testimony Wilson acknowledged that "the settlers have equitable rights which should be recognized," and finally stated that the thirty-three-year statute of limitations proposed by the Snyder bill would be acceptable to him and to the people he represented.[42]

Despite the fact that the Pecos Pueblo grant seemed to have disappeared altogether from active debate, several of the issues raised by the House hearings had important implications for the future of the grant. Wilson returned to the theme of the two different kinds of adverse possession under New Mexico territorial law and emphasized again, more clearly, the fact that one standard (*Maxwell*) applied to land actually used and occupied, while the other (*Montoya*) applied also to those parts of any tract that were not in fact so intensively used. If Congress were to legislate a length of time for non-Indian possession to become valid against a Pueblo claim of ownership, then Congress should at least define the kind of possession it would recognize and limit it as much as possible, so that the legislation would confirm to non-Indians only those tracts actually reduced to ownership by the particular non-Indians. By the end of his extensive House testimony Wilson had repeated so often the difference between *Maxwell*-type adverse possession, under section 3365 of the 1915 New Mexico compilation, and *Montoya*-type title by prescription, under section 3364, that every committee member understood the arcane terminology. Under the broader view, non-Indian claims to irrigated tracts along the river bottoms would reach straight back to the grant boundaries, several miles away. The narrow view would restrict the valid non-Indian claims to the small tracts along the river bottoms and leave the rest clearly to the pueblos.[43]

Wilson also emphasized, for the first time, the effect of the numerous territorial and state court decrees affecting Pueblo Indian land and water. At the least, they should not bind the United States in the land adjudications to be undertaken pursuant to the congressional act. Of course, if the United States could disregard earlier decrees in general, then it could also disregard Wilson's own state court decree quieting title in the Pecos Pueblo grant to the Gross Kelly company. The irony apparently never occurred to Wilson.[44]

The other witnesses who testified succeeded only in further confusing matters. Stella Atwood testified but, according to John Collier, had become so confused she could not remember certain facts. Collier himself spent most of his time in semantic battles over the accuracy of the precise wording he had used to describe the previous performance of the Bureau of Indian Affairs. A. B. Renehan showed pictures of various Indians to prove that the Pueblos in fact had sufficient food. The Indian department brought a young office lawyer to the hearings, who told the committee that the Pueblos' water rights did not differ from those of other Indian tribes and that, in fact, each pueblo was entitled to enough water to irrigate all of its irrigable land before any non-Indian received any. In the confusion of charges and counter-charges, theories and countertheories that ended the House hearings, it became clear that no bill would emerge with broad enough support to pass.[45]

The gap had widened between John Collier's view that most Pueblo land, including parts of Pecos, could be restored, and Francis Wilson's view that non-Indians were entitled to what they had acquired within the Pueblo grants up to the time of statehood. The testimony of the two men had implied as much. As the hearings closed, the tension became explicit. Senator Lenroot, a member of the subcommittee of the Senate Committee on Public Lands and Surveys, introduced a bill of his own. The bill would recognize non-Indian titles based on written documentation in existence for more than twenty years prior to New Mexico statehood and titles based on possession alone more than thirty years old. The so-called Lenroot substitute provided for no compensation to either Pueblos or non-Indians, an element Collier had regarded as a condition precedent to any legislation. While the substitute itself did not enumerate the Pueblo grants to which it applied, it addressed "the lands within the exterior boundaries of any lands granted or confirmed to the Pueblo Indians by any authority of the United States."[46] It would thus cover Pecos and guarantee confirmation of its loss to non-Indians. Francis C. Wilson offered his support to Senator Lenroot. But he had apparently advised Stella Atwood to oppose the bill.[47] These contradictory stances foreshadowed a fatal split to come in the pro-Pueblo forces. For the moment, the Lenroot substitute indicated that the pro-Pueblo opposition could not yet rally around a unified position of its own. With the exception of the Jones-Leatherwood proposal, rejected early on as hopelessly romantic, no legislative proposal promised even the possibility of the restoration of land to the Pecos Pueblo survivors at Jemez. But like the Bursum and Snyder bills before it, the Lenroot substitute also failed for lack of a consensus.

Slowly, through the spring and summer of 1923, a crisis developed for the Pueblo legislation and implicitly for the Pecos Pueblo grant. When John Collier discovered what he considered to be Wilson's duplicitous handling of the Lenroot substitute, he fired him and hired in his place a young New York lawyer, A. A. Berle. In April 1923, Berle composed another Pueblo legal position paper, resurrecting the argument, apparently abandoned by Wilson, that no statute of limitations could run against any land confirmed by the United States to any pueblo, presumably including Pecos.[48] The Pueblo battle had apparently returned to its starting point. But now, in addition to the BIA, the New Mexico congressional delegation, and the politically astute prosettler forces, Collier and Berle had to contend with the Wilson faction of what had once been a united front.

Collier returned to the Pueblos, to try to win their support first. In August 1923, the second pan-Pueblo conference convened to plan strategy, receive reports, and to consider whether to endorse the Collier or the emerging Wilson position. All Indian Bureau personnel were barred from the meeting. No formal minutes were taken. A Pecos Pueblo representative was there, however. He heard Collier present the Berle brief. He listened as Collier outlined a strategy designed to force a much more pro-Pueblo solution to the land dilemma than any previously offered. Collier then asked for and received an endorsement from the All Pueblo Council, including Jesus Baca from Pecos. Sufficient information concerning the otherwise secret meeting reached the superintendent for the northern pueblos, J. G. Crandall, no Pueblo favorite, to allow him to file the following report with Commissioner Burke:

> A very amusing incident occurred at the Santo Domingo meeting August 23 which I failed to mention. The old Pueblo of Pecos was situated near the Santa Fe railway between here and Las Vegas; it was a flourishing pueblo when this country was first discovered 383 years ago. It continued to be a pueblo up to 1837 when from raids from Comanche and Kiowa Indians to the east, and from epidemics, Pecos was about wiped out; the few survivors left in a body, 1837, and moved to Jemez Pueblo where they amalgamated with the Jemez Indians, a Piro tribe and of the same parental stock as Pecos. At this Santo Domingo, meeting John Collier had a Jemez Indian, Jesus Baca, vote for Pecos, and, of course, he voted "yes" to anything that

he was asked. Jesus Baca is not of Pecos blood but in all senses a
Jemez Indian. In 1898 when the Court of Private Land Claims
passed on titles, the Pecos Grant was not considered. I am told,
however, that the Pecos Pueblo was included with other Pueblos
when Congress quitclaimed title to Indian grants in the 1860's. It is
86 years ago since the Pecos Indians vacated their Pueblo, and, of
course, there are none living. The local Indian associations are active
and are taking steps to block Mr. Collier, Mrs. Atwood and others.
They have with them a prominent lawyer from New York, a Mr.
Walker.[49]

Once again the survivors of the Pecos tribe at Jemez were looking for
a solution to the problem of their lost lands. Once again their guardians,
the Bureau of Indian Affairs, hardly considered them a part of the
Pueblo problem. John Collier simply used the Pecos Pueblo situation
for his own purposes.

Bitterness between the previously unified pro-Pueblo forces escalated;
the division between the Collier and the Wilson forces became deeper.
"The split I welcome," A. B. Renehan wrote Indian Commissioner
Burke, "and it is extremely bitter." By October 1923, Clara True would
call her own Indian meeting, in Santa Fe, to try to develop an alternative
Pueblo organization to the one Collier built from the August Santo
Domingo meeting. No Pecos representative appeared at True's meeting.
But A. B. Renehan spoke there, and apparently some heeded his anti-
Collier advice. By January 1924, Taos Pueblo had withdrawn its sup-
port for Collier and had placed it behind the more moderate Wilson.
Now even the Pueblos were divided.[50]

In late November 1923, Francis C. Wilson had sent to Indian Commissioner Burke a new proposal for Pueblo land legislation. The Wilson
bill called for the old commission to adjudicate in the first instance
Indian and non-Indian claims. It called for substantial compensation
to the pueblos if the commission decided, and the court then confirmed,
that the Indians had lost land. The bill defined the prerequisite non-
Indian possession in terms of the *Maxwell* decision. But most importantly, the Wilson proposal set out two specific time periods, one for
non-Indian claims based on color of title, the other for non-Indian
claims based on possession alone. Wilson's bill proposed to recognize
non-Indian written titles dated at least ten years prior to 6 January
1912 and unwritten claims based on possession begun ten years prior
to 16 March 1899. As Wilson explained, he had chosen those particular
dates in order to make his Pueblo land bill conform to the requirements

for *Maxwell*-type adverse possession, under New Mexico territorial law. This would, he said, save the legislation from a possible non-Indian attack based on the claim that different standards would deprive non-Indians of alleged property rights acquired under territorial law. Again, Wilson's proposal precluded any chance of recovering much of the Pecos Pueblo grant.[51]

Through the winter and spring of 1924 the various groups interested in Pueblo land legislation continued to maneuver for advantage. Berle, now as Collier's attorney, at first took the familiar position that no statute of limitation was appropriate. Wilson, Twitchell, and Renehan called the argument foolish at best and asinine at worst.[52] But Congress called for no formal hearings to reconcile the differences. Instead, the entire matter was referred to a special Senate subcommittee, made up of Adams, of Colorado, Lenroot, of New York, and Holm Bursum and Jones, of New Mexico. In the late spring, and without John Collier's direct participation, Berle abandoned his previous position, accepted Wilson's dates, and began to maneuver for other advantages.

Berle added significantly greater compensation provisions for lost Pueblo land to Wilson's original November 1923 draft. He also added a provision which allowed the pueblos themselves to file suit to recover what might be theirs, independent of the bill's terms. Finally, he included a provision that non-Indians be required to have paid real property taxes on the Pueblo land they claimed, before winning it from Pueblo ownership. The Pueblos always had insisted on compensation. The power to maintain suits independent of the act's terms and limitations guaranteed that the Pueblos would have to give up nothing, unless they chose to do so. Berle and Collier apparently believed that few non-Indians would be able to meet the requirement of tax payment that they had added to the bill. They may have lost their fight against a statute of limitations, but they had certainly not abandoned their position entirely.

However, the Pecos Pueblo grant was not saved. Strict adherence to the tax-payment requirements might affect some Pecos land; non-Indians were as lax there as anywhere else in northern New Mexico. Otherwise the concessions won by the Pueblo advocates added little to the Pecos claim. Indeed, once Berle and Collier had finally accepted the applicability of any statute of limitations, Pecos was largely lost as recoverable Indian country.[53]

The Pueblo Lands Act, as enacted on 7 June 1924, did not refer to the Pecos Pueblo grant at all. Like the earlier Lenroot version of the bill, the act applied to "the lands within the exterior boundaries of any lands granted or confirmed to the Pueblo Indians of New Mexico by any authority of the United States." This focus was broad and vague enough to encompass the Pecos Pueblo grant if that had been its authors' intent. But the treatment of Pecos by those who had actively fought over the terms of the 1924 act made it appear that no one considered the grant within the reach of the act's terms. Indeed, the terms themselves almost guaranteed that no recovery could be made for Pecos descendants.

As passed, the 1924 act required the recognition of non-Indian claims to Pueblo lands if they were based on a deed and had begun prior to 6 January 1902, ten years to the day before New Mexico statehood. If the non-Indian claim was not based on a written document, then the claimant had to prove adverse possession dating from 16 March 1889, ten years to the day before the territorial legislature had required written "color of title" for the first time. Under either standard, Hispanic and New York claims would prevail over the Indian claim.

The act did require, in addition, continuous payment of real property taxes assessed under local law. But would anyone use that technicality as a way for the Pecos Pueblo descendants to claim land their ancestors had left a hundred years before? And, the act's *Maxwell* standards might leave that land not intensively used free of non-Indian claims.[54] But would anyone want those rocky, barren, relatively useless acres that made up over half the grant?

If the Pueblo Lands Act promised anything to the Pecos Pueblo survivors at Jemez, it promised only money as compensation for the loss of their ancestral home. In June 1924, no one thought about how much money or to whom it might be paid, because no one at the time suspected that the act might cover the Pecos Pueblo grant at all.

TEN

Unravelling the Pecos Pueblo Knot

In many respects the problems presented in the case of the Pecos
Pueblo Grant, in spite of the fact that there are no Indians living
there, were very puzzling and quite different from those confronting
the Board in any of the other Pueblos.

—Herbert J. Hagerman

In its formulation of the 1924 Pueblo Lands Act, Congress had eliminated the Pecos Pueblo grant from active consideration. The political
process consigned Pecos to the farthest reaches of possible Pueblo claims
and left it there. When the Pueblo Lands Board formed in late spring
1925, none of its three original members considered Pecos part of the
problem the board was supposed to solve. Two members knew too
much of contemporary Pecos to include the grant—Herbert J. Hagerman, a former New Mexico territorial governor, and Roberts Walker,
a wealthy, self-styled Vermont Republican by way of Wall Street, who
had worked for a short while in the 1890s for the railroad, based in
Las Vegas, New Mexico. The third original board member, Charles
Jennings, knew too little. He had never seen New Mexico before.[1] The
Pecos Pueblo grant technically fell within the reach of the 1924 act
by virtue of being a grant previously confirmed to the Pueblo Indians
of New Mexico by an act of Congress. But no one on the initial Pueblo
Lands Board thought of Pecos as Indian country.

As a result, from its formation through the fall of 1928, the Pueblo
Lands Board disregarded the Pecos Pueblo grant. Even in 1930, after
the board had completed its work with Pecos, the chief board spokesman, Herbert J. Hagerman, admitted that the board had always been
in doubt as to whether the apparently defunct Pecos and the moribund
Pojoaque grants should be considered by it.[2]

The subject first arose in 1926. An Albuquerque attorney wrote

245

Hagerman about the claim of a wealthy non-Indian resident of the Pojoaque Pueblo grant. Hagerman responded by saying that "it was too early for the Board to pass on the matter" of non-Indian claims to Pojoaque Pueblo land. In an attached memo, the board's attorney, George A. F. Fraser, noted more honestly that "the fact of the matter is that we do not know whether we will ever hear Pojoaque or Pecos at all in view of the fact that there are no Indians there . . ."[3] Finally, in direct answer to the Albuquerque attorney, Hagerman wrote in the fall of 1926:

> Irrespective of Mr. Fraser's comments on the situation insofar as it relates to your especial case . . . I have myself come to the conclusion, after investigation, that the right course for the Board to pursue . . . is to find that the Indian title to the entire Pecos and Pojoaque grants have been extinguished. I am tentatively, at least, convinced that it has, both that the tribal organization has been long dissolved and that there are no individual Indians who have any valid claim or title to any of the lands within the Pueblo. As far as can be ascertained, all the Pojoaque Pueblo Indians, except perhaps one, have long since abandoned the Pueblo, and this one is said to have abandoned any claim therein and to have disappeared after attempting to convey the whole Pueblo for a certain consideration to a group of promoters.[4]

Eventually the Pueblo Lands Board changed its mind about the Pojoaque Pueblo grant and confirmed almost ten thousand acres to a pueblo it considered dead in 1926. Eventually the Pueblo Lands Board turned its attention to a tract-by-tract analysis of landownership in the Pecos Pueblo grant. At the outset, however, the board linked Pojoaque and Pecos. It regarded the two Pueblo grants, at most, as technically Indian land to be disposed of, rather than to be considered for restoration to the Pueblo communities which once had owned them.

Given that focus, the Pueblo Lands Board did not spend much time in the beginning worrying about how to handle Pecos or Pojoaque. As soon as the board started up in earnest in the fall of 1925, it became embroiled in battles that had nothing to do with the two obscure grants and that succeeded in diverting all attention from them.

The various factions involved in the previous congressional battle now maneuvered for advantage amidst the 1924 act's vague terms. Each did so in private. The Pueblo Lands Board would not let private Pueblo attorneys see the board's work. The board would not specify its interpretation of the law under which it worked. The pueblos and their supporters responded in kind by calling several secret councils of their own in October and November 1925 and encouraging a passive resistance to the board's deliberations.[5]

But as the Pueblo Lands Board began seriously to consider first the Tesuque and Jemez grants and then, in early 1926, the Nambe Pueblo grant, certain techniques emerged for determining which non-Indian claims the board would accept and which it would reject. By the time the Pueblo Lands Board arrived in Pecos, in the spring of 1930, those techniques had hardened into regular procedures that would have an important effect on the adjudication of particular Pecos claims.

In its first consideration of the seventeen adverse, non-Indian claims to the Tesuque Pueblo grant, the Pueblo Lands Board treated each of them as a separate case. The small number of Tesuque claims required five months to adjudicate. Now, as the Board turned, in late 1925 and early 1926, to the hundreds of non-Indian claims to the Nambe Pueblo grant, some expressed concern that the Pueblo Lands Board "would continue until 1940" at the Tesuque pace. Instead, argued the board's first formal chairman, the Pueblo Lands Board should act as a "coarse screen" through which non-Indian claims should be filtered quickly and efficiently.[6]

As a result of criticisms and suggestions, the Pueblo Lands Board adopted a bulk method of processing non-Indian claims. By the time it arrived in Pecos, the Nambe coarse-screen method had become a firm administrative procedure considerably different from the case-by-case approach initially taken at Tesuque.

The board still considered Pueblo grants sequentially, finishing entirely with one before moving on to the next. But within particular grants it no longer considered individual tracts sequentially. Instead, the board first published general notices in the Pueblo grant under consideration, asking non-Indian claimants to produce their written deeds and property-tax receipts. From those written documents and its own work in the county courthouses, the board then compiled an abstract of title to each non-Indian tract. Finally, at mass hearings at the site of the grant under consideration, the non-Indians presented whatever supplemental information they had about the history of use of a particular tract. The approach was definitely coarser. It tended to focus on tracts where there was some doubt as to whether the claim, Indian or non-Indian, met the act's terms.[7]

Other time-saving devices became established as well. Even though the act assumed that non-Indian claimants would prepare and present their own cases, the board soon found that it made more sense for it to make the initial determination itself. While the act required unanimity among board members, they soon found that it made more sense to assign one particular member to each pueblo and to make him primarily responsible for that grant; this policy was operating procedure by 1928.[8]

In addition to this geographical specialization, the board's growing concern with the speed at which it operated resulted, as time went on, in the functional assignment of particular work to paticular members. By 1928 Charles Jennings had become the board's workhorse, taking on the massive, detailed task of assembling tract-by-tract abstracts and tax statements for non-Indian claims. Hagerman specialized in water and compensation matters, leaving what he called the "title end of the game" to Jennings. The third position on the board was filled by several men over the board's life. That member tended to be responsible for Pueblo grants in which there was no particular interest and for functional work not taken up by the other two board members.[9]

In addition, by the fall of 1928 the board had decided that in the interest of economy and speed it would actively consider only those tracts within each Pueblo grant where there was some real controversy as to whether Indians or non-Indians owned it. The issue first arose in the fall of 1926, at Taos Pueblo, when the board discovered that the pueblo itself would recognize the validity of 224 out of 503 non-Indian claims there. Why should the board bother with the cumbersome abstracting investigation with respect to those 224 claims? In the name of thoroughness, Charles Jennings wanted to hear even the uncontested claims. In the name of expedition, Herbert Hagerman did not. At Taos, Hagerman's point of view prevailed.[10] From that point on, the Pueblo Lands Board settled what non-Indian claims it could, rather than formally investigating all of them. The board researched only the balance, the contested non-Indian claims.

For claims not contested, therefore, the board's process of settlement made the initial mapping the first and only stage in the adjudication process. As a result, the Pueblo Lands Board came to depend heavily on whatever maps it could find to define non-Indian claims to Pueblo land in the first place; these the board used to divide and delineate contested and uncontested claims.

Despite the controversy surrounding it in the congressional debates leading to passage of the 1924 act, the old Joy survey came to play an increasingly important role in the actual work of the Pueblo Lands Board. As early as 1925 Hagerman told his superiors that the board could accomplish little without the help of the survey. Where the Joy surveyors had previously mapped, the work of the Pueblo Lands Board sometimes began and ended with a settlement based on the tracts previously described there. In those places, like Pecos, where the Joy surveyors had never worked, the Pueblo Lands Board began by making surveys of its own to detail the nature and extent of non-Indian claims to confirmed Pueblo land.[11]

The board relied primarily on its own surveyor and on whatever previous maps it could find. The surveying of the Pecos Pueblo grant fell to Mark W. Ratcliffe. Ratcliffe had worked for a number of years on the Navajo reservation, under Hagerman's direction, before being brought to Santa Fe to assist the new Pueblo Lands Board. Ratcliffe had had little experience in the irrigated valleys of northern New Mexico and did not speak Spanish. As a result, he worked closely with Joe W. Sena, a Hispano from Santa Fe with considerable experience in local politics.[12]

There had never been a comprehensive survey of non-Indian holdings within the Pecos Pueblo grant. The few previous, partial efforts made there included several attempts in the late nineteenth century to bring the public survey lines up to the borders of the grant itself. In addition, the 1913 Vincent K. Jones survey had grossly delineated the dividing line between the Hispanic and Gross-Kelly claims to Pecos land. Within the Hispanic part of the grant, several enterprising Anglo newcomers had surveyed their large holdings in 1924. Finally, and perhaps most usefully, the New Mexico State Engineer's Office had made a hydrographic survey of the irrigated fields in the summer of 1920, in an effort to determine the nature and extent of irrigation within the Pecos Pueblo grant, but more generally along the extent of the Pecos River in New Mexico. Within the Pecos grant the investigators had found and mapped eighty-one irrigated tracts totaling 674 acres. Sena and Ratcliffe would only have to supplement that work to finish defining privately owned tracts on the grant.[13]

In those Pueblo grants like Pecos where there was no active contest over the validity of a non-Indian claim to Pueblo land, the survey often proved to be the only board work on the claim. Developing internal mechanisms of board procedure guaranteed that, at best, those initial surveying attempts would be checked by one board member only, the one responsible for the grant. The board's concern between 1925 and 1928 with rapid processing brought this situation to the Pecos Pueblo grant adjudication. The board member charged with overseeing the proceedings was Louis B. Warner.

The Pueblo Lands Board members had soon recognized the enormous scope of their task, and had therefore concentrated on administrative speed. But this concern also led to criticism of the initial members' work habits—of Jennings for being too thorough, of Hagerman for being too punctilious, and of Roberts Walker for being too often absent in New York, at his Scarsdale home, or in Europe. Jennings and Hagerman accepted the criticism and went about their business. By June 1926 Roberts Walker had resigned "against," as it was said, "his own judgment." Lucius Embree, an elderly Indianan with political connections, replaced him. The board did not become more efficient. Then, in the fall of 1927, Francis C. Wilson entered Pueblo land affairs once again. This time he complained about Embree's lack of speed on the Pueblo Lands Board and demanded that the new administration replace him in order to facilitate the completion of the board's seemingly endless deliberations. In January 1928, Hagerman was relieved of his responsibilities for the Navajo tribe and was assigned exclusively to Pueblo Lands Board work. That same month, with little warning, President Coolidge accepted Embree's "resignation." Hagerman reported that Embree was "rather bitter about the situation and particularly bitter toward Mr. Jennings and toward Secretary Work."[14]

In Embree's place, President Coolidge appointed Louis H. Warner. Warner was, reported Secretary Work, an "attorney with considerable experience and contact with Congress." At the time of his appointment he resided in Washington. Previously, he had lived and worked in western Massachusetts.[15] Now, in 1928, he came to New Mexico for the first time. Although he was the newest member of the board, he served as its titular chairman. But even in that role he tended to be assigned the work least attractive to other board members. By 1928 board practice appointed one member to each Pueblo grant. When the board finally reached Pecos, Louis H. Warner was put in change of that obscure, slightly romantic, and least controversial grant.

Warner arrived to consider the Pecos Pueblo grant after the board had been at work for three years. In addition to the practical developments that shaped its approach to Pecos, certain legal and theoretical decisions had been made between 1925 and 1928 which also should have affected its final adjudication of the grant. From the beginning of the board's existence, controversy had persisted over the question of whether the two explicit adverse possession standards set out in section 4 of the 1924 act were exclusive or whether, in addition, Congress had intended to adopt the quite different territorial statute of limitations. The board itself wavered on the issue. Finally the New Mexico Federal District Court resolved the question, when it ruled that the act's explicit standards, as set out in sections 4(a) and (b) were in fact exclusive and that the board could allow no claims that rested on the territorial limitations alone.[16]

Regarding the Pecos Pueblo grant, it would not make much difference whether the federal standards were exclusive or not. Under either view, Pecos Pueblo would lose most of the occupied portions of the grant. But if the board viewed the section 4 standards as exclusive, then it had to apply the *Maxwell,* not *Montoya,* view of the extent of adverse possession, since section 4 incorporated only the former standards. In Pecos, that distinction might make a difference. Strict application of the *Maxwell* standard should have meant that the Pecos Pueblo title was extinguished only as to those portions of the grant actually used and occupied by non-Indians.

But the board itself seems to have agreed with the exclusive view of the section 4 standards, even after it had said the opposite and before the federal district court ruled that it had to. The board's handling of the Romero tract claim, at Nambe in 1926, indicates as much. A previous New Mexico territorial court decree had confirmed almost 2,300 acres of Nambe Pueblo grant land in non-Indian ownership. A small portion of the land lay on the north and south sides of the Nambe Creek, in traditional, narrow irrigated strips that extended from the river to the ditch. The much larger balance of the Romero tract lay southwest of the creek in dry, unpopulated, unirrigated, and unused uplands. The territorial court had applied the *Montoya* standard, derived from section 3364 of the 1915 New Mexico compilation, and had awarded the whole tract to the non-Indians. Here the territorial supreme court had made its clearest statement of what it meant to apply New Mexico (as opposed to Pueblo Lands Board Act) standards to non-Indian claims to Pueblo land. Under the 1924 act, the Romero claimants could secure only that small portion of the tract actually occupied and used by them. Under the territorial standards, excluded from the act, they could claim the entire tract. [17]

Early on, the board had stated that it intended to apply territorial standards as well as the explicit 1924 act standards. In August 1928, the New Mexico federal judges Neblett and Phillips ruled that those implicit territorial standards had never applied under the 1924 act. In between the two contradictory declarations, the Pueblo Lands Board iself quietly rejected most of the non-Indian claim to the Romero tract, honored that small portion of it that Hispanos had in fact reduced to ownership, and returned the vast majority of land within the claim to Nambe Pueblo. Despite statements made by board spokesmen, it appears that the Pueblo Lands Board had rejected the most explicit territorial ruling on what local adverse possession statutes meant, well before the federal court ruled the 1924 act's terms exclusive. [18]

In any case, the combination of the Pueblo Lands Board's treatment of the Romero tract and the federal court's ruling of exclusivity for the section 4 standards should have guaranteed that at Pecos the board would recognize non-Indian claims only to the extent that they had been reduced to private, non-Indian possession. Of course, the small house lots, just above the irrigation ditches, and the irrigated lands themselves would meet this test. But less than one thousand acres in the old Hispanic village of Pecos would meet this standard. Perhaps five hundred more acres in the grant were so used. But the balance of the grant, nearly seventeen thousand acres, had never been exclusively occupied by anyone. Certainly the holders of the paper had never put their formal possession to much use.

In addition to developing a position on the extent of non-Indian claims it would recognize, the board also struggled between 1925 and 1928 to determine just what the tax payment provisions of the 1924 act had intended when they required "continuous payment of taxes" in order to sustain a non-Indian claim. The John Collier forces had insisted on those provisions at the last bargaining sessions prior to the passage of the act. They believed that few non-Indian claimants could meet the requirement to have paid all real property taxes assessed and levied on their claims to Pueblo land. The Pueblo Lands Board soon realized that Collier was right. By late 1926, the de facto board leader Hagerman wrote to Indian Commissioner Burke and told him that "not 2% of the claimants whose cases are otherwise good could possibly meet" the strict requirements of section 4 regarding the payment of taxes.[19] As a result, the Pueblo Lands Board relegated its property tax investigations to a secondary status. First the board looked to the length and nature of non-Indian possession of a tract. If satisfied by that, then the board accepted any evidence at all of tax payment, including an occasional tax receipt, an oral statement that the claimant had paid taxes, or, indeed, proof of payment of taxes after the fact. Later Hagerman admitted that in no case had taxes alone determined whether the board would recognize a non-Indian claim.[20]

Some board members did complain about this lax approach. By 1928 Louis Warner, newly arrived on the board, joined Charles Jennings in a battle to insist on a strict application of the 1924 act's tax-payment provisions to non-Indian claims at the San Felipe and then the San Juan pueblo grants. Had Warner persisted in this position and had he therefore based his analysis on the tax-paying habits of non-Indian claimants to the Pecos Pueblo grant, he would have found that a strict application would have disqualified many, if not most, non-Indian claims to Pecos as well.[21]

But the strict reading of the 1924 act's provisions for payment of property tax was forever abandoned when the federal judges Neblett and Phillips, in the same Nambe appeal in which they construed the act's title provisions, also construed the section's tax provisions in a loose way that blatantly favored non-Indian claimants. The decision obviously diminished the role of tax payments in deciding the validity of non-Indian claims. But it also put more of a burden on the Pueblo Lands Board in making initial assessments as to whether non-Indian claimants were required to pay real property taxes in the first place. The Federal Eighth Circuit Court of Appeals delivered the final blow when it confirmed the *per curiam* district court view in *United States v. Wooten*. Neither the United States nor the affected pueblo of Taos appealed.[22]

Thus by the fall of 1928 the Pueblo Lands Board and the courts had deprived Pecos Pueblo of whatever benefits the 1924 act's tax provisions might have promised for the restoration of some Pecos land to the pueblo. Non-Indian possession of the valuable, watered parts of the grant had continued for so long and under such varied circumstances that it did not make much difference with respect to title whether the board regarded the act's section 4 standards as inclusive or exclusive. However, to the equally important, though more subtle, question of the *extent* of titles recognized in non-Indian ownership, the board's own treatment of the Nambe Romero tract and the local federal court's treatment of the section 4 standards made it look as if New Mexico geography would leave some kind of land for every pueblo, including Pecos.

Even without that, the act at least promised compensation to Pecos Pueblo for grant land lost to non-Indians. From the outset of Pueblo Lands Board administration, however, controversy surrounded that issue also. In its initial consideration of non-Indian claims to the Tesuque Pueblo grant, the board awarded the pueblo $18,301.20 for the 179 acres within the grant, the Indian title to which the board found to have been extinguished and which the board determined could have been recovered by the United States in what the act termed "seasonable prosecution." In addition, the board awarded Tesuque Pueblo $11,000 more as "the value of the water rights in the Tesuque watershed above the Pueblo lost to the Indians through failure of the United States seasonably to prosecute such rights."[23] Without the value added for water, the Tesuque award came to $102 an acre. With the value added, the average came to $167 an acre.

Less than a year later, on 12 August 1926, the Pueblo Lands Board submitted its Nambe Pueblo report. There the board approved non-Indian claims to 654 acres, but recommended an award to the pueblo of $19,630.88, an average of $30 an acre, or about one-third of the average per acre award at Tesuque.[24] The difference brought an immediate outcry from Pueblo advocates, who demanded an explanation. The board offered a bewildering variety of justifications at different times, most of them concerned with the board's method for valuing water rights appurtenant to different kinds of land.[25]

But Nambe Pueblo appealed the recommendation. In the trial that ensued, in January 1927, Federal Judge Orie Phillips ruled that the board had erred in figuring the Nambe award. Land with water rights appurtenant to it should be valued, ruled Phillips, at $65 an acre, unless it was absolutely clear that the Indians had lost it before it was irrigated by anyone. If no one could remember the state of the land at the time it passed from Indian to non-Indian use, the board should assume that the Indians had irrigated it and thus make the higher award. On the other hand, ruled Phillips, land that was demonstrably dry was worth only $5 an acre and should be so valued by the board. By the new Phillips calculation, the Nambe Pueblo award increased from $30 an acre to $40.75.[26] The increase ordered by Phillips was not great. It certainly did not approach the $102 or $167 an acre award at Tesuque. But the principle was important: irrigated land should be valued more highly than dry land, and the benefit of irrigation should be presumed to have been instituted by the pueblos before they lost the land.

If the Pueblo Lands Board compensated Pecos Pueblo for the loss of its entire grant according to the Tesuque standards, the award would come to at least $180,000. If, however, the basis for the Pecos award was the judicially approved Nambe standard, then the 650 irrigated acres within the Pecos Pueblo grant would bring $40,000 to the Pecos survivors and the additional dry acres would yield another $90,000, for a total of $130,000. Herbert Hagerman announced, after the Nambe compensation decision by Judge Phillips, that the ruling was law and that the board would follow it thereafter.[27] In fact, the board never did, particularly when it came to Pecos.

But through 1927 Pecos hardly came to mind. Amid all the controversy and confusion that surrounded the Pueblo Lands Board administration in the first years of its operation, the entire act appeared to be ready to collapse. Indeed, John Collier's allies, suffering defeat at every turn, began to think of bringing those independent suits authorized by the act which threatened all the work of the Pueblo Lands Board and so worried those who hoped the act would bring the acrimony between Pueblos and non-Indians to an acceptable end.[28]

As a result, hardly anyone noticed when the subject of the Pecos and Pojoaque grants arose in the fall of 1926. Hagerman treated the casual non-Indian inquiries as a nuisance. He obviously did not contemplate a tract-by-tract adjudication of either Pecos or Pojoaque. By 1928 Hagerman's irritation had increased. He wrote Indian Commissioner Burke that "there are left the pueblos of Laguna, Pojoaque and Pecos which will have to be taken care of in some way." By 1931 the Pueblo Lands Board had extinguished the entire Pecos Pueblo claim to its ancestral grant in an intricate, tract-by-tract treatment of non-Indian claims to Pecos and had also dealt with the Pojoaque Pueblo grant.[29]

The Pecos Pueblo survivors at Jemez did not bring about this apparent reversal in the planned treatment of two Indian communities, both of which were regarded as extinct and therefore not within the purview of the 1924 act. Despite their appearance at various all-Pueblo councils, no Pecos representatives ever publicly suggested to the Pueblo Lands Board any course of action with respect to the Pecos Pueblo grant. Indeed, prior to 1928 John Collier himself received only one communication regarding Pecos. "One of our officials died today," wrote Jemez Pueblo Lieutenant Governor J. M. Baca to Collier, on 15 April 1926,

> like our dear brother Antonio Romero. He was interested in our land fight but is strange the nature God has taken away from us. He was our advisor and wisdom. Also the direct descending of the Old Pueblo Pecos. The head man of Pecos, acting governor. Sad news I'm afraid but God almighty will heal all sorrow.[30]

Six years later Baca wrote Collier again, saying he was glad to hear of the money that the Pueblo Lands Board had awarded Pecos Pueblo for the loss of its ancestral home, and informing Collier that no one at Jemez Pueblo had even been notified of the board's investigations into and rulings on the Pecos Pueblo grant. From the beginning, the Pecos survivors at Jemez had not moved the Pueblo Lands Board to consider the Pecos Pueblo grant at all or to rule on it in any particular way.[31]

The non-Indian claimants to Pecos Pueblo grant lands did not show much more interest. Hispanic Pecoseños only once wrote to the Pueblo Lands Board about their homes. Anglo claimants were a bit more involved. Besides the early 1926 inquiry that set Herbert Hagerman to thinking about Pecos in the first place, only a few post-1928 responses to Pecos Pueblo grant claims survive. In one the country and western singer Tex Austin, who had succeeded to the large interest in the grant confirmed in the Gross Kelly company in 1919, wrote directly to Hagerman, addressing him as "Dear Gov" and asking him how the Pecos Pueblo grant business was proceeding. In another the Atchison, Topeka and Santa Fe Railroad, which claimed a right-of-way through the western edge of the grant, formally approached the board about Pecos, as it did concerning each of the Pueblo grants through which its line ran. The railroad submitted plats and a formal request for confirmation. So too did the American Metals Co., which had built a mill within the grant for copper mined farther up the Pecos Canyon.[32] Otherwise, no one pressured the Pueblo Lands Board to include Pecos in its deliberations.

Instead, the actual impetus for such action came from within the board itself. By the fall of 1928, just as Louis Warner came to the board as its third member, Herbert Hagerman recognized that he would have to do something with the bothersome Pojoaque and Pecos grants:

> The matter is more one of policy and a proper interpretation of the historical facts, perhaps, than anything else. Mr. Warner, the chairman of the Board, has been carefully looking into these complicated situations, and he recently has been at Zuni . . . Mr. Warner has also given a good deal of attention to the Pecos situation which, as you know, is confusing.[33]

What Burke knew of Pecos, he had learned in the 1923 congressional battle between his Indian office and Francis C. Wilson. What Warner knew of Pecos, he had learned between his arrival in Santa Fe, in the spring of 1928, and the time that fall when Hagerman reported on the situation to his superiors. "I have talked," Warner reported, "with some of the Pecos Indians. They tell me that with their inter-marrying, they and their children number about 114 people . . ." (Warner did not say what the Pecos people at Jemez told him they wanted.) In addition, he had gone so far as to write to a University of Texas history professor to ask if the fact that Pecos lay on the east side of the Rio Grande, and therefore within the historic claim of the Republic of Texas, would make any difference to the status of Indian land there. The professor responded, almost scornfully, that it would not.[34]

Sometime during the same period, Warner consulted experienced New Mexico attorneys, including Collier's associate Richard Hanna, about the Pecos Pueblo situation. "Mr. Warner," Hanna reported to Collier,

> has become very interested in the Pecos Pueblo situation and has for the past month been conducting an independent study of old Mexican land grant law, as it would apply to the questions raised by the history of the Pecos Pueblo. I have gone over the situation with him and he seems to feel that a rather sizeable compensation should be made to the remnants of the Pecos Pueblo tribe, which might be possible in the form of a purchase of land adjacent to the Jemez Pueblo for the Pecos Indians to live on.[35]

Even Hanna assumed that the Pecos survivors would recover no land.

Warner's labors bore fruit in an internal Pueblo Lands Board memorandum sometime in the summer of 1928. Eight legal pages long and characterized by half-truths about the Pecos Pueblo grant, the Warner memorandum became the apparent basis for subsequent Pueblo Lands Board dealings with the Pecos Pueblo grant. Warner had discussed, he wrote, with Department of the Interior attorneys, the problem of the 1864 United States patent to the Pueblo de Pecos. The federal attorneys had suggested that the "Pueblo" in the patent referred to any old Spanish town, rather than an Indian community. Hispanic Pecos had attempted that ploy in its unsuccessful 1896 incorporation effort. All available evidence suggested the folly of that approach. Still, Warner suggested in his memorandum, "the 'town' idea" was intriguing.

At least Warner's conclusion was one that the Pueblo Lands Board and its government attorneys could accept:

> It does not seem reasonable under any theory that I can think of,
> that the Pecos Indians have any interest now which could be
> recovered in a Court proceeding. In view of the action of Congress in
> confirming this grant, at least by implication, if not actually, to the
> few remaining Pecos Indians who were then residing at Jemez, the
> Government undertook to assume a position that it did not seem to
> protect insofar as the Indians were concerned. It would seem
> therefore that there was a liability there for their neglect so to do and
> that liability should be the basis for an award. Just what the basis
> should be must be determined . . . This seems to be a case where if
> the earliest recommendations of Indian officials had been followed,
> that this grant would definitely have been recovered to the Pueblo
> and held in their interest.[36]

In other words, none of the Pecos Pueblo grant could be recovered for the Pecos survivors at Jemez. But the Pueblo Lands Board could blame the loss on the United States government. That blame, at best, could provide the basis for a monetary award. Warner's conclusion confirmed everyone's previous assumption: Pecos Pueblo had lost its land to non-Indians.

Warner's conclusion also confirmed his own image among New Mexicans as a slight eccentric. Warner's intense interest in the almost dead issue of the Pecos Pueblo grant won him a nickname with his Pueblo Lands Board coworkers. Alongside Jennings "the mole," and Hagerman "the statesman" sat Warner "the historian."[37]

Each of these nicknames bore derogatory connotations. Jennings worked too hard and saw too little. Hagerman was given to platitudes. Warner was too devoted to archaic questions like Mexican land grant law and the Pecos Pueblo grant itself. While Hagerman engaged in national politics, Warner contributed articles to the *New Mexico Historical Review*. He confirmed his image in the popular mind after the Pueblo Lands Board finished its work, in 1932, by writing, in 1933, a sometimes incomprehensible biography of New Mexico's Archbishop Lamy.[38]

In the fall of 1928, Warner's almost immediate interest in the Pecos Pueblo grant attracted the notice of the Pueblo Lands Board's various Washington supervisors. Sometime in the summer of 1928, Albert Finney, a first assistant secretary of the interior, visited New Mexico to check on the work of the board. On his tour there, he noticed the tracts of non-Indian land that were unsurveyed and unaccounted for in the Pojoaque and Santa Clara Pueblo grants. Finney believed it to be the board's duty to resolve, once and for all, the question of all non-Indian claims to all land confirmed to the Pueblos by the United States. Finney so informed the board. By January 1929, the board had surveyed the non-Indian claims at Santa Clara and had arranged for a survey at Pojoaque.[39]

As in years past, however, attention to the Pojoaque situation brought Pecos back to mind. In November 1928, Hagerman wrote to Secretary of the Interior West. He suggested a full Pueblo Lands Board meeting in Washington to consider other issues, and concluded by mentioning that

> There is too the question of who are to be the beneficiaries in the cases of Pojoaque and Pecos where there are no Indians left, in case the Board, after going into these Pueblos, finds some of the land not extinguished.[40]

Evidently the board had already committed itself to adjudicate the Pecos Pueblo grant by late 1928 and was also still open to the possibility of restoring some land to Pecos Pueblo.

Two months later, in early 1929, when he sent in his Pecos Pueblo memorandum, Louis Warner was not nearly so sanguine about such a possibility. "Is it your idea," he asked Finney,

> that we [the Pueblo Lands Board] should in some way determine the present holders of this area [the Pecos Pueblo grant] as a basis for their getting patents? Under all the facts, of which the skeleton is given above, it does not seem that the Indians have any prospect of making recovery of this land at this late date. It is a question of how far we should go toward determining the present occupant; and also another question, as to just where the balance of the area has gone which is not covered by the decree [the 1919 Gross-Kelly quiet title decree] referred to above.[41]

Possibly, argued Warner, if Indian title to the entire Pecos Pueblo grant was to be extinguished, leaving no land in the pueblo's ownership, then the government could so state for the entire grant, without bothering to identify each individual tract and owner as well. Then the government would not have to sift through Indian and non-Indian parcels, as it had to do where some land was left in Pueblo ownership and other land was awarded to non-Indian claimants. Warner's blanket approach appealed to Indian officials concerned with economy. Charles Burke, still commissioner of Indian affairs, responded to Warner's question as follows:

> it is clear from the foregoing that the Board should make such investigation of the Pecos Pueblo Grant as may be necessary to ascertain whether or not they shall exclude it from their report as provided in section 2, supra—in which case no further action would seem to be required. On the other hand, should the claimants fail to establish good title to all of the lands, then the Board should under the Act cited, make investigation and report as usual in Pueblo lands of such status.[42]

Of course, Burke's suggested procedure actually reversed the board's established methods. Instead of beginning with a survey, as the board had done, the Burke proposal would have started with an assessment of whether any Pueblo claim to the land remained. If no valid claim remained, then the board would not have to go to the trouble of segregating by survey good non-Indian claims from bad ones.

Had the Pueblo Lands Board followed this suggestion at Pecos, the grant's disposition would have been set: Louis Warner had already determined that no Pecos Pueblo grant land would be restored to the Pecos survivors at Jemez. The United States, as guardian of the Indians, could have abandoned all interest in the grant, without the necessity of saying to exactly which owners. However, at the Washington meeting in the spring of 1929, suggested by Hagerman and Jennings, Assistant Secretary Finney instructed the Pueblo Lands Board to proceed with the Pecos Pueblo grant exactly as it had with all the other Pueblo grants it had considered prior to 1928.[43]

No contemporaneous record survives to indicate why Finney reached that decision. By March 1929, Hagerman reported laconically to the new secretary of the interior, Ray Lyman Wilbur, that his board now had the "inactive Pueblos of Pecos and Pojuaque [sic] on its agenda, awaiting adjudication." On 21 March 1929, Warner wrote to the cadastral engineer Guy Harrington, asking him "to survey by metes and bounds all tracts and parcels of land within the Pecos Pueblo grant which are claimed by non-Indians, to enable the Pueblo Lands Board to adjudicate the titles of said holdings." By 1933 other federal officials, then charged with neglecting both Indian and non-Indian interests in the administration of the 1924 Pueblo Lands Act, would point to the government's meticulous (and unnecessary) tract-by-tract designation of non-Indian ownership within the Pecos Pueblo grant as a prime example of the Pueblo Land Board's concern for and fairness to non-Indian interests.[44]

The decision to treat the Pecos Pueblo grant formally brought the entire Pueblo Lands Board procedure, as developed and shaped to that point, to bear on Pecos land. To begin with, there were the maps of non-Indian claims in the Pecos Pueblo grant. The board's surveyor, Ratcliffe, and translator, Sena, did not have the Joy survey to rely on in Pecos. If the board followed established procedure, Ratcliffe and Sena would first assemble what other surveys covering Pecos they could find. Then they would travel to the grant itself and establish the corners of the private tracts claimed by non-Indians. Finally the United States cadastral engineer surveyors would come and formally connect the Sena-Ratcliffe corners. The process would result in formal plat maps, showing by metes and bounds the configuration of each non-Indian claim, identified by number as a certain private claim to the Pecos Pueblo grant.[45]

At the same time, the board's established procedure would call for the assembly of title documents relating to non-Indian claims within the Pecos grant. As a result of the federal district court's 1928 ruling on the 1924 act's tax provisions, the burden had switched from the claimant to the board to prove whether non-Indian claimants met the act's requirements. Charles Jennings ended up in the courthouses of the various counties where Pueblo grants were located, himself searching for evidence of tax payments by claimants. Otherwise, the board depended on the claimants themselves to produce deeds or other evidence justifying their claim to Pueblo land. Those documents, together with the results of the tax research, would be assembled into formal abstracts and assigned to each tract identified on the new survey.[46]

Finally, one board member would convene the now-standard hearings on the site of the grant itself. Individual non-Indian claimants would appear whenever there was any dispute about the status of their claims to the tract. There they would supplement the formal record with oral testimony as to the history of non-Indian possession and use of the tracts claimed. In most cases, the Pueblo Lands Board recorded the testimony and later transcribed it for its own files.[47]

At the Pecos Pueblo grant, the process began according to board procedure when Ratcliffe and Sena went to Pecos in early summer 1929. They had to "make maps of the various areas with all of the adverse claims accurately charted. None of these claims correspond to government sectional surveys and a great many of them are very irregular in shape."[48] The intricate, detailed maps of the 1920 Pecos River hydrographic survey helped. But those maps identified water rights, not property ownership. While they showed individual irrigated tracts as private property, they did not confer that status on them. What were Sena and Ratcliffe to make of the Pecos custom of regadillos, that intimate form of land ownership still alive in 1929, which held that irrigated land was private in the growing season and otherwise public?

There was much less to go on outside of the irrigated acres. The Jones survey of 1913, on the west side of the Pecos River, did show the existing east-west fence that for years had marked the Pecos Pueblo grant dividing line between the outside claim to the entire grant and Hispanic Pecos's centuries-long possession of the northern part of it. But north of that line and west of the irrigated fields and houses, neither formal surveys nor ancient fences divided the high, dry, relatively barren land.

Similarly, east of the river the U.S. Forest Service had built a north-running fence around the turn of the century, to mark the dividing line between Pecos Pueblo grant land, to the west, and the forest reserve, to the east. For the more than two miles between that Forest Service fence and the fences that sometimes divided the houselots and irrigated fields east of the river, once again nothing indicated private property lines.[49]

These large expanses of unfenced uplands still reflected Pecos communal ownerhsip of land. Terrain good primarily for animal grazing and occasional piñon and firewood gathering—important economic activities even in the 1930s—belonged to Pecos as a community, because that land did not depend on intensive, individual labor to yield its bounty.

That traditional areal configuration within the Pecos Pueblo grant duplicated the situation which *Montoya v. Unknown Heirs of Vigil* addressed. Under the *Montoya* rule, the adverse possession by, for example,

East Pecos Hispanos, huddled along the margins of the rivers, would extend to the formal grant boundary, more than two miles away. The drafters of the 1924 Pueblo Lands Act had rejected this *Montoya* rule, in favor of the much more restricted *Maxwell* interpretation. Strict application of the *Maxwell* rule as applied by the Pueblo Lands Board in the case of the Nambe Romero tract would have returned the communal uplands to Pecos Pueblo.

But once the Pueblo Lands Board and Louis Warner had decided that all Pecos Pueblo claims to its grant should be extinguished, there was no way to apply the *Maxwell* rule to either Hispano or Anglo land use there. Clearly, large parts of the Gross Kelly company's one-half of the grant had not been used at all and could revert to the pueblo. Clearly, large parts of Hispanic Pecos east and west of the river fell to individual Hispano claimants only under the *Montoya* rule, discredited by Congress and rejected by the Pueblo Lands Board. But if neither Pecos Pueblo nor individual non-Indian claimants owned the communally held and used portions of the Pecos Pueblo grant, who did? Pecoseños themselves had rejected the 1896 attempt to incorporate the grant in order to create a formal entity which could hold, manage, and own the uplands. There was no other formal Pecos organization that might perform that function. So to achieve its purposes of extinguishing all Pueblo claim to the Pecos Pueblo grant, the Pueblo Lands Board, in an unannounced but total about-face, applied the *Montoya* view of real property law and ecology to Pecos.

None of these finer points occurred to Ratcliffe and Sena when they arrived in Pecos, in the early summer of 1929. They were probably happy enough to find themselves the residual beneficiaries of previous work by Gross Kelly, the state engineer, and a few others who surveyed individual tracts in the grant. For the balance of claims there, Ratcliffe and Sena did what they had done in previous grant work where the Joy surveyors had not come before them. First they sent for the leaders of the community. Then they walked the grant, as the local leaders showed the two Pueblo Lands Board employees the boundaries and corners of the private claims.[50]

In East Pecos, Sena and Ratcliffe selected Octaviano Segura, Donaciano Vigil's son-in-law, to help with the work. Segura, smart, cagey, and progressive, understood the Pueblo Lands Board's problem with the communal claims to the uplands. He cooperated in agreeing that each East Pecos resident's individual claim ran from the Pecos River almost two miles east, to the grant boundary itself. As the northernmost resident of the area purchased by his father-in-law from Preston Beck, Jr., sixty-five years before, Segura found himself in a position to suggest to the board surveyors that the almost three hundred acres at the north end of East Pecos, above the community irrigation ditch, now belonged to him, for lack of any other owner. Pecoseños in fact called the tract "la merced de Donaciano Vigil" (Donaciano Vigil's land grant). But as far as the Pueblo Lands Board was concerned, the large tract belonged to Octaviano Segura, as his private property.[51]

The other East Pecos heirs of Donaciano Vigil agreed that their lands ran from the river to the grant boundary in narrow, very long strips. No upland fences indicated such a division of Pecos properties. But when Ratcliffe, Sena, and Segura had finished with East Pecos, in the summer of 1929, the privitization of land there was more or less complete. It took another thirty years for the legal idea to take practical hold. But in East Pecos, at least, the Pueblo Lands Board maps of non-Indian claims closely resembled the maps of the Alameda Grant, confirmed in *Montoya v. Unknown Heirs of Vigil* and rejected in the 1924 act.[52]

The land within Hispanic Pecos to the west of the river could not be treated the same way. There irrigated tracts could not be extended west to the grant boundary, more than five miles away, without running into other obviously private tracts of land. Houses and gardens, for example, huddled around the arroyo north of the pueblo ruins, between the river, on the east, and the grant boundary, on the west.[53] Small settlements were located near the headwaters of other intermittent, tributary water sources. La Joya, La Cueva del Dentro, and La Cueva Gonzales each had 1929 local identities as established as that of the village of Pecos itself. Such random, scattered settlements must have made surveying Pecos west of the river and north of Tex Austin's fence look like a nightmare.

Once again, Sena and Ratcliffe enlisted prominent local help to find the corners of the private lots west of the river. This time the two Pueblo Lands Board surveyors turned to Jose C. Rivera, long-time *patron* of the Rincon settlement, in northern Pecos, and Manuel Varela y Gonzales, the original Manuel Varela's grandson, a partner in Rivera's various enterprises and a Pecos *rico* in his own right.[54] Rivera and Varela helped the surveyors do their work and took care of themselves as well.

Varela did so by making sure that those vast, little-used upland tracts to the west of his grandfather's irrigated land were surveyed so that they came back into his family's ownership. Where the 1919 decree in the Gross-Kelly litigation had recognized the Varela claim to "no more" than four acres, the Varela corners set out by Manuel Varela y Gonzales, Sena, and Ratcliffe eventually enclosed at least 111 acres of Pecos Pueblo grant land.[55]

Jose C. Rivera played his part by claiming tracts long regarded by the Pecos community as vacant land, open to appropriation by those in need. For example, Rivera bought from Cresencio Lopez a 64 acre tract west of and above the West Pecos settlements, just before Sena and Ratcliffe arrived. He must have known that Lopez had never bought the tract he occasionally used to dry-farm corn. He simply used it. But by the time of the government surveys, Jose C. Rivera had a deed for it. No one in Pecos could contest that.[56]

In the far northwestern reaches of the Pecos Pueblo grant there were three sizable mountainous tracts whose owners could not be identified by anyone. Otherwise the three Pecos men and the two Pueblo Lands Board employees found private owners for each tract. Ratcliffe then mapped in a preliminary way the corners set for each tract, assigned a private claim number to each parcel, and waited for the next step of the established board techniques for the adjudication of grant claims.[57]

In the normal course of Pueblo Lands Board investigations, that next step would have involved the preparation of abstracts of title and real property tax abstracts for each of the non-Indian claimed tracts within the grant. The internal files of the Pueblo Lands Board indicate that workhorse Charles Jennings did go for a short time to the San Miguel County courthouse, in the summer of 1929, to begin this work there. The surviving record indicates that Jennings found the Pecos Pueblo grant tax records in as confused a state as he had found those of the other northern counties. For days Jennings worked on a 40 acre claim by Pedro Ruiz, identified on the 1913 Jones survey as lying just inside the Pecos Pueblo grant's southern boundary. After finding some records of some taxes paid by some Ruiz for some acreage in the Pecos Pueblo grant, Jennings gave up. Thereafter, the working papers of the Pueblo Lands Board show a listing by private claim number and owner. The next column simply notes, "No abstract prepared."[58]

That left the oral hearings. By February 1930, Jennings had advised Hagerman that the board's upcoming work would involve hearings at

Pecos "which Warner and I have agreed can be disposed of in short order." The formal Pecos plat maps, he thought, would not be ready until June or July 1930. But, in the meantime, the board could go ahead at Pecos with the preliminary Ratcliffe drawings.[59]

In March 1930, board employees published notices around the Pecos area advising residents to present their claims for the tracts designated by Ratcliffe. On 20 April 1930, the notices said, the Pueblo Lands Board would consider those claims at the original Adelo store, on the west side of the Pecos River, across the road from St. Anthony's church. This notice did not threaten the existence of Hispanic Pecos, as the nineteenth-century notice of claims had. Still, no one thought to advise the Pecos survivors at Jemez Pueblo of the hearings. No one said anything to the Collier group's attorneys. They had turned their backs on the board's administrative hearings after 1928, deciding instead to contest matters in the courts.[60]

Just six days before the hearings opened in Pecos, the Eighth Circuit Court of Appeals had dealt Pueblo advocates an enormous blow when it confirmed and extended the ruling of the New Mexico district court judges Phillips and Neblett, on the tax-payment question under the 1924 act. Now the appeals court ruled that any non-Indian claimant could meet the 1924 act's property tax requirements by paying those taxes at any time, even after the board's hearings. The ruling nullified whatever promise the original act's tax provisions had held for restoring more Pueblo land.[61]

When the Adelo store opened on 20 April 1930 and the non-Indian claimants marched in to speak up for their century-old possession of what the government still called Indian country, there was no question of who would win. Pecos residents and other claimants had no need to present a case. No one thought to keep a record of the hearing. The entire Pecos Pueblo grant was treated as those parts of Taos had been where the pueblo stipulated that it wanted to make no claim adverse to Hispano ownership.[62] Those non-Indian Pecos Pueblo grant claimants who wanted to make a special case—the AT&SF railroad, American Metals, and Tex Austin, for example—already had done so by mail.[63] For the most part, Pecoseños simply signed up for different tracts of land. Indeed, some of those who could not attend the meeting for one reason or another wrote in afterwards to claim their designated tracts as if from a mail-order house. For example, on 21 April 1930, the day after the Pecos hearings, Manuel Quintana wrote to the Pueblo Lands Board, in elegant English:

> Gentleman: I am today reporting the pieces of land I have in the Pecos Grant as I could not present myself to you on the 21st. The following are the pieces of land: P.C. 302—6.93 acres; P.C. 303—16.20 acres; P.C. 314—0.32 acres; P.C. 316—.008 acres.

On the next day Louis Warner replied. The board would honor Quintana's request; but what was his wife's name? The patent extinguishing the Pecos Pueblo Indian title had to be correctly made.[64] At Pecos the Pueblo Lands Board did not function to determine whether the Pecos Pueblo had lost the tract, but rather how and to whom.

The board's method left the latter decision to Pecos citizens. Individual house lots and the small irrigated tracts connected to them did not create any problems. Everybody in Pecos knew exactly who owned them, despite the fact that most were not fenced. In other instances, where land had been inherited but never partitioned formally or informally between family heirs, family members got together and agreed to send one member to the board to speak for all of them. In other instances, entire Pecos clans united in applying for a single patent to large, unoccupied tracts in the Pecos Pueblo grant's uplands.[65]

The years to come would bring problems to these home-grown solutions. Families sometimes turned against each other when subsequent generations would not honor the representative capacity in which one member supposedly took the patent for all. A Pueblo Lands Board patent to "the Heirs of Donaciano Vigil," a man who had died sixty years before and left two generations of subsequent heirs, none of whom had been formally located or designated, made title to some tracts more confused than they had ever been. But the board accomplished what it had set out to do: somehow to extinguish all Indian claims to the Pecos Pueblo grant. If, in the process of doing so, the board turned public Pecos land into private Pecos land as well, that was not the board's concern.[66]

In the end, the Pueblo Lands Board extinguished the entire Indian claim to the Pecos Pueblo grant in 339 carefully described, separate tracts of land, almost all with an identified non-Indian owner. The number and extent of small Pecos house and garden holdings conformed to the general pattern established in other pueblos considered by the

board. But the Pecos adjudication also involved many more confir-
mations to non-Indians of larger tracts of land than had occurred in
any other Pueblo grant.

That Pecos involved the extinguishment of an entire Pueblo grant
guaranteed the transfer of those larger tracts there. For example, the
Pueblo Lands Board found that Pecos looked ecologically like the
Pojoaque Pueblo grant, with which the Pecos Pueblo grant shared so
much in the popular mind. Of the 13,470 acres in the Pojoaque Pueblo
grant, the Pueblo Lands Board found 210 valid non-Indian claims to
1,652 acres, an average of about 8 acres per claim. In the 10 acre or
less category at Pecos, the Pueblo Lands Board found 224 valid non-
Indian claims, to 1,900 acres. But at Pojoaque the Pueblo Lands Board
had returned the 11,748 acre balance of the grant to the ownership of
the moribund Pojoaque Pueblo. In its Pojoaque report, the board
described those restored acres as lying in the southern and northeastern
parts of the Indian grant, above the irrigated farm lands, and good
only for grazing, if for anything. At Pecos the Pueblo Lands Board
divided among private owners all 16,000 acres of the Pecos Pueblo
grant that were of that type.[67]

The two Pueblo grants always had been viewed in a similar light—
first as not even within the scope of the 1924 act; then as abandoned
Pueblo land; and finally as late irritations to be addressed by the Pueblo
Lands Board. The final difference in treatment between them is not
easy to explain. If the board had treated the Pecos Pueblo grant as it
handled the Pojoaque Pueblo grant, Pecos Pueblo could have recovered
15,000 of the acres within its grant. True, these acres would have been
dry, unirrigated uplands, as they were for the most part at Pojoaque.
There that fact had made no particular difference, although the board
simultaneously awarded the land to the pueblo and recommended that
the pueblo sell it.[68]

But several factors seemed to distinguish Pecos from Pojoaque. For
one, the board was aware of at least one Pecos Pueblo sale of its grant,
as long ago as 1868. Pojoaque Pueblo had not tried to convey its lands
until early in the twentieth century; that sale had been set aside by
the United States District Court for New Mexico, in 1916. Legally,
the 1926 *Candelaria* decision meant that the 1868 Pecos Pueblo sale
had no validity and that no subsequent non-Indian transfers based on
it were binding. But to the board and the public, as a practical matter,
the almost sixty years before the decision did make a difference.[69]

In addition, the public regarded Pecos Pueblo as having abandoned its claim to its ancestral home by moving to Jemez, in the 1830s. Pojoaque Pueblo, on the other hand, had never moved elsewhere. It had simply eroded away. Pojoaque's disappearance must have seemed less drastic than the Pecos diaspora.

And yet, even though they were in residence at Jemez Pueblo, the Pecos band remained a much more easily identified and cohesive social group than did Pojoaque Pueblo, even in the 1920s. As a matter of law, *Candelaria* had completely expunged the *Joseph* decision and had given the 1834 Non-Intercourse Act retroactive effect, as of 1851. Had the Pueblo Lands Act of 1924 not altered that belatedly realized scheme of things, Pecos might have returned to its ancestral home.

However, with the 1924 act, Pecos was lost completely. Warner had intimated as much in his influential 1928 memorandum. The board officially confirmed that view when it completed its tract-by-tract extinguishment of the pueblo's title in its final 4 August 1930 reports, signed by all three members of the Pueblo Lands Board. Herbert J. Hagerman dispatched them to Washington on 5 August 1930, under his own signature. But, in fact, the board reports on Pecos were the work of titular chairman Louis Warner and simply reiterated the distorted history he had previously set out in his internal memorandum of 1928.[70]

The first of the board's 4 August 1930 reports, entitled "Report of Title to Lands Granted or Confirmed to Pueblo Indians," Warner recounted parts of the Pecos Pueblo grant story in Mexican times. Pecos Pueblo, he wrote, "suffered severe epidemics and was from 1825 subjected to every form of coercion and compulsion on the part of local Mexican authorities, according to authenticated records." The report went on to set out the background and terms of the 1829 order of the Diputación Territorial, ordering all non-Indians off the Pecos Pueblo grant. But Warner mentioned nothing of the alleged 1830 sale of the Ciénaga de Pecos to Juan Estevan Pino, even though the document substantiating the transfer, if it had ever taken place, had arrived in the San Miguel County courthouse in 1894. It is doubtful whether Warner ever saw it.

In the next two paragraphs of the first report, Warner described the Pecos Pueblo grant under American rule:

Apparently in desperation because of the continued harassing, the

seventeen remaining members of the pueblo accompanied their
kinsmen to Jemez. There they and their descendants have since lived.

In 1855, an examination of the title to the Pecos Pueblo was made
by the Surveyor General, who approved it and recommended
confirmation of the grant. This action Congress took by Act of
December 22, 1858. In 1864 a patent was issued to the same.

In the files of the Indian office there is at least one specific record
of a request by the Pecos Pueblo to be restored to their lands, or that
they be sold or leased for their account and additional lands
purchased for them in the Jemez section. This was in 1859. It would
appear, therefore, that there was never any intentional abandonment
of their rights by the few surviving Pecos Indians. The records also
show later and similar requests even before they actually signed the
deed of conveyance to John Ward; and subsequent happenings
indicate that they never intended to create the impression that they
had abandoned their rights in the Pueblo.[71]

Warner obviously overlooked many details in his official report. He
never hinted at the surveyor general's ignorance in recommending
approval of the Pecos Pueblo grant in the first place. Warner never
specified what "subsequent happenings" showed Pecos Pueblo's continued assertion of ownership of the grant after the 1868 deed. Instead,
he used his scanty historical exegesis to prove another point: the 1924
Pueblo Lands Act entitled the Pecos Pueblo survivors to money, not
land.

Warner made this explicit in his "Report Concerning Indian Titles
Extinguished," issued under the 1924 act's section 6 compensation
provisions.[72] The board had determined, wrote Warner, that all Pecos
Pueblo claim to its ancestral lands had been extinguished under section
4 standards. But because the Pecos Pueblo survivors had never abandoned their grant and because the federal government could have recovered it for them if it had acted promptly, in 1858, Pecos Pueblo
should be compensated for its loss.

This should have thrown the Pecos Pueblo grant open to the problems
of land valuation that had so involved the board up to that point.
Instead, Warner avoided them by abandoning for Pecos all the previous
methods used for fixing the value of land and water lost by the Pueblos
to non-Indians.

Warner handled water rights most cavalierly. He simply asserted
that "it does not appear that there are any water rights lost to the
Indians to which specific mention should be made."[73] More than seven
hundred acres within the Pecos Pueblo grant had a clear history of

irrigation; the Pecos Indians had first irrigated some, if not all, of those acres. Clearly, once the Pecos Pueblo lost its land it lost its water as well.

Even to the board, making the Pecos Pueblo whole for the losses it had suffered at the hands of the federal government meant securing more irrigated land for the Pecos survivors. Herbert Hagerman, the board member most responsible for the meager initial awards to other pueblos, acknowledged that the Pecos award should be large enough to allow the Pecos survivors commensurate irrigated land at Jemez. But Warner announced for the board in its formal report that water would play no part in determining the recommendation for the Pecos compensation award.

In earlier determinations, both before and after the 1928 Nambe decision, water had played a critical role in the determination of the value of losses to the various pueblos. In the board's 1925 Tesuque Pueblo decision, the pueblo's loss of water, independent of land, had justified an increase in the board's recommended award. Thereafter, the Pueblo Lands Board discounted any incremental value for water on the theory that the pueblos retained a prior and paramount right to water they needed even if they lost irrigated land with appurtenant water rights to certain non-Indians. In other words, the board asserted that while the pueblos may have lost land to which they had applied water, they did not lose the first right to available water. Now they could put it to use on any land they retained after the board's determinations. This argument justified consistently reduced recommendations for awards after that of Tesuque.[74]

Whatever validity the board's theory might have had (and Judge Phillips implied, in 1928, that it had none) depended on a retained land base of dry but irrigable land, to which the pueblo's retained prior right to water might apply. Pecos Pueblo, of all the New Mexico pueblos ruled on by the board, retained no land to which any superior water rights might attach. By the terms of the board's own argument, Pecos should have been the only pueblo where water rights were fully valued. Instead, those rights were not valued at all.

At Pecos, the Pueblo Lands Board adopted no hard formula for determining the monetary value of the loss by the pueblo of all of its ancestral lands:

To determine a fair basis for such an award, in view of all the

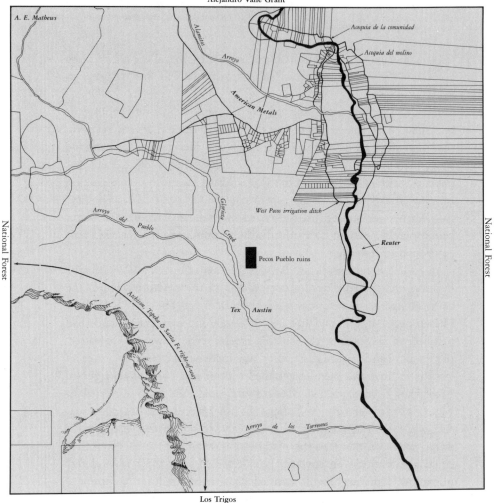

A. E. Mathews

Acequia de la comunidad

Acequia del molino

Alamitos

Arroyo

American Metals

National Forest

National Forest

Arroyo del Pueblo

Glorieta Creek

West Pecos irrigation ditch

Pecos Pueblo ruins

Reuter

Atchison, Topeka & Santa Fe right-of-way

Tex Austin

Arroyo de los Torreones

Los Trigos

MAP 6. The Pueblo Lands Board Finishes with Pecos Pueblo Grant

By 1933 the Pueblo Lands Board and Congress had extinguished all Pueblo claims to the Pecos Pueblo Grant by recognizing non-Indian owners to the 337 tracts Board surveyors had located in the grant. Shown on Map 6 are the results of that determination. The majority of recognized non-Indian claims lay in the northeast quarter of the grant, in and around the *ciénaga* of Pecos, in the area first settled by Hispanics in 1824–1825. There the claims were numerous and small except for the area east of East Pecos where property lines were simply extended to the grant boundary in an artificial effort to include all grant land within non-Indian claims. Otherwise, the land ownership patterns within the grant had simplified between 1915 and 1933, primarily as the result of Tex Austin's consolidation of non-Indian claims to the southern half of the grant.

circumstances, was difficult. The Board has come to a conclusion which in its opinion is fair to all concerned . . . There is now no way to get at the actual value of this land in its entirety as it was at the time the government might have acted or at the time when the members of the Pueblo disposed of their holdings . . . To the Board it seems that the figures for the entire tract might properly be arrived at, not upon the basic value apparently agreed upon in the unconsummated sale of 1912 [the sale from Gross-Kelly to D. C. Collier], but rather should be figured, (having in mind all the conditions), on its approximate average value from the occupancy of this territory in 1846 to the present time.[75]

Nowhere else had the board used this "approximate average value" formula. On a per-acre basis, its use at Pecos resulted in the lowest board evaluation for land lost by any New Mexico pueblo. In eighteen of the twenty pueblos considered by the Pueblo Lands Board, appraisers had gone onto each of the tracts whose Pueblo title the board proposed to extinguish and had formally set a value on the tract, depending on its character (irrigated, irrigable, dry-farmed, grazing, etc.), the improvements made to it (but not on it), and other factors. The board had adjusted these formal appraisers' reports, but had always begun with them.[76] For Pecos the board did not have even this fundamental data to begin with.

But Warner's "approximate average value" formula did allow the board to set a value of $1.50 per acre for all 18,768 acres within the Pecos Pueblo grant. Therefore, concluded Warner in his formal report, "the amount of loss suffered by the Indians through failure of the United States to seasonably prosecute any right of the United States or of the said Indians is $28,144.95."[77]

In the case of other pueblos, recommended awards by the board only began a long period of waiting for subsequent congressional appropriations of actual money. Again Pecos Pueblo proved the exception to the general rule. In the 1931 appropriations bill, passed by Congress less than a year after Hagerman sent in the Pecos Pueblo report, the Department of the Interior requested full awards for Pecos ($28,145), Cochiti ($7,311.62), and Santa Clara ($86,821.87). In addition, the same bill requested much smaller supplemental appropriations for five other pueblos, to cover upward adjustments of original Pueblo Lands Board requests made by the United States District Court for New Mexico. Without much debate, Congress approved. Within less than a year, the Pueblo Lands Board had issued its report on the Pecos

Pueblo grant and Congress had appropriated to the penny the amount the board thought due under the 1924 act.[78]

From the beginning of the board's consideration of Pecos, in 1928, everyone assumed that whatever money Pecos Pueblo received, if any, would go toward the purchase of new land for the Pecos survivors at Jemez Pueblo. Hagerman recommended use of the money to purchase "additional agricultural land" near Jemez Pueblo. Warner's formal report made the same suggestion. At other pueblos, federal officials had argued for using the Pueblo Lands Board awards to repurchase from successful non-Indian claimants lands within the pueblos that the board and the court agreed the pueblo had lost. Indeed, at Jemez Pueblo itself Hagerman urged the use of the pueblo's small award to repurchase the four tracts of 19.994 total acres that the pueblo had lost to non-Indians.[79] But it apparently never occurred to anyone to use the Pecos appropriation to repurchase for the pueblo the more than half of the grant then held by the Gross Kelly company's successor, Tex Austin. There was enough easily irrigable land there to support the Pecos survivors, if they had wanted to return, if Hagerman's water theory was correct, and if government officials had been willing to use the Pecos appropriation to recover lands and water lost under the 1924 act. Instead, officials once again treated Pojoaque and Pecos as special cases. The award of 10,000 acres to Pojoaque they considered ludicrous at best and a cruel joke at worst. Pojoaque, they suggested, would be wisest to sell its land and have done with it. As for Pecos, the only course involved reducing the Pecos survivors' drain on Jemez Pueblo's own resources by purchasing some land for the Pecos at Jemez.[80]

In the meantime, on the Pecos land itself, federal officials proceeded in the final steps toward eliminating all Pueblo claims to the formerly Pueblo land. The General Land Office took on the job of preparing separate United States patents to each of the holders of the 339 perfected claims within the Pecos Pueblo grant. These would represent the second United States patents to the same land; the government had issued the first one to Pecos Pueblo, in 1864. These patents to non-Indians should certainly end the complex federal involvement in the grant. In the spring of 1932, Hagerman wrote officials in Washington to tell them that the last non-Indian patents, for Pojoaque and Pecos, would be ready by 1934, at the latest.[81]

However, other events diverted attention from these last, ministerial details. Increasingly disgruntled with what they considered stingy awards recommended by the Pueblo Lands Board, Collier's Pueblo advocates took the one drastic recourse open to them under the 1924 act. Between December 1930 and January 1932, four Pueblos filed independent suits, based on the still open theory that the Pueblos, as Indians, were entitled to all the land within their grants, no matter how long non-Indians had held them. The suits threatened to upset seven years of Pueblo Lands Board work under the compromise standards of the 1924 act. No one thought to include Pecos in the effort. But a Pueblo victory in any one of the suits would have forced the restoration of all Pueblo land, including that of Pecos.[82]

However, the Pueblo advocates intended to make a political, not a legal, point. This became apparent when they introduced in Congress various bills to increase the amount of money awarded to the pueblos for land and water lost under the 1924 act. In the heat of that battle, Pecos Pueblo neither received consideration nor took any part. J. M. Baca, who had written John Collier in 1926, in 1932 wrote to New Mexico Senator Sam Bratton, to ask if Pecos Pueblo would receive an award in addition to the $28,000 already allocated to it. Bratton, in turn, wrote to the bill's sponsor, John Collier. Collier replied that

> No increase for the extinct Pueblo of Pecos is contained in this bill and about this I was not able to inform Mr. Baca. As for the use of the $28,144.99 already made to the Pecos Indians, they would receive identical protections with those insured by section 5 of the pending bill to all the Pueblo compensation funds.[83]

By late 1933 the Collier forces had wrenched an additional $700,000 from Congress to compensate the pueblos for land and waters lost under the 1924 act. Pecos Pueblo received none of this money, as Collier had previously indicated. Pojoaque Pueblo did receive additional compensation. Both Pueblo advocates and opponents considered this award to be pushing the absolute limits of pro-Indian sympathy. To have increased Pecos's compensation as well, thought the Collier forces, would strain the pueblos' case beyond all possibility of success.[84]

In the end the 1933 act's supplemental awards represented a primarily political solution to the seemingly endless Pueblo land problems. In exchange, the Collier forces dropped the independent Pueblo suits. But in justifying the act Congress explained the monetary increases in ways that reflected ironically, although indirectly, on the previous handling of the Pecos Pueblo award.

The committees which considered the bills proposing increased awards used water to explain their approval. The House committee report preceding passage of the 1933 law justified the proposed increases by referring to the board's "erroneous theory" that the pueblos had not lost water rights, for which they were entitled to compensation, because they retained a prior and paramount right to as much water as they needed on their remaining land:

> The Indian has, accordingly, lost under court decrees, under the doctrine of *res judicata,* certain lands with the water rights appurtenant thereto, for which loss section 6 of the Act of June 7, 1924 clearly provided that he should be compensated. The present bill does no more than bring the awards up to an amount which the appraisers appointed by the Board found to be the value of this land and the water rights appurtenant thereto.[85]

Board members Warner and Hagerman, not formal appraisers, had decided on the vaulue of Pecos lands. Clearly they had not considered the special value of water at all in calculating the amount that Pecos Pueblo had lost with its grant. If Congress, in justifying the increased awards of the 1933 act, had applied the same analysis to Pecos, the pueblo's award would have increased substantially. But by 1933, Pecos had completely disappeared from the national political scene.

There remained two problems with the $28,000 appropriated to Pecos Pueblo: what should be done with it and who should spend it. Everyone agreed that the Pecos funds should go to purchasing additional lands at Jemez. But Jemez Pueblo itself had survived the Pueblo Lands Board adjudications intact. What little land Jemez had lost could be, and was, repurchased with the small Jemez award. To use Pecos compensation funds at Jemez would mean buying additional lands, outside but near the Jemez Pueblo grant, for the Pecos survivors. First Louis Warner and then various other government officials fixed on the possibility of purchasing non-Indian land in the vicinity, then owned by the White Pine Lumber Company but supposedly for sale.[86]

The possible purchase must have stirred some interest at Jemez Pueblo. The Pecos survivors had arrived almost one hundred years before, bearing some of their sacred objects but otherwise carrying nothing more than the clothes on their backs. Now the Pecos Indians at Jemez were suddenly entitled to $28,000, nearly twenty times what Jemez Pueblo had received as damages from the Pueblo Lands Board acts. Should the Pecos Pueblo award be used solely for the benefit of the Pecos survivors at Jemez, or should Jemez Pueblo, including its adopted Pecos members, share the Pecos award? Anthropologists knew, as the residents of Jemez Pueblo had known all along, that the Pecos and Jemez lines had commingled. They also knew that Pecos still retained some of its independent institutions within the Jemez Pueblo framework. Which category should spend the $28,000 award?[87]

In the end, the Jemez and Pecos Indians, with more than a little prodding from the Bureau of Indian Affairs, chose to merge formally. On 27 February 1936, Charles West, acting secretary of the interior, addressed a communication to the Oklahoma congressman and singer Will Rogers:

> Enclosed are copies of resolutions or petitions signed by the officials of the Indian Pueblos of Jemez and Pecos, requesting that Congress give legal sanction to the meger or consolidation of these two tribes.
>
> The merger of these tribes has been accomplished over a period of nearly 100 years by residence of the Pecos Indians within the Pueblo of Jemez and inter-marriage among the members, with the result that there are now very few Jemez Indians who do not have some Pecos blood, and no Pecos Indians who do not have some Jemez blood.
>
> The proposed legislation would make it possible to use the money awarded to the Pecos Pueblo by the pueblo lands board for the benefit of the consolidated Pueblo.[88]

The bill that West attached to his resolution and explanatory letter "consolidated and merged into one tribe . . . known as the Pueblo de Jemez" the distinct Pecos and Jemez communities within Jemez Pueblo. Rogers's House Committee on Indian Affairs approved the bill on 17 April 1936, without amendment, and sent it to the full House. On 4 May 1936, the House passed it without opposition or any comment whatsoever. The Senate Committee on Indian Affairs played its pro forma role on 2 June 1936. Again without amendment, the bill passed the Senate without question. On 19 June 1936, President Roosevelt, who signed the patents to the Pecos non-Indians, also signed the Pecos-Jemez bill into law. As a distinct, legal entity, Pecos Pueblo no longer existed.[89]

The act finally allowed the Department of the Interior to acquire additional, adjoining lands for Jemez Pueblo, using the Pecos Pueblo funds. The 1936 law simply confirmed what had been known since 1870, at the latest: the Pecos community at Jemez still existed, but Pecos Pueblo, that large, peculiar, vital stronghold on the edge of New Mexico's eastern plain, did not.

The Mexican government had treated Pecos Pueblo as a corporate community that owned its lands. In 1846 the first American government had formally made it one. In 1850 Congress approved that early designation and confirmed the grant to the corporation, the Pueblo de Pecos. In 1936 Congress rescinded that status by merging Pecos Pueblo with Jemez Pueblo, thus accomplishing in law what the people themselves had accomplished in fact, one hundred years before.

Through the summer of 1936, non-Indian Pecoseños occasionally traveled into Santa Fe to retrieve the patents the Pueblo Lands Board and the government surveyors had prepared for them. The patents themselves said that they extinguished all claim of Pecos Pueblo and the United States, as the Indians' guardian, to the Pecos Pueblo grant.

At Jemez, the pueblo of Pecos had finally disappeared, more or less. At Pecos, the pueblo's claim to its ancestral home had finally been laid to rest, supposedly once and for all.

Epilog

Pecos Pueblo Church, Pecos National Monument, Pecos, San Miguel County, New Mexico.

Dawn, Sunday morning, 5 August 1979.

In the eighteenth century, the Spanish *padres* reconstructed this church so that the nave would catch the early morning light. A clerestory, high above the altar at the church's east end, directed that light down the rows of waiting Pecos Pueblo worshippers.

Now the clerestory is gone. The church is roofless. For the moment, the ruins are dark and empty and silent.

At this time of year, first light comes gently to this harsh country. Slowly day gains on night, bringing out of obscurity the adobe walls of this church, worn by time, softened by weather, partially destroyed by centuries of neglect.

Then the sun arrives. It climbs the low mountains to the east of the church. It attacks this land with daggers of blinding light. It assaults these ruins. Its light shatters what is left of these walls. The contrast between light and shadow becomes so strong that you cannot see both illuminated and obscured places at once.

Later today, the seeing will become easier. August's rain clouds, gathering by midmorning, will provide some flickering relief from the sun's intensity. Later this morning, crowds will arrive at this church, these ruins. They will come to pray and sing and chat. Their words should soften this deserted, harsh, unforgiving, and unforgetting place.

For the moment, a few local Hispanos and National Park Service employees drift in to begin preparations for the annual celebration of mass in these ruins. This is the Sunday closest to the feast of Our Lady of the Angels. On this day, Hispanic Pecoseños from the Ciénaga de

279

Pecos, the direct descendants of Donaciano Vigil, Manuel Varela, and the others, will come south from the church legitimitized by Juan Estevan Pino to worship at the Pecos Pueblo church. They will bring with them a reproduction of an ancient portrait of Our Lady of the Angels, La Porciuncula. Legend has it that the Pecos Pueblo survivors gave the original of that portrait to Pecos Hispanos before departing for Jemez Pueblo, in 1838. In exchange for the painting the Pueblos requested that the Hispanos celebrate this feast day in their absence. From time to time members of the Kelly family attend this mass. In the recent past, a scattering of Jemez Pueblo Indians of Pecos descent have traveled the eighty miles to Pecos to help celebrate it in these ruins.

Until the National Park Service took over the ruins, in 1965, staging this celebration had become increasingly difficult. Tradition required the Hispanic parishioners to come to the Pueblo church with the Pueblo painting once a year on this day. They had done so until 1953. By then, however, the rubble in the largely neglected ruins had become so deep that the Pecos parishioners could no longer use the pueblo mission church for the annual mass. Beginning that year, they began to celebrate at their own church of St. Anthony's on the Pecos, a few miles to the northeast.

But even prior to 1953, Pecos Hispanos had trouble with the painting that tradition indicated they were supposed to carry, like a banner, on their annual march from the village church to the abandoned pueblo church. The portrait still hung at St. Anthony's on the Pecos, against the wall in the transept. But time had also taken its toll of the painting. For the last celebrations at the pueblo ruins, Pecoseños had had to wrap the portrait of Nuestra Señora de los Ángeles in canvas and foam and then had carefully transported it to the annual mass at the ruins in a pick-up truck, rather than marching the two miles with it, on foot.

Once the pueblo church ruins had so deteriorated that the feast day celebration could not be held there anyway, Pecoseños did not have to worry about the worsening condition of their painting. Between 1953 and 1969 they still took it off the church wall on the designated Sundays. But instead of carrying it all the way to the pueblo ruins, they now complied with tradition and their ancient promise to the departed Indians by carrying the portrait once around their own church on the appointed day.

Then the federal government took over. By 1969 the National Park

Service had sufficiently cleaned up and stabilized the nave of the old Pecos church that mass could once again be said there on the feast day.

The Park Service excavated the church ruins. They exposed the church walls. In the process archaeologists discovered the foundations of an even older, much larger church. In the meantime, Hispanic Pecos church members had begun to show an interest in restoring their ancient portrait. Parish priest Father Leo Lucero had always been intrigued by the painting and the legend behind it. In cooperation with officials of the Pecos National Monument, Lucero arranged for an art expert from the Smithsonian Institution to come to Pecos, to take a look at the portrait, and to advise the parish council on how best to protect and restore it.

The Smithsonian official arrived, took a look, and declared Pecos's portrait of Nuestra Señora de los Ángeles to be worthless. According to the expert, the sacrosanct Pecos painting was nothing more than a cheap, mass-produced religious hoax. He estimated that it would cost fifteen thousand dollars to have the painting restored in the United States. Clearly the Smithsonian did not think the project worth it. Clearly the Hispanic Pecos Parish council could not afford the price itself.

Undaunted, however, Father Leo turned to local help. He knew of a Santa Fe organization called the International Institute of Iberian Colonial Art (IIICA). Several prominent northern New Mexicans, including Thomas Catron, the *Joseph* attorney's great-grandson, sat on the board of directors of the IIICA. The real moving force behind IIICA, however, was none other than Charles Collier, for years a resident of Alcalde, New Mexico, and the second son of John Collier, who had tried to cause Hispanic Pecos such grief in the 1920s, even though Pecoseños might not have known that.

Cantankerous, independently wealthy by virtue of his first marriage, Charles Collier had moved from place to place and job to job, usually returning, as his father did, to New Mexico. In the process of his work and travels through Mexico and Central and South America, Collier had assembled numerous artistic contacts and a collection of about seventy-five historic ecclesiastical paintings. Those paintings became the body of the IIICA's holdings. Collier became the New Mexico expert on them. Naturally, Fathern Lucero turned to him when the Smithsonian turned its back on Pecos's portrait of Nuestra Señora de los Ángeles. John Collier had moved on Pecos in the 1920s, when the federal government had refused to act; Charles Collier now appeared, fifty years later.

With Father Lucero's blessing and the Pecos parish council's consent, Charles Collier took Pecos's portrait to Mexico, where Collier had contacts and the necessary repair work could be done more cheaply. The restorers began by slowly removing the layers of paint that had previously been daubed on the painting.

As they worked, the restorers discovered a remarkable fact. The portrait was not the work of some third-rate copyist. Juan Correa, a famous late-seventeenth-, early eighteenth-century Mexico City religious painter, of the well-known Arteaga school, had done the painting. Correa had also painted the huge, intricate "Assumption of the Virgin" and the "Apocalypse," in the sacristy and in the choir of the Cathedral of Mexico, in Mexico City.

But once the discovery had been made and the *pentamiento* revealed, it took some time, five years in fact, to get Nuestra Señora de los Ángeles back home to Pecos. Experts now valued the painting at twenty-five thousand dollars. Restored but not returned, the portrait somehow became part of the IIICA collection. With the other examples of colonial art collected by Collier, the Pecos painting made it as far as the Guadalupe Church, in Santa Fe, where it hung in an IIICA exhibition. When that ended, the portrait was taken to the third floor of the Fogelson Library, named for Pecos's own Fogelsons, and was stored with the rest of the IIICA collection. Pecos's Nuestra Señora de los Ángeles languished there, propped up against a garret wall, like the other paintings from the Collier collection, gathering dust, awaiting further developments, restored, but again deteriorating.

In the meantime, Pecos parishioners had become increasingly anxious about the fate of their painting. Repeated phone calls to various IIICA officials yielded few answers and no picture. Finally, the parish council reached a board member who told the Pecoseños not to call about the portrait anymore. "Just come to the Fogelson Library and get it." They did. While the rest of the IIICA collection made its way to the University of New Mexico's museum, in Albuquerque, Pecoseños went to Santa Fe and picked up their restored and very valuable Juan Correa portrait of Nuestra Señora de los Ángeles.

In the summer of 1975, a special parish committee drove the portrait from Santa Fe to the Pecos freeway exit, at Glorieta. There the committee and the painting were met by a large contingent of Pecos parishioners. A long line of cars and pick-up trucks escorted Nuestra Señora de los Ángeles the remaining six miles to St. Anthony's on the Pecos. Father Lucero said a special mass before a packed church, in honor of the painting's return.

By then the ruins of the ancient Pecos Pueblo church had been restored. The ancient Pueblo gift to Hispanic Pecos, the portrait of Nuestra Señora de los Ángeles, had come home. All that was lacking was some input from the Pecos descendants at Jemez, to complete the components of the complex system that had moved this remarkable place through the nineteenth and most of the twentieth century.

Between 1936, when Congress merged Pecos and Jemez pueblos, and the 1970s, no one had heard much about the Pecos Pueblo grant from the Pecos descendants at Jemez. For a while in the 1950s, the issue of a Pueblo claim to the ancestral Pecos home had arisen again. But it arrived in the form of a claim by Pecos Pueblo, under the 1946 Indian Claims Commission Act, for increased monetary damages, not for the return of land, to compensate again for the loss of the Pecos Pueblo grant.

Formally filed on 30 July 1951, the case originally was titled *Pueblo de Pecos v. United States of America*. It claimed that the Pueblo Lands Board had not dealt fairly with the Pecos Pueblo grant situation. Specifically, alleged the complaint, the Pueblo Lands Board had awarded the Pecos Pueblo no money for the loss of all of its water rights, in contrast to what the board and Congress had awarded to every other New Mexico Pueblo.

The Indian Claims Commission case dragged on for thirteen years and in the process suggested some new aspects of governmental dealings with New Mexico pueblos. But from the outset several factors suggested weaknesses in the Pecos Pueblo claim.

For one, the Pecos claim came before the Indian Claims Commission as part of a much larger claim for compensation from Jemez Pueblo. The Jemez claim involved no complaint about the Pueblo Lands Board treatment of the Jemez Pueblo grant. Instead, the Jemez claim was for the value of the 298,634 acres once in the Ojo del Espíritu Santo land grant, then in the United States public domain, but always, claimed the Jemez in their suit, part of the aboriginal lands of Jemez, Zia, and Santa Ana pueblos. The equivalent at Pecos would have involved a pueblo claim to those vast acres outside the formal boundaries of the 18,768 acre Pecos Pueblo grant, but obviously used by the Pecos

Indians in ages past. No one had ever thought to claim the value of those lands at Pecos. Instead, the Pecos attorney before the Indian Claims Commission elected to quarrel once again with Herbert Hagerman.

If anyone should have known better, Dudley Cornell, the Albuquerque attorney who represented both Pecos and Jemez pueblos before the Indian Claims Commission, should have. In the mid- and late 1920s, Cornell had worked for the John Collier forces in their battles with the Pueblo Lands Board. In the early 1930s he had begun to represent the Pueblo Lands Board in its battles with the Collier forces. The presiding New Mexico federal court district judge, Colin Neblett, reminded Cornell he could not switch sides quite so easily and threw him off the job. But by the 1950s Dudley Cornell was back on the Pueblo land scene, pressing the Jemez Pueblo claim for a large monetary award and dragging the Pecos Pueblo claim along as a kind of poor relation.

No one would have fought too hard if the Indian Claim Commission had simply dismissed the Pecos Pueblo claim at the outset. But the United States, since 1912 (if not before) the guardian of Pueblo affairs, complicated the situation. The federal government appeared in the suit to oppose the Pecos Pueblo claim, first by delaying. Between November 1951 and November 1954 the United States asked for and received ten separate 120 day extensions in which to answer the Pecos Pueblo claim. Finally, the United States answered the Pecos claim. It said that Pecos Pueblo no longer existed and therefore had no standing to maintain the suit. The basis of the federal claim lay in the 1936 act merging the pueblos of Pecos and Jemez, so that Jemez Pueblo could legally spend the meager amount awarded to Pecos by the Pueblo Lands Board. It was as if a guardian had discharged all obligations by saying that the ward did not exist.

In 1955 Dudley Cornell responded by asking permission to add Jemez Pueblo as an additional claimant to the underlying Pecos Pueblo claim. The commission granted that request. The Pecos Pueblo case went forward under a new and more elaborate name, *Pueblo de Pecos, Pueblo de Jemez and Pueblo de Jemez acting for and on behalf of Pueblo de Pecos v. United States.* Just as in James Seymour's 1880s quiet title suit, the plethora of different names for Pecos Pueblo reflected real uncertainty as to what Pecos Pueblo might legally be. The commission's ruling allowing the suit to go forward, with Pecos Pueblo designated by whatever name, at least suggested that Pecos Pueblo still existed legally.

Nothing more came of the Indian Claims Commission suit than that. Cornell stuck to his Pueblo Lands Board theory when the commission heard the evidence on 10 December 1956. Three years later, on 11 December 1959 the commission ruled against it. No evidence, the commission held, had been presented showing that the United States had not adequately represented Pecos Pueblo before the Pueblo Lands Board. Pecos Pueblo had received no additional compensation in the 1933 supplemental award act. Now the Indian Claims Commission denied it any additional compensation from that source.

The Pecos Pueblo survivors at Jemez had never heard of the Pueblo Lands Board deliberations. Apparently they never heard of the Indian Claims Commission proceedings either. The Pecos clan continued to exist at the Jemez Pueblo. An occasional member would travel to Pecos to look around, perhaps to attend the mass on the feast day of Nuestra Señora de los Ángeles. But, through the 1960s, Pecos descendants at Jemez Pueblo said little about their ancestral home.

By 1970 the National Park Service had restored the ruins of the Pecos Pueblo church so that mass could once again be held there. By 1975 the portrait of Nuestra Señora de los Ángeles had finally found its way back to St. Anthony's on the Pecos. Then Jemez Pueblo interest in the Pecos Pueblo grant rose again.

Part of that resurgence stemmed from Taos Pueblo's final, well-publicized, and successful drive to secure actual title to Blue Lake, a Pueblo shrine some miles east of Taos Pueblo's league. The Pecos Pueblo clan at Jemez found its Blue Lake in a cave at Terrero, fifteen miles upriver from the Pecos Pueblo grant. Negotiations with the cave's owner, the New Mexico State Department of Fish and Game, produced some recognition of an Indian interest in the property. Although hardly a victory, this recognition sparked a renewed Jemez interest in the Pecos Pueblo grant.

The National Park Service and the Pecos National Monument helped to fuel that renewed interest. The federal agency had restored the ruins. It had tried to help restore the sacred painting. Now, in the 1970s, the National Park Service supplied the formal history. Dr. John Kessell, of Albuquerque, a former Park Service employee and premier southwest historian, was hired to prepare an account of Pecos Pueblo and its ancestral home. The federal government was so pleased with the result that it published Kessell's magnificent *Kiva, Cross, and Crown.*

In June 1979, Kessell came to the restored ruins of the Pecos Pueblo church for the book's formal dedication. Several Pecos Hispanic leaders, including the mayor of the village of Pecos, came to the ceremony. At the invitation of monument officials Jemez Pueblo lieutenant governor Roger Madalena attended as well. He brought with him the Pecos clan governor. Madalena said a few words in praise of Kessell's work. In Towa, the Jemez Pueblo Pecos governor said a few words in praise of Pecos. Then Kessell himself spoke of his work.

A small, handsome, energetic man, Kessell talked briefly about Pecos Pueblo's long and complex history. He related several amusing anecdotes about the Indians and the friars. Then, for one eloquent moment, Kessell spoke of what he viewed as the fatal flaw in Pecos Pueblo's long history, the theme of internal dissension and discord that had torn the pueblo apart from within, long before anyone else had tried to dismantle it from without. The small crowd listened and then withdrew to the monument's visitors' center, where Kessell autographed copies of the book.

Kiva, Cross, and Crown received magnificent reviews. The general literate public loved the book for its lively tale. The scholars loved it for its detailed panorama of New Mexico history. Hispanic Pecos loved it because it told something of their own town. But Jemez Pueblo and its Pecos clan loved Kessell's work because, for the first time, the book provided the pueblo with a documentary history of its ancestral Pecos home, a history still very much alive in the oral tradition of the Pecos descendants at Jemez Pueblo, but a history slowly disappearing without the holdfasts of historic facts. *Kiva, Cross, and Crown* supplied those facts in the early summer of 1979 and provided new substance to Jemez Pueblo dreams.

That summer different groups reacted in various ways to the new situation. A new Pecos parish priest, Father Fred, decided to limit the secular aspects of the traditional celebration of the feast of Nuestra Señora de los Ángeles. To the parish council's chagrin, he announced that the local queen of the parish bazaar, which followed the annual mass at the Pecos Pueblo ruins, would no longer be coronated at the mass itself. The coronation, he thought, mixed church and state too much.

Local parishioners grumbled at the priest's decision, but went ahead anyway with plans to make the parish bazaar a genuine historic celebration of Pecos. For the first time, the Hispanic parish council of St. Anthony's on the Pecos sent a delegation to Jemez Pueblo to invite interested Pueblos to Pecos for the mass and bazaar. Jemez Pueblo leaders responded enthusiastically. The Pecos parish agreed to send the church bus to Jemez, at parish expense, to transport any interested Pueblos. The parish council even invited all attending Pueblo guests to a special lunch at the church bazaar, following the mass.

All the threads of the rich Pecos tapestry have begun to converge on the mass at the Pecos Pueblo ruins in honor of the feast day of Nuestra Señora de los Ángeles, to be celebrated on 5 August 1979. The ruins are restored. The painting has come home. The history has been told. The principals will all attend.

On the appointed day, the Pecos parish bus goes to Jemez and returns, to everyone's amazement, fully loaded with interested people from Jemez Pueblo. As the time for mass draws near, more and more Jemez members appear, driving their own cars and pick-ups. The Kellys arrive from Santa Fe. The Vigils and Varelas and Roybals and Riveras and Quintanas and Ruizes arrive from the village of Pecos. The open nave of the church ruins is packed with the descendants of four centuries of Pecos Pueblo grant residents.

The Pecos parish council and the National Park Service have decorated the eastern end of the nave, where the altar rises a few steps. The parish council has provided flowers. The National Park Service has provided a high-quality reproduction of the portrait that no one wants to let out of Saint Anthony's again.

Against the beautiful background, Father Fred begins mass. At his direction, the local fiesta queen will not be coronated here. But the Jemez Pueblo visitors have requested the opportunity to say a few words in what, after all, used to be their church. To local Hispanic dismay, Father Fred has assented to that request. Local Pecoseños do not begrudge the Indian visitors this favor. But fundamental fairness should guarantee them equal time for their coronation, should it not? No matter. Just before the formal offertory begins, Father Fred calls on Jemez Pueblo's Jose Toya, a Pecos Pueblo descendant.

Toya, an older man dressed in traditional clothing, makes his way to the altar. He begins to speak. "So that there will be no misunderstanding," he says to the congregation, "I will say what I have to say in English, in Spanish, and in the language of my people, Towa." And then Toya delivers a harangue on the despicable way the ancestors of the Hispanics now in the audience harassed the last Pecos Pueblo Indians, in the 1830s, to leave their ancestral homes, at Pecos. "Your people poisoned our water, killed our animals, ruined our crops, and drove us from these lands. But these are our lands and we shall return to take them back."

At first a pall hangs over the congregation. Did Toya really say that? He repeats the message, this time in clear but idiosyncratic Spanish. Midway through this rerun, Hispanic parishioners begin to leave the ruins. By the time Toya gets to the Towa version of his message, only Jemez Pueblos and a scattering of mystified Anglo tourists are left in the congregation. Toya finishes. The mass goes on. But the celebration is clearly over.

At the Pecos church bazaar, later that afternoon, the local parish council makes good on its promise to provide the Jemez Pueblo visitors with a meal. A special table is set aside for the guests. And indeed, after church, the Jemez Pueblo contingent shows up at the Pecos High School bazaar site. They sit down at the appointed table and eat the promised meal. But the tension is so thick you could cut it with a knife.

Everyone survives the afternoon, but just barely. In the next year, Father Fred cancels not only the bazaar queen coronation at the annual Pecos Pueblo ruins mass, but also the church bazaar itself. The Pecos parish council extends no invitation to Jemez Pueblo to join in any celebration. The annual mass celebrating the feast day of Nuestra Señora de los Ángeles does take place. But it slips back into the relative obscurity from which it had come.

If you know where to look and how to look at what you see, you can still find telling signs of the intricate, bitter story of the Pecos Pueblo grant. If, for example, you wander today into the Catholic church of St. Anthony's on the Pecos, you can still see the original, restored Juan Correa portrait of Nuestra Señora de los Ángeles.

But it does not hang at eye level, as it used to in the church's transept. When it came back from Charles Collier and the Fogelson Library, parish council member Frank Emerson, a life-long Pecos resident who was raised in an East Pecos family, agreed to use his skills to make sure Pecos would never lose its painting again. Emerson is a skillful metal worker and welder. He invented and patented the metal rack and gate combination that all Pecos pick-ups use to carry huge loads of firewood. Providing a safe place for Pecos's famous portrait stretched Emerson's imagination but not his technical skills.

He welded together the links of two new chains. He hung those chains from the very top of St. Anthony's eighty-foot ceiling. Between them he suspended the painting sixty feet above the alter and pews and transept below.

There Nuestra Señora de los Ángeles hangs today, far removed from the mundane concerns of the present Hispanic parishioners below, now immune from the Colliers and Jemez Pueblos, the Wilsons and Renehans, the Catrons and Varelas, the Becks and Vigils, the Wards and Millers, the Fernándezes and Pinos, the Aguilars and Villanuevas of the Pecos world.

They shot the Pecos Pueblo league with a rope. Nuestra Señora de los Ángeles now hangs on a metal chain from the roof of St. Anthony's on the Pecos. Pecos Pueblo grant history converges, recedes, and converges again. Only the portrait has finally risen.

Notes

Abbreviations

AASF: Archives of the Archdiocise of Santa Fe. Microfilm copy of documents at SRCA.

AGI: Archivo General de Indias, Sevilla, Spain.

BLM: Office of the U.S. Bureau of Land Management, Santa Fe.

HAHR: Hispanic American Historical Review.

HCIA: U.S. House of Representatives, Committee on Indian Affairs, Hearings of Subcommittee, May 1920; reprinted in *Indians of the United States,* vol. 46 (Washington, D.C.: U.S. Government Printing Office, 1943).

JC-Yale: John Collier Papers, Yale University Library, New Haven, Conn.

LHM: Lewis Henry Morgan Collection, University of Rochester, Rochester, NY.

MANM: Mexican Archives of New Mexico, SRCA. In 1970 the state of New Mexico microfilmed them and published a *Calendar of the Microfilm Edition of the Mexican Archives of New Mexico 1821–1846* (Santa Fe: State of New Mexico Records Center, 1970).

NARG–48: National Archives of the United States, Record Group 48; Records of the Office of the Secretary of the Interior. Washington, D.C.

NARG–75: National Archives of the United States, Record Group 75; Records of the Office of Indian Affairs. Washington, D.C.

NARG–200: National Archives of the United States, Record Group 200; Private Papers of Herbert H. Hagerman. Washington, D.C.

NMHR: New Mexico Historical Review.

NMS: Records of the New Mexico Superintendency for the Office of Indian Affairs. Microfilm, SRCA.

NMSA: New Mexico Statutes Annotated.

NMSCt: Archives of the Supreme Court of New Mexico, Santa Fe.

NRJ: Natural Resources Journal (Albuquerque: University of New Mexico School of Law).

PILT: U.S. House of Representatives, Committee on Indian Affairs, Pueblo Indian Land Titles; hearings on S. 3855 and S. 4223, 1–15 Feb. 1923.

PLBSPA: Pueblo Lands Board files, located in the basement of the Southern Pueblo Agency, U.S. Bureau of Indian Affairs, Albuquerque.

PPAAJ: Private Papers of Andreus A. Jones, SRCA.

PPDV: Private Papers of Donaciano Vigil, SRCA.

PPLBP: Private Papers of Lebaron Bradford Prince, SRCA.

Recopilación: Recopilación de leyes de los reynos de las Indias (Madrid, 1681).

RLW: Papers of Ray Lyman Wilbur, Hoover Institute on War and Peace, Palo Alto, Cal.

SANM: Spanish Archives of New Mexico, SRCA.

SCIUS: U.S. Senate, Committee on Indian Affairs, Hearings before a Subcommittee, *Survey on Conditions of the Indians of the United States,* vol. 20 (Washington, D.C.: U.S. Government Printing Office, 1931).

SCPL: U.S. Senate, Committee on Public Lands and Surveys, Pueblo Indian Lands; hearings on S. 3855 and S. 4223, 15–30 Jan. 1923.

SCUNM: Catron Collection, Special Collections, Coronado Room, Zimmerman Library, University of New Mexico, Albuquerque.

SGNM: Records of the Surveyor General of New Mexico, SRCA. The surveyor general assigned to each grant a separate report (R) and file (F) number. New Mexico has microfilmed this archive; the following notes indicate the microfilm reel (r) and frame (f) for documents cited.

SRCA: New Mexico State Records Center and Archives, Santa Fe.

SWHQ: Southwestern Historical Quarterly.

TANM: Territorial Archives of New Mexico, SRCA.

Chapter 1

1. Pedro Bautista Pino to governor, 14 March 1803, SANM I 887.

2. John Kessell, *Kiva, Cross, and Crown* (Washington, D.C.: National Park Service, U.S. Department of the Interior, 1979), 418; *United States v. Sandoval,* 167 U.S. 278 (1897).

3. Eleanor B. Adams and Fray Angelico Chavez, eds., *The Missions of New Mexico, 1776: A Description by Fray Francisco Atanasio Domínguez with Other Contemporary Documents* (Albuquerque: University of New Mexico Press, 1956, 1976), 213–14.

4. Rafael Aguilar to *Diputación territorial,* 12 March 1826, SANM I 1379. For the 1706 Pecos Pueblo census estimates see Charles Wilson Hackett, ed., *Historical Documents Relating to New Mexico, Nueva Vizcaya, and Approaches thereto to 1773, Collected by Adolph F. A. Bandelier and Fanny R. Bandelier,* vol. 3, Fr. Juan Alvarez, 12 Jan. 1706. For 1803 census, see "Noticia de las misiones," 31 Dec. 1803 AGI, Mex., 2737.

5. Pino to governor, 14 March 1803, SANM I 887. For the use of the expression "tierra de pan llevar," see Charles Gibson, *Spain in America* (New York: Harper and Row, 1966), 137–59 and *The Aztecs under Spanish Rule: A History of the Indians of the Valley of Mexico, 1519–1810* (Palo Alto: Stanford University Press, 1964), 285–87. For the term in New Mexico, see grant of

Governor Codallos y Rabal to Sandia Pueblo, 23 January 1748, SANM I 1347.

6. Chacón, marginal note, 30 March 1803, SANM I 887; Juan Bautista Pino, *Noticias históricas y estadísticas de la antigua provincia del Nuevo Mexico en Cádiz, el año de 1812* (Las Vegas, N.M.: Our Lady of Sorrows, 1972), 84; Aguilar and Cota to governor, 1 March 1829, SANM I 288.

7. See David J. Weber, *The Mexican Frontier 1821–1846: The American Southwest under Mexico* (Albuquerque: University of New Mexico Press, 1982), 92–93 for a basic account of the on-again, off-again relationship between the Navajos and settlers. For Taos, see Myra Ellen Jenkins, "Taos Pueblo and Its Neighbors, 1540–1847," *NMHR* 41, no. 2 (1966): 85–114. For Pecos, testimony of Domingo Fernandez, 27 July 1857, Los Trigos Grant, SGNM, R. 8, F. 11; r. 13, f. 31–33.

8. G. Emlen Hall, "Juan Estevan Pino, 'Se Los Coma': New Mexico Land Speculation in the 1820s," *NMHR* 57, no. 1 (1982): 27–42.

9. Alfonso Ortiz, *The Tewa World: Space Time, Being, and Becoming in a Pueblo Society* (Chicago: University of Chicago Press, 1969), 20–23.

10. G. Emlen Hall, "The Problem with Pueblo History: A Review of John Kessell's *Kiva, Cross, and Crown*," *HAHR* 60, no. 1 (Feb. 1980): 115–17.

11. Henry Wagner and Helen R. Parish, *The Life and Writings of Bartólome de las Casas* (Albuquerque: University of New Mexico Press, 1967), 170–78; J. H. Parry, *The Spanish Theory of Empire* (New York and London: Cambridge University Press, 1942).

12. David E. Vassberg, "The 'Tierras Baldías': Community Property and Public Lands in 16th Century Castille," *Agricultural History* 48 (July 1974): 384.

13. Salvador de Madariaga, *Latin America between the Eagle and the Bear* (New York: Praeger and Co., 1962), 60; David E. Vassberg, "The Sale of Tierras Baldías in Sixteenth Century Castile," *Journal of Modern History* 47 (December 1975): 631.

14. José M. Ots de Capdequi, *España en América: El regimen de tierras en la época colonial* (México and Buenos Aires: Fondo de Cultura Económica, 1959), 60. José María Gallego to governor, 1 March 1825, SANM I 887. *United States v. Maria de la Paz de Conway,* 175 U.S. 60 (1899), involving a 1731 Spanish grant for surplus lands (sobrantes) in the then abandoned pueblo of Cuyamungue.

15. Richard E. Greenleaf, "Land and Water 1700–1821," *NMHR* 47, no. 2 (April 1972): 85–112. William B. Taylor, "Colonial Land and Water Rights of New Mexico Indian Pueblos," unpub. ms. (submitted as JP 5 in *State of New Mexico ex. rel. Reynolds v. Aamodt*, no. 6639, USDC, New Mexico, January 1980).

16. *Recopilación,* book IV, title 12, law 18.

17. For example, Myra Ellen Jenkins, "The Baltasar Baca 'Grant': History of an Encroachment," *El Palacio* 68 (Spring 1961): 47; William B. Taylor, "Colonial Land and Water Rights of New Mexico Indian Pueblos," January

1980 (Pueblo Exhibit 17 in *State of New Mexico v. Aamodt,* No. 6639, USDC, NM).

18. *Recopilación,* book IV, title 12, law 9.

19. *Recopilación,* book VI, title 3, law 20. Myra Ellen Jenkins, "Spanish Administration of New Mexico and the Tewa Indians" (SRCA, Santa Fe, mimeographed, 1968), 9–12; Greenleaf, "Land and Water in New Mexico 1700–1821," 85–112.

20. William B. Taylor, *Landlord and Peasant in Colonial Oaxaca* (Palo Alto: Stanford University Press, 1974), 46; Gibson, *The Aztecs under Spanish Rule,* 274.

21. Jenkins, "Spanish Administration," 22–25.

22. Kessell, *Kiva, Cross, and Crown,* 428; Nettie Lee Benson, "Introduction" and Charles R. Berry, "The Election of the Mexican Deputies to the Spanish Cortes, 1810–1822" in Nettie Lee Benson, ed., *Mexico and the Spanish Cortes, 1810–1822: Eight Essays* (Austin: University of Texas Press, 1966); Pino, *Noticias históricas.*

23. Weber, *The Mexican Frontier, 1821–1846,* 27–28 and n. 47.

24. Benson, "Introduction."

25. Berry, "The Election of Mexican Deputies," in Benson, *Mexico and the Spanish Cortes,* 12–42.

26. John H. Hann, "The Role of the Mexican Deputies in the Proposal and Enactment of Measures of Economic Reform Applicable to Mexico," in Benson, *Mexico and the Spanish Cortes,* 153–84.

27. Charles A. Hale, *Mexican Liberalism in the Age of Mora, 1821–1853* (New Haven: Yale University Press, 1968), 248–90.

28. Article V of the act of 9 November 1812, in Manuel Dublán and José María Lozano, *Legislación mexicana,* 1: 396:

> si las tierras de comunidades con respecto a la población del pueblo a que pertenecen *se repartiran,* cuando mas, hasta la mitad de dichas tierras, debiendo entender en todos estos *repartimientos* las diputaciones provinciales, las que designaran la porción de terreno que corresponda a cada individuo, según las circunstancias particulares de este y de cada pueblo. (Emphasis added)

29. Dublán and Lozano, *Legislación mexicana,* 1: 397.

30. Pino, *Noticias históricas,* 19–21; Hann, "The Role of the Mexican Deputies," 160–61.

31. David J. Weber, "Land and Water Rights of the Pueblos of New Mexico under Mexican Sovereignty" (unpub. ms., 1978), 1–11.

32. Bruce T. Ellis, "Fraud without Scandal: The Roque Lovato Grant and Gaspar Ortiz y Alarid," *NMHR* 57, no. 1 (1982): 43.

33. Trujillo et al. to governor, 21 August 1813, SANM I 1005.

34. Trujillo et al. to governor, 26 May 1814, Los Trigos Grant, SGNM, r. 13, f. 4–5.

35. Manrique to ayuntamiento of Santa Fe, 26 May 1814, Los Trigos Grant, SGNM, r. 13, f. 6.

36. Hall, "Juan Estevan Pino," 27–42. The roster of the ayuntamiento of Santa Fe as of 30 July 1814 is from the approval by Santa Fe ayuntamiento on that date in Los Trigos Grant, SGNM, r. 13, f. 5.

37. Juan de Dios Pena et al. to governor, 28 March 1815, Alejandro Valle Grant, SGNM, F. 18, R. 54; r. 14, f. 590. For Pena's roughly simultaneous Taos transactions see Pena to governor, 8 December 1817 and 24 March 1818, and Juan Antonio Martín, alcalde constitucional, to governor, 17 April 1826, all in SANM I 1297. Fr. Angelico Chavez, *Origins of New Mexico Families in the Spanish Colonial Period* (Santa Fe: Gannon, 1975), 256. Kessell, *Kiva, Cross, and Crown,* 441.

38. Will of Faustin Ortiz, Pecos, New Mexico, 17 July 1887, in private papers of Juan Ortiz, Jr., Pecos, New Mexico.

39. Maynez to Ortiz, 29 March 1815, Los Trigos Grant, SGNM, r. 13, f. 9, identifies Ortiz as alcalde constitucional. Minutes, ayuntamiento of Santa Cruz de la Cañada, 4 August 1833, Sender Collection Document no. 121, SRCA (microfilm), identify Matias Ortiz as a member at that time.

40. Chavez, *Origins of New Mexico Families,* 83, 247–51.

41. Kessell, *Kiva, Cross, and Crown,* 435–36, 441.

42. For instance, testimony of Domingo Fernández, 20 August 1855, Preston Beck Grant, SGNM, R. 8, F. 2; r. 12, f. 10.

43. The Los Trigos grant documents identify Padilla only as a Santa Fe resident. The other particulars of his life emerge from the accounts of Padilla's efforts to invade the Pecos Pueblo grant itself.

44. Fernández figures as a principal actor in the Pecos Pueblo grant under Mexican rule; see chapter 2.

45. Ayuntamiento recommendation of 30 July 1814 and Maynez marginal note, 22 June 1815, Los Trigos Grant, SGNM, r. 13, f. 6–9.

46. The difference between community and private land grants is explained in Malcolm Ebright, *The Tierra Amarilla Grant: A History of Chicanery* (Santa Fe: Center for Land Grant Studies, 1979), 1–14, and in Malcolm Ebright, "The San Joaquin Grant: Who Owned the Common Lands? A Historical-Legal Puzzle," *NMHR* 57, no. 1 (1982): 5–27. For grazing grants see Richard Salazar, "Nuestra Senora del Rosario . . .," paper presented at the 22nd Annual Conference of the Western Social Science Association, Albuquerque, 25 April 1980.

47. Pena et al. to governor, 28 March 1815, Alejandro Valle Grant, SGNM, r. 14, f. 592ff. The Alejandro Valle grant was also docketed by the surveyor general under the name *Cañón de San Antonio del Rio Pecos,* or *Cañón de Pecos,* grant.

48. Sandoval to Maynez, 28 March 1815, Alejandro Valle Grant, SGNM, r. 14, f. 593.

49. Sandoval to governor, 17 August 1814, SANM I 18.

50. Matias Ortiz to governor, 30 June 1815; Maynez to Ortiz, 29 March 1815. Both in SANM I 18.

51. Ortiz to governor, 20 October 1815, Los Trigos Grant, SGNM, r. 13, f. 8–9.

52. J. J. Bowden, *Spanish and Mexican Land Grants in the Chihuahuan Acquisition* (El Paso: Texas Western Press, 1971); Bowden, letter to author, 15 July 1974; Jenkins, "Spanish Administration of New Mexico," 48.

53. Juan de Dios Pena deed to Juan Esteban Pino, 17 March 1826, witnessed by Domingo Fernández and Ramón Abréu, both diputación members at the time. Pedro Ortiz to Juan Esteban Pino, 23 September 1826, Alejandro Valle Grant, SGNM, r. 14, f. 614–16.

54. Testimony of Rafael Gonzales, 24 October 1856, Los Trigos Grant, SGNM, r. 13, f. 34–36.

55. Myra Ellen Jenkins, "Taos Pueblo and Its Neighbors, 1540–1847," *NMHR* 41, no. 2 (1966): 85–114.

56. Aguilar to governor, 17 August 1818; Melgares to alcalde, 19 August 1818; alcalde to Melgares, 19 August 1818. All in SANM I 56. For 1567 surveying ordinance see Charles Gibson, ed., *The Spanish Tradition in America* (New York: Harper and Row, 1968), 128–35.

57. Aguilar to governor, 17 August 1818, SANM I 56.

58. Testimony of Domingo Fernández, 27 July 1857, Los Trigos Grant, SGNM, r. 13, f. 34–36.

59. 1804 census of the missions and parishes of New Mexico, AGI Mex., 2737, and Kessell, *Kiva, Cross, and Crown*, 423.

60. Weber, *The Mexican Frontier*, 16–22.

Chapter 2

1. Testimony of Domingo Fernández, 20 August 1855, Preston Beck Grant, SGNM, r. 13, f. 9–10, and 27 July 1857, Los Trigos Grant, SGNM, r. 13, f. 31–33. By 1825, if not before, Fernández served on the Santa Fe cabildo, according to Pino to diputación, 16 August 1825, MANM, r. 4, f. 892–93. Ralph Emerson Twitchell, *The Spanish Archives of New Mexico* (Cedar Rapids, Iowa: Torch Press, 1914), vol. 1, attaches as a note to document 808 a biography of Fernández without source citation.

2. For the 1804 census on Pecos see "Noticia de las misiones," 31 Dec. 1804, AGI, Mex., 2737. For the 1821 census see "Noticia de las misiones," 31 Dec. 1821, SANM II 2950. See also Kessell, *Kiva, Cross, and Crown*, 491–92.

3. David J. Weber, *The Mexican Frontier 1821–1846: The American Southwest under Mexico* (Albuquerque: University of New Mexico Press, 1982), 1–9.

4. Herbert O. Brayer, *Pueblo Indian Land Grants of the "Rio Abajo," New Mexico* (New York: Arno Press, 1979, orig. ed. 1939); Myra Ellen Jenkins, "Taos Pueblo and Its Neighbors," *NMHR* 41, no. 2 (1966): 104; Jenkins, "Nambe Pueblo and Its Neighbors," in *Brand Book,* ed. Al Schroeder (Glorieta, N.M.: Rio Grande Press, 1974); Richard Greenleaf, "Land and Water in Mexico and New Mexico, 1700–1821," *NMHR* 47, no. 2 (1972): 85–112. Each of these works assumes that no fundamental change in Pueblo land status occurred between Spanish and Mexican rule in New Mexico. The assumption

is based either on a misreading or a lack of familiarity with the Mexican archives of New Mexico. Marc Simmons, *Spanish Government in New Mexico* (Albuquerque: University of New Mexico Press, 1968), 213 and n. 80 describes the Pueblo municipal governments. For the description of Pueblos as *ciudadanos* after 1821, see, for instance, Durán to Melgares, 3 Jan. 1821, SANM I 2954, SANM I 1374 (ciudadanos of Picuris Pueblo), and SANM I 1381 (ciudadanos of Picuris Pueblo).

5. Esteban Baca et al. to governor, 10 Feb. 1821, SANM I 130.

6. See minutes of diputación territorial, 12 March 1824, MANM, r. 42, f. 178.

7. Melgares to Ortiz, 12 February 1821, and Ortiz to Melgares, 1 April 1821, SANM I 130. For the general process of grant making see, for example, Myra Ellen Jenkins, "The Baltasar Baca Grant: History of an Encroachment," *El Palacio* 68 (Spring 1961): 47–64; (Summer 1961): 87–105. The contact with La Ciénega, a village south of Santa Fe, began a connection with Pecos Pueblo grant acquisition by non-Indians that continued for twenty years. See Domingo Fernández to teniente de la policia de la Sienega, 2 July 1839, MANM, r. 26, f. 672–76.

8. Simmons, *Spanish Government in New Mexico,* 224; Lansing B. Bloom, "New Mexico under Mexican Administration, 1821–1846," *Old Santa Fe* 1 (July 1913): 27–30; Weber, *The Mexican Frontier,* 16–19; minutes of diputación, 15 April 1822, MANM, r. 42, f. 2. For a list of diputación members as of March 1824, see MANM, r. 42, f. 178. For identification of the merchant class making up the membership see testimony of Domingo Fernández, 20 August 1855, Preston Beck Grant, SGNM, r. 13, f. 9–10. For Pedro Bautista Pino's arrival from Spain and his death in 1827 or 1828, see testimony of Donaciano Vigil, 9 February 1875, Preston Beck Grant, SGNM, r. 12, f. 214ff.

9. For the role of the diputación in land affairs see Nettie Lee Benson, *La diputación provincial y el federalsimo mejicano* (México: El Colegio de Méjico, 1955), 68–73; testimony of Domingo Fernández, 20 August 1855, Preston Beck Grant, SGNM, r. 12, f. 8ff; and John H. Hann, "The Role of the Mexican Deputies in the Proposal and Enactment of Measures of Economic Reform Applicable to Mexico," in Nettie Lee Benson, ed., *Mexico and the Spanish Cortes, 1810–1822: Eight Essays* (Austin: University of Texas Press, 1966), 153–77.

10. Domingo Fernández to governor, 22 April 1822, Eaton–Domingo Fernandez Grant, SGNM, R. 19, F. 16; r. 14, f. 700. The first United States surveyor general originally docketed the claim as a Pueblo Indian one. After Fernández appeared, the designation changed.

11. Felix Guerra and Demetrio Omniveros to diputación, 1 Feb. 1823, MANM, r. 2, f. 709ff.

12. Domingo Fernández et al. to governor, 1 Sept. 1823, SANM I 283.

13. Governor Baca to ayuntamiento of San Miguel del Bado, 1 Sept. 1823, and Alcalde Baca to governor, 18 Sept. 1823, SANM I 283.

14. Baca to diputación, 16 Feb. 1824, and Fernández and Benavídez to

governor, 21 Sept. 1823, SANM I 283; minutes of diputación, 16 Feb. 1824, MANM, r. 42, f. 257.

15. Pino to Baca, 6 Dec. 1823, Preston Beck Grant, SGNM, r. 12, f. 14; minutes of diputación, 20 Dec. 1823, MANM, r. 42, f. 150. A copy of the 23 October 1823 grant to Pino was filed for record in the San Miguel County courthouse, Las Vegas, New Mexico, 27 October 1853, at Book 1 of Deeds, Page 39. See *Pino v. Hatch*, 1 New Mexico 125 (1855). The 31 December 1823 census for the Santa Fe barrio de San Francisco identifies Juan Esteban Pino as a married, thirty-eight-year-old businessman and politician ("comerciante, colonel, y diputado"). The same census identifies as well two sons, Manuel Pino, thirteen years old, and Justo Pino, eight. See G. Emlen Hall, "Juan Estevan Pino, 'Se Los Coma': New Mexico Land Speculation in the 1820s," *NMHR* 57, no. 1 (1982): 27–42.

16. Baca to diputación, 16 Feb. 1824, SANM I 283.

17. Minutes of diputación, 16 Feb. 1824, MANM, r. 42, f. 275. Miguel Ribera et al. to governor, 13 Feb. 1825, and minutes of diputación, 16 Feb. 1825, MANM, r. 42, f. 257, show that the land applied for lay within the Pecos Pueblo grant.

18. Miguel and Felipe Sena to governor, 19 Feb. 1824, SANM I 897. In the application the Senas offered to "obligandose cada uno a cultibarla sin venderla según el tiemp que el dro. previene." For Sena family identification see Weber, *The Mexican Frontier*, 226.

19. Minutes of diputación, 10 March 1824, MANM, r. 42, f. 172–73.

20. Minutes of diputación, 12 March 1824, MANM, r. 42, f. 174–75. Seven years later the battle over the forced allotment of surplus Cochiti and Sandia pueblo lands continued. Minutes of diputación, 14 April 1831, MANM, r. 42, f. 673.

21. Minutes of diputación, 12 March 1824, MANM, r. 42, f. 174.

22. Miguel Ribera to diputación, 13 Feb. 1825, SANM I 808. Domingo Fernandez et al. to governor, 25 Aug. 1826, SANM I 285. This document claims that the two Ortizes put various members of the Fernández group in possession of different parts of the Pecos Pueblo grant in 1824. Narbona to central government, 14 Oct. 1826, SANM I 286, gives the measurements.

23. Minutes of diputación, 1 November 1824, MANM, r. 42, f. 245. MANM, r. 4, f. 1825, shows Fernández as a member of the ayuntamiento of Santa Fe as of 10 Aug. 1825. For the Pablo Montoya grant see Pablo Montoya Grant, SGNM, R. 41, F. 27, r. 17. As surveyed by the United States the Pablo Montoya grant contained 655,000 acres.

24. Miguel Ribera to governor and diputación, 13 Feb. 1825, SANM I 808.

25. Minutes of diputación, 16 Feb. 1825, MANM, r. 42, f. 257–58. The Riberas complained "de haberseles despojado de las tierras que por ordern del Sr. Gefe Politico les habia repardito en el rio de Pecos el Alcalde de Bado a causa de haberse declarado estar yá donado por esta diputación al becino Diego Padilla." At this important meeting, the diputación posed the critical question as "si tienen o no los Pecos drcho a bender tierras o embarrazan las donaciones

que hacia esta diputacion en las tierras que no cultiban; las cuales fueron desechadas a virtud del art. 5 de la ley de 9 de Nobiembre de 1812, que se halla bigente a debe tener efecto segun las circunstancias de cada Pueblo; sobrando estas para beneficarla el Pueblo de Pecos." Obviously the issue was not whether the Pecos Pueblo had the right to sell its land but whether it had the right to sell land already allocated by the diputación to non-Indians. Brayer, *Pueblo Indian Land Grants,* 18–19, badly misreads the document and concludes from it that the general prohibition against pueblos alienating their lands continued into the Mexican period.

26. Minutes of diputación, 16 Feb. 1825, MANM, r. 42, f. 257–58.

27. Miguel Ribera et al. to diputación, 1 March 1825, SANM I 807. The last boundaries are described in Spanish as "por el oriente queda tambien la sierra y al poniente al citado rio." See *Martinez v. Mundy* 65 N.M. 249 (1956) for the difficulty in translating *quedar* as a verb denoting transfer of title.

28. Rafael Benavides et al. to governor, 1 March 1825, SANM I 135. Juan Nepomocino Vigil and José Nestor Armijo joined Benavídez but had not been listed on the 1 Sept. 1823 Fernández application. Pedro Lovato, Jesús Benavídez, and, of course, Rafael Benavídes himself had been in the original Fernández group. José María Gallegos to governor, 1 March 1825, SANM I 388, and Domingo Fernández to governor, 1 March 1825, SANM I 284. In this 1825 reapplication Fernández referred to his 1823 petition, saying that he was making the 1825 petition on behalf of "my companions" from 1823. Only Fernández signed the 1825 request.

29. Benavides to governor, 1 March 1825, SANM I 135: "por el oriente los ojitos que están de este lado del rio de la baca; por el poniente, el rio; por el norte, la vareda que baja del Tecolote, y por el sur, el lindero de Diego Padilla."

30. Minutes of diputación, 3 March 1825, MANM, r. 42, f. 260ff. "Se dio cuenta," the minutes begin, "con una instancia de los Naturales del Pueblo de Pecos, reclamando el derecho de una legua que tenía en tiempo del gobierno español." These minutes do not identify the two members of the commission appointed to apportion the Pecos lands. They are named first in Fernández to governor, 25 August 1826, SANM I 285. In Spanish, the diputación's eloquent message to the Pueblos said, "haciendoles saber a dichos Naturales que así como sesaron sus antiguas cargas, han terminado sus antiguas privilegios, quedando igual, unos y otros, a todos los demás ciudadanos que con ellos forman la gran familia mejicana." For *tierras baldías* as a Spanish legal term of art, see Vassberg, "'Tierras Baldías,'" 383–90.

31. Minutes of diputación, 3 March 1825, MANM, r. 42, f. 262.

32. Luis Benavídez to gefe político and diputación, 8 March 1825, SANM I 897.

33. Minutes of diputación, 19 March 1825, MANM, r. 42, f. 272–73, and Domingo Fernández et al. to gefe político, 25 Aug. 1826, SANM I 285. The Fernández petition says that the allotment took place in 1824. The date is probably mistaken, since the copious details Fernández supplied fit the 1825 procedure exactly.

34. Ortiz to diputación, 19 March 1825, MANM, r. 42. f. 272–73.
35. Ibid.
36. Domingo Fernández to gefe político, 25 Aug. 1826, SANM I 285; Narbona to central government, 14 Oct. 1826, SANM I 1375.
37. Narbona to central government, 14 Oct. 1826, SANM I 1375; Francesco Atanasio Domíngues, *The Missions of New Mexico, 1776,* trans. and annot. Eleanor B. Adams and Fray Angelico Chaves (Albuquerque: University of New Mexico Press, 1956), 213.
38. Rafael Aguilar to diputación, 12 March 1826, SANM I 1370.
39. AASF, B-20, Pecos (box 20), f. 495 shows both Roybals baptized "en esta iglesia de Nra. Señora de Los Angeles de Pecos." But see Kessell, *Kiva, Cross, and Crown,* 552 and n. 38. SANM I 897, SANM I 283, and SANM I 288 place the Roybals, Senas, and Maeses, respectively, on the early Pecos Pueblo scene.
40. AASF, B-20, f. 556.
41. SANM I 288.
42. Minutes of diputación, 19 July 1825, MANM, r. 42, f. 284: petition for land in "el sobrante de la legua que tienen los Naturales de Nambé."
43. Minutes of diputación, 15 Sept. 1825, MANM, r. 42, f. 298. The proceedings of the diputación, covering the same application on the same date, reflect a slightly different disposition. The record of the proceedings for 15 Sept. 1825 show that "se leyó una solicitud de ciudadano J. D. Sena que solicita lo sobrante de las tierras de San Juan." The diputación deferred decision, awaiting the ruling of "supremo gob° sobre la materia para que recarga una resolución gral." MANM, r. 4, f. 855.
44. Minutes of diputación, 17 Nov. 1825, MANM, r. 42, f. 313.
45. Weber, *The Mexican Frontier,* 27–28, dates Narbona's arrival as governor of New Mexico. Minutes of diputación, 17 Nov. 1825, MANM, r. 42, f. 314, lists the members of the diputación as of that date.
46. Minutes of diputación, 18 Nov. 1825, MANM, r. 42, f. 315.
47. Aguilar to gefe político, 12 March 1826, SANM I 1370. See Kessell, *Kiva, Cross, and Crown,* 495, for listing of Aguilar as a notable of Pecos Pueblo.
48. Minutes of diputación, 18 March 1826, MANM, r. 42, f. 390. The composition of the minutes themselves marks the range of debate. They describe Aguilar's 12 March petition as "reclamando las tierras que por posesión y (por tomarlas abandonadas) se donaron a otros individuos." In the actual minutes the parenthetical material is crossed out. The diputación itself was confused about the basis for its distribution of Pueblo lands: either Pecos Pueblo had abandoned its land, as San Cristóbol Pueblo had previously done, or the diputación itself had the right to dispose of sobrante Pueblo land under the 9 Nov. 1812 law of the cortes.
49. Narbona to alcalde del Bado, 21 March 1826, SANM I 1370. Once again, the interlineations in the Spanish text indicate the difficulties Mexican officials in New Mexico had in describing the status of Pueblo lands. Narbona selected "antigua mancomunidad" to describe the Pecos land holdings. "Man-

común" had strong local connotations suggesting joint ownership. Narbona had first used "pertenencia antigua" to describe the Pueblo holdings, then eliminated that in favor of "antigua mancomunidad." Similarly, the interlineations show that Narbona considered "se repartieron" to describe the non-Indian method of acquiring Pecos land and finally settled on the much simpler "se han dado."

50. Cámara to sr. gefe político of New Mexico, 31 May 1826, MANM, r. 5, f. 29ff. The Pecos questions Cámara wanted Narbona to answer included: "cuanta es la estención de las tierras sobre que ha recaido el repartimiento; cual la distribución que se ha hecho de ellas; y el origen y forma de la que Us. llama 'mancomunidades,' su antiguidad, y los terminos en que permanecen."

51. Fernández to San Miguel del Bado alcalde, 19 Aug. 1826, SANM I 285.

52. Alarid to governor, 22 Aug. 1826, SANM I 285.

53. Fernández to governor, 25 Aug. 1826; Narbona, marginal note, 25 August 1826, in SANM I 285; Kessell, *Kiva, Cross, and Crown,* 446–47.

54. Fernandez et al. to governor, 9 Sept. 1826, SANM I 285.

55. Parry, *The Spanish Theory of Empire,* 46.

56. Narbona to central government, 14 Oct. 1826, SANM I 285.

57. Minutes of diputación, 21 Oct. 1826, MANM, r. 42, f. 438–39.

58. Hall, "Juan Estevan Pino," 27–42.

59. Pedro Ortiz deed to Juan Estevan Pino, 23 Sept. 1826, Alejandro Valle Grant, SGNM, r. 14, f. 594. See f. 251ff. for boundary location problems.

60. Minutes of diputación, 3 Dec. 1828, MANM, r. 42, f. 556, for Pino's acceptance as a newly elected member of the diputación. Alarid deed to Pino, 22 June 1823, recorded 18 June 1849, in Santa Fe County deed book A, pp. 56–58, refers to Pino as the "diputado de Excelentísima Diputación de esta Provincia." I find no contemporaneous reference in MANM itself to substantiate this reference. Juan Estevan's father, Pedro Bautista Pino, served as a member then. Pino to Arocha, 17 June 1828, MANM, r. 8, f. 65–66, refers to Pino as in the cañon de Pecos by the time of the communication. Pino to Manuel de Jesús Rada, 24 Nov. 1829, MANM, r. 42, f. 484, on behalf of the diputación, pleads for national Mexican relief from local Comanche and Kiowa raids on herds. Miguel Varela and Jose Roibal to diputación, 29 Feb. 1830, MANM, r. 42, f. 633, requests land "in front of the ranch of Dn. Juan Estevan Pino."

61. Ortiz to Pino, 23 Sept. 1826, Alejandro Valle Grant, SGNM, r. 14, f. 594.

62. Minutes of diputación, 25 June 1827, MANM, r. 42, f. 489. Eaton–Domingo Fernandez Grant, SGNM, r. 14. House of Representatives Report No. 457, 35th Congress, 1st Session (1858), 314–18. Minutes of diputación, 8 Aug. 1827 and 18 Oct. 1827, MANM, r. 42, f. 516 and 532 for the ongoing debate about San Cristóbal.

63. Fernández to alcalde mayor of Santa Fe, 26 Sept. 1828, SANM I 286.

64. Fr. Angelico Chavez, *Origins of New Mexico Families in the Spanish Colonial Period* (Santa Fe: Gannon, 1975), 247–49. At Pecos racial identifi-

cation practices varied from priest to priest. For instance, see Fr. Bragados, AASF B-20, r. 6, f. 452ff, beginning 16 Nov. 1818. The initial Bragados entries reflect no racial identifications until 18 Aug. 1819 where, at f. 458, Bragados designates María Rafaela Apodaca as "española." Bragados keeps the practice up for a while, intermittently designating race and residence. For Juan Manuel Aguilar, see AASF r. 6, f. 631; for Barela (sic) and Gonzales, f. 632.

65. Pedro Gonzales et al. to Ulibarri, 1 March 1829, SANM I 288. The four who appeared on the 1823 and 1829 petitions were Antonio Luján, Juan Rivera, José M. Rivera, and Antonio Armijo.

66. Rafael Aguilar et al. to governor, 9 March 1829, SANM I 288.

67. For instance, minutes of diputación, 17 Nov. 1825, MANM, r. 42, f. 314, signed by Narbona, Francisco Ortiz, Rafael Sarracino, Francisco Ignacio de Madariaga, Severino Martínez, Juan Felipe Vigil, and Juan Bautista Vigil, with minutes of diputación, 24 March 1829, MANM, r. 42, f. 639, which lists José Antonio Chavez, Juan Felipe Ortiz, Santiago Abréu, José Francisco Baca, and Ramon Abréu as members. Starting in 1827, the diputación began to approve Pueblo sales of land to non-Indians, for instance, San Ildefonso, 27–28 June 1827, MANM, r. 42, f. 491–96. Minutes of diputación, 16 March 1829, MANM, r. 42, f. 600, shows the diputación considering Rafael Aguilar's petition.

68. Pecos Pueblo Grant, SGNM, R. F, F. 533; r. 7. I have dated this undated document by use of MANM minutes between 16 March and 24 March 1829. Minutes of diputación, 24 March 1829, MANM, r. 42, f. 605–6 shows the critical diputación addition to the Pino report:

leida y aprovada la acta anterior: la comición encargada de la solisitud de los Naturales de Pecos con los papeles relativos a este asunto remetidos por el alcalde constitucional del Bado presentó su dictamen y puesto a discusión los dos artículos que comprende, fueron aprovados con solo la adición de que las tierras que se han de volver a los hijos de Pecos son las donadas y no las vendidas por ellos.

69. Domingo Fernández to gefe político, 7 May 1829, SANM I 288; minutes of diputación, 12 June 1829, MANM, r. 42, f. 617–18.

70. Pino to governor, 13 June 1829, SANM I 288. Fernandez and Pino had previously sat together as secretary and head, respectively, of the Santa Fe ayuntamiento. Pino to diputación, 16 Aug. 1825, MANM, r. 4, f. 892–93. For real estate transactions shared by the two men see Alarid to Pino, 22 June 1823, witnessed by Fernández; Ortiz to Pino, 23 Sept. 1826, witnessed by Fernández; Baca to Fernández, 4 June 1824, witnessed by Pino. For the shared claim to the San Cristóbal grant, see proceedings of Miguel Antonio Lovato against Manuel D. Pino, 11 Nov. 1837, MANM, r. 23, f. 980ff.

71. Miguel Varela and José Roibal to diputación territorial, 25 Feb. 1830, MANM, r. 42, f. 633. The grant of the tract dates the first occupation of the Vallecitos area of Cow Creek, east of Pecos.

72. José Cota to Juan Estevan Pino, 20 Sept. 1830, recorded 29 May 1894,

in Deed Book 46, p. 474, San Miguel County records. See also Hall, "Juan Estevan Pino."

73. "Indian Deeds: Nambe Pueblo," File nos. 300.5-9-9, 9.1, PLBSPA. The Nambe property abstracts show one Pueblo sale to a non-Indian prior to 1829 and seven sales between 1829 and 1835.

74. Minutes of diputación, 14 April 1831, MANM, r. 42, f. 673. See also SANM I 1291; MANM, r. 42, f. 170–71, 174–75; and Twitchell, *The Spanish Archives of New Mexico*, 1: 377.

75. For instance, Jemez Pueblo league, 1833, SANM I 1245; Santo Domingo Pueblo, SANM I 1380; Picuris Pueblo, 1845 SANM I 1169; and Isleta Pueblo, 1845, SANM I 1381.

76. H. Bailey Caroll and J. Villasna Haggard, "Ojeada of Lic. Antonio Barreiro, 1832," *Three New Mexico Chronicles* (Albuquerque: Quivira Society, 1942), 47–48. Kessell, *Kiva, Cross, and Crown*, 460–62.

77. Kessell, *Kiva, Cross, and Crown*, 463. Charles H. Lange and Carroll L. Riley, eds., *The Southwestern Journals of Adolph Bandelier, 1880–1882* (Albuquerque, University of New Mexico Press, 1966), 77–84.

78. Clara True to Burke, 6 June 1922, NARG–75, pt. 6. Lange and Riley, *The Southwestern Journals*. Affidavit of George Hill Howard, undated, in *In Re the Incorporation of the Pecos Pueblo Grant*, San Miguel County cause no. 4416, 1896, SRCA.

79. Minutes of diputación, 14 April 1831 and 11 November 1831, MANM, r. 42, f. 673, 683.

80. Testimony of Manuel Rodrigues, 28 July 1857, Los Trigos Grant, SGNM, r. 14, f. 42–43. Deed, Estevan Aragón et al. to Manuel D. Pino, 25 July 1840, recorded 13 August 1887, at Book 31, p. 215, deed records of San Miguel County, and Juan Aragón to Juan Estevan Pino, 31 March 1837, recorded 12 August 1887, at Book 31, p. 206.

81. Howard Lamar, *The Far Southwest, 1846–1912: A Territorial History* (New York: W.W. Norton, 1970), 28–29; Hall, "Juan Estevan Pino."

82. Power of attorney, Juan Estevan Pino to Manuel Doroteo Pino, 9 Nov. 1836, MANM, r. 15, f. 452–57, renewed in 1836. MANM, r. 16, f. 308, refers to Pino as at Jemez during the period; SANM I 1236 and MANM, r. 23, f. 480, detail the family interest at Galisteo. Complaint by Manuel Doroteo Pino against José Salaices before Alcalde Felipe Sena, 18 April 1838, MANM, r. 25, f. 389, begins an endless lawsuit over damage Salaices allegedly did Pino's mules hauling goods from Chihuahua. MANM, r. 23, f. 801, identifies Salaices as one of the four members of the *junta departmental* as of 16 April 1837. Testimony of Bernardo Varela, 9 Feb. 1875, Preston Beck Grant, SGNM, r. 13, f. 206ff, tells the story of the Pino ranching operation on the eastern plains. See also Private Papers of A. A. Jones, File: History of Preston Beck Land Grant, SRCA, which dates Juan Estevan Pino's death at around 1840. Milt Callon, *Las Vegas: The Town That Wouldn't Gamble* (Las Vegas, N.M.: Optic Publishers, 1968), suggests that the Las Vegas grant was abandoned at the same time because of increased Indian hostility.

83. Juan Rafael Rascón to Santa Fe, 29 January 1837, MANM, r. 24, f.

809ff; report, José Francisco Terrara from cañon de Pecos, 10 Sept. 1845, MANM r. 24, f. 812. The 1845 renewal of the Pecos church license expressed some concern with the condition of the church and, among other things, recommended construction of a wall around the local cemetery to prevent animals from trampling the ground. Report, Dn. Luis Rubio, 18 Oct. 1850, MANM, r. 24, f. 813.

84. Proceedings of Justo Pastor Pino against Francisco Tomas Cabesa de Baca, 18 March 1846, MANM, r. 41, f. 538ff.

85. Weber, *The Mexican Frontier,* 270–72; Janet Lecompte, "Manuel Armijo and the Americans," in *Spanish and Mexican Land Grants in New Mexico and Colorado,* ed. John R. Van Ness and Christine M. Van Ness (Manhattan, Kan.: Sunflower University Press, 1980), 51–63; George Wilkins Kendall, *Narrative of the Texan–Santa Fe Expedition* (Austin: Stech, 1935), 417–19.

86. Testimony of Rafael Gonzales, 24 Oct. 1856, Los Trigos Grant, SGNM, r. 13, f. 36; testimony of Manuel Rodríguez, 24 Oct. 1856, Los Trigos Grant, SGNM, r. 13, f. 38.

87. Kessell, *Kiva, Cross, and Crown,* 420; Kendall, *Narrative of the Texan–Santa Fe Expedition,* 417.

Chapter 3

1. Annie H. Abel, *The Official Correspondence of James S. Calhoun* (Washington, D.C.: U.S. Government Printing Office, 1915), 3, 327. Alvin R. Sunseri, *Seeds of Discord: New Mexico in the Aftermath of the American Conquest 1846–1851* (Chicago: Nelson-Hall, 1979), 49–65. Robert W. Frazier, ed., *New Mexico in 1850: A Military View* (Norman: University of Oklahoma Press, 1968).

2. Manuel Doroteo Pino to Gertrudis Rascón, witnessed by Manuel Varela, 15 July 1848, in Preston Beck Grant, SGNM, r. 12, f. 409. Ignacio Quintana and Dolores Valencia to José María Valencia, 19 August 1853, recorded 8 October 1853 in the records of San Miguel County Courthouse at Deed Record 1, pp. 62–63.

3. Paul Horgan, *Lamy of Santa Fe* (New York: Farrar, Straus and Giroux, 1975), 148.

4. Abel, *Correspondence,* 21–25, sets out the 9 September 1849 treaty signed by J. N. Ward, bvt. 1st lieutenant, Third Infantry. Annie Heloise Abel, ed., "Indian Affairs in New Mexico under the Administration of William Carr Lane: From the Journal of John Ward," *NMHR* 16, no. 4 (1941): 206.

5. For instance, Malcolm Ebright, *The Tierra Amarilla Grant: A History of Chicanery* (Santa Fe: Center for Land Grant Studies, 1979).

6. 9 Stat. 922; Hunter Miller, ed. *Treaties and Other International Acts of the United States of America* (Washington, D.C.: U.S. Government Printing Office, 1957), 5: 218.

7. J. J. Bowden, "The Texas–New Mexico Boundary Dispute along the Rio Grande," *SWHQ* 42 (1959): 221–37. William C. Binkley, "The Question

of Texas Jurisdiction in New Mexico under the United States, 1848–1850," *SWHQ* 24 (July, 1920): 1–38. Louis Warner to J. Haggard, 4 April 1929, Warner, PLBSPA.

8. *United States v. Pecherman,* 10 US 393 (1833).

9. For example, California began the adjudication of claims originating under its antecedent sovereigns with a board (not a surveyor) instructed to recognize as legitimate any bona fide claims where there was evidence of possession under the previous governments. New Mexico began with the surveyor general, who was asked to scrutinize much more closely the technical compliance of private claims, and ended with the Court of Private Land Claims, established as a full-fledged adversary court, where every claim by a private individual was resisted and denied by the United States government. For a brief but adequate survey of these issues see White, Koch, McCarthy, and Kelly, *Land Title Study* (Santa Fe: State Planning Office, 1971).

10. Sunseri, *Seeds of Discord;* Olen E. Leonard, *The Role of the Grant in the Social Organization and Social Processes of a Spanish-American Village in New Mexico* (Albuquerque: Calvin Horn Publisher, 1970), 103–8.

11. Kearny Code, adopted 1847, set out in 1 New Mexico Statutes Annotated 1978 (NMSA 1978). Testimony of the lawyer and historian Ralph Emerson Twitchell, before the subcommittee of the Senate Committee on Public Lands and Survey's Hearings (SCPL–1923) on Senate Bill 3855, 16 January 1923, 84ff.

12. *De La O v. Pueblo of Acoma,* 1 New Mexico 226 (1857), gives the outlines of the legislative procedure by which the pueblos were incorporated. *Lane v. Pueblo of Santa Rosa,* 249 US 110 (1917), confirms the propriety of that designation.

13. Abel, *Correspondence,* Calhoun to Medill, 1 Oct. 1849.

14. Abel, *Correspondence,* Calhoun to Medill, 15 Oct. 1849.

15. Abel, *Correspondence,* Calhoun to Medill, 10 Dec. 1849.

16. Kearny Code, 1 NMSA 1978, sections 1 and 2 under "Registrar of Lands." As secretary of the government established by the code, Donaciano Vigil served ex oficio as the first registrar of lands. Vigil kept four indexes in that job. See Tipton to Secretary of the Interior, 19 October 1911, National Archives Record Group 75 (NARG–75), series 013, part II, which describes the fate of the four volumes as of 1911. See generally Henry Putney Beers, *The Spanish and Mexican Records of the American Southwest* (Tucson: University of Arizona Press, 1979), 46–47. For a 1923 assessment of the state of public documents until 1856, when New Mexico passed its first mandatory recording statute, see testimony of Francis C. Wilson, 1 February 1923, before the House Committee on Indian Affairs, Hearings on Pueblo Indian Land Titles (PILT–1923), 46.

17. Abel, *Correspondence,* Calhoun to Medill, 1 Oct. and 15 Oct. 1849; Calhoun to Brown, 29 March 1850.

18. Abel, *Correspondence,* Calhoun to Brown, 29 March 1850.

19. Abel, *Correspondence,* Calhoun to Brown, 20 Nov. 1849; Winfield to Lea, 6 Feb. 1852.

20. Abel, *Correspondence,* Calhoun to Medill, 7 April 1849; Calhoun to Clayton, 29 and 27 April 1851.

21. Abel, *Correspondence,* Calhoun to Brown, 20 and 16 November 1849; Winfield to Lea, 6 Feb. 1852.

22. Abel, *Correspondence,* Brown to Calhoun, 28 Dec. 1849. The map is included in a pocket supplement to Abel, *Correspondence.*

23. Abel, *Correspondence,* Grenier to Calhoun, 25 March 1852; Monroe to Jones, 31 May 1851.

24. Abel, *Correspondence,* Calhoun to Brown, 16 July 1850. The letter indicates that Calhoun had negotiated treaties with the Pueblos of Santa Clara, Tesuque, Nambe, Santa Domingo, Jemez, San Felipe, Cochiti, San Ildefonso, Santa Ana, and Cia (*sic*). The proposed treaty documents are set at page 239. The United States government never ratified the treaties. Abel, *Correspondence,* Calhoun to Lea, 29 Feb. 1852. See also 68 *Congressional Globe* 1320, 2 March 1865, where it was reported that the Indians of Arizona wished to live like the Pueblos of New Mexico, who owned their lands by grants from Spain, had been citizens under Mexico, and therefore enjoyed their rights to land not by separate treaty with each tribe but under the Treaty of Guadalupe Hidalgo.

25. Robert W. Larson, *New Mexico's Quest for Statehood, 1846–1912* (Albuquerque: University of New Mexico Press, 1968), 63–68; Abel, *Correspondence,* Calhoun to Medill, 15 Oct. 1849.

26. Records of the New Mexico Superintendency for the Office of Indian Affairs (NMS) 546: 18. A subsequent entry at NMS 547: 16, dated 30 Sept. 1851, indicates that Ward had been employed in the superintendency since Sept. 1851.

27. Abel, *Correspondence,* 484, Grenier to Calhoun, 25 March 1852.

28. Abel, *Correspondence,* 496–97, Grenier to Calhoun, 25 March 1852.

29. John Kessell, *Kiva, Cross, and Crown* (Washington, D.C.: National Park Service, U.S. Department of the Interior, 1979), 459–63.

30. Mariano Galván-Rivera, *Ordenanzas de tierras y aguas o sea formulario geométrico-judicial, amojonamiento y deslinde de las poblaciones,* supplement to Joaquín Escriche, *Diccionario razonado de legislación y jurisprudencia* (Paris: Rosa y Bouret, 1863). Abel, *Correspondence,* Grenier to Calhoun, 25 March 1852.

31. NMS 546: 16, 31 June 1852. In the report Grenier states that Ward is paid only five hundred dollars a year and asks if that sum is fair in light of Ward's substantial duties.

32. Section 7, chapter XIV, act of 27 Feb. 1851, 9 Stat. 587.

33. Chapter CLXI, act of 30 June 1834, 4 Stat. 729.

34. Abel, "Indian Affairs," 217–18.

35. Abel, "Indian Affairs," 220.

36. Act of 22 July 1854, 10 Stat. 308. Victor Westphall, *The Public Domain in New Mexico, 1854–1891* (Albuquerque: University of New Mexico Press, 1965), 3–4. See, for instance, *H.N.D. Land Co. v. Suazo,* 44 N.M. 547 (1940); *Payne Land and Livestock v. Archuleta,* 180 F. Supp. 651 (1960); *Maxwell Land Grant Co. v. Dawson,* 151 U.S. 586 (1894).

37. See Commissioner of the General Land Office John Wilson to the first Surveyor General for New Mexico William Pelham, 17 August 1854, "Misc.," SGNM, r. 23, f. 49ff. In that letter Wilson told Pelham not to concern himself overly with the question of identifying the correct recipient of title originating under the antecedent sovereigns, since the statute specifically said that it would not cut off other rights if there were any. In other words, said Wilson, the statute did not affect private rights but only those of the government. The problem with this point of view was that it potentially pitted decisions of local courts against a legislative determination, not because it was correct, but simply because it was legislative. See, for instance, *Tamelling v. Freehold and Immigration Co.*, 94 U.S. 644 (1876).

38. Westphall, *Public Domain,* 3–4; Beers, *Spanish and Mexican Records,* 46–47.

39. Wilson to Pelham, 21 Aug. 1854, "Misc.," SGNM, r. 23.

40. Westphall, *Public Domain,* 1; Wilson to Pelham, 21 Aug. 1854, SGNM, "Misc.," r. 23, f. 49ff; White et al., *Land Title Study,* 44; Beers, *Spanish and Mexican Records,* 46–47.

41. Beers, *Spanish and Mexican Records,* 48; Howard Lamar, *The Far Southwest, 1846–1912: A Territorial History* (New York: Norton, 1970), 67.

42. Beers, *Spanish and Mexican Records,* 46–47.

43. Wilson to Pelham, 21 Aug. 1854, "Misc.," SGNM, r. 23, f. 49; Pelham to Wilson, 30 Sept. 1855, SGNM, r. 23; Docket Book, Office of the Surveyor General of New Mexico, p. 553, SRCA.

44. Docket Book, SGNM, 553. The listing continued at least until 1872. See "Schedule B, Statement of Confirmed Indian Pueblo Grants and Private Land Claims in New Mexico," in *New Mexico: List of Private Land Claims Reported by the Surveyor General of New Mexico and also Statement of Confirmed Indian Pueblo Grants* (London: John King and Co., 1872), which lists the confirmees to the Pecos Pueblo Grant as the "Indians of the Pueblo," not the "Inhabitants of the Town," as the confirmees of community grants are listed in this unofficial compilation.

45. "Report of the Surveyor General of New Mexico to the Commissioner of the General Land Office," 30 Sept. 1855, in 1 House Message and Documents 383 (1857); Plaintiff's Exhibit 9, in *James Seymour v. George D. Roberts et al.*, San Miguel County cause no. 2723 (1887), SRCA.

46. Taos, Santa Clara, Tesuque, San Ildefonso, and Pojoaque pueblos apparently never produced grant documents. See *Annual Report of the Secretary of the Interior, 1856,* U.S. Congressional Docs., serial no. 893, 411.

47. Pecos Pueblo Grant, SGNM, r. 7, f. 243. The certificate appended to the translation reads: "Surveyor General's Office, Santa Fe, New Mexico, August 8, 1883. The above and foregoing is a correct translation, made by me, of the original paper in Spanish, marked B, not before translated, on file in this office among the papers in the case of Indians of Pueblo claim F in the name of the Pueblo of Pecos. David J. Miller, translator."

48. *Annual Report of the Secretary of the Interior, 1856,* 411.

49. *Annual Report of the Secretary of the Interior, 1856,* 513. Questions by

Surveyor General Pelham. Answers by Pablo Romero, governor; Juan Reyno, war captain; and Benito Casillas, cacique of Taos Pueblo:

Q. Do the lands of the Pueblo extend one league from the church in the direction of the four cardinal points of the compass?

A: By tradition we also know that our lands extend one league to each of the cardinal points measured from the cross in the centre of the burial grounds.

Vigil affidavit, 21 June 1856.

50. *Annual Report of the Secretary of the Interior, 1856,* 519–20. See chapter 1, above, and generally Richard E. Greenleaf, "Land and Water in Mexico and New Mexico, 1700–1821," NMHR 47, no. 2 (1972): 85–112.

51. Preston Beck, Jr., and Donaciano Vigil by mid-1854 had substantial interests in the Pecos Pueblo grant, as well as in other grants, and were actively litigating their interest in New Mexico lands through the adjudications of the surveyor general, at the same time that Pelham was recommending confirmation of the grant to Pecos Pueblo.

52. *Annual Report of the Secretary of Interior, 1856,* 412.

53. For the Chamita problem see, for example, "A Statement Prepared by H. J. Hagerman, Member of the Pueblo Lands Board for Presentation to the House Committee on Indian Affairs in re H.R. 7535," Jan. 1932, NARG–75, 013, part 21. For the Taos situation generally see "Report on Indian Title Extinguished," report II, Taos Pueblo, Jan. 1928, Taos Pueblo Grant, PLBSPA.

54. *Annual Report of the Secretary of the Interior, 1856.*

55. Act of 22 Dec. 1858, 11 Stat. 358.

56. Senate report to accompany Bill H.R. 195, Committee on Private Land Claims, 19 May 1860, 36th Congress, 1st Session, 2–5.

57. House Committee on Private Land Claims, 10 Feb. 1868, 40th Congress, 2d Session, report 71, 4–7.

58. House Committee on Private Land Claims, 15 March 1870, 41st Congress, 2d Session, report 38, 6.

59. T. A. Munson, "Major J. Powell's Paper on Retracing Land Lines," presented to the First Annual Conference on Surveying and Mapping, Austin, Texas, 1940. *United States v. Perat,* 60 U.S. 343 (1856). Manuel Carrera Stampa, "The Evolution of Weights and Measures in New Spain," HAHR 29 (Summer 1949): 2–24; Roland Chardon, "The Elusive Spanish League: A Problem in Measurement in Sixteenth Century New Spain," HAHR 60 (May 1980): 294–302.

60. Laws of New Mexico, 1851–52, Ch. 29 Section 4; Lamar, *Far Southwest,* 79–82.

61. Wilson to Pelham, 21 Aug. 1854, "Misc.," SGNM, r. 23. f. 49.

62. Ibid.

63. E. Boyd, *Popular Spanish Arts of New Mexico* (Santa Fe: Museum of New Mexico, 1974), 321.

64. House Executive Document no. 1, 34th Congress, 3rd Session (1856), 24.

65. Pelham to Wilson, 30 Sept. 1856, "Misc.," SGNM, r. 23; Westphall, *Public Domain,* 1–8.

66. Pelham to Wilson, 22 Aug. 1859, SGNM, r. 49, f. 208.

67. James W. Garretson, "Field Notes of the Survey of the Pueblo of Pecos, 1859" (Santa Fe: Bureau of Land Management, 1859).

68. For instance, Charles Gibson, *The Aztecs under Spanish Rule: A History of the Indians of the Valley of Mexico* (Palo Alto: Stanford University Press, 1964), 247 and map following.

69. United States of America to Pecos Pueblo, 1 Nov. 1864, recorded 11 June 1890, San Miguel County Deed Book 41, 372.

70. *De La O v. Acoma,* 1 New Mexico 226 (1857); *Pueblo of Nambe v. David Herrera et al.,* United States District Court for New Mexico, Cause No. 729, per curiam decision by Judges Phillips and Neblett, Jan. 1928, in Federal Records Center, Denver.

71. The Santa Clara decision in 1852 implied that there was no privatized land in the Pueblo grants. On the other hand, see Gorman, missionary at Laguna Pueblo, to Collins, superintendent of Indian affairs, 2 Oct. 1858, in commissioner of Indian affairs to secretary of the interior, 6 Nov. 1858, Senate Executive Document no. 76, 35th Congress, 2d Session.

72. See *Temelling v. Freehold and Immigration Co.,* 94 U.S. 644 (1876); *Bustamante v. Sena,* 80 NM 274 (1979).

73. The original is still on file at the office of the Bureau of Land Management in Santa Fe. The second is found in Pecos Pueblo Grant, SGNM, R. F, F. 533, r. 7, f. 547. The third was filed on 11 June 1980, at Book 41, p. 372, of the records of San Miguel County, Las Vegas, New Mexico.

74. The only evidence that Toya received a patent comes from a 23 May 1921 letter from Pablo Toya to Lucius Dills of the Bureau of Land Management in Santa Fe, Pecos Pueblo Grant, SGNM, r. 7. Toya says that his father received the patent in 1864 and lost it thereafter. In 1921 the Pecos Pueblo survivors at Jemez and their supporters were pressing the United States attorney to help them sue for the restoration of their Pecos lands.

75. Kessell, *Kiva, Cross, and Crown,* 467. Michael Steck to Dole, 18 June 1864, NMS, r. 552.

Chapter 4

1. *United States v. Lucero,* 1 N.M. 423 (1869); *United States v. Varela,* 1 N.M. 593 (1874); *Territory v. Delinquent Taxpayers of New Mexico,* 12 N.M. 139 (1904). All these cases were overruled in the twentieth century, either by direct congressional act or by Supreme Court decision.

2. Ward to Norton, 2 Aug. 1867, in *1867 Annual Report of the Commissioner of Indian Affairs* (Washington, D.C.: Government Printing Office, 1868), 207–13.

3. *United States v. Antonio Joseph,* 94 U.S. 614 (1876).

4. Victor Westphall, *Thomas Benton Catron and His Era* (Tucson: University of Arizona Press, 1973), 23–30, 100–102, 109–12; William A. Keleher, *Maxwell Land Grant* (Santa Fe: Gannon, 1975); Howard Lamar, *The Far Southwest, 1846–1912: A Territorial History* (New York: W.W. Norton, 1970), 146–47.

5. *De La O v. Acoma,* 1 N.M. 226 (1857); Aurora Hunt, *Kirby Benedict: Frontier Federal Judge* (Glendale, Cal.: Arthur H. Clark, 1961); Arie W. Poldervaart, *Black Robed Justice* (Santa Fe: Historical Society of New Mexico, 1948), 49–66.

6. Deed, Juan Antonia Tolla and ten others to John Ward, 24 Aug. 1868, recorded 22 Sept. 1868 in San Miguel County Deed Book 5, 24.

7. Louis H. Warner, undated "Memorandum on Pecos Pueblo Grant," probably c. 1928, in Warner file, Pueblo Lands Board, Southern Pueblo Agency, Albuquerque, New Mexico.

8. Power of attorney, Juan Antonio and ten others to John Ward, 24 Aug. 1868.

9. Schedule 1, p. 55, precinct no. 3, Ninth Census, Santa Fe County, enumerated 18 July 1870. Original in SRCA.

10. Annie H. Abel, ed., *The Official Correspondence of James S. Calhoun* (Washington, D.C.: U.S. Government Printing Office, 1915), 21–25.

11. At various times different government officials attributed different linguistic skills to the ubiquitous Ward. For example, as late as 20 Feb. 1855 Indian Superintendent Grenier justified Ward's claim for unpaid salary on the grounds that Ward alone among New Mexico Indian agents spoke Spanish fluently (NMS 547, 24). In September 1852, an earlier Indian agent, Abraham R. Wooley, described Ward as a "daring and intrepid man who speaks Apache fluently" (NMS 546, 20). Part of the confusion stems from the fact that the usual Indian agent could speak neither Spanish nor any native language. Since the lengua franca for New Mexico Indians was Spanish, it is likely that Ward used it to converse with all the tribes and that some of the monolingual agents mistook that for a native language.

12. Santa Fe *New Mexican,* 19 May 1868.

13. Brevet Major Carleton, 25 Feb. 1852, NMS 546, 17; Indian Agent Wooley, 9 Sept. 1852, NMS 546, 20; "Note," 1 May 1857, NMS 548, 18a; "Note," 30 Oct. 1852, NMS 546, 21. On 30 Oct. 1852, Territorial Governor Lane chose Ward as his special agent to the existing New Mexico pueblos.

14. Acting Superintendent Yost, 14 Feb. 1858, NMS 549, 57; NMS T-21-3, 9–10; NMS 549, 34; NMS T-21-4, 21.

15. *Territory v. Delinquent Taxpayers of New Mexico,* 12 N.M. 139 (1904). The case involved the question of whether the Territory of New Mexico properly could tax the patented grant lands of the various pueblos. The Territorial Supreme Court held, per Justice Parker, that it could. In the opinion Parker discoursed ex oficio on New Mexico history (12 N.M. at 146):

It is a matter of history, gathered by the writer from conversations
with early residents of the country, that Pueblos were, after the Treaty

of Guadalupe Hidalgo and down to the organization of the Territory, and perhaps down to the act of 1854, regarded by the people as citizens and possessed of all the rights of the same. They are reported to have participated in elections, and held office in Pena Blanca and other places in the Territory. They sat as grand and petit jurors in this same county of Bernalillo while Judge H. S. Johnson presided over the same, at one term of court at least. *It is reported that through the efforts of one John Ward, an agent appointed for them,* there was a tacit agreement reached between them and the people of the counties where they resided, that as long as they refrained from voting, they should not be taxed. They thus drifted out of the political life of the Territory . . . (emphasis added)

16. "Note," 30 Oct. 1852, NMS 546, 21; "Note," 31 June 1852, NMS 546, 18; "Note," 30 Sept. 1854, NMS 547, 16.

17. Lawrence Kelly, *Navajo Roundup* (Boulder: Pruett Publishing, 1970), 17 and n. 32; "Note," 3 May 1861, NMS 551, 4; Collins to CIA, 19 Jan. 1862, NMS 551, 7; Steck to commissioner, 20 Aug. 1863, NMS T-21-5, 24; Ward to agent, 10 Jan. 1863, NMS 551, 14; "Note," 18 April 1863, NMS 551, 13.

18. "Note," 19 Aug. 1863, NMS T-21-5, 23; "Note," 13 July 1863, NMS 551, 20; Steck to CIA, 18 Jan. 1864, NMS T-21-6, 8.

19. "Note, appropriations," 1867, NMS 554, 57; "Note," 12 Oct. 1865, NMS 552, 36.

20. Until the mid-1880s, Congress made no appropriation for an agent for the Pueblos. See, for instance, 13 Stat. 495, ch. 36, section 14, act of 30 June 1887.

21. "Note," 10 Jan. 1864, NMS 552, 8; Power of Attorney, Tolla et al. to Ward, 24 Aug. 1868.

22. *Annual Report of the Commissioner of Indian Affairs, 1867,* 207–13. In his report, dated 10 June 1867, Ward reports that he had written fuller statements in 1866 but that the department had failed to print them because the reports arrived too late in Washington for inclusion in the official reports of that year. Those 1866 reports, if they existed, are now lost.

23. *Annual Report, 1867,* 213.

24. Ward to Norton, July 1867, *Annual Report, 1867,* 24.

25. Ward to Norton, July 1867, *Annual Report, 1867,* 17.

26. Mitchell to CIA, 24 May 1867, NMS 554, 35; CIA investigation, July 1867, NMS T-21-7, 42; Norton to CIA, 20 Aug. 1867, NMS 554, 53–54; Ward to CIA, 6 Oct. 1867, NMS 554, 53–54.

27. Victor Westphall, *The Public Domain in New Mexico, 1854–1891* (Albuquerque: University of New Mexico Press, 1965), 3; *Tamelling v. U.S. Freehold and Immigration Co.,* 93 U.S. 644 (1876): *Pueblo of Nambe v. Romero,* 10 NM. 58 (1900).

28. Deed, Juan Antonio Tolla et al. to John Ward, 24 Aug. 1868. Note that many more of the so-called natives of the Pecos Pueblo residing at Jemez joined in the 12 April 1872 deed from the Pecos remnants to Frank Chapman.

But also note that both deeds were signed by Juan Antonio Tolla, or Toya, who served as the last resident governor of Pecos at Pecos. See John Kessell, *Kiva, Cross, and Crown* (Washington, D.C.: National Park Service, U.S. Department of the Interior, 1979), 469, 477.

29. Power of attorney, Juan Antonio Tolla et al. to John Ward, 24 Aug. 1868.

30. See July 1878, NMS 555, 4: Ward is still listed as special agent to the Pueblos. NMS 554, 77, shows Ward being paid fifteen hundred dollars per year in that same capacity. While there is no formal listing for 1868, the position, and presumably the salary, remained the same.

31. Power of attorney, Tolla et al. to Ward, 24 Aug. 1868.

32. Title to all property ultimately must stem from one sovereign or another. In the case of New Mexico there were three possibilities: Spain, Mexico, or the United States. But ultimately only one counted—title from the United States—because as the most recent sovereign, the United States set out to confirm (or reject) previous disposals of the public domain from antecedent sovereigns. Under United States rule, title had to originate in the United States or be confirmed by it. See, for example, *Tamelling v. United States Freehold and Immigration Co.*, 93 U.S. 644 (1876).

33. Testimony of Francis C. Wilson, 13 Feb. 1913, in Hearings before the Committee on Indian Affairs, 62nd Congress, 3rd Session, on S. 6085, "A Bill to Authorize the Acceptance of Trusts from the Pueblo Indians of New Mexico," 13.

34. David J. Miller, entry, p. 41, Supervisor District 86, Enumerator District 41, Santa Fe County, 1880 census; Malcolm Ebright, *The Tierra Amarilla Grant: A History of Chicanery* (Santa Fe: Center for Land Grant Studies, 1979), 18–19.

35. H.R. Report 321, 36th Congress, 1st Session (1860), 279–90; "Field Notes" of the 1876 survey of the Alejandro Valle Grant, San Miguel County, New Mexico, Office of the Bureau of Land Management, Santa Fe.

36. H.R. Report 321, 36th Congress, 1st Session (1860).

37. "Field Notes," 1876 survey of Alejandro Valle Grant.

38. Julian to Ratliff, 21 Feb. 1887, SGNM, r. 49, f. 86.

39. "Field Notes," 1887 survey of the Alejandro Valle grant, BLM, Santa Fe.

40. Pecos Pueblo Grant, SGNM, r. 7, f. 243.

41. Advertisement for the Historical Society of New Mexico, in *The Legislative Blue Book of the Territory of New Mexico* (Santa Fe, 1882; pages unnumbered). For a general account of the history of the influential Historical Society, see Charles H. Lange and Carroll L. Riley, eds., *The Southwestern Journals of Adolph Bandelier, 1880–1882* (Albuquerque: University of New Mexico Press, 1966), 413.

42. Miller to "Dear Doctor" [Lewis Henry Morgan], 14 June 1878, 12 February 1880, 2 July 1887; "Memo Book of D. J. Miller, Santa Fe, New Mexico, October–December 1877," in Lewis Henry Morgan Collection, University of Rochester Library, Rochester, New York.

43. "Memo Book of D. J. Miller," 58.

44. "Memo Book of D. J. Miller," 69. See also "question 5," p. 6, p. 30, p. 70, p. 72.

45. Miller to [Morgan], 14 June 1878, Lewis Henry Morgan Collection. In that letter Miller recommended that Morgan interview Antonio Joseph and Juan Santistevan of Taos concerning the customs and rites of the members of Taos Pueblo. Joseph and Santistevan speculated in Taos Pueblo land and ended up as defendants in the celebrated *Joseph* case.

46. John Gwynn to David Miller, 5 April 1833, recorded the same day in the records of San Miguel County, Deed Book 23, 222. By the deed Gwynn conveyed to Miller a one-forty-sixth interest in the Pablo Montoya Grant. The deed itself computed the equivalent value of the acreage as 14,249 acres. For a history of the complicated Pablo Montoya grant, see J. J. Bowden, "Private Land Claims in the Southwest," Master's thesis (Southern Methodist University, 1969), pt. 4; and *State v. Red River Valley Co.*, 51 N.M. 207, 182 P2 421 (1947). For Miller's interest in San Miguel County land, see Vigil et al. to Miller, 17 July 1873, recorded the same day in San Miguel County Deed Book 7, p. 269.

47. Miller to Ward, 10 March 1873, San Miguel County Deed Book 7, pp. 140–41. The deed states that Miller conveys to Ward the Pecos Pueblo grant, which was "conditionally conveyed to me by said John Ward and his wife by deed bearing date October 7, 1869." The conditions to which Miller refers in this deed are not set out.

48. Tolla et al. to Chapman, 12 April 1872. Recorded in short form in the records of San Miguel County, but set out in full as Exhibit 8 to *Seymour v. Roberts et al.*, San Miguel County cause no. 2723 (1887), in SRCA.

49. Receipt by Juan Antonio Tolla, Juan Pedro Vigil, Jose Miguel Vigil, and Pablo Toya to Frank Chapman, for $1,300.00, 25 Feb. 1873, attached as exhibit 9 to *Seymour v. Roberts et al.* (1887).

50. Tolla et al. statement before Probate Judge B. Jesus Marquez, 24 Feb. 1873, attached as exhibit 11 to *Seymour v. Roberts et al.* (1887).

51. Miller to Ward, 10 March 1873, and Ward and wife to Frank Chapman, 10 March 1873, San Miguel County Deed Book 7, pp. 142–44.

52. Receipt by Ward to Chapman for thirteen hundred dollars, 26 June 1873, attached as exhibit 4 to *Seymour v. Roberts et al.*, San Miguel County cause no. 2723 (1887).

53. *Las Vegas Gazette*, 15 March 1873.

54. J. Witmar, Jr., to Frank Chapman, 26 Jan. 1871, interest in Pablo Montoya grant recorded in San Miguel County Courthouse, Book 36, p. 18. See Milton Callon, *Las Vegas: The Town that Wouldn't Gamble* (Las Vegas, N.M.: Optic Publishers, 1968), 28, for a description of the early, successful Las Vegas businessman, Juan Maria Baca, who was "born in the Indian Pueblo of Jemez."

55. *Las Vegas Optic*, 2 Jan. 1880.

56. *Las Vegas Optic*, 18 Dec. 1879.

57. *Las Vegas Optic*, 13 Dec. 1879.

58. Chapman and Dold, partnership agreement, 22 Nov. 1873, recorded in San Miguel County Courthouse, 6 Jan. 1881.

59. "Inventory, In re the Estate of Frank Chapman" (1881), San Miguel County Courthouse. Chapman's heirs to Dold, 17 Feb. 1880, recorded 16 March 1881, San Miguel County Deed Book 15, pp. 431–40. For an example of Chapman's connection with other real estate entrepreneurs, see San Miguel County record books for 1 Dec. 1878 and 17 Dec. 1883, which set out Chapman's extensive connection with T. B. Mills, among others. Between 1878 and 1884, at the time the railroad was working its way through Las Vegas, Mills became the biggest subdivider of Las Vegas real estate.

60. Affidavit of Henry Dold, 9 June 1887, exhibit 6 to *Seymour v. Roberts et al.* (1887).

61. *Las Vegas Optic,* 8 Dec. 1879.

62. *Las Vegas Optic,* 30 Dec. 1879.

63. *Las Vegas Optic,* 2 Jan. 1880.

64. *Las Vegas Optic,* 7 Jan. 1880.

Chapter 5

1. *Journal of the Legislative Council of the Territory of New Mexico of the session begun and held in the city of Santa Fe, Territory of New Mexico, on Monday the third day of December, A.D. one thousand eight hundred and sixty-six, it being the sixteenth Legislative Assembly for the said Territory* (Santa Fe: Manderfield and Tucker, 1867), 36; copy at SRCA.

2. For instance, *Journal,* 28, lists Manuel Barela of San Miguel (county) as delegate to the council. This alternate spelling was common for the day.

3. Norton to Bogy, 6 Feb. 1867 and Norton to Taylor, 3 Aug. 1867, NMS 583.

4. George Hebert to Charles E. Mix, 10 Dec. 1867, NMS 583.

5. Martin Kozlowski to C. P. Clever, 12 Feb. 1868; petition attached, signed by Wm. Breeden and fifty others. C. P. Clever to New Mexico Superintendent Charles E. Mix, 23 May 1868. Both in NMS 583.

6. *United States v. Lucero,* 1 N.M. 422 (1869).

7. 4 U.S. Stat. 730, section 11, act of 30 June 1834.

8. 9 U.S. Stat. 587, act of 27 February 1851.

9. *U.S. v. Lucero,* 1 N.M. at 428.

10. For Benedict's judicial career, see Arie W. Poldervaart, *Black Robed Justice* (Santa Fe: Historical Society of New Mexico, 1948), 51. For Benedict's life, see Aurora Hunt, *Kirby Benedict, Frontier Federal Judge* (Glendale, Cal.: Arthur H. Clark, 1961). For an example of Benedict's judicial temperament and prose see *De La O v. Acoma,* 1 N.M. 226 (1857). Underlying Benedict's opinion's masterful irony in this early case there were the seeds of an idea which subsequent New Mexico territorial courts had trouble shaking. To be Indian meant to be uncivilized and thus requiring the government's fostering care. In *De La O* Benedict treated the Pueblos as citizens, thereby giving them

the right to sue to recover their property documents. But by gaining the right to sue, in Benedict's view the Pueblos lost the right to demand special privileges from the government. This dilemma runs through legal treatment of the Pueblos in the nineteenth century; they won respect as humans only by losing the special protection of the federal government.

11. William Clarke Whitford, *Colorado Volunteers in the Civil War: The New Mexico Campaign* (Denver: State Historical Society of Colorado, 1906), 62.

12. *Journal*, 21.

13. Santa Fe *New Mexican*, 1 Aug. 1867.

14. Poldervaart, *Black Robed Justice*, 51.

15. Santa Fe *New Mexican*, 3 Aug. 1867.

16. *U.S. v. Lucero*, 1 N.M. 422, 450–58 (1869).

17. Poldervaart, *Black Robed Justice*, 67–71.

18. For a brief history of the earliest development of what became the 1834 Non-Intercourse Act, see Paul W. Gates, *History of Public Land Law Development* (New York: Arno Press, 1979), 33–35.

19. 4 U.S. Stat. 730, section 14.

20. *U.S. v. Lucero*, 1 N.M. 422, 453–54 (1869).

21. *U.S. v. Lucero*, 1 N.M. 422, 456 (1869).

22. Charles H. Lange and Carroll L. Riley, eds., *The Southwestern Journals of Adolph F. Bandelier, 1880–1882* (Albuquerque: University of New Mexico Press, 1966).

23. Ward to Norton, 2 Aug. 1867, NMS 583.

24. Attorney General to Elkins, 23 Nov. 1867, NMS 583.

25. For the complex political situation, see Howard Lamar, *The Far Southwest, 1846–1912: A Territorial History* (New York: W.W. Norton, 1970), 122–35.

26. *U.S. v. Lucero*, 1 N.M. 422, 426 (1869).

27. Watts represented the heirs of Luis Maria C. de Baca in their claim to the Las Vegas grant, first before the surveyor general for New Mexico and then before Congress. Congress confirmed the land to the Town of Las Vegas, but offered to the C. de Baca heirs five alternative selections of equivalent acreage from the public domain. Watts received four of those five selections as his legal fee. See, for instance, *Wise v. Watts*, 239 F. 207 (CA 9, 1917), adjudicating the claim of Cornelius C. Watts, John S. Watts's son, to Baca Float no. 3. The case describes all the Watts claims arising from the Town of Las Vegas litigation. See also Lamar, *The Far Southwest*, 140.

28. *U.S. v. Lucero*, 1 N.M. 422, 431 (1869).

29. Elkins to Attorney General, 17 Sept. 1870, NMS 583.

30. Arny Report no. 55, in *Report of the Commissioner of Indian Affairs, 1872* (Washington, D.C.: U.S. Government Printing Office, 1872), 309–10. See also Arny Report no. 56, 310. Arny concludes by urging for the Pueblos "the importance of some action in relation to their lands occupied by citizens, and the question of the citizenship of the Pueblo Indians which has caused much trouble since my last report (dated 8/18/1871) . . ." By the time he wrote the second plea for action, Arny had been transferred from New Mexico to

the Los Pinos agency, in Colorado. His replacement in New Mexico, Agent Cole, knew little about the matter, "owing to the short time which I had charge of this agency."

31. N. O. Pope, superintendent for New Mexico, 10 Oct. 1872, report no. 49, in *Report of the Commissioner, 1872,* 308.

32. Commissioner of Indian Affairs, *Report of the Commissioner, 1872,* 55.

33. Victor Westphall, *Thomas Benton Catron and His Era* (Tucson: University of Arizona Press, 1973), 25.

34. Lamar, *The Far Southwest,* 138.

35. Catron to Attorney General, 11 Nov. 1872, NMS.

36. Territory of New Mexico, United States District Court, First Judicial District, *The United States of America v. Martin Kozlowski,* F. 69½, NMSCt.

37. Everyone recognized that a railroad from the East would most likely have to pass through the Pecos Pueblo grant. Similar recognition perked an early and ongoing political concern with the Maxwell Land Grant, through which the railroad route to the East eventually would have to pass as well. See Lamar, *The Far Southwest,* 141–43; David F. Myrick, *New Mexico's Railroads, An Historical Survey* (Golden: Colorado Historical Association, 1970), 46.

38. Kozlowski backed the military-dominated Carleton faction against Arny's. The military faction became the Democratic party faction in territorial politics; that of Arny became the Republican party faction. Catron soon led the state Republican party.

39. See testimony of Donaciano Vigil before the surveyor general for New Mexico, 27 Dec. 1876, Gaspar Ortiz Grant, SGNM, R. 31, F. 67; r. 16, f. 673. Myra Ellen Jenkins, "The Pueblo of Nambe and Its Lands," in *The Changing Ways of Southwestern Indians,* ed. Albert Schroeder (Glorieta, N.M.: Rio Grande Press, 1973), 91–104.

40. Complaint, *U.S. v. Kozlowski,* NMSCt, f. 69½.

41. Whitford, *Colorado Volunteers,* 84, gives the sometimes inaccurate details of Kozlowski's pre-Pecos life. I have selected only those I have been able to verify elsewhere. See also Milton Callon, *Las Vegas: The Town That Wouldn't Gamble* (Las Vegas, N.M.: Optic Publishers, 1968), 55.

42. Hunt, *Kirby Benedict,* 46.

43. Whitford, *Colorado Volunteers,* 84.

44. Martin Kozlowski to Helen Kozlowski, 24 June 1861, in San Miguel County Deed Book 9, pp. 346–47.

45. Mortgage, Martin Kozlowski and Helen Kozlowski to Frank Chapman, 20 June 1879, MR 6, p. 41, San Miguel County Courthouse, Las Vegas, New Mexico. Wm. Osherton, SFe, NM, to Dr. James P. Reid, Broonville, Mo., 1 June 1862, in A. A. Jones papers, SRCA.

46. Deed, M. Kozlowski to H. Kozlowski, 24 June 1861. The translated description of the Spanish warranty deed reads as follows: "the boundaries of the land, on the north the top of the Pecos arroyo; on the south, the top of the same arroyo; on the east the entrance of the arroyo into the river without

including the land beyond; and on the west the fence that is there to this day."

47. Whitford, *Colorado Volunteers,* 84.

48. Act of Assembly of Territorial Legislature of New Mexico, 15 Feb. 1878, "An Act Referring to Rights in Real Property and for Other Purposes." The act authorized New Mexico residents to file documents in the public land records of the state giving notice that they claimed by preemption certain sections of the public domain to which they could make no formal claim until the government surveys had been completed. By the summer of 1879, thirty Pecos residents had filed such claims in the San Miguel County Courthouse. Subsequent federal court decisions made it clear that such state-initiated declarations could have no effect on the federal decision as to who should receive federal title to the land.

49. Mortgage, M. and H. Kozlowski to Frank Chapman, 20 June 1869.

50. "Inventory," *In re the Estate of Frank Chapman, Deceased,* 3 Feb. 1881, San Miguel County Records, Book 8-H, 44; Samuel Chapman et al. to Dold, 17 Feb. 1880, recorded 16 March 1881, Deed Book 15, 431–40.

51. Lange and Riley, *Bandelier Journals,* 411–12.

52. Santa Fe *New Mexican,* 15 March 1881.

53. 1880 census, enumeration district 14, Las Vegas, 2 June 1880; in SRCA.

54. 1880 census, enumeration district 36, p. 4, Town of Pecos; in SRCA.

55. Territory of New Mexico, United States District Court, First Judicial District, *United States of America v. Manuel Varela,* p. 4, NMSCt, F. 69½.

56. See n. 1, above.

57. Manuel Timoteo Pino and Justo Pastor Pino to wives, 15 July 1848, Preston Beck Jr. Grant, SGNM, r. 12, f. 409. Blas Ortega and Manuel Varela witnessed the deed. Varela's name appears on various documents during the 1850s, as justice of the peace. Last will and testament of Donaciano Vigil, 11 May 1877, in private papers of Donaciano Vigil, SRCA.

58. Jesús Lopez et al. to "Señor Barela," 29 Sept. 1855, recorded 28 Nov. 1925 in San Miguel County Deed Book 100, p. 413. The Spanish deed identifies the location of the tract as the "cañon de pecos," even though it almost surely lay within the Pecos Pueblo grant.

59. Visente Armenta et al. to Manuel Varela, 22 Dec. 1857, San Miguel County Deed Book 19, p. 92. The Spanish warranty deed describes the land conveyed as "that land situated in the Cañon de Pecos at the point commonly known as 'La Posada' bounded on the north by land of Miguel Armenta, on the east the crest of the ridge, on the south land of Jesus Armenta and on the west, the river." La Posada is a small settlement on the Pecos River about four miles above the northern boundary of the Pecos Pueblo grant. The Armijo clan still lives there.

60. Manuel Varela, "Aviso de Posesión," 15 July 1879, filed in the records of San Miguel County, Book 34, p. 14.

61. Samuel Ellison, special commissioner in chancery, to Manuel Barela and Jesus Maria Baca y Salazar, 31 May 1862, filed for record 6 Aug. 1862,

San Miguel County Deed Book 34, p. 286. The document identifies the tract
once again as located in the Cañon de Pecos and amounting to 150 acres,
more or less. It says the tract is bounded on the north by lands of Manuel
Barela and Blas Ortega; on the east by the Pecos River; on the south by lands
of Pablo Moya, Manuel Varela, and Vicente Quintana; and on the west by
"public lands." The deed recites that Ellison sold the land as executor of the
estate of Preston Beck, Jr., a year before, on 23 May 1861, at a public auction.
The sale called for payment terms of one-third down, one-third in six months,
and the final one-third at the end of one year. Wm. Street to James P. Beck,
9 May 1861, indicates that the sale proposed for May 23 involved the western
half of the Pino ranch at Pecos. The eastern half had been sold in 1854, to
Donaciano Vigil. The 1862 deed to Varela and Baca y Salazar shows that the
two paid $2601.00 for the 150 acres estimated to be in the western one-half
of the Pino/Beck ranch at Pecos.

62. 1880 census, enumeration district 36, p. 4, "Manuel Varela"; in SRCA.

63. See "Supplemental Plats Showing Private Claims in Sections 28, 33,
29, 32, 31 and 36 within the Pecos Pueblo Grant, 13 November 1934."
BLM, Santa Fe. In particular map sheets 3, 7, 8, 9, 23, 25, and 27 indicate
the tracts confirmed to either Manuel Varela or the heirs of Manuel Varela.

64. Poldervaart, *Black Robed Justice,* 28; Lamar, *The Far Southwest,* 90;
testimony of Joab Houghton before the surveyor general, 25 Feb. 1875,
Preston Beck Jr. Grant, SGNM, r. 13, f. 219–23.

65. Answer and Demurrer, *United States v. Varela* and *United States v. Kozlowski,* 10 Feb. 1873, NMSCt, F. 69¹/₂.

66. "In the Matter of the Pueblo of Pecos and Petition for Incorporation
Thereof," no. 4716, San Miguel County, filed 25 Feb. 1896, SRCA. United
States courts held that Spanish community grants never held title to their
common lands. Therefore those common lands belonged to the United States,
not to the grants. On the other hand, the same courts also held from the very
beginning that Pueblo Indian grants were "perfected" community grants and
that ownership of the common lands vested in the grant, not the government.

67. Transcript, *U.S. v. Kozlowski,* p. 10, NMSCt, F. 69¹/₂.

68. Order Dismissing Complaint, *U.S. v. Kozlowski* and *U.S. v. Varela,*
10 Feb. 1873; transcripts, NMSCt, F. 69¹/₂.

69. Complaint, *U.S. v. Joseph* and *U.S. v. Santistevan,* 13 June and 30 June
1873, NMSCt, F. 70.

70. Testimony of Juan Santistevan, 31 June 1878, Antonio Martinez Grant,
SGNM, r. 24, f. 23–24. Lamar, *The Far Southwest,* 82, notes that the local
office of probate judge, which Santistevan held in Taos, was particularly critical
to land grant maneuvers. Subsequent to the Pueblo litigation, Santistevan
continued in his local political career. Occasionally he represented Taos in the
Territorial Assembly. The 1890–91 Diario del Consejos (SRCA) show Santistevan as a member then. See also *Territory v. Mills,* 16 N.M. 555 (1911), for
a description of his banking career. For Santistevan's ongoing connection to
various members of the Santa Fe Ring see Santistevan to Max Frost, 27 Feb.
1889, in private papers of L. B. Prince, SRCA.

71. TANM, r. 4, f. 554ff., contain the story of the 1872 Taos County embroglio. Robert W. Larson, *New Mexico's Quest for Statehood, 1846–1912* (Albuquerque: University of New Mexico Press, 1968), 96–97, provides the general outline of the battle that involved Joseph, Santistevan, and Catron.

72. Lange and Riley, *Bandelier Journals*, 411, give a brief, sometimes inaccurate sketch of Joseph's life.

73. See, for example, *T. B. Catron v. Antonio Joseph*, Santa Fe District Court, Catron file in PC 29 (Catron Collection), SCUNM, box 203. According to Catron's version of the suit, in November 1873 Joseph had hired none other than Samuel Ellison to induce Congress to confirm the 469,000 acre San Joaquin del Rio de Chama grant. Joseph had acquired, prior to 1873, a large number of undivided interests in the tract. He had promised to pay Ellison if the grant was confirmed. Ellison took Joseph's promisory note and assigned it to Catron for some money he had borrowed but never paid back. Finally, in the 1890s the Court of Private Land Claims confirmed the San Joaquin grant, but for much less acreage than Joseph had anticipated. Catron claimed that that confirmation satisfied the conditions of the promise to Ellison. He now owned Joseph's promise to Ellison and, in 1903, sued to collect. Lamar, *The Far Southwest*, 65, identifies Joseph as "a smiling urbane merchant and land speculator from Taos." For the "rough roasting" Joseph's 1872 land speculation schemes brought on, see Walter John Donlon, "Le Baron Bradford Prince: Chief Justice and Governor of New Mexico Territory, 1879–1893" (Ph.D. diss., University of New Mexico, 1967), 144. Max Frost, one of the most notorious speculators himself, and a Catron Republican, castigated the Democrat Joseph for his sins.

74. Lange and Riley, *Bandelier Journals*, 411. See also advertisement for the Historical Society, in *Legislative Bluebook*, 1880. Joseph joined David Miller, L. Bradford Prince, and Samuel Ellison, among other speculators, on that board.

75. Territorial Archives of New Mexico, r. 4, f. 554ff. show that Joseph ran in the 1871 Taos County election for *jues de pruebas* and lost to the Republican Romulo Martinez, 750 to 844. He did not challenge the results of his own election.

76. Lamar, *The Far Southwest*, 162, identifies Breeden as Catron's law partner, at least for a while. Breeden was a "forceful, aggressive, stubborn lawyer," according to Lamar. He was also a Republican. In 1884 he served as Republican central committeeman for New Mexico. Donlon, "L. B. Prince," 136.

77. See *Quintana v. Tompkins*, 1 N.M. 303 (1853), involving a disputed race for justice of the peace in Santa Fe in 1853.

78. Order in transcripts of *United States v. Santistevan*, NMSCt, F. 69 1/2, and *United States v. Joseph*, NMSCt, F. 68.

79. The alternatives reflected Catron's concern that the appeal not be decided on the narrowest and most arcane procedural grounds. Choosing both helped guarantee that the court would reach the question on its merits.

80. The first collected volume of New Mexico Supreme Court decisions

was not published and distributed until 1880. Earlier systems of printing and distributing decisions left much to be desired. Poldervaart, *Black Robed Justice,* 8–10. Still, Houghton himself had sat on the court that reviewed *Lucero.* The decision had received wide publicity in the local press. The Indian commissioners had printed the decision in its entirety in 1867. It is inconceivable that Houghton did not know about it. Yet neither he nor any other lawyer in the case ever mentioned it.

81. "Brief and Points of Defendant in Error," transcript, filed 14 Jan. 1874, in *United States v. Kozlowski,* NMSCt, F. 69½.

82. *Sunol v. Hepburn,* 1 Cal. 543 (1851). There the California Supreme Court simply held that Pueblo citizenship proved too much, in that citizenship was not necessarily inconsistent with wardship.

83. Mariano Galván-Rivera, *Ordenanzas de tierras y aguas o sea formulario geométrico-judicial, amojonamiento y deslinde de las poblaciones,* supplement to Joaquín Escriche, *Diccionario razonado de legislación y jurisprudencia* (Paris: Rosa y Bouret, 1863), cap. 12, 212ff.

84. *United States v. Ritchie,* 17 U.S. (Howard) 524 (1854), at 541.

85. Breeden's brief does not appear in the surviving archives of the *Santistevan* or *Joseph* cases. I have borrowed his principal arguments from the compiler's summary set out in *United States v. Santistevan,* 1 N.M. 585, 586. Joseph's attorney in the district court, R. H. Tompkins, did not represent him in the Territorial Supreme Court; Breeden took his place.

86. Summary of brief, in *United States v. Santistevan,* 1 N.M. 586. In fact, Calhoun negotiated unratified treaties with many of the pueblos around 1850.

87. Summary of brief, in *United States v. Santistevan,* 1 N.M. 586.

88. In fact, Catron had brought at least 204 Non-Intercourse Act violation suits in 1872. Apparently he was not sure who he would in fact prosecute, and so left the names blank. "Brief and Points of Plaintiffs," *United States v. Joseph,* transcript, NMSCt, F. 70.

89. "Brief and Points of Plaintiff in Error," *United States v. Joseph,* NMSCt, F. 70. Slowly the problem of Congress's so-called plenary control over Indian affairs surfaced from this eliptical reference in the early Catron brief. Eventually the issue would stand the Pueblo question on its head. What started as a question of who the Pueblos were ended as a question of what power Congress had over them. The 1877 *Joseph* decision turned on the issue of whether the Pueblos fit into the definition of "Indians" that Congress had used in the 1834 Non-Intercourse Act. The 1912 *Sandoval* decision turned on the issue of whether Congress retained the power to change that definition. Only the 1926 *Candelaria* decision ruled that the Supreme Court earlier had erred in its 1877 *Joseph* decision. As for his authority, Catron relied in his brief on *Choteau v. Molony,* 16 Howard 202 (1853), to prove that Spain, Mexico, and now the United States owned the Pueblo lands in trust for the Indian inhabitants; therefore, the rules of government lands applied to the Pueblo grants. *Choteau* involved another of those fantastic land claims based on an alleged Indian transfer whose adjudication colored the course of Indian land litigation in the nineteenth and twentieth centuries. Molony was an urban settler in the city

of Dubuque, Iowa, holding land under a patent that the United States had issued when it opened the area to public land law settlement. Choteau claimed that he owned the entire city, because he had purchased from Dubuque who, in turn, had purchased from the original settlers, the Fox Indians. Therefore, argued Choteau, the United States had never had the right to claim the land as public domain and patent it to Malony and others. A determination of the relationship of Spanish law to Indian title was hardly necessary for a decision against Choteau's nineteenth-century claim. Irrespective of their power to convey, held the Supreme Court, the Fox themselves had never intended to sell that much land to Dubuque in the first place. But the court did mention almost incidentally its interpretation of Spanish law as it affected Indians. By the time the Supreme Court reversed its decision on the Pueblos, in *Sandoval* and *Candelaria*, it still relied on *Choteau* for the basic proposition that, under Spanish and Mexican law, Pueblos could not transfer their lands without the consent of the government.

90. Eventually Pueblo Indian land grants came to be treated as so-called perfected community grants and non-Indian Spanish community land grants came to be treated as so-called imperfect community grants. The difference in terminology amounted to a difference in the treatment of the grant's common lands. In a perfected (Pueblo) grant, the grant itself owned those lands around the settled areas that were the private property of no particular resident. In imperfect (Hispanic) municipal grants, the unallotted common lands still belonged to the national government, not to the local grant, and were always subject to national control and disposition. Compare *Joseph* and the 1913 *Sandoval* Pueblo decisions with the 1897 non-Indian Sandoval decision involving the common lands of the San Miguel del Bado grant. *United States v. Sandoval,* 167 U.S. 278 (1897).

91. *United States v. Santistevan,* 1 N.M. 583, 587 (1874).

92. See, for instance, Grant Foreman, *The Five Civilized Tribes* (Norman: University of Oklahoma Press, 1934).

93. *United States v. Varela,* 1 N.M. 593, 595 (1874).

94. *United States v. Varela,* 1 N.M. 597 (1874).

95. See, for instance, State of New Mexico "Brief in Support of Motion for Summary Judgment" against claim of Mescalero Apaches for immemorial priority in *State ex. rel. Reynolds v. Lewis et al.,* Chaves County cause no. 78965 (1980).

96. Docketing Statement, *United States of America v. Antonio Joseph,* no. 226, p. 9, Archives of the Supreme Court of the United States, Washington, D.C.

97. In fact the briefs, pleadings, and record of the argument in the case indicate that Evarts did most of the actual work in the appeal, while Elkins lent his important name to it.

98. See, for instance, *United States v. Sandoval,* 213 U.S. 28 (1913).

99. "Brief and Points of Authority for Defendant in Error, Wm. Evarts, of counsel, Supreme Court No. 226, 227." Archives, U.S. Supreme Court.

100. *United States v. Joseph,* at 616.

101. *United States v. Joseph,* at 616. The Miller opinion is written with such grace that it is easy to miss its pointed accuracy. Miller says that he takes the Slough quote "from the opinion of the chief justice of the court whose judgment we are reviewing . . ." Slough had been, but was not then, the justice of the court which sent Joseph to Washington. However, the court remained the same. To the extent Miller was correct, if misleading.

102. *United States v. Joseph,* at 616.

103. *United States v. Joseph,* at 619.

104. Larson, *Quest for Statehood,* 117–34.

105. Grant Foreman, *The Five Civilized Tribes* (Norman: University of Oklahoma Press, 1934), 68.

106. *Tamelling v. U.S. Freehold and Immigration Co.,* 93 U.S. 644 (1876); *Maxwell Land Grant Co. v. Dawson,* 151 U.S. 586 (1894).

107. No one yet knew how to apportion non-Indian claims to Pueblo lands between those that existed prior to 1846 and those that began only after the inception of American rule. Various claims have been made at different times. Only a comprehensive study of the Pueblo Lands Board records in Albuquerque, the Spanish and Mexican archives in Santa Fe, and the documents of the various county courthouses located in counties where Pueblo grants are situated would yield accurate results.

108. Miller to Morgan, 14 June 1878, Lewis Henry Morgan papers. "By the way," asked Miller in the letter, "did you ever read the United States Supreme Court decision (and pleadings) in the cases of *United States v. Joseph* and *United States v. John Santistevan* wherein much concerning the Pueblo Indians in many material and interesting matters is to be found?"

109. Catron to Commissioner of Indian Affairs, 23 April 1903, NARG–75, 1903, letters received, Office of Indian Affairs.

110. Callon, *Las Vegas,* 71.

Chapter 6

1. F. Stanley, *Giant in Lilliput* (Lubbock, Tex.: Pampa Press, 1963), 23. Howard Lamar, *The Far Southwest, 1846–1912: A Territorial History* (New York: W.W. Norton, 1970), 65; W. G. Ritch, "Gov. Donaciano Vigil," biographical sketch in Ritch Collection, Huntington Library, San Marino, Cal.; Executive Record Book no. 2, TANM, 28 Aug. 1877, r. 21, f. 303.

2. Will in PPDV; the exact date is uncertain.

3. Alejandro Valle Grant, SGNM, F. 18, R. 54; r. 14.

4. Ward Alan Minge, "The Last Will and Testament of Severino Martinez," *New Mexico Quarterly* 33 (Spring 1963): 33–56. Donaciano Vigil's will itself is in PPDV. Apparently it was never formerly probated. It was translated on 14 July 1939 by B. A. Reuter, a resident of the Pecos area, as part of a WPA writers' project. Reuter's translation contains some errors, which I have tried to correct.

5. Pedro Vigil (Donaciano Vigil's great-great-grandson), personal interview, 17 March 1978, Pecos, New Mexico.

6. "Pecos Hydrographic Survey," New Mexico State Engineer's Office, Santa Fe, Map Sheets A-4 and A-5. Fieldwork July–August 1920 by Ed. W. Lighton. G. Emlen Hall, "Of Time and the River," *Santa Fe Reporter,* 8 March 1978.

7. Stanley, *Giant in Lilliput,* 176–77. Stanley offers no authority for either proposition. The subsequent adjudications of the Pueblo Lands Board, in the late 1920s and early 1930s, indicate that claims stemming from the Donaciano Vigil estate were much more varied and not nearly as large as Stanley had guessed.

8. Pedro Vigil interview, 17 March 1978.

9. Lamar, *The Far Southwest,* 65.

10. Lamar, *The Far Southwest,* 73. William A. Keleher, *The Maxwell Land Grant* (Santa Fe: Gannon, 1975). Westphall, *Thomas Benton Catron.*

11. Ralph Emerson Twitchell, *Old Santa Fe: The Story of New Mexico's Ancient Capital* (Santa Fe: New Mexican Publishing, 1925), 155.

12. Testimony of Donaciano Vigil, 20 Aug. 1855, Preston Beck Grant, SGNM, r. 12, f. 43ff. See also f. 204 for Vigil testimony of 9 Feb. 1875, and f. 214 for testimony of 12 Feb. 1875. Lamar, *The Far Southwest,* 167, suggests that late in his life politicians were still "trotting out" Donaciano Vigil as a witness. Testimony of Bernardo Varela, 12 Feb. 1875, Preston Beck Grant, SGNM, r. 12, f. 206ff.

13. Manuel Doroteo Pino to wife, 15 July 1848, for "the Pino ranch at Pecos," Preston Beck Grant, SGNM, r. 12, f. 409. Manuel Varela witnessed the transaction.

14. See the history in *Pino v. Hatch,* 1 N.M. 125 (1855). See also "Preston Beck Grant" file in Private Papers of Andreus A. Jones (PPAAJ).

15. Justo Pastor Pino and Gertrudis Rascon, his wife, to Sr. Alejandro Valle, 2 Jan. 1851, PPDV.

16. Lamar, *The Far Southwest,* 67; Kearny Code, Registrar of Lands, sections 1 and 2, 3 NMSA 1978.

17. Vigil's signature on the document is genuine; he wrote with a unique hand. Pino and Rascon both sign with elaborate rubrics that appear to be Vigil's. Vigil signs as witness as well as registrar. But there is no indication that Pino and Rascon could not write for themselves. The Pino and Rascon signatures on the document definitely differ from those on the one signed the following year, conveying once again the same property to Alejandro Valle. The earlier document was not used in the Surveyor General's Office proceedings leading to the confirmation of the Alejandro Valle grant; it remained among Vigil's private papers. Its presence there suggests that Vigil may have manufactured the earlier deed and then put it aside when a better version was found. See also Pino and Rascon to Valle, 2 Jan. 1851, Alexander Valle Grant, SGNM, r. 14, f. 620.

18. Legend has it that the so-called Pigeon Ranch took its name from the bird-like fandango danced by the ranch's Franco-American owner, Alexander Valle. The myth continues. See *Santa Fe New Mexican* 26 May 1978. In fact,

contemporaneous documents show that Pigeon was Alexander Valle's real last name, and the Franco-American version only a pseudonym. See deed from J. Hyacinth Pigeon of Saint Louis "to my brother, Alejandro Valle of Santa Fe, New Mexico," 16 May 1853, in PPDV. Final government surveys show the Pigeon Ranch located just west of the formal boundary of Pecos Pueblo. Kidder, *Pecos, New Mexico: Archaeological Notes* (Andover, Mass.: Peabody Museum, 1958), 49–51, identifies a fourteenth-century offshoot of Pecos Pueblo in the vincinity of the Pigeon Ranch.

19. PPDV contain at least seven deeds involving Valle's interests in land not in any way connected to Vigil. Stanley, *Giant in Lilliput,* 167.

20. Deed from Catarino and Jesus Maria Archuleta to Alejandro Valle, 15 July 1850, for a tract of land in "Ruedas, County of San Miguel del Bado"; PPDV. Las Ruedas was the name of the town that became Rowe on the arrival of the Southern Pacific Railroad lines, in the 1870s.

21. Mortgage deed, Manuel Pino and wife, Josefa Ortiz, to Hugh N. Smith, as trustee for Preston Beck, Jr., 14 June 1853, recorded 14 Oct. 1854, in San Miguel County Records, Book 1, p. 64. See same deed in Preston Beck Jr. Grant, SGNM, r. 12, f. 72.

22. $2,600 came from the Beck loan. Justo Pastor Pino had received $1,200 from Alejandro Valle for the grant north of Pecos. See NMSCt 7, *Pino v. Hatch,* for the costs assessed against the Pinos as a result of the territorial court litigation.

23. The procedural outlines of the Pino suit are given in *Pino v. Hatch,* 1 N.M. 125 (1855). The details are contained in NMSCt 7, *Pino v. Hatch.*

24. Lamar, *The Far Southwest,* 67, 107.

25. Arie Poldervaart, *Black Robed Justice* (Santa Fe: Historical Society of New Mexico, 1948), 31, 42. Lamar, *The Far Southwest,* 73; Annie H. Abel, ed., *The Official Correspondence of James S. Calhoun* (Washington, D.C.: U.S. Government Printing Office, 1915), 53. The Surveyor General's docket book indicates that Smith's firm first handled Donaciano Vigil's claim to the Los Trigos grant.

26. Twitchell, *Old Santa Fe,* 357. *Cirilia Beck v. Estate of Preston Beck Jr.,* San Miguel County No. 363, SRCA. See also PPAAJ. Jones served as one of the state of New Mexico's first U.S. Senators. As a Las Vegan in the 1880s Jones began purchasing interests in the Preston Beck Jr. grant. By the time the United States actually issued a patent for the grant, Jones had purchased the majority of shares in it. See Jones to Surveyor General, 30 June 1920, Preston Beck Jr. Grant, SGNM, r. 12, f. 356. For testimony in the Beck paternity case see "Notes on Testimony of Josefa Salazar de Manderfield," court journal, summer session, 1879, in PPLBP.

27. See, for instance, "Report of Administrator James P. Beck to Probate Court of Santa Fe County, New Mexico," November, 1862, in PPAAJ, which shows the firm of Beck and Johnson to have received $9,674.88 as payments on accounts due. In addition, by 1862 Preston Beck's administrators had sold parts of his estate and had realized $175,000 from the sales. Various of his heirs bitterly complained that none of the money had been distributed to

them. The financial outlines of Beck's estate are given in "Inventory of the Estate of Preston Beck, Jr.," n.d. but presumably 1862, in PPAAJ. The Kozlowski connection is hinted at in Wm. Asherton, Santa Fe, to Dr. James P. Reid, Boonesville, Mo., 6 June 1862, in PPAAJ.

28. Hugh N. Smith to Preston Beck, Jr., 30 Sept. 1854. Hugh N. Smith to Preston Beck, Jr., 12 Dec. 1854, in San Miguel County Deed Book 3, p. 81.

29. Preston Beck, Jr., to Donaciano Vigil, 26 Dec. 1854, recorded 21 July 1887, in San Miguel County Deed Book 33, p. 36. The deed itself said the tract comprised the eastern half of the Manuel Pino ranch at Pecos, that the tract was bounded on the south by Vicente Quintana, and that the deed did not include the lands of Juan Valencia. In the first comprehensive investigation of landholdings within the Pecos Pueblo grant, the Pueblo Lands Board, in 1929–30, found that the lands just south of the ones confirmed to the heirs of Donaciano Vigil still belonged to the heirs of Juan Valencia. See "Supplemental Plat Showing Private Claims in Section 33, T. 16N, R. 12E NMPM, Pecos Pueblo Grant, 1931," in BLM, Santa Fe.

30. For instance, Renehan to Comm. Burke, 9 Sept. 1923, NARG–75, 013, pt. 7.

31. For instance, Pablo Moya to Donaciano Vigil, 8 Sept. 1874, recorded 5 Aug. 1874, in San Miguel County Deed Book 6, p. 182. The Spanish deed describes the land sold as lying west of the Pecos River, always bounded on the north by Manuel Varela. For the first time, the deed acknowledges that the tract is inside the boundaries of the Pecos Pueblo grant: "adentro de las lineas del Pueblo de Pecos."

32. For a brief but adequate account of the settlement of Cuyamungue, see United States v. Maria de la Paz Valdez de Conway, 175 U.S. 60 (1899).

33. For instance, Ickes to Wheeler, 9 May 1933 NARG–75, 013, pt. 19: "At various times encroachments by non-Indians upon the lands of these tribes took place. These encroachments multiplied during the period subsequent to 1850."

34. Affidavit of Donaciano Vigil, 21 June 1856, "Pueblos: General Documents," SGNM, r. 7, f. 7, and testimony of Donaciano Vigil, 3 Dec. 1856, Sangre de Cristo Grant, SGNM, r. 12, f. 1. Fernández claimed to have been in charge of the papers prior to Vigil, from 1825 to 1846; testimony of Domingo Fernández, 7 Aug. 1855, Preston Beck Jr. Grant, SGNM, r. 12, f. 6–9.

35. See, for instance, John R. Van Ness, "Spanish American vs Anglo Land Tenure and the Study of Economic Change in New Mexico," Social Science Journal 13, no. 3 (Oct. 1976): 45–53; Leonard, The Role of the Land Grant in the Social Processes of a Spanish-American Village in New Mexico (Albuquerque: C. Horn, 1970), 46.

36. Subpoena issued 20 March 1854, directing Manuel Alvarez, Domingo Fernández, and Donaciano Vigil to testify; subpoena issued 14 June 1854 to Fernández and Vigil, in Pino v. Hatch, NMSCt, 7. At the trial, finally held in June 1854, the court rejected the Pinos' offer to prove through Fernández

and Vigil the legitimacy of their father's grant. On that basis the trial court ruled in favor of the defendant, Hatch. The Pinos appealed. The state supreme court reversed in 1855. By then the Pinos had lost both their Pecos and Ojitos de las Gallinas properties to Beck and, through him, to witness Vigil. The new owners did not go back to the territorial courts after they won in the state supreme court. Instead they took up the contest in a new forum, the Office of the Surveyor General.

37. Vigil's signature authenticated the documents necessary to support the following claims to the listed acreages, as determined by subsequent United States surveys:

Name of Grant	Reel, Frame in SGNM	Acres
San Pedro	r. 14, f. 8, 17, 25, 37	35,911
Sangre de Cristo	r. 12, f. 8, 29	998,780
Beaubien-Miranda	r. 15, f. 133, 134	1,414,764
E. W. Eaton	r. 14, f. 715, 722	81,732
Tierra Amarilla	r. 12, f. 19	594,519

The acreage figures are taken from New Mexico State Planning Office, White et al., *Land Title Study* (Santa Fe: New Mexico State Planning Office, 1971), Appendix D.

38. Stanley, *Giant in Lilliput,* 176–77.

39. For instance, testimony of Donaciano Vigil, 23 Aug. 1856, Tierra Amarilla Grant, SGNM, r. 12, f. 36, and 23 March 1857, John Scolly Grant, SGNM, r. 13, f. 8, 10.

40. Testimony of Donaciano Vigil, 23 March 1857, John Scolly Grant, SGNM, r. 13, f. 8, 10; and PPDV.

41. Myra Ellen Jenkins, "The Pueblo of Nambe and Its Lands," in *The Changing Ways of Southwestern Indians,* ed. Albert Schroeder (Glorieta, N.M.: Rio Grande Press, 1973). Robert W. Larson, *New Mexico's Quest for Statehood 1846–1912* (Albuquerque: University of New Mexico Press, 1968). Chapters 5 and 6 give an account of the shifting alliances that surrounded this issue as well as Vigil and Houghton's roles in those alliances.

42. Testimony of Donaciano Vigil, 3 Dec. 1856, in Sangre de Cristo Grant, SGNM, r. 12, f. 1, 10, 29.

43. Harold H. Dunham, *Spanish and Mexican Land Policies in the Taos Pueblo Region* (New York and London: Garland, 1974), 24–46.

44. Testimony of Donaciano Vigil, 24 Sept. 1858, in Town of Anton Chico Grant, SGNM, R. 29, F. 63, r. 19.

45. Testimony of Donaciano Vigil, 23 March 1857 and 12 May 1857, John Scolly Grant, SGNM, r. 13, f. 8, 10. Vigil testified for the first time in the case in March 1857. The surveyor general asked Vigil, "Was it customary under the Mexican government to retain the original title deed to any grant made by the government in the archives of the government and to give the parties interested a certified copy of the original grant, which copy was called a *testimonio?*" Vigil answered, "It was not only customary but a law required

it to be so retained." The problem was that no one could produce the original paper from any source. Two months after his initial appearance, Vigil returned to the Surveyor General's Office and attested to the fact that the allegedly original document the claimants had found between the first and second hearing was in fact genuine. No one bothered to ask where it had come from or why no copy had been retained in the archives that Vigil himself said were in his charge.

46. Affidavit of Donaciano Vigil, 21 June 1856, "General Documents, Pueblos," SGNM, r. 7.

47. Testimony of Donaciano Vigil, 20 Aug. 1855, Preston Beck Jr. Grant, SGNM, r. 12, f. 43ff. The English version of Vigil's testimony appears first in the surveyor general's records, the Spanish one second. Apparently Vigil testified in Spanish, even though Father Stanley says that Vigil learned English from the American traders who entered New Mexico after 1820. The Spanish and English versions of the Vigil testimony demonstrate a different problem with the Surveyor General's Office records: the two versions are remarkably different.

48. Testimony of Donaciano Vigil, 20 Aug. 1855, 9 Feb. 1875, 12 Feb. 1875; Preston Beck Grant, SGNM, r. 13, f. 5, 204ff, 214.

49. Testimony of Bernardo Varela, 9 Feb. 1875, Preston Beck Jr. Grant, SGNM, r. 13, f. 206. Bernardo Varela gave his age as seventy, his residence as Pecos, and his occupation as farmer. He was brother to *Joseph* defendant Manuel Varela.

50. Subpoena issued 23 May 1855, by surveyor general, to Manuel D. Pino and Donaciano Vigil, directing the two to appear before him on 20 Aug. 1855. Vigil came; Manuel Pino did not. Preston Beck Grant, SGNM, r. 13, f. 425.

51. Testimony of Donaciano Vigil, 9 Feb. 1875, Preston Beck Jr. Grant, SGNM, r. 13, f. 206.

52. Application for Los Trigos grant, 17 July 1855, Docket Book, SGNM, r. 13, f. 14.

53. House Report 321, 36th Congress, 1st Session, pp. 109–75. See also J. J. Bowden, "Private Land Claims in the Southwest," LL.M. thesis (Southern Methodist University, 1967), 744ff. See also Los Trigos Grant, SGNM, r. 13. So many technical points of Spanish and Mexican land grant law arose in the course of the adjudication of the Los Trigos claim that the surveyor general had trouble keeping them straight. Did the Santa Fe ayuntamiento have the power to make the grant as and when it did? If the ayuntamiento did have the power, what should the surveyor general make of the additional conditions appended to the original grant by a subsequent governor? Each of these intricate questions would perplex and confuse subsequent surveyors general, Congress, and the courts. In the case of the Los Trigos grant, Surveyor General Pelham took on each issue directly and answered between 17 July 1855, when Vigil filed his claim, and 17 September 1857, when he rendered his decision.

54. Los Trigos Grant, SGNM, r. 13, f. 4.

55. Docket Book, SGNM. File no. 1, registered 7 Feb. 1855, less than a

month after Pelham arrived in Santa Fe and five months before he formally opened his office, lists Alvarez as the present claimant. The surveyor general never reported to Congress on the claim. The second claim filed was that of Preston Beck, Jr. For background on Alvarez see Lamar, *The Far Southwest,* 52–53, 78–81. Cabeza de Baca's claim to the Las Vegas Grandes tract was filed 19 June 1855 and registered as file 6. Cabeza de Baca exchanged his claim to the Town of Las Vegas grant for five so-called floating tracts of land to be selected by him, and, as it turned out, his attorney, from the public domain in the New Mexico territory. For Gervacio Nolan, see file 9; Alexander Valle, file 54; E. W. Eaton, file 16; and Charles Beaubien, file 14. Lamar, *The Far Southwest,* 43, suggests that a pre–Santa Fe ring cabal was at work in New Mexico from the beginning of the surveyor general's regime.

56. Sparks, Comm. of Lands, to Surveyor General Julian, 8 July 1887, Los Trigos Trant, SGNM, r. 13, f. 108.

57. Receipt from attorneys Ashurst and Luby to Donaciano Vigil, 23 Feb. 1850, and receipts dated 25 March 1850 for $35, for "case in San Miguel county" on which "de los Trigos" appears on the back side. Joab Houghton to Señor D. Donaciano Vigil, 23 July 1861, PPDV. The letter says in Spanish that Houghton "has prepared the papers for the following Court term . . ." Houghton says that he must leave for Denver that day but that his partner, Col. Hopkins, will attend to the Vigil business. On 21 Dec. 1863, two years later, Hopkins signed a receipt acknowledging that Vigil paid his fee for the suit "after it was discontinued years ago." No record of any suit survives.

58. Testimony of Rafael Gonzales, 8 Aug. 1857, and testimony of Manuel Rodriguez, 28 July 1857, in Los Trigos Grant, SGNM, r. 13, f. 43ff.

59. Testimony of Domingo Fernández, 28 July 1857, Los Trigos Grant, SGNM, r. 13, f. 32ff.

60. Testimony of Domingo Fernández, r. 13, f. 32ff.

61. PPDV contain several documents from the administration of Domingo Fernández's estate, including administrator's deed to various tracts of land.

62. Testimony of Domingo Fernández, 7 Aug. 1855, Preston Beck Grant, SGNM, r. 12, f. 9.

63. Henry Putney Beers, *The Spanish and Mexican Records of the American Southwest* (Tucson: University of Arizona Press, 1979), 47ff, gives the first, albeit mechanical, description of how SANM I and II came into existence.

64. San Cristóbal Grant, filed 11 Oct. 1855 and approved 12 Sept. 1857, SGNM, R. 19, F. 16; r. 14. In the official files the tract was alternatively referred to as the E. W. Eaton Grant or the Domingo Fernandez Grant. The pueblo of San Cristóbal had disappeared in the smallpox epidemic of 1780–81; Kessell, *Kiva, Cross, and Crown,* 543 n. 60. For San Cristóbal see Domingo Fernández, application for the grant, 22 April 1822, SGNM, r. 14, f. 700; 20 Jan. 1851, Fernández sale to E. W. Eaton and Alejandro Reynolds, r. 14, f. 714; testimony of Donaciano Vigil, r. 14, f. 715ff.

65. "Pueblo Grants File," SGNM, r. 7. After Pelham had segregated Pueblo claims from non-Indian ones, he designated the pueblo of San Cristóbal as Claim LL, in the same manner as other pueblo claims. He also opened a non-

Indian claim under the name of Domingo Fernández's buyer, E. W. Eaton. In his docket book, the surveyor general simply refers the pueblo of San Cristóbal claim to the non-Indian E. W. Eaton claim.

66. SANM I, 283, indicates that the San Cristóbal grant was finally made on 21 Aug. 1827, to Domingo Fernández and thirty others who may or may not have shown up to take possession of the grant. John S. Watts to Surveyor General, 3 May 1871, Eaton-Fernandez Grant, SGNM, r. 14, f. 715–44 makes it clear that a dispute continued through the nineteenth century as to the rights of settlers other than Fernández. The issue continued into the twentieth century and was finally laid to rest in the 1970s, when the California successors to the original Fernández claim finally acknowledged the rights of the community of Galisteo to be where it had been for centuries.

67. Testimony of Domingo Fernández, 28 July 1857, Los Trigos Grant, SGNM, r. 13, f. 32, 36ff.

68. Testimony of Rafael Gonzales, 28 July 1857, Los Trigos Grant, SGNM, r. 13, f. 44ff.

69. "Final Brief of Donaciano Vigil," Los Trigos Grant, SGNM, r. 13, f. 46.

70. "Contestants Complaint," Los Trigos Grant, SGNM, r. 13, f. 51ff.

71. For instance, Twitchell, *Old Santa Fe,* 312.

72. English deed, Catarino and Jesus Maria Archuleta to Alexander Valle, 15 July 1850, in PPDV. Vigil's certificate is attached as follows: "Recorded in book letter b, page 242, to which I certify and sign in testimony thereof. Santa Fe, July 24 1850. Donaciano Vigil, Recorder." Beers, *Spanish and Mexican Records,* 321, claims that Book B of the documents recorded by Vigil in his tenure as registrar was lost and never found. Will Tipton, who had gained earlier fame as a document examiner for the Court of Private Land Claims and who had exposed the so-called Cruzate grants to the Pueblos as clumsy forgeries, claimed to have located Vigil's lost Book B in 1911, while working as an inspector in New Mexico for the Department of Interior. See Tipton to Secretary of the Interior, 12 Sept. 1911, NARG–75, 013, pt. 6.

73. Undated deed from Catarino and Jesus Maria Archuleta to "Señora Dolores," PPDV.

74. Decision, 15 Sept. 1857, Los Trigos Grant, SGNM, r. 13, f. 68ff.

75. H.R. 321, 36th Congress, 1st Session, pp. 1–2 (1860). The report of the Committee on Private Land Claims, which first considered the Los Trigos recommendation by the surveyor general, despaired of any fair review of Pelham's grant recommendations. The committee, said the report, "has no time to scrutinize the evidence and the application as made by the Surveyor General of the Spanish and Mexican laws and usages of each of them in detail." If the special committee had no time, of course Congress itself had less. The act which confirmed the grant itself rolled through Congress without debate.

76. As finally surveyed, the Los Trigos grant contained 9,646 acres. Less than 1,500 of them were actually fenced and occupied as exclusive, private property. The remaining 8,000 or so acres were owned in typically quasi-corporate status by the vaguely defined communities of Los Trigos, Las Ruedas,

and the other small settlements that dotted the grant. For the railroad's arrival see David F. Myrick, *New Mexico's Railroads: An Historical Survey* (Golden: Colorado Historical Association, 1970), 17–18. Letter from J. Houghton, Attorney for the Los Trigos Grant, to Surveyor General James K. Proudfoot, 20 June 1874 (Los Trigos Grant, SGNM, r. 13, f. 191), indicates something of the problems faced by purchasers who bought undivided interests in the grant: "In the meantime, the owners of the [Los Trigos] grant, not doubting but that the survey and plat [of the grant] had been approved in good faith, accepted them and used them in negotiating undivided portions of that tract." Surveyor General to Col. Abreu and Mr. Chapman, 7 June 1878 (Los Trigos Grant, r. 13, f. 101), calls for the payment of amended Los Trigos grant survey costs by the owners of the grant, Abreu and Chapman. Frank Chapman had previously purchased the Pecos Pueblo grant from John Ward and by 1878, two years before his death, apparently had begun to speculate in Los Trigos land as well. The technique of purchasing undivided interests in grant land had become common in New Mexico by the 1870s; see Westphall, *Thomas Benton Catron,* 39–46. Around the time the railroad arrived, in 1879, Los Trigos community residents abandoned the townsite of Las Ruedas, near the Pecos River, and moved west, along the tracks, where they founded the present town of Rowe. At the turn of the century, Donaciano Vigil II lived there. He was the son of Deciderio Vigil, the first Donaciano Vigil's middle son. Donaciano Vigil II lived in a sprawling adobe house just west of the railroad tracks. See G. Emlen Hall, "Genealogy of Donaciano Vigil Family," unpub. ms. in possession of the author, and Las Vegas Title and Abstract Co. Abstract No. S-149, Wanda Clayton, Rowe, New Mexico. Records in the attic of Donaciano Vigil II's home indicate that he served as local justice of the peace in the first decades of the twentieth century.

77. On this point, *Joseph* in 1877, *Sandoval* in 1913, and *Candelaria* in 1926 were all consistent. See Leo Crane, *Desert Drums* (Boston: Little, Brown, 1928), 280–82. By the mid-nineteenth century, if not earlier, individual Pueblo Indians regarded themselves, and were regarded by their neighbors and the governing authorities of the pueblos, as the absolute owners of the small, irrigated tract each farmed alone. See, for example, Henry R. Poore, Special Agent, "Condition of 16 New Mexico Pueblos, 1890," in *Report on Indians Taxed and Indians not Taxed at the Eleventh Census* (Washington, D.C.: Bureau of the Census, 1890), 410–53.

78. *United States v. Sandoval,* 167 U.S. 278 (1897), involving the common lands of the San Miguel del Bado grant. Other cases dealing with the status of non-Indian community land grants included *Grisar v. McDowell,* 73 U.S. 363, 373–74 (1867); *Rio Arriba Land and Cattle v. United States,* 167 U.S. 298 (1897); *Bond v. Barelas Heirs,* 229 U.S. 492 (1914); *First National Bank v. Town of Tome,* 23 N.M. 255 (1917). See also Malcolm Ebright, "The San Joaquin Grant: Who Owned the Common Lands? A Historical Legal Puzzle," *NMHR* 57, no. 1 (1982): 5–26.

79. U.S. Department of the Interior, General Land Office, Santa Fe, "Spe-

cial Instructions to Govern Surveys within the Pecos Pueblo Grant, New Mexico, Group 230," 25 March 1929, in BLM, Santa Fe.

80. David Vassberg, "The Tierras Baldías: Community Property and Public Lands in 16th Century Castile," *Agricultural History* 48 (July 1974): 383–90.

81. I have calculated the irrigated acreage figures from "Pecos Hydrographic Survey," July–Aug. 1920.

82. Felix Sena, personal interview, 24 March 1979, Pecos, New Mexico; Vassberg, "Tierras Baldías." *Rastrojos* means literally *stubble*. In Pecos terminology it described community rights in irrigated land during the fallow season.

83. *Mancomún* and the associated verb form, *mancomunar,* had a common use in eighteenth- and nineteenth-century New Mexico land terminology that defies precise definition. The word connotes the joining together of two estates, each of which is incomplete alone.

Chapter 7

1. U.S. Census, 1880, Las Vegas precinct 26, enumeration district 32, p. 30. Census enumerated 9 June 1880. SRCA.

2. *Las Vegas Optic,* 7 Jan. 1880.

3. Ralph Emerson Twitchell, *Leading Facts of New Mexico History* (Cedar Rapids, Iowa: Torch Press, 1917), 4: 222, n. 586.

4. Milt Callon, "The Merchant Colonists of New Mexico," in *Brand Book of Denver Westerners* (Denver: Pruett Publishing, 1965), 21: 21–23.

5. Milt Callon, *Las Vegas, New Mexico: The Town that Wouldn't Gamble* (Las Vegas, N.M.: Optic Publishing, 1962), 27, citing a 2 April 1854 report from a correspondent traveling with the district judge and attorney general.

6. *Las Vegas Optic,* 25 March 1881.

7. Callon, *Las Vegas,* 38. For traditional New Mexico business at the time, see William Jackson Parish, *The Charles Ilfeld Co.: A Study of the Rise and Decline of Mercantile Capitalism in New Mexico* (Cambridge, Mass.: Harvard University Press, 1961). For Dold's real estate dealings with Alexander Hatch and others see Dold and Taylor to Alexander Hatch, 8 Feb. 1860, recorded 12 April 1861, in San Miguel County Deed Book 2, p. 53; Dold and Taylor to Alexander Hatch, 8 Feb. 1860, recorded 11 Dec. 1865, in Deed Book 3, p. 82; and Archbishop Juan B. Lamy to Dold, 2 Aug. 1869, recorded 11 Aug. 1869, in Deed Book 5, pp. 357–58.

8. See "Dissolution of Partnership of John and Andres Dold," 16 April 1861, filed for record 4 Jan. 1867, in San Miguel County Records, Book 3, p. 107. *Las Vegas Optic,* 5 April 1881.

9. Kihlberg affidavit, 13 May 1887, exhibit 7, *Seymour v. Roberts et al.,* SRCA.

10. *New York City Directories* list an Andres Dold in 1875–77 residing at 220 E. 60th Street; in 1877–78 at 108 E. 57th Street; in 1878–80 at 105 E. 65th Street; and in 1880 at 101 E. 60th Street. The 1880 directory

information would have been gathered in late 1879, at which time Dold still lived in New York. No Andres or Andrew Dold appears after 1880 in this area of the city, a fact which lends plausibility to the identity between the Dold listed in the directories and the New Mexico patriarch described by the *Optic*. By 1881 Dold was back in New Mexico for good.

11. Parish, *Charles Ilfeld*, 46.

12. Callon, *Las Vegas*, 45; *Las Vegas Optic*, 28 Jan. 1881. For Las Vegas's newspapers see Callon, *Las Vegas*, 97–100. Two small papers, the *Las Vegas Daily Gazette* and the *Las Vegas Herald*, preceded the *Optic*, which editor Kistler brought to town with the railroad. The *Optic* soon surpassed its competitors and still survives today. For opium market allegations see *Las Vegas Optic*, 28 Dec. 1880 and 26 March 1881.

13. *Las Vegas Optic*, 30 and 31 Jan. 1880.

14. The *Las Vegas Daily Gazette*, 5 March 1881, reported the laying of the cornerstone. For Dold's mining interests see mortgage, Andres Dold to owners of the Hannover Copper Mine, securing a Dold loan of $13,000, reported in San Miguel County Records, Book 5, p. 160. See *Las Vegas Optic*, 28 Dec. 1880, for notice of a lawsuit involving a Dold interest in a Raton mine in the opposite corner of the territory. See also *Las Vegas Optic*, 19 April 1881, for Dold interest in mining tailings at Tijeras Canyon, near Albuquerque. Finally, for Dold's interest in the power proposal, see Callon, *Las Vegas*, 118. On 11 March 1881, T. B. Catron, titular head of the Santa Fe Ring; Marcus Brunswick, among other things administrator of the estate of Frank Chapman; Trinidad Romero, the single largest property owner in Las Vegas; F. O. Kihlberg, a long-time Dold henchman; and Dold himself incorporated the New Mexico Electric Light Co.

15. "In the Matter of the Estate of Frank Chapman Deceased, Petition for Appointment of Administrator," 3 Jan. 1880, San Miguel County cause no. 24671, SRCA. Frank Chapman's nephew, John, at the age of twenty-one, had come from Illinois to join his uncle in 1876. Affidavit of John Chapman, 27 April 1887, in *Seymour v. Roberts et al.*, SRCA.

16. San Miguel County Records, Book 18, pp. 137–40. A straightforward deed from Chapman to Dold would have accomplished the same result, but under existing state law, the deed would have to have been notarized before it was filed by the county clerk. There was no such requirement for partnership agreements. Neither of the two partnership agreements between Chapman and Dold was notarized.

17. Exhibit 7, *Seymour v. Roberts et al.*, SRCA.

18. For the Pecos subdivision called Sulzbacher, see *Las Vegas Optic*, 28 April 1881 and 4 March 1881. For the incorporation of the mining company, see *Las Vegas Optic*, 25 March 1881. For John Sulzbacher in New York, see *Las Vegas Optic*, 26 April 1881 and 9 May 1881.

19. "In the Matter of the Estate of Frank Chapman, Deceased." See also "Affidavit of John Chapman," 27 April 1887, in *Seymour v. Roberts et al.*, SRCA.

20. Deed, Heirs of Frank Chapman to Andres Dold, 17 Feb. 1880, recorded

16 March 1881, in San Miguel County Deed Book 15, pp. 431–40. Technically the deed conveyed to Dold only that one-half interest that Chapman retained at this death. Dold already owned the other half by virtue of the 1879 partnership agreement. Confirmation of that half-interest awaited the final arrangement of Frank Chapman's estate. Finally, on 10 March 1881, the *Optic* reported that "a deed conveying property from M. Brunswick, administrator of the estate of Frank Chapman, deceased, to Dn. Andres Dold, has been filed in the clerk's office. It covers 15 pages of legal cap" and presumably covered the Pecos grant as well. For other problems with the administration of Chapman's estate, see *Las Vegas Optic*, 5 and 6 Jan. 1881.

21. Kihlberg affidavit, 13 May 1887, *Seymour v. Roberts et al.*, SRCA.

22. *Las Vegas Optic*, 24 March 1881.

23. *Las Vegas Optic*, 28 Jan. 1881.

24. For logging prospects on the Pecos Pueblo grant see Kihlberg and Henry Dold affidavits, 13 May 1887, in *Seymour v. Roberts et al.*, SRCA. For railroad calls for tie contracts see *Las Vegas Optic*, 28 March 1881, in which one railway line asked for proposals to supply 350,000 ties, 3,000 telegraph poles, 125,000 board feet of pine, 40,000 board feet of 2 in. plank, and 10,000 board feet of 3 in. plank. *Las Vegas Optic*, 1 May 1881, reported Kihlberg's trip to Pecos to check on lumber. For timber business operated by Walsh and Levy on the Pecos Grant see *Las Vegas Optic*, 17 and 28 Jan. 1881 and 4 March 1881. *Las Vegas Optic*, 4 March 1881 reported that the company had obligated itself "to get out 500,000 cross ties for a special order to be delivered at the Pecos crossing, this county." Walsh and Levy had headquarters at Walsenburg, Colorado, and a growing timber operation in and around the Pecos grant. The company paid first Chapman and then Dold five hundred dollars a year for the right to cut and then paid, in addition, a percentage based on the amount of timber actually cut.

25. *Las Vegas Optic*, 7 May and 4 June 1881. In Hispanic Pecos stories had floated for generations about buried and lost Spanish and Indian treasures on the grant. After 1881 those stories gained power until they ascended from any possible reality into the realm of myth. See J. Frank Dobie, *Coronado's Children: Tales of Lost Mines and Buried Treasures of the Southwest* (Dallas: Southwest Publishing, 1930), chapters 12 and 13 for the account of "la mina de Jose Baca," still discussed as a kind of cosmic joke around Pecos today.

26. *Las Vegas Optic*, 7 Nov. 1879.

27. *Las Vegas Optic*, 7 April 1882.

28. For the beginnings of the U.S. Forest Service in the Pecos area see John W. Johnson, *Reminiscences of a Forest Ranger, 1914–1944* (Dayton, Ohio: private publication, 1976). As to Pecos's climate, there is a local saying which describes the Pecos year as "ocho meses de invierno y cuatro meses de infierno" (eight months of winter and four months of hell), because of the heat.

29. See Lance Edwin Davis, "Capital Immobilities and Southwestern Land Prices, 1865–1875: A Study of Historical Market Paradox," Plaintiff's Exhibit 4043, Indian Claims Commission, *Navajo Nation v. United States*, Table 1 page 3. Borrowed money had always cost a lot in New Mexico. In the 1820s Juan

Estevan Pino charged 15 percent on his loans. Preston Beck, Jr., lent the Pino brothers the money necessary to finance their suit against Alexander Hatch at 13 percent interest in 1852 and 1853. The fact that the Pinos repaid neither principal nor interest (and lost the ciénaga de Pecos in the process) suggests just how difficult and risky borrowing money was at the time. Just before the advent of the railroad in New Mexico, banks were formed for the first time. But particularly early on, most local banks had no capital to lend, since they had not had time to accumulate capital of their own. As a result, the drive for New Mexico improvements brought on by the railroad further strained local capital markets and drove the market price for money even higher than it had been in earlier days.

30. For Elkins's role in Europe, see William A. Keleher, *The Maxwell Land Grant* (Santa Fe: Gannon, 1975), 148–49; for European interest in New Mexico and Australian land see James Pearson, *The Maxwell Land Grant* (Norman: University of Oklahoma Press, 1963); for the general financial situation see Davis, "Capital Immobilities," 16.

31. *Las Vegas Optic,* 12 March 1881.

32. *Las Vegas Optic,* 17 March 1881.

33. *Las Vegas Optic,* 9 May, 21 March, and 14 May 1881.

34. *Las Vegas Optic,* 8 July 1881. At least Chapman and Dold acknowledged the presence of Hispanic Pecos when each published his notice of claim to the entire grant in 1873 and 1881. Curious passers-by had noted the ruins of the Pecos Pueblo church, near the center of the grant, at least since the early 1850s. Kessell, *Kiva, Cross, and Crown,* 446. Accounts contemporaneous with Dold's sale to Wright treated the Indian presence in Pecos as a historical anachronism; see *Las Vegas Optic,* 5 May 1881, reprinting an article from the *Reading* (Pa.) *Eagle,* describing the ruins of the church. The author belonged to that party of wealthy Philadelphians who had ventured through Las Vegas two months before, in search of investment possibilities. See *Las Vegas Optic,* 21 March 1881, and Callon, *Las Vegas,* 130–31. For his own part, *Optic* editor Kistler took a disparaging view of Indians, calling them in print "Uncle Sam's Pets" and "copper-colored curiosities," *Las Vegas Optic,* 9 and 17 May 1881. Kistler was aware of the Non-Intercourse Act and its application to New Mexico; *Las Vegas Optic,* 7 May 1881. But he was probably also aware that the 1877 *Joseph* decision had held that that law did not apply to New Mexico Pueblos or their land. By 1880, Adolph Bandelier, the first trained American archeologist, had already visited Pecos, his first stopping place. Suffice it to say that Dold, Wright, and Bandelier did not run in the same circles. Dold to Wright, 6 July 1881, recorded 9 July 1881, in San Miguel County Deed Book 16, pp. 154–55.

35. 1880, U.S. Census, 27th Ward, Philadelphia, Pa., enumerator district 580, p. 8. Enumerated 4 June 1880.

36. *Gopsill's City Directories: Philadelphia,* for the years indicated and 1880 Philadelphia census. "James W" and "J Whittaker" Wright are listed at the same address for 1880 in the census and the city directory.

37. *Directory of Members,* American Institute of Mining Engineers, 1887–

1904. From 1887 to 1890, directories list "Whitaker Wright, Philadelphia" as a member. From 1891 to 1894 the same directory lists Wright as a member with a post office box in San Francisco.

38. For instance, R. W. Paul, *Mining Frontiers of the Far West, 1848–1880* (New York: Holt, Rinehart and Winston, 1963). For example, the infamous Emma Mine, in southwest Utah, supported the float of a five million dollar stock issue in London, even after everyone knew that a lawsuit challenged the validity of the mining claim in the first place and after everyone had guessed that whatever mine was there had already been worked out.

39. Davis, "Capital Immobilities," 33–34.

40. In 1873 Chapman had paid John Ward and the Pecos elders $5,500 for the Pecos Pueblo grant. In 1880 Dold had paid Chapman's heirs $21,500 for their one-half interest in all Chapman's real estate holdings, a small and speculative part of which included the grant. At most Wright paid Dold $18,678 for the entire grant he purchased. At $1 an acre, Wright would profit on the resale of the grant in the East and Dold would much more than recoup his investment.

41. For Roberts, see *New York City Directories,* 1883–84. J. Whitaker Wright and wife to George D. Roberts, 31 March 1883, recorded 11 June 1884, in San Miguel County Deed Book 24, pp. 522–23.

42. Roberts to Seymour, 3 June 1884, recorded 11 June 1884, in San Miguel County Deed Book 25, p. 330, executed before "William H. Clarkson, Commissioner of the Territory of New Mexico in New York, 117 Broadway, New York City."

43. Deed, Roberts to Seymour, 3 June 1884.

44. The gravestones in the Rosedale Cemetery, Essex County, New Jersey, mark some of the history of the Seymour family. Four Celtic-cross headstones, side by side, indicate the graves of Caroline Shaw Seymour, 1848–1908; James Madison Seymour, Sr., 1847–1919; James Madison Seymour, Jr., 1871–1929; and Fred Seymour, 1874–1947. Also buried in the family plot was Maud Carter, Fred Seymour's wife, 1881–1930. New York City directories for 1884 provide the business addresses of both Seymour and Fox.

45. Affidavit of T. B. Mills, *Seymour v. Roberts et al.,* 1887, San Miguel County cause no. 2723, proofs offered 30 March 1887; SRCA.

46. Callon, *Las Vegas,* 212. Koogler edited and published the *Las Vegas Optic's* only competitor at the time, the *Las Vegas Gazette.* He later served as superintendent of public instruction in the Las Vegas schools. In between he practiced law.

47. Keleher, *Maxwell Land Grant,* 112n, for an adequate biographical note on Springer's life. The text itself tells the story of the litigation. The date of the oral arguments in Washington is given on p. 109.

48. Complaint filed 20 Jan. 1887, in *Seymour v. Roberts et al.,* SRCA. The naming of a large number of defendants under the vacuous "unknown heirs" style showed that something fishy had emerged in the Seymour strategy for the suit. Mills and Koogler at least knew who Andres Dold's heirs were. The San Miguel County District Court had determined Frank Chapman's heirs in

a previous 1880 proceeding. That information was on public record in Las Vegas. Yet the *Seymour* complaint named none of those known living heirs as defendants. So long as there were no living heirs, the plaintiff, Seymour, did not have to serve any of them personally. He could proceed simply on the basis of publication of notice of the suit in the Las Vegas newspapers. Apparently Seymour and company were arranging things so that no one would know about, let alone contest, the New Yorker's claim to the grant. In addition, in 1887 information was available about the whereabouts and identities of the Pecos Pueblo survivors at Jemez. Several of the Pueblo deeds identified them and said they lived at Jemez. Yet in the *Seymour* suit, a Kihlberg affidavit provided all the information that the court had about the Indians. That affidavit said that the Pecos survivors had dispersed, that some had ended up at Cochiti Pueblo, while the final destination of the rest was unknown. Finally, Preston Beck, Jr., Donaciano Vigil, and Manuel Varela had each filed deeds laying claim to Pecos Pueblo land well before the *Seymour* suit. Legally, this fact would have put Seymour on notice of the existence of these other claims. Yet the *Seymour* complaint named none of the Hispanos living on the grant. For the published version of notice in the *Las Vegas Optic,* see "Notice of Publication and Proof of Publication," filed 15 March 1887, in *Seymour v. Roberts et al.,* SRCA.

49. For the simultaneous Las Vegas land grant suit see *Millheiser v. Padilla,* 1 N.M. 436 (1885).

50. Exhibits filed 3 Nov. 1887 in *Seymour v. Roberts et al.,* SRCA. Marcus Brunswick gave his statement on 30 March 1887; Henry Dold, 9 March 1887; John L. Chapman, 29 April 1877; and Frank O. Kihlberg, 13 May 1887. The proofs were taken 30 March 1887. The exhibits attached to the T. B. Mills statement included certified copies of the chain of title from the United States to Seymour. Mills stated that he had tried to contact Seymour in New York about securing original copies of the various deeds, but that he had not succeeded.

51. Koogler brief, 14 May 1887, *Seymour v. Roberts et al.,* SRCA.

52. "Report of the Special Master," filed 14 November 1887, in *Seymour v. Roberts et al.,* SRCA, pp. 1 and 8. Special Master Johnson cited John Arnold Rockwell's *A Compilation of Spanish and Mexican Law in Relation to Mines and Titles to Real Estate* (New York: J.S. Voorhies, 1851), 458, article 18.

53. Cancelled "Final Decree" in *Seymour v. Roberts et al.,* SRCA.

54. "Order Striking Decree," 17 Dec. 1887, *Seymour v. Roberts et al.,* SRCA.

55. For instance, Juan Estevan Aragon to Juan Estevan Pino, 31 March 1837, recorded 12 Aug. 1887, in San Miguel County Deed Book 31, p. 206; Estevan Aragon to Manuel D. Pino, 25 July 1840, filed 13 Aug. 1887, in San Miguel County Deed Book 31, p. 215; Jose Ulibarri to Juan E. Pino, 14 May 1832, filed 9 May 1888, in San Miguel County Deed Book 35, p. 417; Juan E. Pino to Amado Quintana, 2 Nov. 1855, filed 3 Aug. 1887, in San Miguel County Deed Book 31, p. 154. The last deed is clearly a forgery, executed, as it purports to have been, by Juan Estevan Pino, fifteen years after his death.

56. Seymour to Fox, 6 May 1889, recorded 4 Dec. 1889, in San Miguel County Deed Book 40, pp. 593–94. *New York City Directories,* 1885–95, under James W. Fox. From 1887 to 1888 Fox listed himself as in mines, in 1889 as a broker, and from 1900 on as a banker.

57. Quitclaim deed, 7 May 1889, Fox and wife to Flushing Bank of Flushing, New York, recorded 4 Dec. 1889 in San Miguel County Deed Book 40, pp. 595–96.

58. The facts of Prince's life, including the Flushing connection, are given in Walter John Donlon, "Lebaron Bradford Prince: Chief Justice and Governor of New Mexico Territory, 1879–1893," Ph.D. diss. (University of New Mexico, 1967). From 1877, when he came to New Mexico, until 1917, Prince went from New Mexico east to attend every national Episcopal convention (Donlon, "Prince," 161). In 1882 Prince somehow obtained from a Pecos Pueblo emigrant to Jemez, Agustin Cota, a wooden plaque of Our Lady of the Angels from the mission church at Pecos (Kessell, *Kiva, Cross, and Crown,* 465). In early 1889, the year the Flushing Bank of New York secured the Pecos Pueblo grant, Prince was in New York. See, for instance, letter from S. B. Elkins, at No. 1 Broadway, NYC, to Prince, at 39 Nassau St., NYC, 19 Jan. 1889, on the subject of New Mexico territorial politics (File F-10, Letters received, beginning 1–1889, in PPLBP). See also J. W. Hasten to Prince, at Flushing, New York, 26 Feb. 1889. In 1889 Prince was actively campaigning for territorial governor. In that campaign he had to answer charges of "unloading a worthless New Mexico mine on innocent and confiding New Yorkers." Whether the charge involved Pecos is not known. But from the outset of his public New Mexico career, Prince had sought to attract eastern capital to New Mexico as a way of boosting the local economy. Donlon, "Prince," 122–25.

59. Flushing Bank of New York to Mattie G. Smith, 14 Dec. 1895, recorded 28 Dec. 1895, San Miguel County Deed Book 46, pp. 308–9; Mattie G. Smith and Pascual R. Smith to John L. Laub, 26 Dec. 1895, recorded 28 Dec. 1895, in San Miguel County Deed Book 46, pp. 310–11.

60. Affidavit, John L. Laub, Nov. 1916 in *Gross-Kelly Co. v. Juan Quintana et al.,* San Miguel County cause no. 7613.

61. Complaint filed 15 April 1899, *John L. Laub v. Rosario Valencia,* San Miguel County cause no. 5124, SMCR. The suit involved 101 varas of land from north to south, adjoining the land of Antonio B. Vigil or Pablo Vigil, his son, on the north; land of Melquiades Armijo, deceased, on the south; and bounded on the west by the Pecos River. This description placed the tract in East Pecos. See also *John Laub v. Atanacio Casaus and Pedro Casaus,* filed 15 April 1899, San Miguel County cause no. 5123, involving a tract in West Pecos; and *John L. Laub v. Juan Sena and Ecarnacion Sena,* filed 17 May 1898, San Miguel County cause no. 5025, also involving a tract of West Pecos land.

62. *Territory of New Mexico v. Pecos Pueblo Grant,* filed 21 July 1886, San Miguel County cause no. 2617. *Territory v. Delinquent Taxpayers,* 12 N.M. 139 (1904) tells the story of the first territorial efforts to impose real property taxes on Indian as well as non-Indian land. The earliest return for tracts of

land within the Pecos Pueblo grant that I have found is evidenced by tax receipt of J. L. Lopez by Wm. G. Hayden, deputy, to Mariano Ruiz, 2 Oct. 1891, for $16.80, for "payment in full for year ending 1 May 1890," Tax Roll 1889, p. 12, precinct no. 12, San Miguel County Records, for land described as 160 acres within the Pecos Pueblo grant. Lorenzo Lopez, sheriff of San Miguel County, New Mexico, to James L. Bridge, 25 July 1889, recorded 26 July 1889, in San Miguel County Deed Book 40, pp. 270–72.

63. J. L. Bridge to Frank Keeler, 3 Feb. 1890, recorded 3 Feb. 1890, in San Miguel County Deed Book 46, pp. 95–96. J. L. Bridge to W. M. Mahin, 17 Dec. 1889, recorded 2 Jan. 1891, San Miguel County Deed Book 42, pp. 22–23; W. M. Mahin to J. A. Bell, 17 Dec. 1889, recorded 2 Jan. 1891, in San Miguel County Deed Book 42, pp. 23–24; and W. M. Mahin to F. W. Blair, 17 Dec. 1889, recorded in San Miguel County Deed Book 43, pp. 1–2.

64. James L. Bridge and wife to John L. Laub, 18 Jan. 1895, San Miguel County Deed Book 45, p. 188; F. W. Blair and wife and J. A. Bell and wife to J. L. Laub, 17 June 1895, recorded 14 Sept. 1895, in San Miguel County Deed Book 46, pp. 243–44; Frank Keeler and wife to J. L. Laub, 2 March 1896, San Miguel County Deed Book 46, pp. 407–8.

65. *Territory v. Delinquent Taxpayers of New Mexico,* 12 New Mexico 139 (1904).

66. Jose Cota to Juan Estevan Pino, 20 Sept. 1830, recorded 29 May 1894, in San Miguel County Deed Book 46, p. 474. G. Emlen Hall, "Juan Estevan Pino, Se Los Coma: New Mexico Land Speculation in the 1820s," *NMHR* 57, no. 2 (1982): 26–42.

67. The classic example is the Town of Las Vegas grant itself. Through the 1860s Congress confirmed a number of so-called community grants to so-called towns, even though, legally, there were no municipal governments in place to run the towns or even to give them existence. The 1891 act addressed itself to this anomaly.

68. See *Territory v. Delinquent Taxpayers,* 12 N.M. 139 (1904) for a discussion of the Pueblo incorporation act. For the legal status of non-Indian so-called community property within community land grants, see Malcolm Ebright, "The San Joaquin Grant: Who Owned the Common Lands? A Historical Legal Puzzle," *NMHR* 57, no. 1 (1982): 5–26.

69. "Petition for Incorporation of Pecos Pueblo Grant," in *In the Matter of the Pueblo of Pecos,* San Miguel County cause no. 4716, filed 25 Feb. 1896, SRCA.

70. Affidavit of Emerijildo Vigil and Hilario Roibal, 1 March 1896, *In the Matter of the Pecos Pueblo Grant,* SRCA.

70. Affidavits of Agapito Lucero, Aniceto Deabueno, and Juan Jose Martinez, 17 April 1896, *In the Matter of the Pecos Pueblo Grant,* SRCA.

72. "Minutes of a Junta or Meeting of the residents of the Pueblo Pecos, and owners of real property in the Pecos Pueblo Grant held 26 April 1896 at the school house in the town of Pecos," *In the Matter of the Pecos Pueblo Grant,* SRCA.

73. "Tally of Ballots Returned by the Judges of Election 4 May 1896," *In the Matter of the Pecos Pueblo Grant,* SRCA.

74. Kessell, *Kiva, Cross, and Crown,* xiii.

Chapter 8

1. Vincent K. Jones, "Survey of the Pecos Pueblo Grant, 1914," attached as Exhibit F to *Gross-Kelly Co. v. Juan Quintana et al.,* San Miguel County cause no. 7613, SRCA. In addition, Charles H. Erickson, who had succeeded to the Baca rights west of the Pecos River, had prepared in 1920 a map of his considerable holdings in the present village of Pecos. The map indicates the location of the Baca ranch house and the East Pecos residences. For the Ortiz holdings at the site of the Reuter tract, see Ignacio Quintana and Dolores Valencia, his wife, to Jose Maria Valencia, 19 Aug. 1853, recorded 8 Oct. 1853, in San Miguel County Deed Book 1, pp. 62–63. See also the will of Faustin Ortiz, 30 May 1922, filed in San Miguel County Will Record, p. 157.

2. Daniel T. Kelly, *Buffalo Head* (Santa Fe: Vegara Publishing, 1972), 207. Evaristo Lucero, personal interview, Pecos, New Mexico, January 1978. Lucero, eighty-one years old in that year, lives in part of the original Manuel Varela house in the village of Pecos.

3. Richard W. Bradfute, *The Court of Private Land Claims: The Adjudication of Spanish and Mexican Land Grant Titles, 1891–1904* (Albuquerque: University of New Mexico Press, 1975), gives the court's general history as well as the dates of its operation.

4. On Tipton, see, for instance, Bruce T. Ellis, "Fraud Without Scandal: The Roque Lovato Grant and Gaspar Ortiz y Alarid," *NMHR* 51, no. 1 (1982): 49ff. Hanke, 2nd commissioner of Indian Affairs to Secretary of Interior, 26 Oct. 1911 (NARG–48, 5.1, Northern Pueblos), indicates the government's increasing dependence on Tipton for archival work in organizing Pueblo and other Indian title papers. For Tipton and Donaciano Vigil II's work on the Taos survey at the turn of the century, see "Fieldnotes," survey, T. 18N R. 14E, June 1904, BLM, Santa Fe.

5. John W. Johnson, *Reminiscences of a Forest Ranger, 1914–44* (Dayton, Ohio: Private Printing, 1976), 26ff.

6. Samuel Adelo, Sr., personal interview, Pecos, New Mexico, 11 November 1979.

7. John L. Laub and wife to Henry W. Kelly, 30 Oct. 1897, recorded 13 Nov. 1897, in San Miguel County Deed Book 45, p. 283.

8. Kelly, *Buffalo Head,* 72–73.

9. See the history and list of congressional "gratuities," set out in the district court's opinion in *United States v. Sandoval* (DC, NM, 1912), 198 F. Supp. 539, 550–51.

10. See the reports by government officials on the Pueblos, set out in the Supreme Court's opinion in *United States v. Sandoval,* 213 U.S. 28 (1913).

11. On the territorial imposition of real property taxes and federal removal of them, 33 Stat. 1069 (1905), see testimony of Francis C. Wilson, in "Hearings before the Committee on Indian Affairs, United States Senate, 62d Congress, third session on S. 6085, a bill to authorize the acceptance of trusts from the Pueblo Indians of New Mexico," 13 Feb. 1913 (Washington, D.C.: U.S. Government Printing Office, 1913), 9–10; see also Wilson testimony, 5 Feb. 1923, PILT, 61.

12. See 30 Stat. 571 at 594 (1898), for first congressional appropriation for special attorney for Pueblos. See also Ortiz v. Suazo, 91 N.M. 45, 570 P.2 304 (1977). Contemporaneous information suggests that no one knew for sure how long the Pueblos had had a special attorney. See, for instance, testimony of Ralph Emerson Twitchell, 5 Feb. 1923, in PILT, 76. Twitchell said that the Pueblos had had a special attorney "before the establishment of that court [Court of Private Land Claims, established in 1891] for a long time."

13. Abstract of title, Juan Jose Lovato Grant, Forest Service, United States Agriculture Department, Albuquerque, New Mexico.

14. For instance, Acequia Llano et al. v. Acequia de Nueva et al., Santa Fe County cause no. 4414 (1902) and Jose A. Rivera v. Pueblo of Nambe, Santa Fe County cause no. 4088 (1900) show Howard's role in the suits. The two Nambe water cases are listed on the dockets of Santa Fe County District Court, Santa Fe, N.M. The records themselves, however, have disappeared. Surviving documents are located in SCUNM.

15. Rhoads to Commissioner, 12 July 1929 (NARG–75, 13, pt. 8), gives the exact dates of Wilson's appointments to New Mexico. See also Ortiz v. Suazo and B. Alan Dickson, "The Professional Life of Francis C. Wilson: A Preliminary Sketch," NMHR 55, no. 1 (1976): 35–57. The Dickson article provides the skimpiest and often self-serving details of Wilson's complex, multifaceted life. The Wilson estate has just released the Francis C. Wilson papers to SRCA. My account is based on materials drawn from the Collier papers at Yale University and in the National Archives.

16. Robert W. Larson, New Mexico's Quest for Statehood 1846–1912 (Albuquerque: University of New Mexico Press, 1968).

17. Act of June 20, 1910, ch. 310, 36 Stat. 557. See United States v. Sandoval.

18. United States v. Mares, 14 N.M. 1 (1905), construing act of Jan. 30, 1897, ch. 109, 29 Stat. 506. See Merritt, 15 Feb. 1923, 371.

19. Larson, New Mexico's Quest for Statehood, 253ff.

20. Wilson testimony, 13 Feb. 1913, PILT, 9–10.

21. Milt Callon, Las Vegas: The Town that Wouldn't Gamble (Las Vegas, N.M.: Optic Publishing, 1968), 220–23.

22. United States v. Sandoval, 198 F. Supp. 539 (1912). The opinion indicates that the infraction took place on Santa Clara Pueblo land, west of Espanola. The private attorney A. B. Renehan later swore that in fact the so-called crime took place on San Ildefonso land. That and other technical defects in the government's case, he claimed, could have won the case for his non-Indian clients. But he was so anxious to settle the point that he overlooked

those technical faults. See Renehan testimony, 23 Jan. 1923, SCPL, 211, and Renehan testimony, 14 Feb. 1923, PILT, 329.

23. Wilson testimony, 3 Feb. 1923, PILT, 19; R. E. Twitchell, 6 Feb. 1923, PILT, 145.

24. A. B. Renehan, "Brief for Appellee," *United States v. Sandoval,* no. 222 on Supreme Court of the United States Docket, fall term, 1913. Renehan complained bitterly about the lateness of filing of the government brief. See Renehan, 13 Feb. 1923, PILT, 292.

25. Solicitor General, "Brief for Appellant, United States of America," no. 222 on Supreme Court of the United States Docket, fall term, 1913.

26. *United States v. Sandoval,* 13 U.S. 28 (1913).

27. "Brief for Appellant, United States of America," *United States v. Sandoval.* As the years passed, the esoteric point of whether *Sandoval* overruled the earlier *Joseph* decision or simply went around it became increasingly important. If *Joseph* survived *Sandoval,* then non-Indian property rights acquired between 1877 and 1913 would still be valid. If *Sandoval* expunged *Joseph,* however, then rights acquired under the *Joseph* doctrine would no longer be valid.

28. *United States v. Candelaria,* 271 U.S. 432 (1926).

29. Leo Crane, *Desert Drums* (Boston: Little, Brown and Co., 1928), 170–71. As late as 1920, A. B. Renehan, the attorney who had lost the *Sandoval* case, still referred to the decision as limited to liquor; testimony of A. B. Renehan, 16 May 1920, HCIA, 651.

30. Testimony of Charles Burke, 15 Jan. 1923, SCPL, 231. Myra Ellen Jenkins, "The Baltasar Baca 'Grant': History of an Encroachment," *El Palacio* 68 (Spring 1961): 47–64; (Summer 1961): 87–105. *Ortiz v. Suazo,* 91 N.M. 45 (1977). Dorr report on Wilson, 28 Dec. 1911, in NARG–48, 5.1.1, Northern Pueblos. Clara True to F. C. Wilson, 3 Dec. 1922, JC-Yale. Wilson testimony, 5 Feb. 1923, PILT, 23.

31. Testimony of Francis C. Wilson, 13 Feb. 1923, PILT, 9–12.

32. For the earliest suggestion of the trusteeship proposal see Lange to Samuel Adams, 27 Sept. 1911, NARG–48, 5.1. Thereafter see Dorr to Secretary of the Interior, 28 December 1911, 5 March 1912, and item 20, in NARG–48, 5.1.1. See also "Hearings Before the Committee on Indian Affairs," Sixty-second Congress, Third Session on S.6085, a Bill to Authorize the acceptance of trusts from the Pueblo Indians of New Mexico, 1913.

33. Dorr to Secretary of the Interior, 28 Dec. 1911, recommendation no. 5, in NARG–48, 5.1.

34. Dorr to Secretary of the Interior, 6 April 1912, NARG–48, 5.1.1, Northern Pueblos, p. 3.

35. Lang to Samuel Adams, 27 Sept. 1911 (NARG–48, 5.1.1), suggests strongly that at the time government officials believed that the Pueblo Indian land was fully alienable without government assent. Valentine to Commissioner of Indian Affairs, 19 April 1912 (NARG–48, 5.1.1), shows the Indian department's handling of the Dorr suggestions. West, Assistant Attorney

General, to Secretary of the Interior, 20 Jan. 1914 (NARG–48, 5.1.1), argues that the United States could still accept Pueblo land in trust if it chose to.

36. J. P. Harrington, *Ethnogeography of the Tewa Indians* (Andover, Mass.: Phillips Academy, 1919), 122, 336.

37. Dorr to Secretary of the Interior, 5 March 1912, NARG–48, 5.1.1.

38. E. L. Hewitt, "Ancient America at the Panama-California Exposition," *Art and Archaeology* 2 (Nov. 1915): 65–104.

39. See Edgar L. Hewitt, *Ancient Life in the American Southwest* (New York: Bobbs-Merill, 1930). For Hewitt's knowledge of the abandoned pueblo of Pecos, see Edgar L. Hewitt, "Studies in the Extinct Pueblo of Pecos," *American Anthropologist* (1904), 6: 426–39.

40. Affidavit of Antonio Tapia, 18 Feb. 1914, attached as Exhibit H to the answer in *D. C. Collier and Co., a corporation v. Petro L. Boquet et al.,* no. 301 Equity, Federal District Court, New Mexico, in FRC: Denver.

41. Juan Ortiz and Luz Duran Ortiz, widow and sole heir of the late Antonio J. Ortiz, to Collier and Owen, a partnership, incorporated and doing business under the laws of New Mexico, 22 Jan. 1913, recorded 23 Jan. 1913 in San Miguel County Deed Book 75, p. 58. See also mortgage of the same date, between the same parties, in San Miguel County Mortgage Records, Book 23, p. 67. An 1853 sale of the same property brought $56.50. Interestingly, the D. C. Collier suit involving Pojoaque Pueblo was brought in the United States District court on the basis of the alleged fact that the D. C. Collier company was a foreign, California corporation. The Pecos papers show that there was a New Mexico organization as well. Had the Collier Company gone to court in the Pojoaque litigation as a New Mexico corporation, it would have to have brought suit in state, not federal, court.

42. Complaint, 22 Jan. 1914, in *D. C. Collier v. Boquet et al.*

43. For Tapia answer see n. 40. Most of the information in this narrative is drawn from that affidavit. Francis C. Wilson, "Answer of Certain Defendants," 7 March 1914, *D. C. Collier v. Bouquet et al.*

44. Louis H. Warner, "Memorandum regarding Pojoaque Pueblo Grant situation," attached to Hagerman to Wilbur, 4 Aug. 1930, NARG–75, 013, pt. 6-A.

45. PPAAJ, "Irrigation," detail Jones's interest in the Preston Beck and Anton Chico grants. Callon, *Las Vegas,* 235–38 suggests Jones's interests in the Las Vegas grant. Shortly after the Office of the New Mexico Territorial Engineer was established, in 1907, Jones and some business associates filed for the appropriation of all surplus waters in the Gallinas and Pecos rivers, part of a grandiose plan to create of the Upper Pecos watershed an agricultural paradise that would attract new settlers to the arid desert.

46. Exhibit F, *Gross-Kelly Co. v. Juan Quintana et al.,* San Miguel County cause no. 7613 (1914). Complaint filed 5 June 1914. The only extant file of this case is located in the basement of the San Miguel County Courthouse, Las Vegas, New Mexico. On 13 April 1920, attorney Francis C. Wilson signed a receipt for most of the formal papers in the suit. He returned only a few. As a result I have reconstructed the story of this suit from the remaining court

docket sheets, which indicate filings made and then borrowed by Wilson, and from various other private papers. Exhibit F, the Jones survey map of the Pecos Pueblo grant, is still housed in the San Miguel County Courthouse.

47. Testimony of Francis C. Wilson, 25 January 1923, SCPL, 248. See Callon, *Las Vegas*, 235–38.

48. Answers of various defendants, 26 June and 30 June 1914, in *Gross-Kelly v. Juan Quintana et al.*

49. *Ortiz v. Suazo;* Dickson, "The Professional Life of Francis C. Wilson." Possibly Wilson let the Pecos suit lag because D. C. Collier's bubble was about to burst in New Mexico. In any case, when asked in 1923 what had happened to the Pecos suit, Wilson disingenuously said that it had been a straightforward lawsuit that took "about three years" to complete. See testimony of Francis C. Wilson, 25 Jan. 1923, SCPL, 248.

50. For Wilson's involvement in Taos Pueblo's claim to the Tenorio tract, see *Ortiz v. Suazo*. For Wilson's involvement in the Paguate purchase litigation, see *United States v. Candelaria,* 271 U.S. 432 (1926). At the end of the lengthy litigation in the 1920s, the federal courts finally held that Laguna Pueblo was bound by the adverse results of a suit brought by Wilson in the period between 1916 and 1918.

51. Lang to Secretary of Interior, 3 Oct. 1911 (NARG–48, 5.1.1), and Hanke to Secretary of Interior, 26 Oct. 1911, NARG–48, 5.1.1.

52. Lang to Adams, 27 Sept. 1911; Valentine to Secretary of Interior, 19 April 1912, NARG–48, 5.1.1.

53. Testimony of Francis C. Wilson, 13 Feb. 1923, PILT, 72, 255–56. On 22 Jan. 1923, Wilson told the Senate subcommittee (SCPL, 151) that "when I was Pueblo attorney about the year 1912, the question of filing blanket suits, one for each Pueblo, to quiet title on these grants, was being agitated and I was trying to get somewhere." On 13 February Wilson told the House committee that he had actually begun two of the suits that he halted, pending the results of the Joy surveys. The only evidence of any Wilson Pueblo quiet-title suits remain the Pojoaque and Pueblo suits, brought not to confirm Pueblo ownership of land but to confirm the sale of it to non-Indians.

54. Parrott to Comm. of Indian Affairs, 25 Aug. 1917, NARG–75, 013, pt. 8.

55. Testimony of Francis C. Wilson, 13 Feb. 1923 (PILT, 255–56), where Wilson himself bitterly complained about the unfair manner in which the surveys were conducted, alleging that they favored expansive and expanding non-Indian claims to Pueblo land. The scant evidence suggesting that Wilson himself manipulated the survey to favor non-Indians is based on his alleged refusal to have the surveyors consider a tract east of the Rio Grande, within the Santa Clara grant. See Hagerman to West, 23 Nov. 1928, NARG–75, 013, pt. 16. For Pueblo charges of the Joy survey's unfairness, see Reeves to Sells, 18 May 1917, and Archuleta and Ortiz to Commissioner, 25 March 1922, NARG–75, 013, pt. 6.

56. Crane, *Desert Drums,* 211; Wilson testimony, 2 Feb. 1923 (PILT, 24)

and 5 Feb. 1923 (PILT, 129). See also Renehan testimony, 14 Feb. 1923 (PILT, 286).

57. "Motion by plaintiff for notice by publication and motion to make certain persons party defendant," 3 Jan. 1916, in *Gross-Kelly v. Juan Quintana et al.*, San Miguel County cause no. 7613.

58. "Exception of certain defendants to plaintiff's motion praying for reinstatement on the court docket," 28 Feb. 1916; "Plea in abatement by certain defendants," 22 April 1916; "Demand of W. W. Wagner that he be served with a copy of the complaint," 24 April 1916; "Summons on a number of defendants," 13 Sept. 1918; "Petition of Donaciano Gonzales to intervene and order," 12 Dec. 1918, all in *Gross-Kelly v. Juan Quintana et al.*, San Miguel County cause no. 7613.

59. For instance, quitclaim deed, Gross-Kelly and Co. to Juan Sena y Ortega, 16 July 1918, San Miguel County Records.

60. "Final decree," 30 June 1919, in *Gross-Kelly v. Juan Quintana et al.* The acreage was based on the 1913 Jones survey and came in one large tract of 10,835 acres, minus twelve recognized claims totaling 824.04 acres and two smaller ones of 503.2 acres and 357.6 acres. The additional 6,100 acres within the Pecos Pueblo grant were covered neither by the decree in favor of Gross-Kelly nor by the specific exceptions to it. The 1919 court decree simply did not treat them at all. At least a part of those additional acres may have been covered by quitclaim deeds intermittently issued by the company between 1914 and 1919.

61. See, for instance, Hagerman to Ray Lyman Wilbur, 22 July 1929, NARG–75, 013, pt. 17, where the head of the Pueblo Lands Board described True as "a well-known character in the annals of the Pueblo country who has for years been fighting the Indian office and has been looked upon par excellance as the defender and champion of the Indian people." Her correspondence to the Indian department became so voluminous that the government assigned to her a separate file designation of her own.

62. Memorandum to file, 30 Dec. 1922, by Charles Burke, NARG–75, 013, pt. 8. I have used the Burke memorandum to supply the details of the 1919 investigation into Wilson's activities. The Linnen report is itself attached to the Burke memorandum of 1922.

63. Burckhardt to Attorney General, 25 March 1920 and 25 May 1920, NARG–75, 013, pt. 8. Called to defend himself again in 1923, Wilson introduced before the subcommittee of the Senate Committee on Public Lands a statement by James R. Garfield, saying that the 1920 Linnen report's charges were "not substantiated and unjustifiable"; 9 Feb. 1923, NARG–75, 013, pt. 10.

64. Crecencio Vigil of Chamita, in the San Juan Pueblo grant, to Commissioner of General Land Office, 5 March 1920; R. H. Hanna to Commissioner of General Land Office, 13 April 1920; both in NARG–75, 013, pt. 9.

65. John Collier, *From Every Zenith: A Memoir; and Some Essays on Life and Thought* (Denver: Sage Books, 1963), 68, gives the basic account of Collier's ar-

rival in New Mexico. Collier gave a more contemporaneous and slightly different account of his arrival in New Mexico on 10 Feb. 1924, in PILT, 180ff.

Chapter 9

1. Subcommittee of House Committee on Indian Affairs, hearings 16 May 1920 (hereafter HCIA:1920), reprinted in *Indians of the United States,* vol. 46 (Washington, D.C.: U.S. Government Printing Office, 1943), 616, the subcommittee chairman, Homer Snyder, declared the authority under which the subcommittee convened.

2. Testimony of H. Snyder, 3 Feb. 1923, PILT, 21. Recalling the 1920 Tesuque hearings, Snyder said in 1923 that "We did not know a thing about it [the pitched war over non-Indians on Pueblo lands]. We went there for the purpose of advising ourselves on what the conditions were." Later, Snyder admitted that the *Garcia* suit at the Sandia Pueblo had brought the committee to Tesuque. For confirmation see testimony of A. B. Renehan, 14 Feb. 1923, PILT, 243.

3. Hernandez translation of Archuleta Spanish testimony, 16 May 1920, HCIA, 596. For testimony and translation see HCIA:1920, 594ff. For complaints about the accuracy of the Hernandez translations see statement of Ortiz and Archuleta, 17 Feb. 1923, SCPL, 251.

4. Testimony of A. B. Renehan, 16 May 1920, HCIA, 650–56. Three years later Congressman Snyder described the Renehan meeting as "practically an all night session," PILT, 284.

5. Elston to Renehan, 16 May 1920, HCIA, 658.

6. Testimony of A. B. Renehan, 16 May 1920, HCIA, 661, and submissions to the committee, HCIA:1920, 667–69.

7. For instance, testimony of A. B. Renehan, 13 Feb. 1923, PILT, 283, in which Renehan described his own first legislative attempt as "just for starters." He based his first attempt, he then said, on a model drawn from the situation San Francisco found itself in at the turn of the century, when an earthquake destroyed all property records within the city.

8. The outline of the events is given in Superintendent of Pueblos to Commissioner of Indian Affairs, 12 Feb. 1922, NARG–75, 013, pt. 11.

9. Pablo Toya to Lucius Dills, 23 June 1921, Pecos Pueblo file, BLM, Santa Fe. The letter is countersigned by Lansing Bloom, one of the first serious historians of New Mexico's Mexican period. See Malcolm Ebright, "Manuel Martinez's Ditch Dispute," *NMHR* 54, no. 1 (1979): 21–34. Lansing Bartlett Bloom, "New Mexico under Mexican Administration," *Old Santa Fe* 1 (1913): 242. By 1923 Bloom joined that influential group of Santa Fe residents pushing the Pueblo cause. See, for instance, PILT, 232, where John Collier inserted in the records of the hearing a 5 Feb. 1923 letter from Margaret McKittrick, for the New Mexico Association on Indian Affairs, to Judson King. The letter describes the near-starvation faced by the Pueblos. The letter is signed by McKittrick, Edgar L. Hewitt, and Lansing Bloom, among others.

10. True to Burke, 7 Feb. 1922, NARG–75, 013, pt. 8.

11. Testimony of Ralph Emerson Twitchell, 16 Jan. 1923, SCPL, 91; testimony of A. B. Renehan, 23 Jan. 1923, 234ff.

12. Donald R. Moorman, "A Political Biography of Holm O. Bursum, 1899–1924," Ph.D. diss. (University of New Mexico, 1962), 237–45, 261–63. Testimony of Francis C. Wilson, 2 Feb. 1923, PILT, 13, in which Wilson sets out the Republican platform verbatim. For the Hernandez bill see testimony of Ralph Emerson Twitchell, 16 Feb. 1923, PILT, 136, and testimony of A. B. Renehan, 23 Jan. 1923, SCPL, 236, where the Santa Fe attorney testified on Senate Bill 2274, introduced 19 July 1921. "In that bill," said Renehan,

I provided for a commission, not that I was wedded to that form of adjudication, but because it was the method used in the act which I employed as my model, on the San Francisco situation. But there were not there the complexities which are to be found in New Mexico, which were more developed through the Indians and the Mexicans than in that part where San Francisco existed.

13. The details of the hammering out of the final so-called Bursum bill have been told elsewhere. Kenneth Philp, *John Collier's Crusade for Indian Reform 1920–1954* (Tucson: University of Arizona Press, 1977), 26ff, sketches the details but relies too heavily on the Collier Papers at Yale to provide a balanced assessment. Lawrence C. Kelly's *History of the Pueblo Lands Board: 1922–1933* (Office of the State Engineer: Santa Fe, 1980) tells a much fuller story. In neither account do the details of the negotiations prior to the Bursum bill introduction bear on the particular handling of the Pecos Pueblo grant. I will not dwell on those details here. Interestingly, Collier described Twitchell's 1922 report as "a very beautiful piece of scholarship and literary composition and the most valuable single document we possess," Collier testimony, 7 Feb. 1923, PILT, 212. For Twitchell's assessment of his chances in court, see Twitchell to Burke, 16 Dec. 1922, NARG–75, 013, pt. 8. Others agreed. See, for instance, Hayden testimony, 2 Feb. 1923, PILT, 22: "In any event, it was known to many interested people that the federal government, through its attorney, contemplated action in the courts which under existing law would undoubtedly result in ejecting every one of them from the Pueblo lands."

14. Testimony of Francis C. Wilson, 2 Feb. 1923, PILT, 27, outlines the sequence of political events surrounding the Bursum bill through withdrawal of the approved bill by the Senate from the House.

15. Testimony of Francis C. Wilson, 5 Feb. 1923, PILT, 119ff.

16. Wilson to Burke, 17 Oct. 1922, NARG–75, 013, pt. 8.

17. For Collier's work, see Philp, *John Collier's Crusade,* 26ff. For the government's assessment of the strength of the opposition to the Bursum bill, see Burke to Atwood, 8 March 1923, NARG–75, 013, pt. 11. For Wilson's version of the Pueblo initiative behind the Bursum bill opposition see testimony of F. C. Wilson, 15 Jan. 1923, SCPL, 15ff.

18. Philp, *John Collier's Crusade,* 35–36, gives a general description of the

meeting without indicating Pecos participation. Burke to Deming, 29 Sept. 1922, NARG–75, 013, pt. 6, describes the initial position of the Pueblos.

19. Statement from the November meeting, NARG–75, 013, pt. 9. JC-Yale, contains Collier's notes on the minutes of various other Pueblo meetings between Oct. 1922 and Aug. 1924. Pecos references flicker in and out. Sometimes Pecos appears on the list of pueblos called. Other times it does not. Sometimes Pecos Pueblo shows on the roll call and then does not vote. Other times Pecos does not appear on the roll call and then appears as voting. SCPL, 77–78, also contains a copy of the 1922 protest signed by and for Pecos Pueblo.

20. See, for instance, Archuleta and Ortiz statement, undated, SCPL, 251.

21. See testimony of F. C. Wilson, 15 Jan. 1923, PILT, 54, for the basic chronology in the fight against the Bursum bill. For Collier's basic position on Pueblo land claims and his differences with Wilson, see Collier to Wilson, 29 Nov. 1922, JC-Yale.

22. Renehan's letter to the *New York Herald Tribune* is printed in *Congressional Record: House* 64 (1): 498, 14 Dec. 1922. Francis C. Wilson's version of the "sundry slanderous statements" in the letter is set out in testimony of F. C. Wilson, 2 Feb. 1923, PILT, 27–28. Renehan to Burke, NARG–75, 013, pt. 7, March 1922 to August 1923, shows the amount and kind of information Burke was provided by Renehan.

23. True to Wilson, 3 Dec. 1922, JC-Yale. For True's charges against Wilson, see Burke to File, 14 Dec. 1922, NARG–75, 013, pt. 8. In her letter to Wilson, True said that she herself no longer owned any interest in Pueblo lands. Subsequent non-Indian claims in the San Juan and Santa Clara Pueblo grants belie that assertion.

24. Wilson to George Vaux, 15 Dec. 1922, JC-Yale.

25. Wilson to Collier, 20 Dec. 1922, JC-Yale.

26. Collier to Wilson, 22 Dec. 1922, JC-Yale. See Burke to file, 30 Dec. 1922, NARG–75, 013, pt. 8, for the preparation by the commissioner of Indian affairs of a dossier on Wilson's handling of Pecos Pueblo affairs.

27. Wilson to Collier, 29 Dec. 1922, JC-Yale. Wilson himself provided a different, and equally inaccurate, timetable for his Pecos Pueblo grant involvement at the Senate hearings in January 1923 (SCPL, 248). Either Wilson did not remember when the Pecos Pueblo grant work was done and how long it took, or he was hedging for political advantage, trying to disarm his opponents.

28. Philp, *John Collier's Crusade,* 32–48 and Kelly, *History of the Pueblo Lands Board,* 1–27, describe the bills and alternatives during the period.

29. A. R. Manby to Reed Smoot, 9 Jan. 1923, in SCPL, 12–13, and Manby to Jones, 1 Jan. 1923, NARG–75, 013, pt. 3-A.

30. Collier to Atwood, 23 Jan. 1923, JC-Yale. Alfred Kidder, *The Pottery of Pecos* (New Haven: Yale University Press, 1931). Leo Crane, *Desert Drums* (Boston: Little, Brown, 1928), 288. The quote comes from "Anonymous pamphlet signed by 'A Friend of the Pueblos Who Has Spent Four Years Among Them and Knows Whereof He Speaks,'" in NARG–75, 013, pt. 4.

Charles Burke to Mrs. Stella Atwood, 3 March 1923, NARG–75, 013, pt. 4.

31. Testimony of Ralph Emerson Twitchell, beginning 15 Jan. 1923, in SCPL, 34ff.

32. Collier to Johnson, 19 Jan. 1923, reprinted in PILT, 242. The *New Mexican* editor ran the Collier dispatch as if it had come from United Press International. When government officials, under attack by Collier, discovered this, they lept on Collier's unauthorized use of the UPI imprimatur as an example of Collier's unbridled and unprincipled propaganda.

33. Testimony of A. B. Renehan, 23 Jan. 1923, SCPL, 222, 223.

34. Testimony of A. B. Renehan, 23 Jan. 1923, SCPL, 224–25.

35. *Montoya v. Unknown Heirs of Vigil,* 16 N.M. 349 (1911), affm'd 232 U.S. 375 (1914), contains the fullest discussion of the effect of New Mexico's two statutes dealing with so-called adverse possession. The two statutes were codified in 1915 as sections 3364 and 3365 of the New Mexico code in existence at the time of the Pueblo Lands Board debates. References to these two sections during the Pueblo hearings in 1923 bear these designations. The sections were recodified in 1978 at 37-1-21 and 37-1-22. Section 3364 of the 1915 compilation and 37-1-21 of the 1978 compilation deal with land within Spanish and Mexican land grants. Sections 3365 and 37-1-22 deal with all land, whether inside or outside Spanish and Mexican land grants. *Maxwell Land Grant v. Dawson,* 7 N.M. 133 (1891), reversed in part in 151 U.S. 586 (1893), and *Jenkins v. Maxwell Land Grant Co.,* 15 N.M. 281 (1910), discuss section 3384. The *Maxwell* cases held that New Mexico's general land grant statute affected only real estate actually possessed by a claimant to land who did not legally hold full title to it. Prior to 16 March 1899, that statute did not require a written instrument to begin the tolling of the adverse possession. On 16 March 1899, the territorial legislature amended the act to require a written document. Subsequently the New Mexico Supreme Court reversed itself and held that adverse possession under color of title after 1899 extended to the limits of the written document on which the possession was based, whether occupied in fact or not. See *Archuleta v. Pino,* 86 N.M. 94 (1974). In very recent years the state legislature has done away altogether with the special land grant statute. See generally "Adverse Possession in New Mexico," 4 *NRJ* 559 (1964) and 5 *NRJ* 96 (1965).

36. Testimony of F. C. Wilson, 9 Feb. 1923, SCPL, 247–48, and attached Statement of Hon. James R. Garfield on behalf of Francis C. Wilson.

37. Testimony of F. C. Wilson, 22 Jan. 1923, SCPL, 175ff. For a similar plea from the office of the commissioner of Indian affairs, see PILT, 6.

38. Remarks of Chairman Snyder, 1 Feb. 1923, PILT, 6–7. Snyder announced that the House committee would make a broad inquiry, "to ascertain what the conditions are in New Mexico" (PILT, 44).

39. Testimony of Stella Atwood, 1 Feb. 1923, PILT, 73–110; Collier's defense of Atwood, PILT, 255; Chairman Snyder's characterization of Wilson as principal Pueblo witness, PILT, 65; and Wilson's refusal to testify on the committee's terms, PILT, 175–79.

40. Testimony of A. B. Renehan, 13 Feb. 1923, PILT, 296, 339.

41. Statement of Archuleta and Ortiz, undated, in SCPL, 251.

42. Statement of F. C. Wilson, 1 Feb. 1923, PILT, 46: "No statute of limitations can be passed which will not do injustice to the Indians or the settlers. They say we have no statute of limitations in the Leatherwood bill. I think any statute of limitations is a mistake." Statement of F. C. Wilson, PILT, 62, where Wilson acknowledged that non-Indian settlers had some interest in Pueblo land. Statement of F. C. Wilson, PILT, 64, where Wilson accepted the Snyder bill's proposed statute of limitations. Statement of F. C. Wilson, PILT, 118, where Chairman Snyder asked Wilson, "You want a bill passed that will give to the Indians the land they had in 1848?" and Wilson responded, "No. Not at all. If my discussion of it has given that impression to the committee, I am very sorry."

43. Testimony of F. C. Wilson, 1 Feb. 1923, PILT, 14, 23, 27, 46–47, 55, 60–61, 68.

44. Testimony of F. C. Wilson, 2 Feb. 1923, PILT, 31–33, 35.

45. Testimony of J. Collier, 10 Feb. 1923, PILT, 246; of A. B. Renehan, 10 Feb. 1923, PILT, 288.

46. *Congressional Record: Senate,* 28 Feb. 1923, 4876, 4878, set out the text of the Lenroot substitute.

47. Burke to Renehan, 29 Aug. 1923, and Renehan to Burke, 23 Aug. 1923, in NARG–75, 013, pt. 7.

48. Renehan to Burke, 23 Aug. 1923, NARG–75, 013, pt. 7. For Berle's version of events, see Beatrice B. Berle and Francis B. Jacobs, eds. *Navigating the Rapids* (New York: Harcourt, Brace, Jovanovich, 1973), 15–19. See also Burke to Renehan, 6 Sept. 1923, NARG–75, 013, pt. 7.

49. Crandall to Burke, 29 Aug. 1923, NARG–75, 013, pt. 7.

50. Renehan to Burke, 1 Sept. 1923, NARG–75, 013, pt. 7. See Philp, *John Collier's Crusade,* 26–54.

51. F. C. Wilson to Burke, with bill and analysis attached, 26 Nov. 1923, 6 Dec. 1923, and 11 Jan. 1924, NARG–75, 013, pt. 8. 6 January 1912 was the date on which New Mexico formally became a state and accepted the terms of the enabling act under which the new state disclaimed any right to or jurisdiction over Pueblo Indian land. On 16 March 1899 the territorial legislature amended section 3365 of the 1915 compilation to require, for the first time, color of title in order to maintain the defense of title by adverse possession under New Mexico's general adverse possession statute. See also E. H. Meritt memorandum, 30 Dec. 1926, NARG–75, 013, pt. 13. In January 1924 Wilson told Burke that the Senate subcommittee had rejected the notion, now pushed by the new Pueblo attorney, A. A. Berle, that no statute of limitations had ever run against New Mexico Pueblos. Wilson reported that "our Federal district court agreed in the Laguna case this summer." In fact, the Senate subcommittee had never been so clear. In addition, the Laguna case proved Wilson wrong in the end as well. The lower courts had held that New Mexico's pueblos were subject to the territorial law of adverse possession. But when the Laguna cases finally reached the United States Supreme Court,

in 1926, under the name *United States v. Candelaria,* that court held that the territorial laws of New Mexico had never applied to the New Mexico pueblos. Years later, Pueblo advocate John Collier said that if *Candelaria* had been decided before, rather than after passage of the Pueblo Lands Act, in 1924, the act would have been considerably different, and much more pro-Pueblo, than it turned out. Wilson's faulty reasons for adopting the territorial statutes of limitation bear out the Collier analysis, though only in hindsight. See generally Twitchell to Burke, 28 June 1924, NARG–75, 013, pt. 9; H. J. Hagerman to Walker, 1 Jan. 1926, NARG–200, and Hagerman to Walker, 1 Oct. 1926, NARG–200.

52. Twitchell to Burke, 22 Dec. 1923, and Wilson to Burke, 2 January 1924, in NARG–75, 013, pt. 8.

53. Kelly, *History of the Pueblo Lands Board,* 20–23; Adams to Burke, 27 March 1924, NARG–75, 013, pt. 9.

54. Act of 7 June 1924, 43 Stat. 636.

Chapter 10

1. H. J. Hagerman to Hubert Work, 13 May 1926, NARG–200; Work to Hagerman, 22 Aug. 1924, NARG–75, 013, pt. 9. See Walker to Burke, 2 June 1925, NARG–75, 013, pt. 9. Jennings's background can be gleaned from the records of the Department of Justice, Employment, 1923. Before coming to New Mexico to work on the Pueblo Lands Board Jennings served with the Department of Justice as a title examiner, primarily of sites proposed for post office acquisition.

2. Hagerman to Wilbur, 4 Aug. 1930, NARG–75, 013, pt. 7A.

3. Hagerman to Burke, 24 Sept. 1926, NARG–75, 013, pt. 7A, reporting on correspondence from New Mexico Senator A. A. Jones on behalf of Albuquerque attorney George S. Flock. Flock in turn had asked Jones about the holdings of Adine Turner Bridges in the Pojoaque Pueblo Grant. Fraser's undated memo is attached.

4. Hagerman to Flock, 9 Sept. 1926, NARG–75, 013, pt. 11.

5. Hagerman to Work, 1 Dec. 1925, NARG–75, 013, pt. 7; Walker to Hagerman, 10 Nov. 1925, NARG–200; Fraser to Hagerman, 5 Jan. 1926, Misc., PLBSPA; Rt. Rev. Msgr. Wm. Hughes to Burke, 27 Nov. 1925, NARG–75, 013, pt. 9, enclosing Fr. Fridolin Shuster to Hughes, 22 Nov. 1925. The accounts do not say whether Pecos Pueblo participated in these meetings in the fall of 1925. The Collier notes in the Yale University Collier collection make no mention of the attendance by Pecos either.

6. Transcript of Pueblo Lands Board meeting, Washington, D.C., 18 Jan. 1926, NARG–75, 013, pt. 10; Roberts Walker to Hagerman, 10 Nov. 1925, NARG–200. "It should be borne in mind," Walker wrote Hagerman, "that there is no finality about the Board's report . . . The Board is at most only a coarse screen."

7. Hagerman to Wilbur, 8 March 1929, in Ray Lyman Wilbur papers,

Hoover Institute on War and Peace, Palo Alto, Cal., box 16 (hereafter cited as RLW). In this and other letters, Hagerman emphasized the paucity of hard information to be gleaned from the extremely vague written deeds and the necessity for oral testimony to explain them. See, for instance, pp. 4–5 of the Wilbur letter and Hagerman to United States Senate, 9 Sept. 1926, NARG–75, 013, pt. 11.

8. Hagerman to Burke, 5 Aug. 1925, NARG–75, 013, pt. 6; Cornell to Collier, 21 March 1928, JC-Yale; Hagerman to Burke, 3 Sept. 1928, NARG–75, 013, pt. 16; and Hagerman to file, 30 March 1928, NARG–75, 013, pt. 15.

9. Hagerman to Walker, 14 Aug. 1925, Misc., PLBSPA. As early as the board's consideration of the Tesuque Pueblo grant, Jennings was described as "absorbed with the title end of the game." Hagerman described Jennings as assembling the documents for the seventeen Tesuque non-Indian claims himself. "He has done this," wrote Hagerman, "in a most thorough way and I have before me on my desk as I write a set of thirteen abstracts which he has laboriously produced. The situation here is enough to make any man of his exact turn of mind crazy." The following members filled the third slot on the Pueblo Lands Board: Roberts Walker, 1924–26; Lucius Embree, 1926–28; Louis H. Warner, 1928–31; and Guy Harrington, 1931–33.

10. Hagerman to Work, 23 Sept. 1926, NARG–75, 013, pt. 10, describes the Taos debate and its resolution by the board. The 224 uncontested tracts lay primarily within the town of Taos proper, an area in the southwest corner of the Taos Pueblo grant occupied by non-Indians with pueblo permission since 1790. The board surveyor Mark Ratcliffe went around the external boundaries of the non-Indian town with chosen members of Taos Pueblo, selecting those points where the Indians recognized the limits of the non-Indian claims. The points were set and surveyed. Hearings were held only on those tracts which did not fall within the area segregated by Ratcliff and the Taos Pueblo leaders.

11. Hagerman to Work, 1 Dec. 1925, NARG–75, 013, pt. 8; Hagerman to Wilbur, 8 March 1929, RLW, box 16: Of the Pueblo grants and reservations considered by the Pueblo Lands Board, at least Sandia, Pojoaque, Santa Ana, Zuni, and Pecos pueblos were never mapped by the Joy surveyors.

12. See, for instance, Hagerman, "Notes for Memoirs, 1934," in NARG–200 for a general discussion of Ratcliffe and Sena's indispensable roles in the board's work in northern New Mexico's Spanish-speaking counties. Sena had previously worked as clerk of the state district court in Santa Fe.

13. For the written results of the 1920 hydrographic survey see *United States of America v. Hope Community Ditch et al.,* No. 712 Equity, *USDC for New Mexico,* General Index, Volume I, "For Adjudicated Water Rights to Lands Situate in the Counties of San Miguel and Guadalupe Counties, Section II, Being the Pecos River from Irwin's Ranch to the mouth of Cow Creek." See also "Pecos Hydrographic Survey, Map Sheet No. A-2 to A-5, Field Work July–August 1920, Ed W Lighton, Inst." Both documents are in the State Engineer's Office, Santa Fe, New Mexico.

14. Hagerman to Walker, concerning Jennings, 16 Dec. 1925, NARG–200: "The whole trend of Mr. Jenning's thought as to the operation of the Pueblo Lands Board, as opposed to my own, is towards thoroughness as opposed to expedition." NARG–75, 013, pt. 7, contains the correspondence concerned with Walker and the problems that first his travels and then his illness caused the board. For Wilson's role in removing Embree, see Wilson to Work, 12 Dec. 1927, NARG–75, 013, pt. 12. Hagerman to Merritt, 3 Feb. 1928, NARG–200, suggests Embree's bitterness.

15. Secretary Work to Pueblo Lands Board, 19 Jan. 1928, NARG–75, 013, pt. 11.

16. Fraser to Burke, 20 Jan. 1926, NARG–75, 013, pt. 10, explains Fraser's differing opinions. Fraser's briefs, taking opposite sides of the section 4 question, are located in Misc., PLBSPA, Walker to Hagerman, 10 Nov. 1925, NARG–200, and Fraser to Hagerman, 5 Jan. 1926, Misc., PLBSPA. For the judicial resolution of the issue see *United States of America as the Guardian of the Pueblo of Nambe v. Herrera et al.*, no. 729 USDC, New Mexico. Per curiam opinion, August 1928, in FRC: Denver. Hagerman to Burke, 3 Sept. 1928, NARG–75, 013, pt. 16.

17. *Pueblo of Nambe v. Romero*, 10 N.M. 58, 61 P. 122 (1900).

18. Hagerman to Jennings, 10 June 1926, Jennings General, PLBSPA. Just prior to the letter the United States Supreme Court decided *United States v. Candelaria*. The case represented the third attempt by the Pueblo of Laguna to litigate its claim to the so-called Paguate purchase, a large area of Spanish land grant terrain the pueblo claimed to have purchased from its Spanish neighbors. See Myra Ellen Jenkins, "The Baltazar Baca Grant: History of an Encroachment," *El Palacio* 68 (Spring 1961): 47–64, (Summer 1961): 87–105. Special Pueblo Attorney Francis C. Wilson had tried twice, once in the territorial courts and then in the federal courts created after New Mexico became a state. The territorial court ruled against the pueblo's claim. The federal court then ruled that the question could not be relitigated. Thereafter, Special Pueblo Attorney Ralph Emerson Twitchell, stating that he was trying to "revive this 'dead horse' with a little 'legal oxygen,'" brought a third suit concerning the pueblo's claim to the Paguate purchase. This time he did so not in the name of the pueblo, but in the name of the United States, as guardian for the pueblo. The local federal district court ruled against Twitchell. He filed a timely appeal, this time to the circuit court of appeals. In turn, that court could not decide two questions it considered critical to the case and certified them to the United States Supreme Court for an answer. In the spring of 1926, Justice Willis Van Devanter wrote his third and last opinion on New Mexico–Pueblo legal matters. This time he ruled that New Mexico Pueblos had always been covered by the 1834 Non-Intercourse Act. The *Candelaria* decision may have influenced the board to view the Romero tract problem at Nambe as it did. At least that is what Hagerman himself said when he wrote, "the *Candelario* [sic] case, as far as I can see, while it is very unsatisfactory in many respects, absolutely cuts out the Romero tract." Later Hagerman maintained that the board had always given retroactive effect to

the *Sandoval* decision, thus holding that federal law exclusively had governed Pueblo affairs since 1846, despite *Joseph,* in 1877.

19. Hagerman to Burke, 11 Nov. 1926, NARG–75, 013, pt. 11.

20. Hagerman to Burke, 10 Aug. 1927, NARG–75, 013, pt. 12. "I do not know," Hagerman told Burke, "of a single case that has been disposed of by the Board solely on the question of the payment or non-payment of taxes."

21. Hagerman memo, re tax provisions of 4(a) and 4(b) of the 1924 act, 30 March 1928, NARG–75, 013, pt. 15. See Hagerman to Ray Lyman Wilbur, 22 April 1929, NARG–75, 013, pt. 14A. Had the board applied the San Juan standards to Pecos, few tracts in Pecos would have gone to the non-Indian claimants.

22. Per curiam opinion, *United States as the Guardian of the Nambe Pueblo v. David Herrera et al.,* no. 729, USDC, New Mexico, August 1928, in FRC: Denver. See Hagerman to Burke, 3 Sept. 1928, NARG–75, 013, pt. 16. See also *United States v. Wooten,* 147 F. 926 (1930), and Charles Elkus to Rhoads, 13 Nov. 1930, NARG–48, 5.1.

23. Pueblo Lands Board, "Tesuque Pueblo, Report on Indian Titles Extinguished," 9 Nov. 1925, Tesuque Pueblo, PLBSPA.

24. Pueblo Lands Board: "Nambe Pueblo, Report on Indian Titles Extinguished," 12 Aug. 1926, Nambe Pueblo, PLBSPA.

25. For instance, testimony of R. H. Hanna, Senate Committee on Indian Affairs, *Hearings Before a Subcommittee . . . Survey on Conditions of the Indians in the United States* (hereafter SCIUS), vol. 20 (Washington, D.C.: U.S. Government Printing Office, 1931), 10743. Testimony of C. Jennings, SCIUS, 10787.

26. *Nambe Pueblo v. the United States,* no. 1729, USDC, New Mexico, 1927, FRC. Note that this case represented Nambe Pueblo's own appeal of the compensation awarded to it and was a different suit from the one brought by the United States as guardian of the Nambe Pueblo to quiet title to all the lands within the Nambe Pueblo grant to which the Pueblo Lands Board found that Pueblo Indian title had not been extinguished.

27. Hagerman to Burke, 3 Sept. 1928, NARG–200. Wrote Hagerman, "The decision of the Federal court is now law, and unless appealed from, it will govern the Board in its decisions on future claims."

28. *United States v. Candelaria,* 271 U.S. 432 (1926).

29. Hagerman to Burke, 5 Sept. 1928, NARG–75, 013, pt. 16.

30. Baca to Collier, 15 April 1926, JC-Yale.

31. Baca to Collier, 25 Jan. 1932, JC-Yale.

32. Austin to Hagerman, 14 April 1929, and Hagerman to Austin, 14 Dec. 1930, in NARG–200. File, "ATSF Claim: Pecos Pueblo Grant," no. 300-14, and "American Metals Inc. Claim: Pecos Pueblo Grant," no. 300-18, in Pecos Pueblo Grant, PLBSPA.

33. Hagerman to Burke, 23 Sept. 1928, NARG–75, 013, pt. 16.

34. Warner to Haggard, 6 July 1928, and Haggard to Warner, 16 July 1928, in Warner, PLBSPA.

35. Hanna to Collier, 13 March 1929, concerning Pueblo Lands Board progress, in JC-Yale.

36. "Memorandum on Pecos Pueblo," undated, in Misc., Pecos Pueblo, PLBSPA.

37. For the Hagerman and Warner characterizations, see Jennings to Attorney General, 3 March 1930, NARG–75, 013, pt. 21. For the Jennings characterization, see Hagerman to Burke, 4 April 1929, NARG–75, 013, pt. 20.

38. Louis H. Warner, "Conveyance of Property, the Spanish and Mexican Way," *NMHR* 6, no. 3 (1931): 334–59; and Warner, *Archbishop Lamy: An Epoch Maker* (Santa Fe: New Mexican Publishing Co., 1933).

39. Warner to Finney, 23 Jan. 1929, NARG–75, 013, pt. 17.

40. Hagerman to West, 23 Nov. 1928, NARG–75, 013, pt. 16.

41. Warner to Finney, 23 Jan. 1929, NARG–75, 013, pt. 17.

42. Burke to Finney, 2 Feb. 1929, NARG–75, 013, pt. 17.

43. Hagerman to Wilbur, 4 Aug. 1930, NARG–75, 013, pt. 21.

44. Hagerman to Wilbur, 8 March 1929, RLW, box 16; Warner to Harrington, 21 March 1929, NARG–75, 013, pt. 17; Finney to Burke, 3 March 1929, NARG–75, 013, pt. 17.

45. For instance, Hagerman to Work, 19 Feb. 1927, NARG–200, describing the preliminary work of Ratcliffe and Sena in the town of Bernalillo, within the Sandia Pueblo grant.

46. Hagerman to Work, 25 Feb. 1927, NARG–75, 013, pt. 12.

47. For example, Jennings to Hagerman, 16 June 1926, in General: Jennings, PLBSPA. For transcript preparation see Hanna to Collier, 5 Oct. 1926, JC-Yale. Most of the transcripts of the hearings are housed in the Southern Pueblo Agency in Albuquerque.

48. Hagerman to Wilbur, 8 March 1929, RLW, box 16.

49. John W. Johnson, *Reminiscences of a Forest Ranger, 1914–1944* (Dayton, Ohio: Privately Published, 1976), 58.

50. For this and the following account of the Pueblo Lands Board procedure in Pecos, I am indebted to the following people for interviews: Gabino Varela (103 years old at the time of our interviews in 1979), Pedro Vigil (77), Jose Asisclo Vigil (84), and Adelaido Quintana (68). Their recollections were invaluable; I am aware of no written references to surveying practices in the Pecos Pueblo grant.

51. For instance, Exception 170, surveyed as Private Claim 207, containing 353.544 acres on "Supplemental Plat Showing Private Claims in Sections 26, 27, 34 and 35, Pecos Pueblo Grant, Township 16 North, Range 12 East," BLM, Santa Fe, prepared 13 Nov. 1934.

52. For instance, Exceptions 217 to 227 on "Supplemental Plat Showing Private Claims in Sections 26, 27, 34 and 35, Pecos Pueblo Grant," BLM, Santa Fe.

53. For instance, Exceptions 298 to 303 on "Supplemental Plat Showing Private Claims in Sections 31 and 36, Pecos Pueblo Grant," BLM, Santa Fe.

54. Manuel Varela y Gonzales, Jr., personal interviews, 1977–78, Pecos.

55. For instance, Exception 61 (13 irrigated acres), Exception 38 (60 dry acres), Exception 297 (3 dry acres), Exception 293 (27 dry acres) and Exception 18 (8 irrigated acres). In this tally I have included only those tracts patented to either Manuel Varela or to the heirs of Manual Barela. Numerous other tracts were confirmed in other Varela individuals, also descendants of the first Manuel Varela.

56. For instance, Exception 292, containing 235 acres, patented to Jose C. Rivera and wife.

57. For instance, Exception 333 (46 acres), Exception 335 (60 acres), Exception 339 (189 acres).

58. Pecos Pueblo Grant, File 301.17, PLBSPA. The file bears the listing of all private claims within the grant by number and the "no abstract" designation. In addition, the file contains Jennings's rough notes of the beginning of his ad valorem property tax investigation in the San Miguel County Courthouse.

59. Jennings to Hagerman, 23 Feb. 1930, and Hagerman to Jennings, 5 Oct. 1929, in Jennings, PLBSPA.

60. Manuel Quintana to Pueblo Lands Board, 22 April 1930, "Misc.," Pecos Pueblo Grant, PLBSPA. Baca to Collier, 25 Jan. 1932, JC-Yale. Samuel Adelo, Sr., personal interview, Pecos, 1979.

61. *United States v. Wooten et al.,* 40 F2 882 (1930), decided 14 April 1930.

62. Hanna to Collier, 5 Oct. 1926, JC-Yale, describes the handling of the adverse claims within San Fernando de Taos itself.

63. Files on AT&SF, American Metals, and J. V. Austin, in Pecos Pueblo Grant, PLBSPA.

64. Manuel Quintana to Pueblo Lands Board, 22 April 1930, and Warner to Quintana, 24 April 1930, "Misc.," Pecos Pueblo, PLBSPA.

65. For instance, certain members of the East Pecos Varela clan maintain that the family members agreed to send Liberato Varela to the Pueblo Lands Board to secure the patent in his name for the heirs of his deceased father. See Exception 295, in the name of Donaciano Gonzales, and Exception 304, in the name of the heirs of Epifanio Lucero.

66. For instance, Exception 118, surveyed as private claim 320 to the Pecos Pueblo grant. The genealogy of Donaciano Vigil's heirs in 1979 revealed over three hundred living members (genealogy in the possession of G. Emlen Hall). The *eras* and *mancomunes* lost their official status with the Pueblo Lands Board designations, as did the tradition of the *regadillos*.

67. In preparing for the 1933 Congressional hearings on bills proposing a large increase of awards to the Pueblos, staff members of the Pueblo Lands Board prepared several tables, from which these figures are drawn. See "Summary of Reports and Court Actions by the Pueblo Lands Board, September, 1933," in Misc., General, PLBSPA.

68. Fraser to Rhoads, 30 Nov. 1932, and 19 Jan. 1933, in NARG–75, 013, pt. 31.

69. In fact the Pojoaque Pueblo grant had not been sold sooner since no one could find any resident Indians who would speak for the so-called moribund Pojoaque Pueblo.

70. Hagerman to Wilbur, 5 Aug. 1930, NARG–75, 013, pt. 21, enclosing the proposed reports and indicating that the actual filing of the 4 Aug. 1930 Pecos reports would be delayed "for a few days" by final preparation of the survey maps.

71. Pueblo Lands Board, "Report No. 1, Report on Title to Lands Granted or Confirmed to Pueblo Indians, Pecos Pueblo Grant," "Misc.," Pecos Pueblo, PLBSPA.

72. Pueblo Lands Board, "Report No. 2, Report Concerning Indian Titles Extinguished, Pecos Pueblo Grant," "Misc.," Pecos Pueblo, PLBSPA.

73. "Indian Titles Extinguished, Pecos Pueblo Grant," 4.

74. The history of the board's treatment of Pueblo water rights is extraordinarily complex and arcane. See, for instance, House Report 820, on House Bill 9071, 72d Congress, 1st Session (1932), which describes the history of the board's water treatment and suggests that it was built on an erroneous theory.

75. "Indian Titles Extinguished, Pecos Pueblo Grant," 6.

76. Hagerman to Scattergood, 30 June 1931, NARG–75, 013, pt. 26, includes all eighteen completed appraisals. The letter describes the method by which the board adjusted the appraisals downward in figuring recommended awards to the pueblos.

77. "Indian Titles Extinguished, Pecos Pueblo Grant," 7.

78. "Appropriation Bill, Department of the Interior, for the Fiscal Year Ending June 30, 1932," PLCh 187, 46 Stat. 1122, "Indian Lands, for Carrying out the Provisions of the Act of June 7, 1924, . . . to Quiet Title in Pueblo Indian Lands, New Mexico, and in Settlement for Damages for Land and Water Lost . . ."

79. Hagerman to Wilbur, 4 Aug. 1930, NARG–75, 013, pt. 21; Hagerman to President of U.S. Senate, 9 Sept. 1926, NARG–75, 013, pt. 11, 11.

80. For the board's attitude toward Pojoaque Pueblo and its award, see Fraser to Rhoads, 22 Nov. 1932, NARG–75, 013, pt. 31. For Pecos, see Hagerman to Wilbur, 4 Aug. 1930, NARG–75, 013, pt. 21.

81. Hagerman to Rhoads, 27 May 1932, NARG–75, 013, pt. 30.

82. Armijo to Hagerman, 11 Jan. 1932, NARG–75, 013, pt. 30, lists the independent suits filed by Taos (two suits), Sandia, Picuris, and San Felipe pueblos. For an adequate discussion of these suits and the companion bills for added compensation in Congress, see Richard Frost, "Relations Between the Pueblo Indians and the Federal Government, 1910–1933, with Particular Reference to Water Rights," unpub. ms., Center for the History of the American Indian, January 1980, Chicago, Ill.

83. Collier to Bratton, 6 Feb. 1932, JC-Yale.

84. For instance, Fraser to Rhoads, 22 Nov. 1932, in NARG–75, 013, pt. 31.

85. As quoted in State ex. rel. Reynolds v. Aamodt et al., 537 F² 1102 (10th C.A., 1976).

86. For instance, Elkus to Wilbur, 15 Aug. 1932, RLW, box 16.

87. Elise Clews Parsons, *The Jemez Pueblo* (New Haven: Yale University Press, 1925), 46.

88. West to Rogers, 27 Feb. 1936, Report no. 2447, to accompany H.R. 12074, House of Representatives, 74th Congress, 2d Session (1936), p. 1.

89. Act of 19 June 1936, 74th Congress, 2d Session. The Indian Claims Commission, in *Pueblo of Pecos and Pueblo of Jemez and Pueblo of Pecos v. United States,* no. 174, decided in 1955 that the 1936 act had merged the two pueblos but had not necessarily extinguished Pecos Pueblo as an entity joined with Jemez Pueblo.

Index